David Winter was Editor of New Daylight *from 1998 to 2000 and is now Consulting Editor. An honorary canon of Christ Church Oxford, he is former Head of Religious Broadcasting at the BBC and author of many books, including* After the Gospels, *a selection of readings from the first two centuries of the Christian Church (BRF, 2001).*

A YEAR WITH New Daylight

DAILY READINGS FROM THE BIBLE

Edited by

David Winter

Published by
The Bible Reading Fellowship
First Floor, Elsfield Hall
15–17 Elsfield Way, Oxford OX2 8FG
ISBN 1 84101 234 3

First published 2001
10 9 8 7 6 5 4 3 2 1 0

Acknowledgments
Scripture quotations taken from The New Revised Standard Version of the Bible, Anglicized Edition, copyright © 1989, 1995 by the Division of Christian Education of the National Council of the Churches of Christ in the USA, are used by permission. All rights reserved.

Scripture quotations taken from The Revised Standard Version of the Bible, copyright © 1946, 1952, 1971 by the Division of Christian Education of the National Council of the Churches of Christ in the USA, are used by permission. All rights reserved.

Scripture quotations taken from the *Holy Bible, New International Version*, copyright © 1973, 1978, 1984 by International Bible Society, are used by permission of Hodder & Stoughton Limited. All rights reserved. 'NIV' is a registered trademark of International Bible Society. UK trademark number 1448790.

Scriptures quoted from the Good News Bible published by The Bible Societies/ HarperCollins Publishers Ltd, UK © American Bible Society 1966, 1971, 1976, 1992, used with permission.

Scriptures taken from the New Jerusalem Bible, published and copyright © 1985 by Darton, Longman and Todd Ltd and les Editions du Cerf, and by Doubleday, a division of Bantam Doubleday Dell Publishing Group, Inc. Used by permission of Darton, Longman and Todd Ltd, and Doubleday, a division of Random House, Inc.

Scriptures taken from the New English Bible copyright © 1961, 1970 by Oxford University Press and Cambidge University Press.

Extracts from the Authorized Version of the Bible (The King James Bible), the rights in which are vested in the Crown, are reproduced by permission of the Crown's patentee, Cambridge University Press.

A catalogue record for this book is available from the British Library

Printed and bound in Slovenia

Contents

Waiting for the Lord

Editor's Introduction

Margaret and her family lived in a village in southern Uganda during the civil war some years ago. The countryside was overrun with armed gangs, the local shop had been destroyed and supplies of food came through sporadically if at all. Each morning the family said the Lord's Prayer together, pausing on the words 'Give us this day our daily bread'. When the fighting finally stopped and things returned more or less to normal, they realized that they could look back and say that the simple daily prayer had been answered. Each day, sometimes against all the odds, they had just enough to eat. God had given them very literally their 'bread for the day'.

All of us are familiar with the prayer, of course, but not the experience. Most of us have no idea what it would be like to suffer anxiety every morning about whether or not the family would have enough, or indeed anything, to eat. But—rightly—we pray the words, recognizing that God is the source of our daily food, as of every other gift of his creation. Perhaps we don't notice (and our traditional translation somewhat disguises it) that what we pray for is our 'bread for the day'. Like the Israelites in the wilderness, we are not to gather tomorrow's manna today, but to trust God to meet our daily needs. That is the straightforward meaning of the petition.

However, in the Bible—as in ordinary speech—'bread' stands for more than food. When we describe someone as the family's 'breadwinner' we don't imply that they bring home a couple of sliced loaves every day, but that by their work they are able to supply the family's necessities of every kind. Beyond that, the Bible tells us not to live 'by bread alone'. Simply to set out to satisfy our bodily hunger, while neglecting other essentials of life, would leave us seriously under-nourished. We don't just need to eat, but to experience love and companionship, trust and security and hope. We are much more than machines needing fuel.

Most of all, according to the Bible, we need the words that God speaks to us. Jesus quoted a saying from the Hebrew scriptures when he was being tested in the desert: 'We shall not live by bread alone, but by every word that comes from the mouth of God.' This is the true spiritual manna, nourishment for the soul, as necessary to a full life as food itself.

That strange phrase 'the words that come from God' reminds us that we believe in a God who speaks. Indeed, it is a distinctive characteristic of his nature. The very first thing God did, in the Genesis creation story, was to speak: 'God said, "Let there be light."' It was by those words that creation itself was set in motion—words of power, indeed.

And God has gone on speaking, down the centuries—to prophets and seers, but also to ordinary men and women at turning points in their lives or in the unfolding of the divine story. God spoke to Abraham and Gideon, to Moses and Elijah, to Mary and to John the Baptist. Finally, as the magnificent opening to the book of Hebrews puts it, 'Long ago God spoke to our ancestors in many and various ways by the prophets, but in these last days he has spoken to us by a Son.'

That 'Son', of course, was the One who is given in John's Gospel the elusive title of *Logos*, 'the Word'. *Logos* is in fact more than just a piece of isolated vocabulary. It suggests a whole 'idea', the meaning or explanation of something, an insight into truth. Jesus is God's 'explanation'. Indeed, for Christians he is very much what we call 'the last word on the subject'. Here is God's message for the human race in its clearest and most accessible form.

All of these ideas are brought together in the phrase 'the Word of God'. For us today, that word which was once visible and incarnate in Jesus is most obviously available in the scriptures. Certainly a balanced and healthy Christian diet will include attention to scripture. To hear or read the Bible with faith is to open our ears to 'every word that comes from the mouth of God', and it can never be an optional extra for the disciples of Jesus. Indeed, it is and has always been an absolute necessity.

The prayer 'Give us this day our daily bread' encompasses this need. Feed us, we pray, not only with the perishable bread from the oven, but also with the imperishable bread which is the Word of God—everything that God wishes to say to us.

This book is intended to help those who would like to embark on a year's readings from the Bible, helped on their way by a team of gifted and experienced teachers. It offers 366 readings (in case you choose a Leap Year), selected from many different parts of the Bible, though usually in sections of readings based on a book or a theme. They are arranged to match, as far as possible, the seasons of the year, though obviously it was impossible to provide dated readings for movable Christian festivals like Lent, Easter and Pentecost. Under four quarterly titles, they embrace fundamentals of Christian discipleship—Light on the Way, The New Life, Under the Hand of God and Waiting for the Lord.

The readings are taken from *New Daylight* for the three years from 1998 to 2000. *New Daylight* is the very popular daily reading scheme of the Bible Reading Fellowship, which draws its writers from across the spectrum of Christian denominations and traditions. It is unlikely that any reader will find nothing in these pages with which to disagree, but the common factor for all our writers, from whatever background, is a deep and reverent respect for the scriptures as bringing to us the Word of God. Between them—Anglican, Roman Catholic, Free Church, evangelical or charismatic—they offer a veritable supermarket of biblical spirituality. They draw from a deep well, and it is our prayer that no one dipping into it will fail to draw living water.

David Winter

FIRST QUARTER

Light on the Way

2 Peter 3:8–10, 13 (NRSV)

New things for a new year

Thinking in thousands

With the Lord one day is like a thousand years, and a thousand years are like one day. The Lord is not slow about his promise, as some think of slowness, but is patient with you, not wanting any to perish, but all to come to repentance. But the day of the Lord will come like a thief, and then the heavens will pass away with a loud noise, and the elements will be dissolved with fire, and the earth and everything that is done on it will be disclosed… But, in accordance with his promise, we wait for new heavens and a new earth.

Today, on this first day of a new year, we ponder the mystery of time, and 2 Peter uses a gripping analogy, derived from Psalm 90:4, to impress upon us the vast timescale whereby the Supreme Intelligence is working his purpose out.

The ancients reckoned on a much briefer lifespan for the world than we do. They reasoned that if a day equals a thousand years and the Creator took seven days to make our world, then his plan must allow for seven thousand years in all. In their quaint reckoning, they calculated that history had lasted for three to four thousand years when BC became AD. On this basis, the third millennium, in which we are living, could be the last.

What are we to make of the writer's counsel concerning the final wind-up? He cannot say when, but he does explain how. As at the beginning, the end will come with a second 'big bang' and a totally destructive conflagration. But the patient Lord will allow plenty of time for us to change our wicked ways. It was the Lord's long-term patience that led General Booth, longing to switch on an instant light in darkest England, to remark, 'The trouble is that God is not in a hurry, and I am.'

Scripture here tells us that God himself will finally destroy his own creation. We tend to think that human beings will do it as a consequence of their careless tampering with the environment and their heedless attacks on the ozone layer. Verse 13, however, with its hope of renewal, gives us our topical theme centred on the word 'new'.

Reflection

What does it mean to live 'a godly, righteous and sober life' in today's world which might end tomorrow?

CE

Revelation 21:1–5 (NRSV)

Back to the drawing board

Then I saw a new heaven and a new earth; for the first heaven and the first earth had passed away, and the sea was no more. And I saw the holy city, the new Jerusalem, coming down out of heaven from God, prepared as a bride adorned for her husband. And I heard a loud voice from the throne saying, 'See, the home of God is among mortals. He will dwell with them as their God; they will be his peoples, and God himself will be with them; he will wipe every tear from their eyes. Death will be no more; mourning and crying and pain will be no more, for the first things have passed away.' And the one who was seated on the throne said, 'See, I am making all things new.'

The visionary named John the Divine (i.e. theologian) must have been a dangerous dissident to get himself exiled to the lonely Greek island of Patmos. It was there that he wrote his Revelation for the immediate encouragement of his fellow Christians fiercely persecuted by the Emperor Domitian (AD81–96).

This kind of so-called apocalytic writing, so full of weird obscurities, hardly appeals to our more literalistic western minds. We ask what John actually saw in his vision of a new heaven and earth. In what way will God, at the last, make all things new? And, to begin with, why the relief at getting rid of the sea?

The Hebrew people were total landlubbers; they feared and hated the sea, but not only for its destructive powers. More pertinently here, they believed that the depths of the sea provided a home for evil spirits. To be rid of the sea was to be rid of them. So, with evil destroyed, the need now was for a heaven and earth wrought from a new design. Back to the drawing board to dump the old plans and create new!

Although we cannot envisage John's vision of the future, the words and terms in which it is expressed on the final page or two of scripture must inspire us and give us hope. 'His world-view,' wrote William Neil, 'is that beyond the rise and fall of world empires, the afflictions of the righteous and the chances and changes of fortune, lies the purpose of God, a good purpose which will in the end prevail.'

Reflection

What oxygen is to the lungs, such is hope for the meaning of life.

Victor Hugo (1802–85)

CE

3

2 Corinthians 5:17–20 (NRSV)

New world vision

So if anyone is in Christ, there is a new creation: everything old has passed away; see, everything has become new! All this is from God, who reconciled us to himself through Christ, and has given us the ministry of reconciliation; that is, in Christ God was reconciling the world to himself, not counting their trespasses against them, and entrusting the message of reconciliation to us. So we are ambassadors for Christ, since God is making his appeal through us; we entreat you on behalf of Christ, be reconciled to God.

I knew an optician who devised a simple advertising slogan: 'See Jones and See Better'. The classic effect of Christian conversion is improved vision. See Christ and see better!

'Everything has become *new*!' stated Paul, describing what happens when someone is 'in Christ'. A young man converted in a mission among the Welsh hills was showing a nasturtium leaf to a young boy. 'Do you know,' he said, 'I never knew how beautiful that leaf was until six months ago when I gave myself to Christ.' Years earlier, the drunken reprobate Billy Bray, a hell-raising Cornish miner, was dramatically converted by the Methodists. In November 1823, he said, 'Everything looked new to me—the people, the fields, the cattle, the trees. I was like a man in a new world.'

Paul next underlines the word 'reconciliation'. Humans, at loggerheads with God, desperately need to make friends with him. Christ died for this. The saving arms of God are always open to receive the sinner, for it is we who need to be reconciled to God, not the reverse. All thought of the cross as an instrument to placate an angry God is alien to Paul's thinking. We could say that all the blood shed in sacrifices made by human beings to pacify a supposedly hostile deity has been a wicked waste. It is we who need the change of attitude. 'The very essence of Christianity,' wrote William Barclay, 'is the restoration of a lost relationship.'

Paul sees the Church as an *embassy* of God's unfailing friendship and love set down in the midst of a disordered world. The major task of the followers of the reconciling Lord is to be his ambassadors, pointing to the cross and saying, 'This is how much God loves you, erring child though you are. He longs for you to come home and he waits to welcome you with those open arms of love.'

Reflection

See, everything has become new!

CE

Matthew 9:14–17 (NRSV)

The new wine

Then the disciples of John came to him, saying, 'Why do we and the Pharisees fast often, but your disciples do not fast?' And Jesus said to them, 'The wedding guests cannot mourn as long as the bridegroom is with them, can they? The days will come when the bridegroom is taken away from them, and then they will fast. No one sews a piece of unshrunk cloth on an old cloak, for the patch pulls away from the cloak, and a worse tear is made. Neither is new wine put into old wineskins; otherwise, the skins burst, and the wine is spilled, and the skins are destroyed; but new wine is put into fresh wineskins, and so both are preserved.'

Everyone in Israel was expected to fast at least once a year. Those adhering to a stricter religious regime fasted twice a week. Fasting belonged to days of mourning, like black ties, but otherwise, it seems, Jesus and his disciples didn't fast. In fact, he warned against the hypocrisy that sometimes accompanied fasting, like putting on a miserable facial expression (Matthew 6:16–18). He envisaged life in the kingdom as a wedding feast full of joy.

In the above verses, Jesus warned against mixing the new and the old by using two domestic illustrations. One is a warning about patching clothes. The other has profounder implications.

The process of making wine involved drawing it out of the vat into large jars or wineskins to undergo an initial fermentation, and then another when it was poured into smaller jars and skins. If an old skin was used, the explosive nature of the fermentation would almost certainly cause the skin to burst. New skins must at all costs be used if loss was to be avoided.

Jesus commended the new again and again. In the Sermon on the Mount, he offered a new charter for living as against the old, prefacing each part of it with the phrase: 'You have heard that it was said to those of ancient times… But I say to you…'

'What is this?' they asked with feeling. 'A new teaching!' Such was the impact of the revolutionary Christ upon his contemporaries. A new commandment, a new covenant; and when BC became obsolete and AD replaced it in our calendars, God effected a new beginning. Someone described the gospel as 'planned obsolescence'—a making of all things new.

Reflection

No one open to the moving of the Spirit will cling to the old and fear the new.

CE

1 John 2:7–10 (NRSV)

New age commandment

Beloved, I am writing you no new commandment, but an old commandment that you have had from the beginning; the old commandment is the word that you have heard. Yet I am writing you a new commandment that is true in him and in you, because the darkness is passing away and the true light is already shining. Whoever says, 'I am in the light,' while hating a brother or sister, is still in the darkness. Whoever loves a brother or sister lives in the light, and in such a person there is no cause for stumbling.

John, now very old, is looking back over more than half a century since the first Easter. The old yet ever new commandment is, of course, Jesus' instruction to his inner circle of disciples that they should love one another as he has loved them (John 13:34–35).

We are bound to ask what was new about this exhortation. Listed among the many Old Testament laws of holiness and justice is, 'Love your neighbour as yourself (Leviticus 19:18). That meant a fellow Israelite but also the foreign settler living in Israel (v. 34). But did Jesus narrow that love down to the Christian community? Only to emphasize the value of an example of fellow-love to show the world… 'See how these Christians love one another!'

Jesus actually broadened the scope of that love. He made it indiscriminate. The neighbour is anyone of whatever class, creed or nation, not just one of our own circle or someone we happen to like. Jesus chose a hated Samaritan as the hero of his parable. No Israelite in those days would have picked a battered Samaritan out of the gutter. Even enemies must be loved, Jesus insisted. 'Give me such love for God and men,' said Bonhoeffer, 'as will blot out all hatred and bitterness.' And he meant that love even for the men who would string him up with piano wire in a woodland one April morning.

Jesus came to inaugurate a new age of enlightenment in which his kind of love would be the dominating characteristic. His love has nothing to do with 'liking'. It is the love of a determined will-power, not subject to mood and feeling, like or dislike. Jesus didn't *invite* us to adopt and practise his kind of love. He *commanded* us to do so.

Reflection

The atheist who is moved by love is moved by the Spirit of God; and the atheist who lives by love is saved by his faith in the God whose existence (under that name) he denies.

William Temple (1881–1944)

CE

Matthew 2:9–11 (NRSV)

Led by the light to the Light

When they had heard the king, they set out; and there, ahead of them, went the star that they had seen at its rising, until it stopped over the place where the child was. When they saw that the star had stopped, they were overwhelmed with joy. On entering the house, they saw the child with Mary his mother; and they knelt down and paid him homage. Then, opening their treasure chests, they offered him gifts of gold, frankincense, and myrrh.

Today's reading reflects on the story of the so-called 'wise men' and their journey to worship the newborn king, Jesus. I say 'so-called' because 'wise men' is rather a flattering title for them, I think! They were magi, the origin of our word 'magic'—astrologers, soothsayers, fortune-tellers. In the ancient world, especially the Greco-Roman world, such people held enormous influence. Indeed, it would be no exaggeration to say that millions of people lived in fear and dread of the 'fates', of which such men were regarded as being the mediators.

So why does the Gospel story give them the huge privilege of being among the first to worship the new Messiah? Is this a biblical endorsement of astrology, or soothsaying? Well, that was certainly not how the early Church saw this story. Unanimously, they held it as the final demonstration that God had broken the malign hold of superstition on the human race. Far from being nice, godly old men out on a pious search for truth, the magi were seen as the representatives of a failed and discredited order, who were brought by the power and leading of God to the holy house, and there 'laid their treasure' at the feet of the infant King. For those Christians of the first centuries, the key phrase was 'they knelt down and paid him homage'—literally, they abased themselves before him.

So God in his love draws all the earthly powers and systems to acknowledge his Son. 'Every knee *in heaven and on earth* shall bow, every tongue confess, that Jesus Christ is Lord' (Philippians 2:10–11).

The Collect

Eternal God, who by the shining of a star led the wise men to the worship of your Son: guide by his light the nations of the earth, that the whole world may behold your glory; through Jesus Christ our Lord.

DW

Genesis 37:3–10 (NRSV, abridged)

Selfish dreamer

Israel loved Joseph more than any other of his children... and he had made him a long robe with sleeves. But when his brothers saw that their father loved him more than all his brothers, they hated him... Once Joseph had a dream, and when he told it to his brothers, they hated him even more. He said to them, 'Listen to this dream that I dreamed. There we were, binding sheaves in the field. Suddenly my sheaf rose and stood upright; then your sheaves gathered around it, and bowed down to my sheaf.' His brothers said to him, 'Are you indeed to reign over us?...' He had another dream, and told it to his brothers, saying, '...the sun, the moon, and eleven stars were bowing down to me.' But when he told it... his father rebuked him, and said to him, 'What kind of dream is this that you have had? Shall we indeed come, I and your mother and your brothers, and bow to the ground before you?'

The story of Joseph is a little masterpiece. It is full of psychological insight, dramatic tension and well-drawn characters. Unlike the earlier parts of Genesis, which consist of short episodes strung together, this is (with a few brief intrusions) a single well-told story.

The tale does not start well. We are introduced to an obnoxious youth who is his father's pet. His special status is marked by the coat he is given; although he is supposedly assisting his elder brothers in their work, its long sleeves show that here is one who does not have to do much. Joseph doesn't expect to get his hands dirty, much less the cuffs of his robe. Of course, the kind of favouritism he has been shown is bound to have its effect. The spoilt boy is sure of his own superiority, and he bolsters his sense of his own importance by telling tales. It's no surprise, then, that he is hated by his older brothers. The scene is already set for disaster.

When he tells of two dreams which portray him as ruling over the rest of his family, we are not surprised. They are the kind of dreams that he might well be expected to have. The double irony is that the dreams are indeed true; and yet their real meaning remains hidden. Jospeh has been given a gift by God, but sees it merely as a way to swell his own importance.

Reflection

What gifts have I been given?
How do I use them?

MM

Genesis 37:18–28 (NRSV, abridged)

Revenge

They conspired to kill him... But when Reuben heard it, he delivered him out of their hands, saying, 'Let us not take his life.' Reuben said to them, 'Shed no blood; throw him into this pit here in the wilderness, but lay no hand on him'—that he might rescue him out of their hand... So when Joseph came to his brothers, they stripped him of his robe... and threw him into a pit... They saw a caravan of Ishmaelites coming from Gilead... on their way... down to Egypt. Then Judah said to his brothers, 'What profit is it if we kill our brother and conceal his blood? Come, let us sell him to the Ishmaelites...' And his brothers agreed. When some Midianite traders passed by, they drew Joseph up, lifting him out of the pit, and sold him to the Ishmaelites for twenty pieces of silver. And they took Joseph to Egypt.

Revenge comes when Joseph is sent to see how his brothers are getting on with their flocks. Far from home, and smarting at Joseph's cockiness, his brothers go so far as to suggest murder. It's a dreadful moment, made all the more telling for its realism. It is those closest to us whom we abuse the most, and not necessarily by direct action. Taking them for granted, assuming they are there for our needs, is all too easy to do. Our family relationships do not prosper automatically. Like any other, they need working at, so that love rather than resentment may grow.

Reuben, the eldest brother, comes to the rescue. Make Joseph suffer, by all means, but murder is going much too far. Yet this is not enough for Judah, and Joseph is sold to some passing merchants. It may be that here we have traces of two earlier versions of the story. In one, Joseph is stolen by Midianites, in another he is sold by his brothers. In either case, through his brothers' actions, he ends up on the road to a life of slavery in Egypt.

Where is God in all this? So far, in Genesis, we have become used to God as a central player in the stories. He speaks to the patriarchs, sends angels and even drops in himself. In the Joseph story, he is apparently in the background. As we shall see, though, his presence pervades the whole tale. It is a story of how God turns tragedy to victory, and works out his purposes through the very sins of his people.

Prayer

Lord, Joseph could hardly know that everything was following your will. Neither can we. Yet give us faith to trust that you are in charge of our lives.

MM

Genesis 37:29–36 (NRSV, abridged)

Tragedy strikes

When Reuben returned to the pit and saw that Joseph was not in the pit, he tore his clothes. He returned to his brothers, and said, 'The boy is gone; and I, where can I turn?' Then they took Joseph's robe, slaughtered a goat, and dipped the robe in the blood. They had the long robe with sleeves taken to their father, and they said, 'This we have found; see now whether it is your son's robe or not.' He recognized it, and said, 'It is my son's robe! A wild animal has devoured him; Joseph is without doubt torn to pieces.' Then Jacob tore his garments, and put sackcloth on his loins, and mourned for his son many days... He refused to be comforted, and said, 'No, I shall go down to Sheol to my son, mourning.' Thus his father bewailed him. Meanwhile the Midianites had sold him in Egypt to Potiphar, one of Pharaoh's officials.

The story of Joseph has been described as the Bible's soap opera. Certainly, it runs the full gamut of human emotions, and pitches its characters into just about every situation. Grief now strikes the household of Jacob. To be sure, Joseph is not really dead, but his father does not know that. His distress is real, and the desolation he feels is that of every parent who has lost a child.

If God is really in charge, and the adventures of Joseph are working out God's purposes, it may seem cruel that he allows his servant Jacob to suffer in this way. To think that way is too simplistic, however. We should not think of God as simply pulling strings like a cosmic puppeteer. Rather, he uses the opportunities (and setbacks) afforded by the world he has made and the actions of the people he deals with. No doubt, if Joseph's brothers had been more forgiving or less violent, he would still have ended up in a position to help them to safety in Egypt. But that kind of speculation is pointless. God works with us as we are, in the situations that really exist.

The great encouragement in all this is that God can turn any situation to his advantage. We may keep messing things up, but he still keeps putting us on the right track.

Prayer

Father, help me to realize that you are with me wherever I am, and that I can still follow you, even when things seem to go wrong.

MM

Genesis 39:1–6a (NRSV, abridged)

Blessings in Egypt

Now Joseph was taken down to Egypt... The Lord was with Joseph, and he became a successful man; he was in the house of his Egyptian master. His master saw that the Lord was with him, and that the Lord caused all that he did to prosper in his hands. So Joseph found favour in his sight and attended him; he made him overseer of his house and put him in charge of all that he had. From the time that he made him overseer in his house and over all that he had, the Lord blessed the Egyptian's house for Joseph's sake; the blessing of the Lord was on all that he had, in house and field. So he left all that he had in Joseph's charge; and, with him there, he had no concern for anything but the food that he ate.

Put your trust in the Lord, honour him and follow his way, and he will honour you. He will pour blessings on you, your family, your home and your business. For those whom the Lord blesses will prosper.

No, it's not really my opinion, it's a (more or less accurate) quote from a preacher I once heard, and whom I won't name. I suppose the story of Joseph could look a bit like that. He starts off as Jacob's favoured son, ends up in Egypt as a slave, but the Lord blesses him and he ends up in charge of Potiphar's household.

Those who preach that strange gospel of God-given prosperity would say it was a sign that Joseph was OK with God. On the other hand, if his brothers had known at the time, they might have thought it was just typical of the jammy little so-and-so, and it just goes to show there's no justice in the world.

Of course, it was God's doing; the story tells us that. But why was God doing it? Is he really so capricious? The answer will be revealed at the end of the story: he is doing it for Jacob's whole family, because of his promise to Abraham, and for the sake of his plan of salvation. Joseph, of course, doesn't know that. He merely knows what we all know, that God is to be served wherever we are, and whatever we do.

Prayer

Lord, keep me faithful to you, not because that is the way to prosperity, but because it is the way to you.

MM

Genesis 39:6b–10 (NRSV)

Chastity

Now Joseph was handsome and good-looking. And after a time his master's wife cast her eyes on Joseph and said, 'Lie with me.' But he refused and said to his master's wife, 'Look, with me here, my master has no concern about anything in the house, and he has put everything that he has in my hand. He is not greater in this house than I am, nor has he kept back anything from me except yourself, because you are his wife. How then could I do this great wickedness, and sin against God?' And although she spoke to Joseph day after day, he would not consent to lie beside her or to be with her.

To be honest, I don't know what attitude the ancient Egyptians had towards sex with a slave. Much later in Rome, it was not considered adultery, and the sexual abuse of slaves was common. Perhaps Mrs Potiphar thought nothing of her attempted seduction, until she was spurned.

What is most interesting, and in our culture, rather surprising, is Joseph's attitude. To him it is both a sin against his master's trust and a sin against God.

Nowadays, there are many who would ask, 'What is the harm?' Recently a man boasted to me about how he had seduced a seventeen-year-old girl. As long as his wife never knew, what did it matter?

The answer is found in Joseph's attitude. His relationship to Potiphar was based on trust, and that was something he would not betray. To treat our promises and responsibilities as something to be honoured only when they are in the foreground is to devalue them and ultimately to lose them. This is why the Bible consistently places sex within marriage. It is by necessity to do with relationships. It is the closest we can get to another person. To be that close physically, and yet distant in every other way, is about as dishonest as you can get.

Although he has so far come over as a spoilt brat, Joseph's integrity is intact. In Egypt he is growing up fast.

Prayer

Lord, help me to do what is right, not because it is easy or fun, but because it is what you desire.

MM

Genesis 39:11–18 (NRSV, abridged)

Lies

One day... she caught hold of his garment, saying, 'Lie with me!' But he left his garment in her hand, and fled and ran outside. When she saw that he had left his garment in her hand and had fled outside, she called out to the members of her household and said to them, 'See, my husband has brought among us a Hebrew to insult us! He came in to me to lie with me, and I cried out with a loud voice; and when he heard me raise my voice and cry out, he left his garment beside me, and fled outside.' Then she kept his garment by her until his master came home, and she told him the same story, saying, 'The Hebrew servant, whom you have brought among us, came in to me to insult me; but as soon as I raised my voice and cried out, he left his garment beside me, and fled outside.'

Potiphar's wife fails in her pursuit of Joseph and turns vindictive. Or was it just self-preservation? The sight of a naked youth running from her room might just have been conspicuous. Perhaps there is a bit of both—anger rising from her bruised ego and an attempt to save face. Either way, she takes refuge in deceit.

It's amazing just how often lies seem to rescue us. We can tell lies to avoid punishment, or to turn aside condemnation. We try often enough to persuade ourselves that the facts are not as they appear. We can even, God help us, try to lie to God.

In each case, the reason is much the same. We would rather not face up to the consequences of our actions. Yet lies have their own consequences, both for others and for those who tell them. For one thing, they stop us from growing. We cannot become more responsible, more trustworthy or more mature. They lock us into the situation we lie about, and there we fester.

Even more tragically, lies deny us the hope of forgiveness and reconciliation. The lies we tell lie between us and the one we lie to. Because we don't want to face reality, we can shut ourselves off from those we love, and especially from God—which is a shame, because he wants nothing more than to forgive us, and equip us for a fresh start.

Prayer

Father, let me be truthful to others, to myself and to you, and so find healing.

MM

Genesis 39:19–23 (NRSV)

Top underdog

When his master heard the words that his wife spoke to him, saying, 'This is the way your servant treated me,' he became enraged. And Joseph's master took him and put him into the prison, the place where the king's prisoners were confined; he remained there in prison. But the Lord was with Jospeh and showed him steadfast love; he gave him favour in the sight of the chief jailer. The chief jailer committed to Joseph's care all the prisoners who were in the prison, and whatever was done there, he was the one who did it. The chief jailer paid no heed to anything that was in Joseph's care, because the Lord was with him; and whatever he did, the Lord made it prosper.

A colleague of mine, faced with a church building that had rampant dry rot, shallow finances, an ageing congregation and more than his share of squabbles among the worshippers, asked me what I thought he had done to deserve it all. Later, when he had moved to another parish, he told me what it was—preparation. In the new place, he had a bigger building with worse rot and more disharmony in his elderly congregation. But he knew how to cope with it. Both churches are doing well.

God often prepares us for what we will have to do for him. The trouble is, the preparation can seem a little difficult at times. That, I think, is the lesson that Joseph was learning. Once he is in jail, he bounces back again, and ends up in a position of responsibility. He may be a prisoner, but he is at least the top prisoner.

Of course, it didn't just happen. We have already seen Joseph's integrity. In the light of that, it is pretty clear that Joseph's own diligence was a factor in the favour he earned from the chief jailer.

God is always prepared to see us through. But we need to work with him. Even God doesn't do magic.

Prayer

Father, make me willing to work with you, to show trust and integrity in all I do.

MM

Genesis 40:2–8 (NRSV, abridged)

Restless dreams

Pharaoh was angry with his two officers, the chief cupbearer and the chief baker, and he put them in custody in the house of the captain of the guard, in the prison where Joseph was confined. The captain of the guard charged Joseph with them, and he waited on them... One night they both dreamed—the cupbearer and the baker of the king of Egypt, who were confined in the prison—each his own dream, and each dream with its own meaning. When Joseph came to them in the morning, he saw that they were troubled. So he asked Pharaoh's officers, who were with him in custody in his master's house, 'Why are your faces downcast today?' They said to him, 'We have had dreams, and there is no one to interpret them.' And Joseph said to them, 'Do not interpretations belong to God? Please tell them to me.'

Of course, we all know the story. Joseph interprets the dreams accurately, and the cupbearer is restored to his position, while the baker is executed. Yet, we are told, the cupbearer did not remember Joseph, but forgot him.

Well, what did you expect, a fairy-tale ending? It's a very realistic moment in the story. The restored servant is no doubt overjoyed to get his job back, but why jeopardize it by speaking out on behalf of a man who is in obvious disfavour? He knew Joseph's story, but then, what prisoner ever admits to guilt? Whatever the reasons, Joseph was left imprisoned for another two years.

One of the strange things that puzzles me is the way Christians often seem to think that their faith has brought them into the realm of fairy-tale. They seem to think that, somehow, if their marriage hits difficulties, if they succumb to (major) temptations, if they lose their job or their health, or are bereaved, then God cannot possibly be doing his job, or there is no God, or the Bible has got it wrong. I've come across all these situations and complaints, and more besides. Most of us probably have. Come to think of it, I've made most of these complaints!

Once again, we have to say that we are called to live in the real world, and that is where God works. That is why we need faith. Joseph's disappointment was not the end of the story. Neither is ours.

Prayer

Father, give me faith to see you working in the same world as I am.

MM

15

Genesis 41:1–8 (NRSV)

Uneasy lies the head

After two whole years, Pharaoh dreamed that he was standing by the Nile, and there came up out of the Nile seven sleek and fat cows, and they grazed in the reed grass. Then seven other cows, ugly and thin, came up out of the Nile after them, and stood by the other cows on the bank of the Nile. The ugly and thin cows ate up the seven sleek and fat cows. And Pharaoh awoke. Then he fell asleep and dreamed a second time; seven ears of grain, plump and good, were growing on one stalk. Then seven ears, thin and blighted by the east wind, sprouted after them. The thin ears swallowed up the seven plump and full ears. Pharaoh awoke, and it was a dream. In the morning his spirit was troubled; so he sent and called for all the magicians of Egypt and all its wise men. Pharaoh told them his dreams, but there was no one who could interpret them to Pharaoh.

So now the chief cupbearer remembers Joseph, who interprets Pharaoh's two dreams. Dreams are obviously a major motif in the Joseph story, and it is worth asking at this point whether we should really think of them as a way in which God communicates with us. Not too long ago, I saw a book which claimed that we should look for the spiritual significance of our dreams, since they are a common biblical vehicle for divine messages.

On the other hand, ever since Freud, we have become used to seeing dreams as the product of our subconscious wishes, guilt and desires. Freud was certainly right to a great extent. If, as an adolescent, I had a fevered dream featuring a famously well-endowed actress, it is unlikely that I was receiving a divine revelation. Other dreams are less obviously self-generated, but in fact, they probably are.

The story of Joseph was written in a time when the psychological mechanism of dreams was less well understood. Even then, Joseph was clear that the interpretation of them lay with God. It is there that we should seek the answer to what troubles us, be it dreams or anything else—in prayer and reflection, and conscious awareness of God.

Prayer

Father, help me to bring to you in prayer whatever unsettles my peace.

MM

Genesis 41:33–36, 45 (NRSV, abridged)

Prime minister

'Now therefore let Pharaoh select a man who is discerning and wise, and set him over the land of Egypt. Let Pharaoh proceed to appoint overseers over the land, and take one-fifth of the produce of the land of Egypt during the seven plenteous years. Let them gather all the food of these good years that are coming, and lay up grain... That food shall be a reserve for the land against the seven years of famine that are to befall the land of Egypt, so that the land may not perish through the famine.' ... Pharaoh gave Joseph the name Zaphenath-paneah; and he gave him Asenath daughter of Potiphera, priest of On, as his wife. Thus Joseph gained authority over the land of Egypt.

So Joseph ends up as the chief minister of Egypt. He is given an Egyptian name, takes an Egyptian wife, and assumes the mantle of Pharaoh's authority. Yet he does not turn his back on the God of his fathers, and his two sons are given Hebrew names. After many ups and downs, he has achieved the highest possible worldly success. But he has learnt his lesson. This success has come about through his faithfulness to God, and he will not abandon God now.

It's a lesson worth learning. There are many people who are willing to turn to prayer when they are in difficulty. There are lots who will testify that 'something' helped them in their time of need. Yet when stability is recovered, or sorrow wanes, that something once again takes a back seat.

God is infinitely loving and gracious, and he hears all who turn to him in distress. None the less, what he calls for are people who will remain faithful servants through good times as well as bad.

Another point is that Joseph is now fully a part of Egypt. He has not kept himself aloof, but plunged into the work of the pagan nation which has been put in his charge. He knows that God is served wherever his people find themselves, and that God's work is done in the everyday world, not in some separate religious enclave. It is just as holy a task to be Prime Minster of Egypt as to be the missionary to Egypt.

Prayer

Father, whatever I do, and in whatever circumstances, remind me that I do it for you.

MM

Genesis 42:14–16; 43:8–9; 44:18, 33–34 (NRSV, abridged)

Transformations

But Joseph said to them, '...You shall not leave this place unless your youngest brother comes here! Let one of you go and bring your brother, while the rest of you remain in prison.' ... Then Judah said to his father... 'Send the boy with me... I myself will be surety for him...' Then Judah... said, 'O my lord... please let your servant remain as a slave to my lord in place of the boy; and let the boy go back with his brothers. For how can I go back to my father if the boy is not with me? I fear to see the suffering that would come upon my father.'

The close of the story is, on the surface, the tale of how Joseph plays cat and mouse with his brothers, who have been driven by the famine to buy grain in Egypt. He accuses them of spying, and keeps Simeon hostage as they return to bring Benjamin, the new young son of old Jacob. Then he accuses Benjamin of theft and threatens to keep him in Egypt as a slave. Our few verses cannot do justice to the whole story, but they bring out the point which is easily lost.

Judah, who had been fiercest in his hatred of Joseph, now puts his own life on the line for another young brother, who is his father's favourite. The attempted murderer who was willing to return home without Joseph cannot now return without Benjamin. Just as Joseph is unrecognizable to his brothers, so Judah is unrecognizable to the reader. Much has happened in both Joseph's and Judah's lives. Both bear the marks of their experience, but above all, both bear the marks of the work of God.

We often hear of the change that God promises in the lives of those who put their faith in him. And then perhaps we wonder where that change is, either in our own life, or that of other Christians. The answer is that it is there. But it takes time. God doesn't wave a magic wand, and change sinners into instant saints. 'Instant' is a word which is meaningful only to coffee (and then isn't as good as the real, slow brew).

In people's lives, change comes slowly, through experience, through prayer, and through the steady drip of the grace of God. He works, as we have seen in the story of Joseph, through the circumstances and events of our lives. If we trust him, we will be transformed. That transformation may not seem a miracle, but it often is. It's just a slow one.

Prayer

Father, take charge of me, my life, and my whole being, that I may become what you desire me to be.

MM

Genesis 45:4–10 (NRSV, abridged)

A new home

Then Joseph said... 'I am your brother, Joseph... Do not be distressed... because you sold me here; for God sent me before you to preserve life. For the famine has been in the land these two years... God sent me before you to preserve for you a remnant on earth, and to keep alive for you many survivors. So it was not you who sent me here, but God... Hurry and go up to my father and say to him, "Thus says your son Joseph, God has made me lord of all Egypt; come down to me, do not delay. You shall settle in the land of Goshen, and you shall be near me, you and your children and your children's children, as well as your flocks, your herds, and all that you have."'

It is easy to see how the story of Joseph could be held up as a shining example of worldly success. It is a classic tale of rags to riches, and it could easily be a TV 'mini-serial' with the full Hollywood gloss. Joseph triumphs over all adversity, turning each descent into tragedy into victory. It could be a story of the unquenchable nature of the human spirit, showing how, with the right attitude, and with a good appreciation of his natural talents, Joseph pulls himself up and attains a glorious destiny.

Joseph, however, knows better. 'God sent me before you to preserve life.' It is God who has been in charge all along, and the story is not Joseph's but God's. God is being faithful to the promise he gave to Abraham, and keeping his chosen people safe for the long task which lies ahead of them.

Of course, Joseph has a part to play. He has been gifted above the average. He has a God-given ability to interpret dreams. He is good-looking, and so attracts attention, both good and bad. He is an able administrator, and a man of integrity. He seems, to the onlooker, to be gifted with the strange ability always to land on his feet. He has been specially favoured by his father, by Potiphar, by the jailer, and by Pharaoh. And yet none of this is for him. All his gifts, talents and good fortune are in the end for the good of others. The presumptuous boy of the opening scenes is now the man who has learnt a lesson that many fail ever to grasp—that we find our true fulfilment in the service of others, and of God.

May we too learn the same lesson.

Prayer

Father, thank you for the gifts you have given me. Help me to identify them, not for my sake, but so that they may be a help to others.

MM

Luke 8:22–25 (NRSV)

Boat in a storm

While they were sailing Jesus fell asleep. A windstorm swept down on the lake, and the boat was filling with water, and they were in danger. They went to him and woke him, shouting, 'Master, Master, we are perishing!' And he woke up and rebuked the wind and the raging waves; they ceased, and there was a calm. He said to them, 'Where is your faith?' They were afraid and amazed, and said to one another, 'Who then is this that he commands even the winds and the water, and they obey him?'

Two good questions may be asked in approaching a story like this: (1) what happened? and (2) what does it mean? It is not every day that a man with such charism, authority and power appears in the midst of our problems and confusion. But such a man was Jesus, and his power was exercised not to display any magical talents, but in response to human need. What happened was that when the disciples were in desperate need, with no one else to turn to, they woke and called upon the sleeping Saviour, and cast themselves before him in utter dependence. The power he exercised not only calmed the storm, but stirred up awe, wonder and amazement in the fearful hearts of the disciples.

What does it mean? Well, it means that whatever storms and calamities overtake you in your frail vessel as it sails life's choppy seas, the Saviour is asleep in the depths of your heart. It means that if you realize your utter dependence upon him for salvation, for healing, for deliverance, and if you wake him by the exercise of faith and trust, he will come to your aid. It may not be plain sailing from then on, for his actions will not always be to the measure of your requirements. But as in the experience of the disciples, he will evoke awe, wonder and amazement and you will realize that he is a disturber of your peace. Jesus' action brought a calm, but the disciples were shaken to the foundations, and they trembled before the one they thought they knew, but who now caused them to quake in fear and gladness.

Prayer

Jesus, Lord of wind and waves, I have not been truly aware of your dynamic power dwelling within me. Let me not wait for the storms of perplexity, sickness or mortality to overwhelm me, but waken within me your faith and power. Grant me a godly sense of reverence and calm that can face all my future storms, secure in your love.

R/SSF

A different way of looking at this story can be found later, on page 40.

Luke 8:26–39 (NRSV)

A possessed man

When the swineherds saw what had happened, they ran off and told it in the city and in the country. Then people came out to see what had happened, and when they came to Jesus, they found the man from whom the demons had gone sitting at the feet of Jesus, clothed and in his right mind. And they were afraid. Those who had seen it told them how the one who had been possessed by demons had been healed. Then all the people of the surrounding country of the Gerasenes asked Jesus to leave them; for they were seized with great fear.

During these next three days we shall read the stories of a man, a woman and a child; of the terror of demons, of disease and death and of the authority of Christ over the powers of darkness and over the last enemy.

The primary thing in today's story of deliverance is the centrality of Christ as Saviour and Lord. But there are also some intriguing points in the narrative. The first is that although Jesus dealt with the fears of the populace in healing this wild and fearful man who had oppressed them, they immediately wanted to see the back of Jesus. Was it that he interfered with their commercial lives, or that he had exposed the fears, the madness and the uncontrollable passions within *themselves*?

Then there is that wonderful picture of the man who had been healed and delivered. We find him 'sitting at the feet of Jesus, clothed and in his right mind'. What a marvellous picture of a redeemed soul! He is at peace with the Saviour and with himself.

Thirdly, there is the yearning plea of the man to follow after Jesus. But Jesus responded: 'Return to your home, and declare how much God has done for you.' This saddened the man for the moment, but can you imagine the joy of perhaps wife and children—plus perhaps the opposition of the community who would have preferred the Lord not to have intervened?

I wonder what this story says about our own lives, our relationship with the Christ who stirs up trouble and confronts all that offends grace and compassion in our life and society?

Prayer

Lord Jesus, Light of the world, your power dispelled the demonic darkness from this tormented man, and your redeeming love scared the mediocre people who wanted to preserve their selfish lives. Dispel all the darkness in my life, and give me grace to witness in the community in which you have placed me.

R/SSF

Luke 8:43–48 (NRSV, abridged)

A suffering woman

There was a woman who had been suffering from haemorrhages for twelve years; and though she had spent all she had on physicians, no one could cure her. She came up behind him and touched the fringe of his clothes, and immediately her haemorrhage stopped... When the woman saw that she could not remain hidden, she came trembling; and falling down before him, she declared in the presence of all the people why she had touched him, and how she had been immediately healed. He said to her, 'Daughter, your faith has made you well; go in peace.'

Yesterday the possessed man; today the suffering woman. And what suffering it was—twelve years of internal bleeding, all that time ritually unclean and unable to worship in the temple with God's people, with all the loneliness and derision that went with it. Luke is a bit reticent of complaining about the physicians (he was one!) but Mark says, 'She had endured much under many physicians, and had spent all that she had; and she was no better, but rather grew worse' (5:26).

Perhaps it is because I am in this hermitage where prayer is primary that, in spite of all the progress in medicine and surgery, I receive more and more prayer requests from people in desperate need and terminal illness. Maybe they seem to be increasing because of my age, as my peer group is exposed to the consequences of mortality! However that may be, this poor woman was in desperate straits and there are many (perhaps you) who can identify with her physical, mental and spiritual suffering. For her, it was a matter of physical contact—and how important that is in the sharing of emotional life. We need to be held, embraced and touched in love—and she was not allowed to touch anyone. In today's reading she took the risk, moved forward, and touched Jesus.

We can reach out and touch Jesus in faith today. It works through prayer and sacrament. If you are seriously ill, have you not only laid your case before the Lord in prayer, but also asked priest, pastor, elders of your church, for anointing and laying on of hands for healing? This may be the next step for you—why not take it?

Prayer

Jesus, Compassionate Physician, look on my need and the needs of those I love. Help us to reach out and touch you in faith, and may we experience your healing in body, mind and spirit.

R/SSF

Luke 8:40–42, 49–56 (NRSV)

A dead child

Jesus replied, 'Do not fear; only believe, and she will be saved.' When he came to the house, he did not allow anyone to enter with him, except Peter, John and James, and the child's father and mother. They were all weeping and wailing for her; but he said, 'Do not weep; for she is not dead but sleeping.' And they laughed at him, knowing that she was dead. But he took her by the hand and called out, 'Child, get up!' Her spirit returned, and she got up at once... Her parents were astounded; but he ordered them to tell no one what had happened.

We have thought about a possessed man and a suffering woman, and today we come to the death of a child, and our Lord's tender and amazing ministry in a house full of mourning.

The tension builds up as Jesus' journey to Jairus' house is interrupted by the episode of the woman who touched his garment. A messenger arrives in the commotion and says it is too late—the child is dead—and Jairus must have despaired in grief. Into such pain Jesus spoke faith and encouragement, and they went forward together. A whole wall of unbelief and negativity met them at the house, culminating in the derision of the mourners—and Jesus cast them all out.

He took three believers, Peter, John and James, and the grieving parents, and they gathered around the child. Jesus touched her, took her hand and spoke the saving word. Mark gives us the actual Aramaic words, '*Talitha cum*', which means, 'Little girl, get up!' The miracle took place, light shone in the darkness, life drove out the spectre of death, and Jairus and his wife were astounded as they received the newborn child from the hand of Jesus.

I am thinking today of children who need the healing touch of Jesus; children who need loving human care; children who need to be protected from the abuse of families and predators. Children are the apple of God's eye, and they are given to us in trust, for our nurture, care and example. Do you spend time in prayer, in play and in sharing with your children, or with the children of your family, church and neighbourhood? If you have no children, start today and enter into a new dimension of joy!

Prayer

Jesus, Friend of Children, let me love little children with your love, and communicate to them your warmth, joy and healing.

R/SSF

Luke 9:18–27 (NRSV)

A secret messiah

(Jesus) said to them, 'But who do you say that I am?' Peter answered, 'The Messiah of God.' He sternly ordered and commanded them not to tell anyone, saying, 'The Son of Man must undergo great suffering, and be rejected by the elders, chief priests and scribes, and be killed, and on the third day be raised.' Then he said to them all, 'If any want to become my followers, let them deny themselves and take up their cross daily and follow me.'

We come today to what has been called 'the messianic secret'. Jesus sternly forbids his disciples to say that he is messiah. Why? Was it that the time was not ripe? Was it that he was not certain? Or was it that the word 'messiah' conjured up in most Hebrew minds an apocalyptic conquering hero riding a war horse out of the dreams of the Maccabean period? Here is the nub of the matter. Jesus needed to purify the word, to place before his disciples the understanding of messiah as the suffering servant, the one who would bear Israel's sins and sorrows in pain and silence, and by such suffering bring redemption, forgiveness and the reign of righteousness and peace. This was only to be accomplished by his death and resurrection, by the coming of the Holy Spirit at Pentecost and by the disciples' entering into the harrowing path of suffering and new life to which Jesus' passion would expose them. Our lesson from these verses is that the Master's way is our way, and that the path to the crown is only and always via the cross. If we confess Jesus as Lord, we must accompany him to the garden of Gethsemane and to the cross of Calvary. It means that our passions and sins are to be nailed to the cross and that we die and rise with him.

It was a radical and difficult lesson for the disciples to learn what kind of messiah Jesus really was. But (apart from Judas) they learned it well, and faithfully lived and proclaimed the suffering messiah as the Lord of love. Our path of discipleship may seem easier and more comfortable than this—so perhaps we had better look again at the role and pattern of the suffering messiah.

Prayer

Jesus, Messiah and King, teach us that your crown was of thorns, that your throne was the cross and that the weapons of your kingdom were those of love and equity. Help us to take up our cross and follow you in humility, and thus enter with you into glory.

R/SSF

Luke 10:1–20 (NRSV, abridged)

Lambs among wolves

The Lord appointed seventy others and sent them on ahead of him in pairs to every town and place where he himself intended to go. He said to them, 'The harvest is plentiful but the labourers are few, therefore ask the Lord of the harvest to send out labourers into his harvest. Go on your way. See, I am sending you out like lambs into the midst of wolves... Whatever house you enter, first say, 'Peace to this house!'

One of the amazing things about Jesus' ministry is the way in which he sent out the disciples to preach. They frequently misunderstood his message, were often unforgiving and filled with ambition, and sometimes drove mothers and children away. Yet he trusted them to represent him and to go before him in his ministry. He expected them to be like lambs in the midst of wolves, to proclaim and live the peace and reconciliation that was part of the kingdom message.

If Jesus had waited until their theology was perfect, their PR image acceptable and their communicative skills honed, he could never have sent them forth. They were full of paradox, vulnerability and the risk of failure. When they returned with joy at the marvellous things that had happened, he had to remind them that it was by his grace that they had become channels of his message, and that this same grace had inscribed their names in the book of life.

We live on the glory side of Easter and yet we are still weak, vulnerable and confused if we trust in our own ability. Without Jesus we can do and be nothing (John 15:5), yet he still calls us and equips us for his service. How can our preaching accord with his truth? How can our lives reflect his compassion? And how can we live like lambs in this wolfish world, where it is so easy for us to be affected by the materialistic philosophy which is in the very air we breathe?

When St Francis and his first companions heard today's passage at the beginning of their gospel adventure, they cried out, 'This is what we have been searching for—this is what we want!' And by the sheer grace and joy of God they set out as lambs among wolves to live and proclaim the saving gospel which illumined the world.

Prayer

Jesus, the Way, the Truth and the Life, conform our lives to the pattern of your simplicity and anoint our preaching with the grace of the gospel. Then our ministry will be fruitful and the harvest be gathered in.

R/SSF

Luke 10:25–37 (NRSV)

The good Samaritan

A man was going down from Jerusalem to Jericho, and fell into the hands of robbers who stripped him, beat him, and went away, leaving him half dead. Now by chance a priest was going down that road; and when he saw him, he passed by on the other side. So likewise a Levite, when he came to the place and saw him, passed by on the other side. But a Samaritan, while travelling, came near him; and when he saw him he was moved with pity. He went to him and bandaged his wounds, having poured oil and wine on them. Then he put him on his own animal, brought him to an inn, and took care of him.

Early on a Sunday morning I often take Mungo, the monastery dog, through the woods to Astley Church where there is a lovely window in the nave, depicting the story of the good Samaritan. There is portrayed the poor Jewish traveller, wounded and bleeding upon the ground; the priest and Levite are moving away in the distance; the beautiful donkey stands patiently waiting, and the outsider Samaritan kneels before the victim, pouring wine and oil into his wounds.

Can we excuse the priest and the Levite? Perhaps the first was afraid to transgress the Levitical law of purity, and in any case he had religious services to perform! Perhaps the Levite was attending a committee for the cleaning up of the Jericho road! Jesus' story was revolutionary, for it showed the unclean, heretical Samaritan as the channel of God's love and mercy, and the religionists neglecting the primary law of love.

Lovers of this story have always seen it portraying the gospel. Upon the Jericho road of life, the representative of our humanity is attacked by the powers of sin and darkness. Religion and social systems pass by and neglect him, but the Saviour comes to where he is, pours in the antiseptic wine symbolizing his cleansing blood, and the soothing oil symbolizing the balm of the Holy Spirit. St Augustine does a lot more allegorizing, but it is difficult *not* to relate the story to the compassionate work of Christ the Saviour.

Do you find yourself as one of the characters in this story? If so, which one?

Prayer

Jesus, Good Samaritan, grant that I may dispense the cleansing of your precious blood, and the healing of your Holy Spirit, to my neighbour.

R/SSF

Luke 10:38–42 (NRSV)

Sitting at Jesus' feet

Mary sat at the Lord's feet and listened to what he was saying. But Martha was distracted by her many tasks; so she came to him and asked, 'Lord, do you not care that my sister has left me to do all the work by myself? Tell her then to help me.' But the Lord answered her, 'Martha, Martha, you are worried and distracted by many things; there is need of only one thing. Mary has chosen the better part, which will not be taken away from her.'

Today's passage is not meant to castigate activists and commend contemplatives! Both have their place and both roles can be abused. Jesus is on his way to Jerusalem and the shadow of the cross looms over his life. It is not appropriate to cook three-course meals and to fuss over external comfort at *this* time. The place to be is at Jesus's feet—for his sake as well as our own. He needs the comfort and solace of an understanding heart—and we need the place of quiet and receptive listening, waiting, resting in his love.

It is sometimes appropriate simply to *be* with Jesus, to feel his suffering, to enter more deeply into his passion. There are times in my hermitage when I lay aside the saying of prayers simply to kneel, or lie, at the feet of Jesus. It is then that the Holy Spirit moves me to tears, to adoration, to intercession, and the mingling of joy and sorrow that assures me that the Christ-life is being expressed within my human life.

This is the 'one thing needful', the 'better part' which is indispensable to a gospel life. For if this waiting at the feet of Jesus has its primary place, then our service will not be energized by fussy activism, but by the still dynamism of the indwelling Spirit. The life of Martha will then flow from the life of Mary, and sitting at his feet will lead to serving his needy people. The difference will be that it will proceed not from a fussy and self-pitying martyr complex, but from the interior stillness of the divine love. Charles Wesley understood it in the words of today's prayer.

Prayer

O that I could for ever sit
With Mary at the Master's feet!
Be this my happy choice:
My only care, delight, and bliss,
My joy, my heaven on earth, be this,
To hear the Bridegroom's voice.

R/SSF

27

Luke 12:8–12 (NRSV, abridged)

Proving the promise

Everyone who acknowledges me before others, the Son of Man also will acknowledge before the angels of God; but whoever denies me before others will be denied before the angels of God... When they bring you before the synagogues, the rulers, and the authorities, do not worry about how you are to defend yourselves or what you are to say; for the Holy Spirit will teach you at that very hour what you ought to say.

In today's passage I want to bear witness! It was a powerful incentive to confidence in the gospel message when I was seventeen years of age to *prove* God's promise in personal experience. At that time, being among the last to be called up under conscription to the armed forces, I had an overwhelming pacifist conviction which led me to register as a conscientious objector. I am not prescribing this pattern to others, though I would do the same again. The day came when I had to appear at an appellate tribunal before judge and jury to give account of my persuasion. After much thought and prayer, I had been led to the last lines of today's passage, and determined not to plan or scheme what to say, but simply to trust the Holy Spirit.

There was a particular question which I had wrestled with, and committed to God, and it was the very question which was addressed to me in the dock. There was a tiny Quaker woman in the front row of the court praying for the four conscientious objectors who were appearing that day. I answered the impossible question simply, honestly and (apparently) convincingly, and it carried great weight. At that very moment I felt the fulfilment of the words of verses 11 and 12 actually taking place in my experience, and I left the court dazed with such a happening. Ever since that time it has remained a precious experience which has undergirded much of my witness and faith.

As I say, I am not preaching pacifism here, but I am bearing witness to the reality of God's living presence in the midst of the circumstances in which we find ourselves. Risk it—venture on his call and prove him!

Prayer

Lord of Promise, in the difficult circumstances of our lives make your presence and power known. May we prove you in days of darkness and trust you to carry us through— for you are faithful!

R/SSF

Luke 13:10–17 (NRSV)

Bent double!

He was teaching in one of the synagogues on the sabbath. And just then there appeared a woman with a spirit that had crippled her for eighteen years. She was bent over and was quite unable to stand up straight. When Jesus saw her, he called her over and said, 'Woman, you are set free from your ailment.' When he laid his hands on her, immediately she stood up straight and began praising God. But the leader of the synagogue (was) indignant because Jesus had cured on the sabbath.

This was one of the stories in my scripture examinations as a boy, and I can remember now the dramatic imaginative vision of this woman straightening up by the laying on of Jesus' hands, and her sheer delight and praise for his compassion and power.

The religionists and legalists in the story were concerned with the breaking of the law, and the regulations which dictated what kinds of knots *could* be untied on the sabbath—even to release an animal! Jesus would have none of this legal disputation, and he cut through the theology of knots which kept a daughter of Abraham and a child of God in such bondage. The Greek text says that Jesus affirmed it was 'necessary' (*dei*) for the woman to be set free. He does not engage in ritualistic argument but takes the initiative, sets before the congregation and religionists a woman redeemed and set free—whatever they may make of it!

Of course the result depended on the attitude of the onlookers. For Jesus it was the necessary liberation of the woman; for the woman it was the exhilaration of freedom; for the religious killjoys it was a breaking of ritual law. What is it for us? Perhaps we can share in the sheer extemporaneous exultation of the common people: 'All his opponents were put to shame; and the entire crowd was rejoicing at all the wonderful things that he was doing' (v. 17).

Prayer

Jesus, Liberator of Captives, you straightened the woman's spine so that her eyes could be raised to the sun. Grant that I may stand straight today, lifting my eyes from the base things of earth to gaze into your wonderful face. Then those around will share in the joy, the praise and the gratitude.

R/SSF

Luke 14:7–14 (NRSV)

Invite the poor!

(Jesus) said to the one who had invited him, 'When you give a luncheon or a dinner, do not invite your friends or your brothers or your relatives or rich neighbours, in case they may invite you in return, and you would be repaid. But when you give a banquet, invite the poor, the crippled, the lame, and the blind. And you will be blessed, because they cannot repay you, for you will be repaid at the resurrection of the righteous.'

I once heard a good definition of the gospel: 'one beggar telling another beggar where to get food'. Jesus, in today's reading, is not giving lessons on etiquette or commending some subtle 'power game' rules on how to get to the top of the table by pretending humility until the host notices you. If you read on into the next section, you'll find that in the kingdom of God everyone at the feast is a beggar, or lame, or blind—we're all unworthy, and we're all in it together.

Jesus begins by contrasting true humility with the fact that he sees the guests sliding into the honourable places (v. 7), and he carries the story into the eternal feast of the kingdom (v. 14). But on the way he makes a significant point which needs to be taken to heart by the comfortable Christians who populate our churches of all denominations. The question is: do we often go out for expensive meals, and exchange invitations to exotic and competitive meals with our own peer group, but never dream of inviting a poor family from the neighbourhood, let alone anyone from cardboard city?

Jesus is saying that our place in the eternal kingdom is linked to our attitude and behaviour in our present lives (the story of Dives and Lazarus is relevant in Luke 16:19–31). But Jesus does not mean that we should 'earn our place' in the kingdom by calculated good deeds or penances in this world. It is all of grace, and we are all unworthy and undeserving sinners. Love bids us welcome, and our response should be that our hearts, homes and bank balances are open to the poor, the needy, and the abused of the world. How about it?

Prayer

Jesus, Master of the Feast, you have called us freely to the gospel feast, and we come in from the highways needing to be cleansed and made worthy. Enable us to open our hearts in generosity as you have opened your heart in mercy. So shall we rejoice with you in the feast of your love.

R/SSF

Matthew 21:18–22 (NRSV)

Failing grace

In the morning, when he returned to the city, he was hungry. And seeing a fig tree by the side of the road, he went to it and found nothing at all on it but leaves. Then he said to it, 'May no fruit ever come from you again!' And the fig tree withered at once. When the disciples saw it, they were amazed, saying, 'How did the fig tree wither at once?' Jesus answered them, 'Truly I tell you, if you have faith and do not doubt, not only will you do what has been done to the fig tree, but even if you say to this mountain, "Be lifted up and thrown into the sea," it will be done. Whatever you ask for in prayer with faith, you will receive.'

The Church is not very good at failing, is it? I can hear you gasping in disbelief as you read those words, so let me put it another way—the Church is not very good at *visibly* failing. The cursing and death of the fig tree is not a miracle that receives much attention, perhaps because many people secretly and guiltily feel that it was a rather petulant act on the part of Jesus, but it says something very important to the modern Church about freely and openly allowing things that are not bearing fruit to die.

I was once invited to the launch of a major Christian project initiated by one of those 'never visibly wrong' groups, and very impressive it was too. Prophecies, words of knowledge and amazing coincidences had apparently abounded, and the thing took off in a victorious blaze of publicity. A few months later I happened to notice, in the tiniest of tiny paragraphs in a corner of the same organization's newsletter, that this project, 'planted to grow for years', had already been terminated. I really wished that they could have given as much attention to explaining why it unexpectedly died as they had done to celebrating its birth.

There is nothing wrong with ending something that is no longer doing what God wants or wanted it to do, whether huge, corporate undertakings or small personal areas of our lives. I meet many people who are trapped in little prisons of obsolete activity, not realizing that God himself has already opened the door which will allow them to leave. Of course we have to be careful to get it right, but wouldn't you rather be wrong than fruitless? I would. God will always let us start again…

Prayer

Father, if we are wasting our time,
give us the courage to stop.

AP

This is the first of a series by Adrian Plass on Gospel miracles.

Mark 4:37–41 (NRSV)

Don't you care?

A great windstorm arose, and the waves beat into the boat, so that the boat was already being swamped. But he was in the stern, asleep on the cushion; and they woke him up and said to him, 'Teacher, do you not care that we are perishing?' He woke up and rebuked the wind, and said to the sea, 'Peace! Be still!' Then the wind ceased, and there was a dead calm. He said to them, 'Why are you afraid? Have you still no faith?' And they were filled with great awe and said to one another, 'Who then is this, that even the wind and the sea obey him?'

It is remarkable how little people change.

I have just re-read my first sentence and realized it could be saying that hugely significant alterations tend to occur in persons of small stature. I'll leave it in as a good example to other contributors of how not to write.

No, what I meant was that, in this story of the calming of the storm, the disciples say to Jesus what many of us say to him nowadays: 'Don't you care?' What an extraordinary thing to ask so soon after the feeding of thousands of people by means that must have been supernatural. (The bring-and-share system hadn't got going by then, and quiche was yet to be invented.)

The disciples had still not grasped two vital points. First, matters of physical safety, sustenance and finance were never unimportant to Jesus, but actually securing them was a piece of cake—or bread, or fish. When money is needed to pay tax, for instance, he sends Peter off to do what seems to be the first thing that comes into his head. I dunno, he says, catch a fish, look in its mouth, you'll find a coin. That'll do...

Second, they hadn't understood, like so many Christians in the West, that the crucial and most endangered part of them, the part that will live for ever *somewhere*, was as safe as houses (well, houses built on a rock, anyway).

Today some people try to shake Jesus awake because their mortgage arrangements haven't worked out. 'Don't you care?' they cry. 'Look what's happening! Don't you care?' Of course he cares. Jesus cares about everything. But isn't it difficult sometimes to take strength from remembering what he's done for us in the past, and what the top priorities for followers of Jesus really ought to be? We'll go on trying, eh?

Prayer

Thank you for caring. Forgive us for not trusting you.

AP

Matthew 8:1–4 (NRSV)

Feeling the touch

When Jesus had come down from the mountain, great crowds followed him; and there was a leper who came to him and knelt before him, saying, 'Lord, if you choose, you can make me clean.' He stretched out his hand and touched him, saying, 'I do choose. Be made clean!' Immediately his leprosy was cleansed. Then Jesus said to him, 'See that you say nothing to anyone; but go, show yourself to the priest, and offer the gift that Moses commanded, as a testimony to them.'

As I write, it is five days since millions of people watched the funeral procession and memorial service of Diana, Princess of Wales. On that Saturday morning a hush fell over the entire country as the princess who did *not* live happily ever after went to her rest. What a staggering response to her death! Never have I seen this country as united as it has been over this tragedy, and I doubt if I shall see it again. That experience of togetherness is an injection that the thin bloodstream of this country sorely needed, and is a quite unexpected aspect of Diana's legacy. It proved that what millions of ordinary people really want, despite what cynics say, is to look up to and admire someone who is *good*.

Di was not perfect, and would never have claimed to be, but Jesus was and is. I long for more people to see the beauty and goodness of Jesus, and to learn that he is still alive and still touching people. And, of course, it was the whole business of 'touch' that made me think of Diana when I read this passage about the leper. It is said that the Princess of Wales broke new ground by making physical contact with AIDS sufferers—the 'lepers', I suppose, of modern times.

Here is the Son of God, though, two thousand years ago, doing exactly the same thing with a power of practical love that is impossible to comprehend, and an unfathomable depth of compassion. Did the leper find the miracle of actually being touched less astounding than the miracle of being healed? Given a choice, and not being a complete loony, he would have gone for the latter, of course, but, oh, the sweetness of being touched by the hand of the Prince of Peace! I do hope you have felt that touch.

Prayer

Touch us with your love, Lord, and help us to touch others.

AP

Matthew 14:15–19 (NRSV)

An amazing adventure!

When it was evening, the disciples came to him and said, 'This is a deserted place, and the hour is now late; send the crowds away so that they may go into the villages and buy food for themselves.' Jesus said to them, 'They need not go away; you give them something to eat.' They replied, 'We have nothing here but five loaves and two fish.' And he said, 'Bring them here to me.' Then he ordered the crowds to sit down on the grass. Taking the five loaves and the two fish, he looked up to heaven, and blessed and broke the loaves, and gave them to the disciples, and the disciples gave them to the crowds.

Birthdays are always special occasions for us, but mine have not generally involved huge expenditure because I prefer things made by the children. This year, though, my wife indulged my childish whim to own my very own Nintendo 64, which, for the uninitiated, is a computer console allowing one to play incredibly complex games on a television screen. The only game I have been able to afford so far stars a little red-capped Italian workman who takes amazing risks in a bewildering variety of worlds, dies repeatedly by falling over precipices and being attacked by monsters, and is always resurrected to continue his search for the imprisoned princess whose rescue is his ultimate goal.

Please don't assume I've gone completely mad, but I think the Christian life, at its best, is not unlike the adventures of Mario. This feeding of the five thousand, for instance. Imagine it being your turn to use the controller for that one. I've often wondered if Jesus knew in advance that problems like this would need solving, or whether he simply had to think and plan (pray) on his feet. There they were, a bunch of five thousand assorted people with no lunch, and what an extraordinary solution he came up with.

It must have been similar throughout that action-packed three-year ministry, every day bringing new adventures and problems to be solved. The exhilarating thing about it is that nothing has changed. There were and still are no limits. Because it's God on our side, *anything can happen*, and, whatever does happen, we cannot die the second death. Stop and have a really good think about that. When you get up tomorrow—enjoy the adventure.

Prayer

Some of us have got a bit stale, Lord.
Please remind us that we are on an
adventure with you.

AP

Luke 22:47–51 (NRSV)

Friend or foe

While he was still speaking, suddenly a crowd came, and the one called Judas, one of the twelve, was leading them. He approached Jesus to kiss him; but Jesus said to him, 'Judas, is it with a kiss that you are betraying the Son of Man?' When those who were around him saw what was coming, they asked, 'Lord, should we strike with the sword?' Then one of them struck the slave of the high priest and cut off his right ear. But Jesus said, 'No more of this!' And he touched his ear and healed him.

I have always felt a great sympathy with Peter over this incident. I suspect that the resultant mixture of humiliation and frustration was an extremely potent cocktail.

As a teenager, and in the early part of my marriage, I was destructively possessive of those close to me. Looking back, I am embarrassed about the ploys I used in trying to chain those I cared about to myself. If a new person arrived on the immediate social scene, I looked carefully for negative aspects of their personality or behaviour and pointed out these deficiencies to my wife, or to friends who might be 'seduced' into liking them more than me. This ridiculous behaviour, growing out of the deep and poisoned soil of insecurity, aimed to separate the world into two warring camps, one being me and those who loved me without reservation, and the others being a shadowy crowd of beings who needed to be kept at arm's length in case they threatened my fragile world.

Did Peter feel a little like this on that awful night? He had been brave enough to defend his master with a sword, and actually managed to do some damage. How did he feel when the man he loved and was prepared to support with his blood showed such tenderness to the wounded enemy? It is as difficult for us to understand today as it was for Peter all those years ago, that we can only do things for God in *his* way, and that he truly does require us to dispose of our enemies by making them into our friends.

We share Jesus or we don't have him at all. There can be no safe little holy huddles in the Christian Church, however tempting such situations may be. If that's what's happening with your lot—watch it!

Prayer

Father, give us a willingness to share Jesus
with anybody and everybody.
Any friend of yours...

AP

Luke 10:16–20 (NRSV)

Are you in the book?

'Whoever listens to you listens to me, and whoever rejects you rejects me, and whoever rejects me rejects the one who sent me.' The seventy returned with joy, saying, 'Lord, in your name even the demons submit to us!' He said to them, 'I watched Satan fall from heaven like a flash of lightning. See, I have given you authority to tread on snakes and scorpions, and over all the power of the enemy; and nothing will hurt you. Nevertheless, do not rejoice at this, that the spirits submit to you, but rejoice that your names are written in heaven.'

Twin notes of delight and warning echo from these verses down the passage of two thousand years.

Jesus' eyes shone with joy on seeing his disciples so thrilled and inspired by 'their' success. He was deeply proud of them, and elated by this early confirmation that the devil was finally faced with defeat. Whether the disciples themselves really understood what was happening is a different matter. I suspect that much of their satisfaction was based more on the 'magical' thrill of healings and deliverance than on strictly spiritual aspects. They had experienced sensations of exhilarating power on discovering that even demons did what they were told when commanded by the servants of the living God in the mighty name of Jesus.

Power is a dangerous drug. It makes slaves out of men and women, not just in the secular world, but also, with disastrous effects, in some sections of the Christian Church. That is why Jesus tempered his enthusiasm with a warning. He had to. When he told the disciples that nothing could hurt them, he certainly did not mean that they would never suffer physically, because many of them did. He meant that their eternal souls were safe with God, whatever else happened. Never mind the thrill of power, he was saying, and never mind anything physical or verbal that anyone throws at you—just be thankful that you're going to live happily ever after.

What shall we pray about today? Let's pray that churches all over the world will hear these words of Jesus and learn from them. He delights in his name being used as a powerful force for good, but gifts and spiritual power can be seductive. The real cause for rejoicing is the fact that he's got our names down.

Prayer

May your words be dark glasses to our eyes when glittering irrelevancies threaten to blind us.

AP

John 2:6–10 (NRSV)

Filling the pots

Now standing there were six stone water jars for the Jewish rites of purification, each holding twenty or thirty gallons. Jesus said to them, 'Fill the jars with water.' And they filled them up to the brim. He said to them, 'Now draw some out, and take it to the chief steward.' So they took it. When the steward tasted the water that had become wine, and did not know where it came from (though the servants who had drawn the water knew), the steward called the bridegroom and said to him, 'Everyone serves the good wine first, and then the inferior wine after the guests have become drunk. But you have kept the good wine until now.'

So would I have put my faith in him? Goodness gracious—you'd have had a job to keep me away from a man who reveals his glory by turning large pots of water into top-quality wine. I love the fact that Jesus' first miracle was so practical and recreational. This event is precisely what an earthly committee set up to plan the Son of God's visit to the third planet would have rejected out of hand.

'For his first miracle let's have him turn some water into wine at a wedding,' the youngest committee member might have suggested. 'That'd be ace!'

'That would not be ace—I mean, good,' one of the more serious-minded members replies sternly. 'The initial earthly revelation of the miraculous power of God incarnate is *not* going to occur in a catering context.'

Fortunately, such a committee did not exist, and we are privileged to witness the really quite extraordinary ordinariness of the character of God over and over again in stories like this, and in the life of Jesus generally.

Not that the water pots story does not have its own very significant spiritual interpretation. Insights into some areas of scripture become tools that last you for ever, don't they? Years ago, Bridget and I read in somebody or other's daily notes the simple suggestion that if we obediently fill the water pots in our own lives, doing all the things that we are actually able to do, God will transfigure them just as Jesus turned water into wine.

That very basic divine principle has inspired and sustained us again and again over the years, and I thank God for the miracle which revealed it.

Prayer

Take our best, Lord, and turn it into yours.

AP

Luke 8:41–42, 49–55 (NRSV, abridged)

Clear sight

There came a man named Jairus, a leader of the synagogue. He fell at Jesus' feet and begged him to come to his house, for he had an only daughter, about twelve years old, who was dying... While he was still speaking, someone came... to say, 'You daughter is dead; do not trouble the teacher any longer.' When Jesus heard this, he replied, 'Do not fear. Only believe, and she will be saved.' When he came to the house, he did not allow anyone to enter with him, except Peter, John, and James, and the child's father and mother. They were all weeping and wailing for her; but he said, 'Do not weep; for she is not dead but sleeping.' And they laughed at him, knowing that she was dead. But he took her by the hand and called out, 'Child, get up!' Her spirit returned, and she got up at once. Then he directed them to give her something to eat.

Jesus was quite often astonished or (apparently) impatient in response to lack of faith. I find it very warming. It shows he was genuinely functioning as a human being on the most important levels, and it resonates with the sense that he was aware of a 'real life' that offered a taste of heaven. In fact, he called this real life the kingdom of heaven, and he knew it was at hand because he could see it so clearly. He seems to have been genuinely surprised that others couldn't.

The practical consequences of such clear sight are apparent in this story. Jesus is not handicapped by the common and reasonable view that the little girl's illness is a matter for despair. He knows what can happen when faith meets impossibility. Learning of her death doesn't diminish his confidence. In the kingdom of God, illness and death are fully negotiable, and are, in any case, not the worst things that can befall human beings.

His divinely human certainty survives the mourners' scorn, and that kingdom vision of a healed child becomes reality. The little girl lives. Then, being a very nice, practically caring person, as well as being God incarnate, Jesus tells her shocked parents to feed their healthy daughter. Hungry work, coming back from the dead!

I'm not keen on phrases like 'kingdom vision' (it sounds like one of those awful magazines produced in grey and red by desktop publishers), but I think we need it, don't you?

Prayer

Open our eyes, Lord.

AP

John 9:1–7 (NRSV) (but please read the whole chapter)

Seeing is believing

As he walked along, he saw a man blind from birth. His disciples asked him, 'Rabbi, who sinned, this man or his parents, that he was born blind?' Jesus answered, 'Neither this man nor his parents sinned; he was born blind so that God's works might be revealed in him... As long as I am in the world, I am the light of the world.' When he had said this, he spat on the ground and made mud with the saliva and spread the mud on the man's eyes, saying to him, 'Go, wash in the pool of Siloam' (which means Sent). Then he went and washed and came back able to see.

I include this story of the healing of the man born blind because of two features, one being the subsequent conversation between the newly healed man and the furious Pharisees. I mention this snappy piece of dialogue not because of its spiritual implications, but because it's so funny. There's no room to set it all out here, but do read it—it's wonderful stuff!

The second feature is the interplay between the disciples and Jesus at the beginning of the chapter. Jesus' followers assumed every now and then that they had finally established a pattern or norm in their master's approach to the world. It remains a common tendency today. Gettling things *settled*, drawing up lists of conditions or rules, building in safeguards, knowing where we are—these constructs make Christians feel better, and can be important, but only if they are allowed to bend or break when God's truth changes our understanding.

Whether the disciples' question was culturally based, or whether they were being a bit cocky in thinking they knew the only two possible reasons for this man's lifelong affliction, I don't know, but I suspect that Jesus' interesting reply was a loud bell in their heads saying 'WRON-N-NG!!' I have made the same mistake. I must have been unbearable on some of the occasions when I have lectured others on the exact way in which God thinks and works, and I'm sure I shall do it again.

Now, do get your Bible out and read the whole of this chapter. It's well worth it!

Prayer

Break up the unhelpful patterns that we hide in, and lead us out to where you are, Lord. Thank you for laughter.

AP

Luke 13:10–13 (NRSV)

Getting straight

Now he was teaching in one of the synagogues on the sabbath. And just then there appeared a woman with a spirit that had crippled her for eighteen years. She was bent over and was quite unable to stand up straight. When Jesus saw her, he called her over and said, 'Woman, you are set free from your ailment.' When he laid his hands on her, immediately she stood up straight and began praising God.

This account of a sabbath day miracle might also be seen as a splendid little parable of spiritual and emotional revival. I have known many people (been one myself) who are bent double with worrying introspection. All we can see in that state is our feet, an uninspiring sight for most of us at the best of times. Some of us have been looking downwards for so long that we have forgotten there is a sky at all, let alone what it looks like.

Is it really possible that God could heal such a painful twisting and distortion of the spirit? Books, preachers and the Bible itself seem continually to say that he can and does, but some of the people who are reading these notes have known inward pain for a very long time and have lost heart after 'trying everything'.

Well, we might take a crumb of comfort from the fact that, just as Jesus noticed the suffering of the woman in this story, so he must notice and care about all those who are in mental and emotional pain. Then there is the fact that, in this case, the healing seems to have taken place quite independently of the faith of the sick person. Jesus simply laid hands on her and, perhaps rather to her surprise, she was instantly healed, much to the disgust of the synagogue ruler, so lost in religion that he had forgotten what God was really like. What a wonderful moment after that, when she straightened up and praised God!

Do you want to straighten up and praise God? Or do you know someone who has a desperate need to be unlocked, to be freed to look up and see the sky that God made? Let's talk to Jesus.

Prayer

Lord Jesus, some of us have been bowed over with pain for so long that we don't think we shall ever look up again. We trust that you have noticed us. Please put your hands on us and release us to worship you.

AP

John 11:32–35 (NRSV) (but please read vv. 1–44)

When everything is just too much

When Mary came where Jesus was and saw him, she knelt at his feet and said to him, 'Lord, if you had been here, my brother would not have died.' When Jesus saw her weeping, and the Jews who came with her also weeping, he was greatly disturbed in spirit and deeply moved. He said, 'Where have you laid him?' They said to him, 'Lord, come and see,' Jesus began to weep.

Why did Jesus weep?

I have read so many theories that I can no longer see the question very clearly. On reading through the story again, though, I see that for Jesus this event marked a terribly significant crossroads in his life.

He was on his way to be with people who seem to have provided the kind of refuge that all public figures in great demand long to have, a place of total acceptance where you can take your sandals off and let your hair down even further than it already falls. One of those close friends was four days dead, Martha and Mary were distraught and somewhat accusing, and he was about to say a prayer that would result in the resurrection of Lazarus. In the back of his mind the knowledge of his own impending death and resurrection, and the consequent potential rescue from destruction for the entire world, would have been pressing constantly for space in his consciousness. Nobody—*nobody*—could possibly begin to understand the wild conflicts of hope, sadness and fear that were happening inside him at this time. There was no other human being like Jesus for Jesus to talk to.

Standing outside the tomb, no doubt seeing in the emergence of that shrouded figure seeds of the unimaginably vast redemptive process that only his willing death would facilitate, his heart must have come as close as it ever could to failing him.

What a tension Jesus felt as he approached Bethany, a place of warmth and escape, but situated only two miles from Jerusalem, which was so soon to be a place of death. For him, the raising of his friend Lazarus was bound to bring those two worlds into dramatic mental collision.

No wonder he wept.

Prayer

Father, we have not even begun to understand the suffering of Jesus, have we? Thank you for allowing him to go through all that he did for us. We are so glad that he is in a place of warmth and safety now. Thank you for making it possible for us to join him.

AP

Luke 5:4–11 (NRSV, abridged)

Jackpot!

When he had finished speaking, he said to Simon, 'Put out into the deep water and let down your nets for a catch.' Simon answered, 'Master, we have worked all night long but have caught nothing. Yet if you say so, I will let down the nets.' When they had done this, they caught so many fish that their nets were beginning to break... But when Simon Peter saw it, he fell down at Jesus' knees, saying, 'Go away from me, Lord, for I am a sinful man!' For he and all who were with him were amazed at the catch of fish that they had taken... Then Jesus said to Simon, 'Do not be afraid; from now on you will be catching people.' When they had brought their boats to shore, they left everything and followed him.

It would have needed a miracle like this to persuade Peter finally to leave behind his life as a fisherman. The ease with which Jesus organized a huge catch must have had a bewildering effect on men who never knew how successful their work would be from day to day.

Gamblers dread winning. A friend of mine told me how, for a long time, he was addicted to playing fruit machines in pubs and station waiting-rooms. 'The thing I dreaded most,' he said, 'was winning a lot of money the first time I pulled the handle.'

'Why?'

'Well, it's obvious, isn't it?'

'It is?'

'Yes, you see, there'd have been no point in going on playing if I'd won a lot straight away, but then I would have put it all back in anyway, and I wouldn't have been able to kid myself that it was worth playing the machine because I'd have known deep down that there was no chance of coming out on top, so I wouldn't have enjoyed it.'

'I see.' Well, I did—sort of.

Peter wasn't a gambler. Fishing was very hard work, but in a way his experience with the big catch would have been the equivalent to Jesus coming up behind my friend as he played the fruit machine and 'fixing' the machine so that only jackpots came up. Not much fun any more.

Peter's priorities as a working man were displaced—eclipsed by this miracle—and he thereby gained a little more freedom to commit himself to the master. To follow Jesus in any meaningful way, I shall have to learn the same lesson.

Prayer

Shift our priorities, Lord; we want to come with you as well.

AP

John 10:1–4 (NRSV)

Called by name

'Very truly, I tell you, anyone who does not enter the sheepfold by the gate but climbs in by another way is a thief and a bandit. The one who enters by the gate is the shepherd of the sheep. The gatekeeper opens the gate for him and the sheep hear his voice. He calls his own sheep by name and leads them out. When he has brought out all his own, he goes ahead of them, and the sheep follow him because they know his voice.'

There are so many wonderful things to pick up from this chapter about the good shepherd that it is very easy to miss the truth that Jesus calls his own sheep by name. To a stranger all sheep look alike. The true shepherd, though, spends a great deal of time with his flock. Indeed, he enters into a very real relationship with them, just as we might with a dog. Each one is unique and special and the name emphasizes that.

Emily came from a very disturbed background. She was taken for a weekend in the country, and on the Saturday morning, during a game, she hid in the broom cupboard. All day the staff of the house were looking for her and calling her by name. It took them many hours before they found her. She had heard them calling but would not reveal herself because, she said, 'I just loved to hear you calling my name. It made me feel wanted and special.'

Everyone in India spoke of the very poor as 'untouchables'. Instead Gandhi called them 'the children of God'. That very name emphasized their importance. No wonder the ordinary people loved him.

In Britain, the dog leads and the shepherd follows the sheep. However, in the Middle East the shepherd is very much the leader. He prepares the way and makes sure it is safe for the sheep to follow. Mark 16:7 tells us that after the resurrection, Jesus went ahead of the disciples into Galilee, the place where they had first heard the call to follow him. John's Gospel virtually ends with the same call (John 21:22). Because Jesus loves us enough to call us by name, we know it is safe to follow and be true disciples.

Prayer

Thank you, Lord, for being my shepherd and friend. Help me never to forget that I am special to you, for you call me by my name. Amen.

PG

Hebrews 11:8–10 (NRSV) (also read Genesis 12:1–9)

Wilderness unknown

By faith Abraham obeyed when he was called to set out for a place that he was to receive as an inheritance; and he set out, not knowing where he was going. By faith he stayed for a time in the land he had been promised, as in a foreign land, living in tents... For he looked forward to the city that has foundations, whose architect and builder is God.

Pulling up roots, wandering as a nomad, not knowing the direction of your pilgrimage, all these are great demands to make of obedience—unless the obedience is grounded in faith and love. During these next two weeks we shall encounter many wilderness experiences, and there will be times when we shall see, in the Bible and in our own experience, that wilderness is a time of drought, emptiness, pain and suffering—and only in a relationship of faith and love can these things yield positive blessing.

In Abraham's case, we have the promise of blessing and increase in the Genesis passage, and the Hebrews commentary of faith in a 'God-horizon' that was not even part of the revelation back in the time of Abraham. However dark the path may have seemed to him, he held on, not by grim determination, but by faith and trust in a God who called him from over the horizon of love.

When you are called to pull up your roots, when you have to face a future which calls for faith and challenge, when you have to face unknown problems which have reason to cause you fear in your present ignorance, then it is well to think about the qualities attributed to Abraham in his wilderness journeyings.

Cultivate the kind of faith that is grounded in love today. For who knows when the call may come to you—a call hitherto unimagined, and one which, if it came today, you would be unable to respond to. But when the time comes, the strength will be given—and the rewards will be 'over the horizon' of present imagination.

Prayer

God of the unknown, let me be known by you, and let me know you in those deep and secret places of my soul, so that I may answer at your call and find in you my joy.

R/SSF

This is the first of a series by Brother Ramon on 'Wilderness Experiences'.

Genesis 28:10–12, 16–17 (NRSV, abridged)

Wilderness dream

Jacob left Beer-sheba and went toward Haran. He came to a certain place and stayed there for the night, because the sun had set. Taking one of the stones of the place, he put it under his head, and lay down... and dreamed... Then Jacob woke from his sleep and said, 'Surely the Lord is in this place—and I did not know it!' And he was afraid, and said, 'How awesome is this place! This is none other than the house of God, and this is the gate of heaven.'

Strange place, lonely journey, rocky terrain, darkness and exhaustion. This was the context and setting of Jacob's dream as he ran away from the anger of his deceived brother Esau and sought a new place and new roots.

He didn't realize that though his journey seemed accidental and decided by unforeseen circumstances, God had an appointment with him. The place and the time were right!

It was not an easy and comfortable meeting—not a relaxing period of meditation to bring peace to a worried mind or to lower his blood pressure! This was a prophetic encounter, a numinous vision, and one which shook him to his very foundations.

The Celtic tradition speaks of 'thin places' in our world, where heaven is so near, and there are universal sites which have been blessed and made sacred by divine visitations, or made unholy by demonic attacks of evil. Our spiritual perception is often too blunt or atrophied to be made aware of such spiritual dimensions.

But when God appoints his time and place, then our circumstances will bring us there. It may be a wilderness for us, but it will have a visionary quality, it will shake us to our foundations, and communicate God's will for our personal or social lives. Our task is to continue our journey, see it as a moving pilgrimage, and be prepared to encounter God in the most likely or unlikely places. Then we shall have reason to say: 'How awesome is this place! This is none other than the house of God, and this is the gate of heaven.'

Prayer

Help me to realize, dear Lord, that you are in control of my life and can transform it from a journey into a pilgrimage. Sharpen my spiritual awareness, and enable me to discern your voice and vision along the way.

R/SSF

Genesis 32:24, 29–31 (NRSV)

Wilderness wrestling

Jacob was left alone; and a man wrestled with him until daybreak... Then Jacob asked him, 'Please tell me your name.' But he said, 'Why is it that you ask my name?' And there he blessed him. So Jacob called the place Peniel, saying 'For I have seen God face to face, and yet my life is preserved.' The sun rose upon him as he passed Penuel, limping because of his hip.

This passage of scripture makes me tremble. Partly because it has always had a numinous, mysterious, aweful quality in my reading and experience, as I have linked it with Charles Wesley's beautiful hymn *Come, O thou traveller unknown*, indicating the mystical depths of its meaning. But also because it has to do with my own exploration of the mystery of God's love, which has wounded me in all manner of ways, has ordered my life in its joys and sorrows, and has brought me to where I am today.

Wilderness is like that—it mingles in our experience divine yearning and mortal pain. 'You have striven with God and humans' (v. 28). This striving is part of being in the wilderness.

This is not the beginning of Jacob's spiritual life—we saw something yesterday of his early confrontation with God. Today's passage occurred years later, in the time of his maturity. We must expect God's revelation and our experience to grow in maturity, for we are only able to receive that for which we have been prepared in earlier lessons of joyful and sorrowful relationship with God.

It can be sheer joy and holy expectation on the level of faith and trust, but none of us is immune also from the rocky wilderness of the journey. Jacob's fears of Esau are not the same as they had been. They too have grown with maturity, and now comes the day of reckoning and of confrontation. He need not have been afraid—but he was. And that is often the case with us. Our heavenly Father works always and only for our good, and even when he wrestles with us in the wilderness, laming us in the process, it will be for us as for Jacob: 'The sun rose upon him as he passed Penuel, limping because of his hip...'

Prayer

In the darkest hour, Lord, when I am wrestling with your loving will, enable me not to let go. For you will never let go of me—even into eternity.

R/SSF

Mark 1:9–13 (NRSV)

Wilderness temptation

Jesus came from Nazareth of Galilee and was baptized by John in the Jordan. And just as he was coming up out of the water, he saw the heavens torn apart and the Spirit descending like a dove on him. And a voice came from heaven, 'You are my Son, the Beloved; with you I am well pleased.' And the Spirit immediately drove him out into the wilderness. He was in the wilderness forty days, tempted by Satan; and he was with the wild beasts; and the angels waited on him.

Matthew and Luke say that Jesus was 'led' by the Spirit into the wilderness; Mark says that he was 'driven'—but always by the Holy Spirit! It depends upon which way you look at it. Some of our spiritual guidance is gently led, and some is powerfully driven. We cannot always sort out one from the other, for there is a wilderness aspect in which leading and driving speak of the profound movement which turns our lives upside down.

Here we are faced with the fact that ecstatic high experiences are often followed by harrowing low moments in our pilgrimage. Baptism is followed by temptation in the path of Jesus, and it is a principle that this is a human pattern of high and low, light and darkness, blessing and pain. The River Jordan speaks of refreshment, cleansing, fertility and the descent of the dove; the wilderness speaks of weariness, hunger, thirst, sweat and barrenness. Both are necessary in the path that Jesus has chosen, and to which he is drawn by the divine love. Therefore the Spirit both leads and drives him to fulfil his own role and destiny.

As you read these words, you can doubtless count the trials and temptations that have beset you thus far in your pilgrimage, and which stretch out before you into the foreseeable future. Yet there are not only beasts and Satan in the wilderness, there are also ministering angels. The Spirit calls us forward, from Jordan to wilderness, and that same Spirit will lead, empower, and bring us home at last.

Prayer

Your Spirit leads me into pastures of blessing and refreshment, Lord, and then drives me into the dry aridity of the desert. Keep me faithful whatever my circumstances, for you will sustain me in my deepest need, and keep me ultimately from falling from love.

R/SSF

Genesis 37:26–28 (NRSV)

Wilderness betrayal

Judah said to Joseph's brothers, 'What profit is it if we kill our brother and conceal his blood? Come, let us sell him to the Ishmaelites, and not lay our hands on him, for he is our brother, our own flesh.' And his brothers agreed. When some Midianite traders passed by, they drew Joseph up, lifting him out of the pit, and sold him to the Ishmaelites for twenty pieces of silver. And they took Joseph to Egypt.

Betrayal was a real wilderness for Joseph! He had been promised by God, by terrestrial and celestial dreams, that he would rise in glory and be some kind of chosen leader. No doubt his mind and heart were full of such ambitious dreams when he set off from his father to Shechem and Dothan to find his brothers. But he was dreaming, they were scheming!

When they saw him, they made up their minds. First of all, it was to abandon him in a pit (Reuben wouldn't allow them to kill him), but when Reuben was not around, they sold him to the Midianites for profit, dipped his 'technicolour dreamcoat' in blood, and returned to convince poor Jacob of his son's death. A real wilderness experience.

Everything may seem to have gone wrong in your life. There are unfulfilled dreams, unattained visions, unaccomplished plans; and so many problems have overtaken you that those youthful aspirations have now faded like castles in the air. Were those early dreams God's movement in your soul, or simply your own plans which have come to naught?

If any wilderness pilgrimage reveals the providential care of God, it is the life of Joseph. Early promise… years of contradiction and denial… then a strange turn of events, so that all the wonder and glory of early dreams begin to find fulfilment—and such fulfilment that filled the dreamer with amazement.

So wherever you are today, don't give up. The providence of God is often hidden, and frequently slow—but beneath the surface of things, God is at work. As we shall see.

Prayer

My Lord, you are both father and mother to me, and I am your child. Help me to remember this when things go awry and dreams and hopes collapse. Grant me present faith—and future glory.

R/SSF

Genesis 39:19–21, 23 (NRSV, abridged)

Wilderness prison

When… (Potiphar's) wife spoke to him, saying, 'This is the way your servant treated me,' he became enraged. And Joseph's master took him and put him into the prison… But the Lord was with Joseph and showed him steadfast love; he gave him favour in the sight of the chief jailer… The chief jailer paid no heed to anything that was in Joseph's care, because the Lord was with him; and whatever he did, the Lord made it prosper.

When Joseph was purchased by Potiphar in the Egyptian slave market, he thought his fortune had changed—and it had for a while! Things went well—so well. The Lord's blessing was such that he became the wholly responsible first servant of the household.

But there was a problem. Some scholars think that Potiphar was a eunuch. Joseph 'was handsome and good looking' (39:6), and Potiphar's wife had her eye on him. The fuse was lit, and the explosion was inevitable. It was not a matter of Potiphar's ignorance, the wife's fault or Joseph's naïvety or integrity. It just seemed that circumstances brought things to a head, together with the hurting of pride, the indignation of the boss, and the consequential false accusations which were both convenient and face-saving. I wonder if Potiphar really understood the situation?

Human relationships can be a web of compassion or intrigue, and although these are two extremes, we are all aware of the moral mazes into which we, or our friends, can be caught up, sometimes in all innocence, though sometimes engineered for a special purpose.

For Joseph it was a second betrayal, and this time it landed him in prison. Did he still believe that the Lord was in control? Some of God's best saints have been in prison, and we shall see that at the end of the story, Joseph says to his brothers, 'Though you intended to do harm to me, God intended it for good, in order to preserve a numerous people… So have no fear' (50:20–21).

Prayer

Even in prison, Lord, Joseph planted some seeds in his wilderness. Bless the Prison Phoenix Trust, the Howard League for Prison Reform, and all those, including prisoners, who carry the light of your Spirit into the prison cell.

R/SSF

Exodus 3:3–6 (NRSV, abridged)

Wilderness fire

Moses said, 'I must turn aside and look at this great sight, and see why the bush is not burned up.' When the Lord saw that he had turned aside to see, God called to him out of the bush, 'Moses, Moses!' And he said, 'Here I am.' Then he said, 'Come no closer! Remove the sandals from your feet, for the place on which you are standing is holy ground.' ... And Moses hid his face, for he was afraid to look at God.

This wilderness is at Horeb, where Moses fled after killing an Egyptian for the ill-treatment of the Hebrews—after the deed had been discovered. He must have wondered if, with the end of his Egyptian sojourn, his exciting life was over. Here he was, looking after the sheep of his father-in-law, Jethro, and nothing was happening. It was a wilderness.

Why do we think that we must initiate great matters? It is the Lord who moves both among nations and in the deep places of our lives, and what he initiates he will bring to fulfilment and final consummation. But in the process he will use us—for our good and his glory.

The basic need, from our side, is to let there be a 'place' where God can speak. In the Bible, that is usually solitude, and often a desert place. We need to make such places in our lives, away from the marketplace values of our consumer society, away from the vociferous opinions of politicians, fellow workers, and even the legitimate domestic and social round of our lives. It is when we purposely find a place of interior quiet and sometimes geographical solitude that God will speak to us.

Moses did not plan the confrontation with fire in the wilderness, but he did plan his day of quiet caring for the sheep, his journey to that place at the back of the desert, and a receptive soul, so that God could call and speak and command.

Prayer

Lord, enable me to create a pool of quiet,
a small wilderness in which the fire of
your Spirit may descend, not only
warming, but burning up the dross,
and spreading the flame of glory
from my heart.

R/SSF

Exodus 13:20–22 (NRSV) (also read Hebrews 11:23–31)

Wilderness pilgrims

The Israelites set out from Succoth, and camped at Etham, on the edge of the wilderness. The Lord went in front of them in a pillar of cloud by day, to lead them along the way, and in a pillar of fire by night, to give them light, so that they might travel by day and by night. Neither the pillar of cloud by day nor the pillar of fire by night left its place in front of the people.

It would be wonderful to be able to write of a united company of God's people, led by an inspired prophetic leader to whom they listened as they left behind them the city of destruction and went on to Canaan, inspired by the Spirit, and led by a pillar of cloud by day and a pillar of fire by night.

But it wasn't like that, as we shall see tomorrow. It was meant to be like that, and the journey could have been accomplished in a much shorter time. Everything was in place for their guidance and sustenance on the way, though conditional upon their response and obedience—such a pattern can be found in Hebrews 11:23–31.

Many of them didn't want to leave Egypt. Their hearts were still there and they were suspicious about this wilderness journey, especially its ascetic disciplines and challenge. In the following chapter we read of the mysterious deliverance at the Red Sea, with the continuing leading of the pillars of cloud and fire. But a life of bondage in Egypt was more familiar to them, and more attractive than the promise of liberty and an increasing horizon of faith.

Imagine you were confronted with Jesus today, saying simply, 'Follow me!' Could you do it? Would you? Your Egypt may be too comfortable, the financial and domestic security too tempting. The invitation to abandoned faith and love in Christ is challenging, but if we turn away, there will be no pillar of cloud and fire to lead, and no ultimate guidelines into eternity. The world's offer constitutes a poor bargain—and we have to decide.

Prayer

Father, the image of pilgrims in a barren land is not an attractive one, and the world has conditioned me to expect something more material and lucrative. But how substantial is it? Grant me clear vision, and genuine faith.

R/SSF

Exodus 16:13–15, 18 (NRSV, abridged) (also read John 6:26–36)

Wilderness manna

In the morning there was a layer of dew around the camp... there on the surface of the wilderness was a fine flaky substance... on the ground. When the Israelites saw it, they said to one another, 'What is it?' ... Moses said to them, 'It is the bread that the Lord has given you to eat.' ... When they measured it with an omer, those who gathered much had nothing over, and those who gathered little had no shortage; they gathered as much as each of them needed.

Much devotional writing has been given over to manna as symbolic of the bread of the eucharist, a sort of *panis angelicus* or food of angels, or of Christ as the heavenly manna. Indeed, when Jesus refers to himself as the bread of life he speaks of the manna in the wilderness, and tells people not to rest in the literal figure, but to go on to the spiritual reality of feeding upon his own life and teaching.

Yet there is some basic truth about wilderness pilgrimage in our Exodus passage today which gives us teaching about the gathering, sharing and not stockpiling of material food, thus avoiding a widening gap between the poor and the rich. There is an inbuilt corrective in this account in Exodus, because the greedy entrepreneurs who grabbed more than their share found that it bred worms and became foul (16:20). And Moses was very angry with them!

The primary truth is that we need to feed upon the life and teaching of Christ. If we followed that as individuals, families, societies and nations, we would not have people around us today who earn £120 an hour, speaking of the folly of fixing a ground-level wage of less than £4 an hour for others. This is not meant to be a political, but a Christian, humane statement. And it has to do with manna! If we do not listen, as some of the Israelites did not (v. 20), one day someone will be angry. And that anger will be the searing aspect of love!

Prayer

Help me to become aware of the levels of teaching in today's passage, Lord. Then enable me to pattern my life a little more closely to the teaching of the gospel of Jesus.

R/SSF

Hebrews 3:16—4:1 (NRSV) (also read Numbers 14:1–25)

Wilderness complaining

Who were they who heard and yet were rebellious? Was it not all those who left Egypt under the leadership of Moses? But with whom was he angry forty years? Was it not those who sinned, whose bodies fell in the wilderness? And to whom did he swear that they would not enter his rest, if not to those who were disobedient? So we see that they were unable to enter because of unbelief. Therefore, while the promise of entering his rest is still open, let us take care that none of you should seem to have failed to reach it.

There was a great deal of complaining in the wilderness, for we have seen that it was not a united nation, inspired by godly hope and disciplined by obedience and loyalty, that left Egypt, but a gaggle of unresolved and warring tribes and clans, for whom appetite and security were primary, and who lacked vision, faith and hope. What a task Moses had taken in hand, and how impossible it seemed along the way.

The New Testament is full of 'comparison and example' teaching, based on the wilderness journey. 'These things happened to them to serve as an example, and they were written down to instruct us' (see 1 Corinthians 10:1–12). This long-term perspective is from a vantage point of faith, and what emerged from that multitude of warring tribes, half-hearted in their quest for liberation, was a united nation under a chosen leader with prophetic and leadership gifts, called by God who led them out of bondage into a freedom which was beyond their wildest imagination.

And what about us? Are we willing to stay in our Egypt? Are we reluctant to take that step of faith, to rise to the challenge of freedom, and to lay our humble and obedient hearts at the feet of the Lord who calls us to the glorious liberty of the children of God? We may choose to drag our feet, to complain along the way. Jesus is our heavenly Moses, and he calls us out of our lethargy, blazes the trail by his life of compassion and joy. Shall we prefer anything else?

Prayer

Am I among the complainers on life's way, Lord, with heavy heart and dragging feet? Liberate me today, lift up my heart, my eyes and my spirit, and then I shall be a source of encouragement to other discouraged fellow pilgrims.

R/SSF

Mark 8:31–33 (NRSV)

Wilderness passion

Then Jesus began to teach them that the Son of Man must undergo great suffering, and be rejected by the elders, the chief priests, and the scribes, and be killed, and after three days rise again. He said all this quite openly. And Peter took him aside and began to rebuke him. But turning and looking at his disciples, he rebuked Peter and said, 'Get behind me, Satan! For you are setting your mind not on divine things but on human things.'

Here we see Jesus already treading the way of his passion—his mind and heart leading his feet on to the *Via Dolorosa*, the Way of Sorrows. The word 'passion' means suffering, it means being acted upon, being taken over, having pain inflicted—and yet Jesus is not simply a victim, but the One who willingly elected to undergo such a path of passion for our redemption. It is the kind of desolate wilderness into which the scapegoat of ancient Israel was banished, bearing the sins of the people (Leviticus 16:2–22). Yet for Jesus, this was the way to transform the wilderness into the fertile blossoming of the Holy Way of the Lord (Isaiah 35).

If you read the rest of today's passage, you will see that Jesus does not tread this path of suffering in order that we may go scot-free. Certainly he does for us what we cannot do for ourselves, and in that way obtains for us salvation by grace alone. But then he calls us to follow him in cross-bearing, entering into participation in his redemptive work, united with him in his sufferings, in order that we may share his glory.

These are the suffering aspects of the Calvary passion, but they are shot through with a passionate love for souls, and a passionate love for God. It is not an easy way—but it is the path we are called to tread. Dare we take up the invitation?

Prayer

Lord, I tremble before such an invitation to share your passion. I am scared not only that I shall be unable to follow to the end, but that I shall turn tail and run away. If you call me, then, Lord, you must provide the impetus, the energy and the love which endures.

R/SSF

Exodus 19:2, 16, 20 (NRSV, abridged)

Wilderness mystery and glory

The Israelites had journeyed from Rephidim, entered the wilderness of Sinai, and camped... there in front of the mountain... On the morning of the third day there was thunder and lightning, as well as a thick cloud on the mountain, and a blast of a trumpet so loud that all the people who were in the camp trembled... When the Lord descended upon Mount Sinai, to the top of the mountain, the Lord summoned Moses to the top of the mountain, and Moses went up.

This is a strange chapter, full of mystery and glory, and full of that numinous quality which makes our hair stand on end when we become aware of the truly holy. Unfortunately, we have so substituted our religion or our book-knowledge for real experience of the holy that 'God' has become the name of a kind of heavenly pal or mate who is there at our disposal or for our benefit. How far astray we have wandered, and how true are the objections which thinking people make against religion when they observe our lives.

This chapter is a good antidote to easy religion or establishment Christianity. It speaks of the God of mystery, the summons to holiness, the experience of fire, and the call to ascend higher, to go deeper, into the wonderful and fearful presence we call God. We ought to learn more about the profound meaning of such a mystical journey before we find ourselves cast into some wilderness of unknowing where all our former faith proves insufficient for the trials or challenges of such a place. (See 'Mount Sinai' in Brother Ramon SSF, *The Prayer Mountain*.)

Perhaps the warning is sufficient today to make us realize that there are deeper levels for us to discover, higher heights for us to climb; and even the awareness of the poverty of our spatial language indicates that there is more, much more, to the spiritual path than we had dreamed. Then God may call you from the heights of his holiness, to begin a new ascent, and live a new experience of mystery and glory.

Prayer

I realize, Lord, that I have hardly begun to know the depths of your ways or the heights of your glory. Make me more aware of these dimensions of faith, and then show me the first steps to take.

R/SSF

1 Kings 17:1–3, 5–6 (NRSV, abridged)

Wilderness drought

Elijah said, 'As the Lord the God of Israel lives, before whom I stand, there shall be neither dew nor rain these years, except by my word.' The word of the Lord came to him, saying, 'Go from here and turn eastward, and hide yourself by the Wadi Cherith, which is east of the Jordan.' ... So he went... The ravens brought him bread and meat in the morning, and bread and meat in the evening; and he drank from the wadi.

Many of God's people live in a wilderness experience of drought! It is possible to bring it upon ourselves by neglect, selfishness or giving ourselves to consumer priorities instead of walking the way of Jesus. But in my pastoral ministry I have frequently found some of God's dearest people in a personal or family wilderness which is dried up and barren because of sickness, poverty, depression or family claims and failures which take their mental and spiritual toll upon life. Yet I have also found something else—as parish priest, university chaplain, ministering friar or simply as a functioning Christian. It is that for those who trust him, who call upon him, who lay their lives before him in utter need, God causes a secret spring to rise in the wilderness, or sends ravens of different kinds, to sustain the needy soul.

During my three years living as a hermit in a caravan in the grounds of Tymawr convent, near the Redbrook, I felt like Elijah at the Wadi Cherith. In my 'departure homily' at the end of the three years, I told the SSC sisters that I had read a commentary in which the 'ravens' were a group of wandering nomads who sustained Elijah, and that in their habits the nuns had been nourishing ravens to me. They loved the analogy and listened to Elijah's homily!

What is your wilderness drought today? Have you ministering ravens? And if they do not seem to be on the scene, lay your life before the Lord; cry out to him in thirsty need—and ravens will come!

Prayer

There comes a time, Lord, when I can dig for water no longer, and only your supply will meet my need. Provide for me a watering-place; minister to me by the ravens of your choice; help me thus to see your providential care.

R/SSF

1 Kings 17:7–11 (NRSV, abridged) (also read vv. 12–24)

Wilderness sustenance

After a while the wadi dried up, because there was no rain in the land. Then the word of the Lord came to Elijah, saying, 'Go now to Zarephath, which belongs to Sidon, and live there; for I have commanded a widow there to feed you.' ... When he came to the gate of the town, a widow was there gathering sticks; he called to her and said, 'Bring me a little water in a vessel, so that I may drink... Bring me a morsel of bread in your hand.'

This is a wonderful story. The wadi dries up; Elijah moves on; the widow woman says that she has only enough for one drink and one loaf before she and her son die of famine. Then things begin to happen!

Yesterday we saw that the pilgrim in the wilderness has to undergo many different experiences on the journey, and though difficulties and trials are part of the way, they are precisely to teach us humble dependence on God. Even the outward circumstances of life which seem to be fortuitous are taken by God and made into moments of meeting and providence, not for us alone, but also for those who help us on the way, and whom we meet in our travels. Some call it synchronicity, and others call it providence!

This poor woman was ready to die with her little boy. After the deliverance brought about by Elijah's visit (have you read the *whole* passage?), the boy falls ill and dies. An extreme situation. But again, by prayer and faith a remarkable intervention and restoration take place. The result is not only confirmation of Elijah's mission, but life for the boy and enlightenment for the woman.

We don't engineer such occasions of providential grace, but if we are 'in the way' of their happening when the Lord is at work, we are taken up into such acts of grace and mercy, and blessings will abound in all directions—even from a place of famine and drought!

Prayer

There have been times, Lord, when you have taken my simple acts of prayer and hope and caused them to bear fruit beyond my intentions. Today let me be in the way of your providential care, not only for myself, but for others in need. Here I am, Lord!

R/SSF

1 Kings 19:3–5 (NRSV, abridged)

Wilderness cowardice

Then Elijah was afraid [of Jezebel]; he got up and fled for his life, and... went a day's journey into the wilderness, and came and sat down under a solitary broom tree. He asked that he might die: 'It is enough; now, O Lord, take away my life, for I am no better than my ancestors.' Then he lay down under the broom tree and fell asleep. Suddenly an angel touched him and said to him, 'Get up and eat.'

It had to happen, didn't it? Nevertheless, we are surprised. How could a wild, fiery, fearless and faithful man like Elijah suddenly get scared out of his wits when Queen Jezebel issues her threat of revenge?

Perhaps it is a matter of that steep decline after a time of mental or spiritual blessing—an emotional low after a spiritual high! Whatever it is, we are subject to attacks from without and within, and we are not always the master of our own feelings and emotions. Simple and hitherto trivial things can make us scared. But Jezebel's threat was not trivial!

Here is Elijah in his wilderness, under the broom tree. Depression has led to despair, and despair to seeking a termination of his life. Things have got wholly out of perspective, and he seems to have no soul-friend or loved one with whom he can share. The Lord seems far away.

Yet beneath the surface, in the hidden place, God was at work. That is something we must note for our own pilgrimage. We shall have our wilderness of depression, sadness, sickness, verging on despair. And it may not be simple but clinical depression! Yet God's will for us is hope and faith, joy and love. In Elijah's experience a heavenly messenger came and first of all listened; then caused him to sleep; then woke him to feed him physically. This physical and mental therapy was repeated, and then he was sent on his continuing journey (oh no, it was *not* the end of things!). The Lord knows what he is about, and sometimes we need to trust him when he does not make the pattern of our lives immediately clear to us.

Prayer

In whatever circumstances I find myself, help me to remember, Lord, that you are always there. And when I am not aware of your presence, continue your ministry, so that I shall eventually come to understand the mystery of your ways.

R/SSF

1 Kings 19:8–10 (NRSV, abridged)

Wilderness cave

Elijah went... to Horeb the mount of God... He came to a cave, and spent the night there. Then the word of the Lord came to him, saying, 'What are you doing here, Elijah?' He answered, 'I have been very zealous for the Lord, the God of hosts; for the Israelites have forsaken your covenant, thrown down your altars, and killed your prophets with the sword. I alone am left, and they are seeking my life, to take it away.'

A cave can be a place of exploration, a place of adventure, or a place of regression and negative retreat. Caves are different things at different times. Since my childhood scary explorations on the Gower peninsula, they have held a fascinating attraction for me, with a sense of creepy mystery.

Elijah was certainly cowardly in retreat as we saw yesterday, and his perspective was out of focus, thinking he was the only faithful one left. (Obadiah had fed one hundred prophets of Yahweh secretly in another cave, and there continued to be a hidden remnant in Israel.) Yet in spite of Elijah's funk, cowardice, depression and despair, the Lord was at work. It began yesterday with the angelic ministry of rest, refreshment and revitalization in the wilderness (vv. 1–8), and now continues as Elijah realizes that this cave to which he had run in fear was God's appointed place. There is no evading such divine synchronicity.

Contemplative language speaks of 'the cave of the heart', the meeting place where God confronts the human soul and the work of transformation begins, and from which the renewed soul ventures out into avenues of service. This is where we are today, and we can profitably read on to verse 16 which gives promise for the future, and then we can sing John Whittier's hymn, *Dear Lord and Father of mankind*, where the 'still small voice of calm' speaks to our condition, showing the way forward. The cave of the heart is the place of revelation.

Prayer

Breathe through the heats of our desire
Thy coolness and thy balm;
Let sense be dumb—let flesh retire;
Speak through the earthquake,
wind and fire,
O still small voice of calm!

John Greenleaf Whittier (1807–92)

R/SSF

Luke 1:26–31 (NRSV)

Wilderness oasis

In the sixth month the angel Gabriel was sent by God to a town in Galilee called Nazareth, to a virgin engaged to a man whose name was Joseph, of the house of David. The virgin's name was Mary. And he came to her, and said, 'Greetings, favoured one! The Lord is with you.' But she was much perplexed by his words and pondered what sort of greeting this might be. The angel said to her, 'Do not be afraid, Mary, for you have found favour with God. And now you will conceive in your womb and bear a son, and you will name him Jesus.

The feast of the Annunciation falls in Lent, and is an oasis in the wilderness. In this chapter we have a young woman who was a virgin, and an old woman who was barren (v. 36). If we seek for fertility in the desert and wilderness, then we need an oasis, and here it is. Even if we are in a desert, and there is quite a way to go, we can be refreshed by the glorious message of Gabriel, rightly called the Annunciation.

It does not at first seem to Mary that this is an oasis—a place of refreshment and fertility—for she is startled, frightened, perplexed, by the manner and content of the angelic message. It often takes a time for the believer to learn to rest at the oasis of God's refreshing love—we are too busy striding through the desert organizing our own and other people's lives. Be still today, and give yourself to God's word in our annunciation passage.

But Mary got the message—the annunciation was made complete, and her glad answer to the amazing and creative word is a pattern for our response. God calls us to be receptive to his work in our lives, to allow him to perform his miracle of grace within us. Our response, like Mary's, should be, 'Here am I, the servant of the Lord; let it be with me according to your word.'

Prayer

In my wilderness experiences, Lord, there has been an oasis, though I have not always recognized it. Let me learn to rest in the oasis of your love and promise, and let my response be as immediate, as clear and as simple as Mary's, and let the result be divine fruitfulness.

R/SSF

Psalm 74:1–3, 9–11 (NRSV, abridged)

The cry of despair

O God, why do you cast us off for ever? ... Remember your congregation, which you acquired long ago, which you redeemed to be the tribe of your heritage. Remember Mount Zion, where you came to dwell. Direct your steps to the perpetual ruins; the enemy has destroyed everything in the sanctuary... We do not see our emblems; there is no longer any prophet, and there is no one among us who knows how long. How long, O God, is the foe to scoff? Is the enemy to revile your name for ever? Why do you hold back your hand; why do you keep your hand in your bosom?

Why does God allow his people to suffer and perish? Why does he allow evil seemingly to triumph? This is the question the people of God are crying out to him in their anger and desolation. They had been driven out of the land he had promised them, to exile in a pagan land. They had no prophets to guide them, no holy places for worship. His covenant to care for and protect them seemed to have been forgotten. They felt exiled from God himself. And they let him know how they felt about it. God, look at us. *Your* people destroyed as a nation. *Your* holy temple in ruins. *Your* city taken over by your enemies. Why don't you do something about it? Why? ... Why? ...

The exiled Jews were not alone in their cry of despair. There are still countless refugees cruelly driven from their country. There are still thousands of politically oppressed people who can see no end to their situation, and have no leaders to call upon. And in the personal tragedies that befall most of us at some time in our lives, we can know the same despair of feeling forsaken by God, with none of the old familiar supports at hand.

Psalms like this one certainly take on the problem of why our loving Father God lets so much evil and suffering go on in the world. We will look at the problem more deeply in the next few days. Meanwhile we remember that Jesus himself, from the desolation of the cross, cried out, 'My God, my God, why have you forsaken me?'

Yet even in death, when evil appeared to have won, Jesus trusted that, somehow, his Father would bring redemption and new life out of his suffering and death.

Prayer for those in despair

God, my loving Father, hear me as I cry out to you now. I don't understand why you have let this happen, but help me to trust you as Jesus did. Amen.

CC

This reading is the 'extra' one for a Leap Year.

Psalm 74:12–17 (NRSV)

Focusing on God

Yet God my King is from old, working salvation in the earth. You divided the sea by your might; you broke the heads of the dragons in the waters. You crushed the heads of Leviathan; you gave him as food for the creatures of the wilderness. You cut openings for springs and torrents; you dried up ever-flowing streams. Yours is the day, yours also the night; you established the luminaries and the sun. You have fixed all the bounds of the earth; you made summer and winter.

The psalms teach us that it is all right to tell God how we feel, even when we are angry or depressed, for it is God who created us and the world in which we live. For a while it is right to stay with our darkest feelings before God. And this psalm expresses in no uncertain terms what it feels like to be apparently abandoned by God.

But then, look at what the psalmist does. Suddenly he stops focusing on his people's feelings and troubles, and focuses on God himself: 'Yet God my King is from old, working salvation in the earth.' You can almost feel the momentary lifting of those downcast spirits. He switches from talking *about* God to talking *to* God.

He remembers that God is Israel's own king and also the king of all creation. With mighty power he overcame the evil of chaos in order to create the order of the world—water and dry land, light and dark, the seasons of the year. With mighty power he delivered his people out of the evil they were suffering in Egypt. Their God *has* shown that he is able to work through hostile powers in order to save his people. He actually created good out of evil.

The power of God is greater than any power of evil. When we remind ourselves of this fact we may pray with more confidence that God will work his way through our troubles. How often we can look back on our suffering and realize that God has created *something* good out of it all—some strength in ourselves, some change in lifestyle or relationship, some meeting. Perhaps we would have preferred it to happen by another way, but at least some good has come because of the evil.

Prayer

O Lord, my God, I know that you are with me as I open up my feelings to you. Thank you for creating new, good things out of my sufferings. Amen

CC

Psalm 74:18–23 (NRSV)

Our prayers are heard

Remember this, O Lord, how the enemy scoffs, and an impious people reviles your name. Do not deliver the soul of your dove to the wild animals; do not forget the life of your poor for ever. Have regard for your covenant, for the dark places of the land are full of the haunts of violence. Do not let the downtrodden be put to shame; let the poor and needy praise your name. Rise up, O God, plead your cause; remember how the impious scoff at you all day long. Do not forget the clamour of your foes, the uproar of your adversaries that goes up continually.

The psalmist pleads with God to deliver his people from their suffering. They are his beloved, his dove, who are now his desperately poor and needy. He urges God, too, to defend himself against his enemies, to do something, *anything*, to show the world that he is God.

How often have we pleaded with God to take our troubles away and give us the help we want so much? How often have we felt that God *should* protect us from the dangers and tragedies of this life when we do our best to be faithful Christians?

Does God need to defend himself? He did not cause evil and tragedy to happen. It was because the people turned away from God that they allowed the power of evil to have its way, albeit unwittingly. It was because God loved his people so infinitely that he forgave them again and again, and provided new ways for their starting again.

If only we can shift from our perspective of wanting our lives to be just as they were before tragedy hit us, God can, and will, restore us in a way that we could not have envisaged before. Justice, as we see it, may not happen in our lifetime. But we may, with confidence, commit our loved ones who have died into God's safe and loving hands. We may pray for the qualities we need to cope with our troubles. We may offer ourselves and our situation to God and ask him to work his will through it all.

Our prayers will be heard. We can do far more than we think to open the way for God's power to flow through the evil we suffer, by our faith and by our prayers.

Prayer

God of hope, who raised Jesus Christ from the dead to give us new life in him, grant us the gift of faith, to fight against evil through the power of prayer and to keep up our hope for change. Amen

CC

Psalm 77:1–9 (NRSV)

No easy answers

I cry aloud to God, aloud to God, that he may hear me. In the day of my trouble I seek the Lord; in the night my hand is stretched out without wearying; my soul refuses to be comforted. I think of God, and I moan; I meditate, and my spirit faints. You keep my eyelids from closing; I am so troubled that I cannot speak. I consider the days of old, and remember the years of long ago. I commune with my heart in the night; I meditate and search my spirit: 'Will the Lord spurn for ever, and never again be favourable? Has his steadfast love ceased for ever? Are his promises at an end for all time? Has God forgotten to be gracious? Has he in anger shut up his compassion?'

What utter hopelessness! Crying out to God is useless, even thinking about God makes matters worse, because he does not do anything. Sleep refuses to come, talking is too painful, and looking back at the good times makes the present seem all the more unbearable. Thinking about it all, questioning God endlessly, is useless. Where is God's love and compassion now? Where is God?

Have you ever felt like that? The psalms were written many centuries ago. They were the words of the men and women of Israel speaking from their hearts to God about their situation. Yet they are as relevant today as they were then.

This psalm expresses the personal anguish of one who seems to have lost all that was ever dear to him. And there are times when we ourselves are in that position. We lose someone we love, or our home, our job, our old lifestyle—and, so it seems—God. Our whole world is turned upside down. We feel utterly devastated, hopeless and helpless.

The psalm plunges into the depths of human grief, and gives us no easy answers. But then there *are* no easy answers. But the psalm does not stay in the depths. And we do not have to stay in the depths for ever. At times like this, when we cannot know God's presence through prayer, we may begin to know a glimmer of God's love through the people who walk alongside us, who listen to our pain, who reach out to us. A hand outstretched can be taken hold of—as a channel of God's comfort and love to us.

Prayer

Lord, give me the strength to respond to the people who are trying to help me. Give me the grace to receive comfort from their presence.

CC

Psalm 77:10–15 (NRSV)

A way through

And I say, 'It is my grief that the right hand of the Most High has changed.' I will call to mind the deeds of the Lord; I will remember your wonders of old. I will meditate on all your work, and muse on your mighty deeds. Your way, O God, is holy. What god is so great as our God? You are the God who works wonders; you have displayed your might among the peoples. With your strong arm you redeemed your people, the descendants of Jacob and Joseph.

Where is God in all this? In addition to all his human pain, the thought that God has cut him off is too much for the psalmist to bear. It jolts him into moving a little in his depression. He knows really that God has not changed. It is he who has been so overwhelmed by his pain that there is no longer room for God in his life. Understandably, yes. But it does not mean that God is not there, waiting, loving.

And so he makes the conscious decision to think about God, his ways and his deeds. At times when there seemed no way through, humanly speaking, God found a way. He inspired the leaders of the Israelites. He made a way for the people by dividing the waters of the Red Sea so that they were able to pass through. And he can still make a way through our troubled waters now.

As Christians, we look to God's decisive act in sending his Son, Jesus Christ, to live in our world, in its darkness. He entered into suffering and death and transformed it through the power of his resurrection. He does not take away our suffering, but he does offer a way through. He reaches out his hand to us from the other side of his human suffering and death and offers us his hand to lead us gently through.

He may lead us by means of other people, who give us strength and new vision. He may place us in the way of new situations and 'coincidences'. He may convict us of some truth through our reading or listening. He may give us a sense of inner peace or a new motivation to forgive and lay aside resentment. He leads us in ways that we would never have imagined.

Prayer

I come to you, Lord Jesus, for you, too, suffered and felt for a moment that God had abandoned you. But you trusted your Father for your resurrection, and you want me to trust you now to lead me through my grief into your new life and light. Help me to trust you, Lord. Amen

CC

Psalm 77:16–20 (NRSV)

From despair to hope

When the waters saw you, O God, when the waters saw you, they were afraid; the very deep trembled. The clouds poured out water; the skies thundered; your arrows flashed on every side. The crash of your thunder was in the whirlwind; your lightnings lit up the world; the earth trembled and shook. Your way was through the sea, your path through the mighty waters; yet your footprints were unseen. You led your people like a flock by the hand of Moses and Aaron.

'Yet your footprints were unseen.' God did not seem to be there. His presence could not be felt. The way ahead was frightening, impossible. These verses express the majesty and power of God in terms of thunderstorms and earthquakes, which opened up the Red Sea. God was there all the time. He made a way through. He led them 'by the hand of' Moses and Aaron.

Sometimes we feel unable to pray. We are too anxious, too fearful, too upset. God just does not seem to be there for us. And we may feel angry with him for not intervening. But just because his footsteps are not seen, it does not mean that God is not there, working things out for us in ways we cannot foresee. He is present in Spirit, but our spiritual eyes are closed by our anxiety or anger or fear. God will find ways of opening our eyes—often through ordinary everyday experiences —if we cry out to him and seek his help and try to be open to him.

Sometimes we may experience the new life God has for us through people outside our immediate circle of family and friends: leaders like Moses and Aaron; professionals such as doctors or counsellors. It can be helpful to talk our feelings through with people who accept us unconditionally, who accept our feelings without judging us, who restore our self-respect and self-worth by hearing us, who may see ways forward that we could not see for ourselves. Such people may or may not be Christians, but they can still be used by God to bring his healing and his way through.

Like the psalmist who moves from despair to hope without any concrete answers to his problems, let us have the courage to walk on through the storms, in faith that our unseen Lord will lead us through.

Reflection

The Lord is my shepherd, I shall not want. He makes me lie down in green pastures; he leads me beside still waters; he restores my soul.

Psalm 23:1–3

CC

Psalm 1:1–3 (NRSV)

Choose your way with care

Happy are those who do not follow the advice of the wicked, or take the path that sinners tread, or sit in the seat of scoffers; but their delight is in the law of the Lord, and on his law they meditate day and night. They are like trees planted by streams of water, which yield their fruit in its season, and their leaves do not wither. In all that they do, they prosper.

It is so easy to accept bad advice. Somehow it is always so attractive, so plausible, with its 'you know it makes sense' overtones. 'Beware,' says the psalmist, 'learn the lesson of true happiness which is to be found in studying and obeying the law of the Lord.' 'The law' perhaps conjures up for us dry and dusty tomes of legal rules, regulations and restrictions, shot through with dire warnings of penalty clauses. But the law of the Lord refers to the first five books of the Bible, the wonderful history of God's dealings with his people, of his love and guiding hand, enabling them to live out their lives.

The Hebrew word for law, 'Torah', means guidance, or instruction, on how to enjoy the full life God intends for all of us. Surely it's worth giving it our full attention? Then we shall draw strength and insight, gain vision and purpose, and become the people God intended we should be, fruitful in service for him and for our fellow men and women.

The analogy of the fruitful healthy tree and the person who delights in knowing and obeying God's word brings home the joy and value of God's word for us each day. We draw from the water of life our nourishment, our strength. We are enabled to grow and develop; to stand tall and straight; to provide sustenance for others, so that they too might know and grow; to be 'something beautiful (and useful) for God' and to be truly happy, 'blessed' in our daily lives.

Reflection and prayer

Thus says the Lord: Stand at the crossroads, and look, and ask for the ancient paths, where the good way lies; and walk in it, and find rest for your souls.

Jeremiah 6:16

Lord, help me to choose the right way,
to listen to your voice, to grow in
understanding, to be fruitful in service,
and to praise your name every day
of my life.

MC

Psalm 8:3–9 (NRSV)

Creator and sustainer

When I look at your heavens, the work of your fingers, the moon and the stars that you have established; what are human beings that you are mindful of them, mortals that you care for them? Yet you have made them a little lower than God, and crowned them with glory and honour. You have given them dominion over the works of your hands; you have put all things under their feet, all sheep and oxen, and also the beasts of the field, the birds of the air, and the fish of the sea, whatever passes along the paths of the seas. O Lord, our Sovereign, how majestic is your name in all the earth!

On the last night of our 'winter sun' holiday in Tenerife, I stood on our balcony looking up into the sky, the bright moon shining over the sea, the stars like jewels, the air like wine. The following night I stood in our garden in North Yorkshire, well wrapped up on that cold frosty evening, and looked up into the sky again. The same moon, stars, brilliant clear sky, and I marvelled at the glorious majestic creation of God, the world he has made and given us to enjoy and share. I found myself singing a children's chorus: 'There are hundreds of planets, thousands, millions, way out in space each has a place in God's decree; there are hundreds and thousands and millions of planets, but God knows every one, and God knows me!'

The psalmist in his time sang a hymn of praise to God for the gift of creation, realizing how tiny and insignificant he was in relation to it all, yet recognizing the awesomeness of being a steward of creation, in relationship with the creator God. He speaks of 'our Sovereign', the one worshipped and praised in heaven, as Isaiah saw in his vision of seraphs around the throne who cried, 'Holy, holy, holy is the Lord of hosts; the whole earth is full of his glory' (Isaiah 6:3). Yet he is also the one who reaches down from heaven to earth to enable humanity to know him, to love him, and to tend the creatures of land, sea and sky.

Prayer

Creator of the universe, watch over us and keep us in the light of your presence. May our praise continually blend with that of all creation, until we come together to the eternal joys which you promise in your love, through Jesus Christ our Lord. Amen.

Celtic prayer

MC

Psalm 13 (NRSV)

How long, O Lord?

How long, O Lord? Will you forget me forever? How long will you hide your face from me? How long must I bear pain in my soul, and have sorrow in my heart all day long? How long shall my enemy be exalted over me? Consider and answer me, O Lord my God! Give light to my eyes, or I will sleep the sleep of death, and my enemy will say, 'I have prevailed'; my foes will rejoice because I am shaken. But I trusted in your steadfast love; my heart shall rejoice in your salvation. I will sing to the Lord, because he has dealt bountifully with me.

In the NRSV this psalm is headed 'Prayer for deliverance from enemies'. The enemy referred to may have been an opposing power waging war, physical illness, depression, or the fear of death—that 'last enemy' that Paul writes about in his first letter to the Corinthians ('The last enemy to be destroyed is death', 1 Corinthians 15:26). Whoever or whatever the enemy was, the psalmist felt ignored, forgotten by God, isolated, alone, almost to the point of being totally overwhelmed. The God who he knew loved him had somehow turned away from him, for there was no answer to his prayer for help, and he was sinking into the depths from which there would be no escape. He could almost hear his enemy celebrating the victory over him, and still no help came. The love he had trusted in was steadfast, he knew that; but it was in the past, so what about now? But the reminder of that steadfast love gave him hope for the future, in spite of how it seemed, and he knew within himself that he would again rejoice and sing for joy, and praise the Lord for bringing him through his trouble.

There are times in our life when perhaps we too cry, 'How long, O Lord, how long?' God seems distant, even uncaring, and yet we know he cannot and will not forsake us, even though the circumstances we find ourselves in seem to deny it. Jesus himself went through that, but he came through to know again the joy of the steadfast love of his Father which had always been there, and which would bring him—and us—through to victory.

Reflection

Thanks be to God, who gives us the victory through our Lord Jesus Christ.

1 Corinthians 15:57

MC

Psalm 16:5–11 (NRSV)

The joy of each day

The Lord is my chosen portion and my cup; you hold my lot. The boundary lines have fallen for me in pleasant places; I have a goodly heritage. I bless the Lord who gives me counsel; in the night also my heart instructs me. I keep the Lord always before me; because he is at my right hand, I shall not be moved. Therefore my heart is glad, and my soul rejoices; my body also rests secure. For you do not give me up to Sheol, or let your faithful one see the Pit. You show me the path of life. In your presence there is fullness of joy; in your right hand are pleasures forever more.

I had just been reading and reflecting on this psalm when the post arrived. A letter came from an old friend telling me of her change of address, and the reason for it, namely to be nearer her grandchildren following the death of their mother, her daughter. My friend is a widow. She has had a busy life, experiencing quite a number of very tough times, sadnesses and bereavements. Yet her letter was full of joy, contentment and enthusiasm for life. She ended her letter with these words: 'God has been very good to me—"my lot has fallen in a pleasant place".' Like the psalmist, she has complete trust in God, and knows the security of putting everything into his hands.

Here in this psalm we share in the experience of one who chose the way of the Lord, and followed it throughout his life, listening and watching, seeking God's guidance and direction and delighting in it. Nothing can shake him, for he holds to the one who is there beside him. As for the future, it is with God, and God will take him safely into the future. He walks towards the future on a secure path, the path of life, knowing that all the joys of the journey will be perfected in heaven, in that face-to-face meeting. He sees a vision of the welcoming hand of God filled with gifts for him as he reaches journey's end.

To pray and to sing!

Forth in thy name, O Lord, I go,
My daily labour to pursue,
Thee, only thee, resolved to know
In all I think or speak or do.
The task thy wisdom has assigned,
O let me cheerfully fulfil,
In all my works thy presence find,
And prove thy good and perfect will.

Charles Wesley (1707–88)

MC

Psalm 19:1–6 (NRSV)

Look up and see the glory of God

The heavens are telling the glory of God; and the firmament proclaims his handiwork. Day to day pours forth speech, and night to night declares knowledge. There is no speech, nor are there words; their voice is not heard; yet their voice goes out through all the earth, and their words to the end of the world. In the heavens he has set a tent for the sun, which comes out like a bridegroom from his wedding canopy, and like a strong man runs its course with joy. Its rising is from the end of the heavens, and its circuit to the end of them, and nothing is hid from its heat.

In the symphony orchestra of the sky, chorus and principals combine to make music to inspire and delight us. God himself is author, choreographer and conductor, and all we need to do is to look up and listen with our eyes, our hearts, our minds and our souls to the wordless, soundless music of heaven—the song of creation with its light and shade, its bursts of dramatic power and energy, the gentle harmony of the passage of time through to the whisper of a new dawn. The story is retold day by day; we are welcomed without charge to the performance, and nothing is spared that we might personally experience the almighty power and glory of God. There is no need for words—God's glory seen in the heavens transcends speech, and yet it spells out the story so that even a child can look, marvel and receive.

From the dawn of creation, men and women have gazed into the sky and marvelled at the glory of it all, sensing the existence of a power that has made and held it—a power so great that it must be God, for the glory could not have happened just by chance.

What marvellous pen-pictures we have here of the sun, likened to the bridegroom coming in his glory on his wedding day, and the proud runner striding out, enjoying his physical power. Here are beauty, excitement, glory and confidence to be seen, admired and enjoyed. As we read these verses, may we get a vision of the glory of God, written large in his heaven.

Reflection

The glory of God is there for me to see and hear if I will lift my eyes and heart to heaven.

MC

Psalm 19:7–14 (NRSV)

Delight in the law of the Lord

The law of the Lord is perfect, reviving the soul; the decrees of the Lord are sure, making wise the simple; the precepts of the Lord are right, rejoicing the heart; the commandment of the Lord is clear, enlightening the eyes; the fear of the Lord is pure, enduring forever; the ordinances of the Lord are true and righteous altogether. More to be desired are they than gold, even much fine gold; sweeter also than honey, and drippings of the honeycomb. Moreover by them is your servant warned; in keeping them there is great reward. But who can detect their errors? Clear me from hidden faults. Keep back your servant also from the insolent; do not let them have dominion over me. Then I shall be blameless, and innocent of great trans-gression. Let the words of my mouth and the meditation of my heart be acceptable to you, O Lord, my rock and my redeemer.

Yes, we are looking at Psalm 19 again, this time the second part. In verses 1–6 we saw God's glory in creation; now we see it in black and white, the written word of God, which contains rules and guidance to enable us to live in the light of his glory. The psalmist delights in God's word, and commends it to us. What pleasure there is in getting to know it. But in case we are content just to happily read and applaud what it says, there comes the word of warning. The word that reveals God to us reveals our selves too. Our lives, thoughts, feelings and actions are an open book, and we need to take note and action. We can drift into sin and error so easily that we fail to recognize what is happening. We can also try to cover up, or close our eyes to those sins of 'negligence, weakness and our own deliberate fault' which, if allowed to go on unrecognized, unchecked or unconfessed, will take hold of us in a vice-like grip, until we are no longer concerned or aware of the dangers we have succumbed to. The psalmist ends by offering himself to God in quiet confidence, knowing that God is his total security, the one who protects, forgives, enables and provides. The creator and sustainer of all life, the one who knows and loves him, will never let him go.

Prayer

Let the words of my mouth and the meditation of my heart be acceptable to you, O Lord, my rock and my redeemer (v. 14)

MC

Psalm 22:1–5 (NRSV)

The cry of the heart

My God, my God, why have you forsaken me? Why are you so far from helping me, from the words of my groaning? O my God, I cry by day, but you do not answer; and by night, but find no rest. Yet you are holy, enthroned on the praises of Israel. In you our ancestors trusted; they trusted, and you delivered them. To you they cried, and were saved; in you they trusted, and were not put to shame.

Christians cannot read this psalm without hearing Jesus crying out in agony on the cross, being engulfed in the darkness, deeper than that which covered the world during the time of his dying and death. He cries out in the words of a psalm that he would have known from childhood, words of his ancestor David.

These words may have described David's own feeling of desolation at some point in his life, or were words of prophecy concerning his descendant. In Acts, Luke speaks of David as a prophet foretelling the suffering, death and resurrection of the Messiah (Acts 2:25–35). They also echo the cry of the human heart today, the cry of those going through intense pain, calling out to the God they know is there, the God they trust, but who somehow seems to have deserted them.

This psalm can help, for while it begins with that cry 'Why?' it goes on to recall God's love and care even from before birth, remembering the sustaining power of God along the way, and giving a sure hope for the future. The psalmist looks forward to praising God, testifying of his experience of salvation, with a glorious vision of all nations worshipping the God who answers and saves. He also sees the promise of salvation for all the generations yet unborn—including our own! What began with 'My God, why?' ends in assurance, confidence, praise.

We look forward in hope, too, to the day when there will be no need for questions, only songs of praise and thanksgiving. Until then, psalms like this one will enable us to realize that we are not alone. Even in our darkest hour, God is with us, will save us, and will never let us go.

Prayer

Hold thou thy cross
before my closing eyes,
Shine through the gloom
and point me to the skies.
Heaven's morning breaks,
and earth's vain shadows flee,
in life, in death, O Lord,
abide with me.

Henry Francis Lyte (1793–1847)

MC

Psalm 23 (NRSV)

The good shepherd

The Lord is my shepherd, I shall not want. He makes me lie down in green pastures; he leads me beside still waters; he restores my soul. He leads me in right paths for his name's sake. Even though I walk through the darkest valley, I fear no evil; for you are with me; your rod and your staff—they comfort me. You prepare a table before me in the presence of my enemies; you anoint my head with oil; my cup overflows. Surely goodness and mercy shall follow me all the days of my life, and I shall dwell in the house of the Lord my whole life long.

David was a shepherd all his life, first of all caring for his father's sheep, then leading and caring for his nation as king. His experience in killing marauding wild animals who were attacking the sheep proved to be the perfect training for disposing of those who would attack Israel, and the account of his victory over Goliath is probably one of the best-known Bible stories.

David was a good shepherd: he loved his flocks, both sheep and people, and he would have given his life for them. But David, the shepherd king, also needed someone to care for him, to guide and protect him, rescue him from danger and provide for him. He knew that God himself was his shepherd, so that he was safe and secure for all time, and would be brought through all dangers and temptations to share the joys of his Shepherd King in heaven. So in this psalm he describes the joy of the relationship he shares with God—the assurance and peace he knows through trust and obedience; the comfort of being guided and protected throughout his life; and the goodness and mercy of God who is his shepherd and friend, providing food and refreshment along the way and a shared home for eternity.

This psalm has brought comfort and strength to millions, given hope and peace and joy to those going through their own dark valleys, and the assurance of a welcome home when life is done. It is a very personal testimony, but one that opens the way for others to share in that personal relationship with God too.

Reflection

Jesus said, 'I am the good shepherd. The good shepherd lays down his life for his sheep.' He said it and he did it so that we might live.

MC

Psalm 30:1–5 (NRSV)

Thanksgiving for healing

I will extol you, O Lord, for you have drawn me up, and did not let my foes rejoice over me. O Lord my God, I cried to you for help, and you have healed me. O Lord, you brought up my soul from Sheol, restored me to life from among those gone down to the Pit. Sing praises to the Lord, O you his faithful ones, and give thanks to his holy name. For his anger is but for a moment; his favour is for a lifetime. Weeping may linger for the night, but joy comes with the morning.

The words of this psalm dance and sing—you can feel the throb of excitement, relief and pure joy. The psalmist's prayer for healing had been answered, he had been brought back from what seemed certain death—*Sheol* is the grave, the Pit—and now he wants to share the good news, and tell of the love and power of God. This is not only a psalm of thanksgiving for one very special answer to prayer but a recognition of the loving purposes of God in every situation, even in those that seem so hard, so hopeless.

Suffering is real, tears flow, hearts come to breaking point, but just as night ends and morning comes, so light will return to our life. God will lift us out of death so we might dance for joy in his presence, testifying to his wonderful love for us, singing songs of praise to him.

The psalmist had also learned another very important lesson, one we do well to learn too. He had thought that when things were going well, nothing could move him, nothing could topple him—but he was wrong! It was only by the grace and love of God that he was preserved, not by his own strength and power. Trouble brought him to his senses, to admit his pride, and to cry out for mercy (vv. 6–8).

Sometimes we need reminding that pride goes before a fall, but God will restore us and set us free in company with all those who also have discovered not only the rhythm of life, but the author of life. Then one day, as we enter into the glorious reality of eternity, what a party it will be, joining 'with angels and archangels, and all the company of heaven' in the presence of our Lord, for ever.

Prayer

Lord, give me the grace and the humility to see your hand in all things, and to sing your praise at all times.

MC

Psalm 33:16–22 (NRSV)

A sure hope

A king is not saved by his great army; a warrior is not delivered by his great strength. The war horse is a vain hope for victory, and by its great might it cannot save. Truly the eye of the Lord is on those who fear him, on those who hope in his steadfast love, to deliver their soul from death, and to keep them alive in famine. Our soul waits for the Lord; he is our help and shield. Our heart is glad in him, because we trust in his holy name. Let your steadfast love, O Lord, be upon us, even as we hope in you.

This psalm is a hymn of praise to God who is creator, ruler, judge and saviour. The whole of the psalm should be read, so as to put into context our portion for today. It tells of our God who knows, watches and acts, and it tells of the futility of putting our trust in armies and weapons of war. But, in the words of the folk song, 'When will they ever learn, when will they ever learn?'—and for 'they' read 'we' and 'I'. The power struggles for supremacy go on between nations, groups and individuals. History is littered with terrible accounts of the suffering inflicted one upon another, and today it still continues. Wars, fighting, destruction, suffering, death. Winners rise and fall; victory is hollow, paid for in the currency of human misery. Yet, thank God, there are always those who work for peace and understanding, who seek a better way—peace makers and peace keepers in 'the corridors of power'; aid organizations, and those who take out that aid and expertise to suffering people caught up in conflict; those who risk, and often give, their lives to get help to the needy, regardless of which side they are on. Such people are often unsung and unknown, but they are agents of God's love for all human beings. Whose side is God on? Verses 18 and 19 may help us think that through. And what about our response? Where is our ground for hope? Surely the power of love is our only hope, the steadfast love of the Lord, for it is the way of peace and victory, of freedom and life.

Prayer

O God, our help in ages past,
Our hope for years to come.
Be thou our guard while life shall last,
And our eternal home.

Isaac Watts (1674–1748)

MC

Psalm 40:1–3 (NRSV)

Firm on the rock

I waited patiently for the Lord; he inclined to me and heard my cry. He drew me up from the desolate pit, out of the miry bog, and set my feet upon a rock, making my steps secure. He put a new song in my mouth, a song of praise to our God. Many will see it and fear, and put their trust in the Lord.

A friend of mine once told me how, when he was a small boy in Ireland, he fell into a bog. He had the terrifying experience of being sucked down into the mud, until a boy, only a couple of years older than himself, heaved him up and out of it. He remembers then lying filthy and frightened, but safe, on firm ground again. He said, 'When I read Psalm 40, I relive it. I have been there—I know what it's like first hand.'

Recently, when my colleague David and I were reading this psalm together, I recounted the story. 'Yes, Margaret, but our trouble is, we don't always realize we are stuck in the bog and need rescuing, do we?' he said. I need to remember that, and I pass it on to you! Sometimes we fall into the miry bog of trouble and sin; often we jump in; but either way, we get stuck, and the more we struggle, the deeper we get. All we can do is to cry out to God, and wait. God does hear and answer, and will bring us to firm ground again, so that we might walk in his way on the right path. King David knew that through personal experience. He had everything to sing about: he had been rescued and restored; he was a walking, singing testimony. So we too can rejoice in what God has done for us—his saving power, restoration and renewal. We can share the good news with others, just as David does in this psalm.

But read on in the psalm from verse 12, where he writes of 'evils' and 'iniquities': it has happened again, and again... as it does in our lives. And yet the good news is that God keeps on reaching down, lifting us out of the mire, giving us another chance, setting us on the rock of his salvation. May we, like David, 'say continually, "Great is the Lord!"' (v. 16).

Reflection

What did it cost God to stoop down and rescue me out of the mire? Read John 3:16.

MC

Matthew 21:8–11 (NRSV)

Who is this?

A very large crowd spread their cloaks on the road, and others cut branches from the trees and spread them on the road. The crowds that went ahead of him and that followed were shouting, 'Hosanna to the Son of David! Blessed is the one who comes in the name of the Lord! Hosanna in the highest heaven!' When he entered Jerusalem, the whole city was in turmoil, asking, 'Who is this?' The crowds were saying, 'This is the prophet Jesus from Nazareth in Galilee.'

On Palm Sunday it is usual to speak of Jesus riding into Jerusalem 'in triumph', but in one sense that's to miss the point of the event. Everything in this story is significant; every detail is important to our understanding of the true answer to the question posed by 'the whole city': 'Who is this?'

I remember, twenty years ago, standing on the Mount of Olives on a Palm Sunday morning, looking across the valley to the old city of Jerusalem, bathed in April sunshine. It wasn't hard to imagine this scene, the donkey picking its way down the stony slope, Jesus on its back, the crowds cheering and cutting palm branches to lay in his path. Indeed, one could almost hear the cries of 'Hosanna to the Son of David!'—'Save us now!'—and the crowd's blessing on the one who 'comes in the name of the Lord'. Clearly the disciples from Galilee had made up their minds (whatever the people of Jerusalem thought) that Jesus was the 'Messiah', the one God was to send to save his people. There's no other explanation either for the 'hosannas' or for the title 'Son of David'. And Jesus didn't tell them to stop. Quite the contrary. Luke tells us that the Pharisees asked him to do so, but he answered, 'If these were silent, the stones would shout out' (Luke 19:40).

And what about the donkey? The prophet Zechariah, in a clearly messianic prophecy, had spoken of Israel's king coming to her 'humble, and mounted on a donkey' (Zechariah 9:9), so this whole event, 'stage-managed' by Jesus so skilfully (see 21:1–3), was the clearest possible claim to messiahship. It was a claim that was to seal his human fate. The city wanted its messiah, of course it did. But not this one, unarmed, on a donkey, and escorted by peasants.

Reflection

The people of Jerusalem wanted a conquering king, not a suffering servant. How easy it is to rewrite God's plan according to our own wishes!

DW

This is the first of a series 'From Olivet to Calvary'—and beyond!

John 12:1–7 (NRSV)

The fragrance of true worship

Six days before the Passover Jesus came to Bethany, the home of Lazarus, whom he had raised from the dead. There they gave a dinner for him. Martha served, and Lazarus was one of those at the table with him. Mary took a pound of costly perfume made of pure nard, anointed Jesus' feet, and wiped them with her hair. The house was filled with the fragrance of the perfume. But Judas Iscariot, one of his disciples (the one who was about to betray him), said, 'Why was this perfume not sold for three hundred denarii and the money given to the poor?' (He said this not because he cared about the poor, but because he was a thief; he kept the common purse and used to steal what was put into it.) Jesus said, 'Leave her alone. She bought it so that she might keep it for the day of my burial.'

This story appears, with differences of detail, in other Gospels. John's story, and Mark's very similar one, are about a woman (Mary, presumably the sister of Lazarus) who was deeply devoted to Jesus and who sensed that his suffering and death were near. Now, she felt, was the time to anoint him with the 'costly perfume' she had kept for this moment. (Could it, one wonders, have been the ointment that would have anointed the body of her brother, had he not been brought back from the dead?)

In any case, such questions are irrelevant to the main thrust of this lovely story. It's about *worship*—costly worship, worship that is filled with the beauty of true love and devotion, worship that is, as some would see it, extravagant and extreme.

However, two points need to be made clear. Firstly, Jesus wasn't indifferent to the problems of poverty. No one who reads the gospels could have any doubt that Jesus cared for the poor, perhaps beyond any others—'the poor have the good news preached to them'. Secondly, this story is not an endorsement of a kind of self-indulgent spending on religious adornment—shall we say, copes of gold or thick pile carpets in the sanctuary! It is about the *pure* extravagance of gratitude, a worship that doesn't even ask, 'What does it cost?'

Reflection

What would it mean for me to throw off caution and worship God 'extravagantly'?

DW

John 12:27–32 (NRSV)

Lifted up from the earth

'Now my soul is troubled. And what should I say—"Father, save me from this hour"? No, it is for this reason that I have come to this hour. Father, glorify your name.' Then a voice came from heaven, 'I have glorified it, and I will glorify it again.' The crowd standing there heard it and said that it was thunder. Others said, 'An angel has spoken to him.' Jesus answered, 'This voice has come for your sake, not for mine. Now is the judgment of this world; now the ruler of this world will be driven out. And I, when I am lifted up from the earth, will draw all people to myself.'

There is no 'Garden of Agony' in John's Gospel, but some have described this scene as John's 'Gethsemane'. Clearly Jesus, with his arrest and crucifixion just ahead, is deeply troubled in soul. Here it is not 'Let this cup pass from me' but the equally desperate 'Father, save me from this hour.' It is a very human cry, and one that will have been echoed in the experience of many people.

The reply is the voice of God, no less! The Father responds to the Son's affirmation of faith and prayer only that the Father's name should be glorified, with a ringing assurance that it has been (presumably in Christ's earthly ministry) and would yet be (in his death and resurrection). The bystanders don't quite hear it like that, but react exactly as people do when confronted with any demonstration of the power of God. Some rationalized it: 'It thundered.' Some both spiritualized it and at the same time distanced themselves from it: 'An angel spoke to *him*.' But Jesus gave them the true interpretation of the event. It was not for his benefit (had he not already expressed his total faith in the Father?) but for *theirs*. Failure on their part to recognize the divine action in Jesus would be a form of judgment, no less.

It's impossible not to be reminded of the picture in the other gospels of Jesus weeping over Jerusalem, for its failure to 'recognize the time of (its) visitation from God' (Luke 19:44). Now that city was to be the scene of God's greatest act of salvation, as his Son was 'lifted up'—not in military triumph, but on a cross. By this he would 'draw all people to himself'—but only those, of course, who were willing to be drawn.

Reflection

Help me to recognize the work of God, not to rationalize it, nor distance myself from it.

DW

John 12:42–47 (NRSV)

Coming out of darkness

Nevertheless many, even of the authorities, believed in him. But because of the Pharisees they did not confess it, for fear that they would be put out of the synagogue; for they loved human glory more than the glory that comes from God. Then Jesus cried aloud: 'Whoever believes in me believes not in me but in him who sent me. And whoever sees me sees him who sent me. I have come as light into the world, so that everyone who believes in me should not remain in the darkness. I do not judge anyone who hears my words and does not keep them, for I came not to judge the world, but to save the world.'

This passage stands as a kind of freeze-frame snapshot of the situation in Jerusalem halfway through what we now call Holy Week. Jesus divides the people, as he said he would. There were his disciples, of course, who had by now recognized him as the Messiah and Saviour. There were the 'crowds', quite a feature in the Gospels, now enthusiastic, now drawing back—attracted by the miracles, but fearful of the demands that Jesus made on their commitment. Now, we learn, there was even division among the 'authorities', the people John rather oddly calls 'the Jews' (after all, just about everyone in the story is Jewish!) Apparently some of them were secret believers in Jesus—perhaps Nicodemus, the ruler who came to Jesus by night (John 3) was one of them. But they couldn't bring themselves to come out and confess it 'for they loved human glory more than the glory that comes from God'. What a terrible judgment! And yet, what a common failing.

I remember a young man whose wife was a practising Christian saying that he was very impressed by her faith and the change it had made in her. But he felt unable to follow her example. His reason? 'What would my mates say?' I suggested to him that that was a pretty unconvincing reason for rejecting something so vitally important, yet he was adamant. He wouldn't be able to face the ridicule if his friends found out he had 'gone religious'. Yet, as Jesus says here, believing in him is the way out of darkness into 'light'. How sad to pass that experience by simply because of what other people would think.

Reflection

We are all susceptible to peer pressure, of course. But if that pressure deprives us of the most important thing in the world, it must be rejected. Before God, we stand alone.

DW

John 13:1–5 (NRSV)

The Servant King

Now before the festival of the Passover, Jesus knew that his hour had come to depart from this world and go to the Father. Having loved his own who were in the world, he loved them to the end. The devil had already put it into the heart of Judas son of Simon Iscariot to betray him. And during supper Jesus, knowing that the Father had given all things into his hands, and that he had come from God and was going to God, got up from the table, took off his outer robe, and tied a towel around himself. Then he poured water into a basin and began to wash the disciples' feet.

John's Gospel has no institution of the Lord's supper (though the deep truths of this gospel sacrament are taught by Jesus in the discourse in chapter 6). Instead, we are allowed the privilege of 'eaves-dropping' on other aspects of the last supper, with marvellous teaching about the coming of the Holy Spirit, and the wonderful 'high priestly prayer' of Jesus in chapter 17. What an evening that must have been, during which Jesus drew back the veil of heaven, as it were, and shared with his disciples the deepest purposes of God.

But before the meal begins we have this astonishing little incident, when Jesus washed the disciples' feet. That should have been the task of a servant, or perhaps of the most junior person present. Perhaps the disciples had all held back, none wishing to assume the most menial role. If that was so, they must have been embarrassed and ashamed when Jesus—their 'Teacher and Lord' (13:13)—took on the task himself. John's introduction to the story sets the scene in all its stark contrasts. There is the intention of Judas (sitting there at the table with the others) to betray Jesus. There is the fact that Jesus was fully aware of his own identity—'that he had come from God and was going to God' and that the 'Father had put all things into his hands'. And then, a lovely touch, that those divinely authorized hands took a basin, poured water into it, and began to wash his disciples' feet. They were to learn a lesson they would never forget: 'servants are not greater than their master' (v. 16). To follow Jesus is not to enjoy privilege and status, but to share in loving, humble service.

Reflection

Christ is our Teacher and Lord, but he is also a 'Servant': the paradox is the lesson for us!

DW

John 19:25–30 (NRSV)

The task accomplished

Standing near the cross of Jesus were his mother, and his mother's sister, Mary the wife of Clopas, and Mary Magdalene. When Jesus saw his mother and the disciple whom he loved standing beside her, he said to his mother, 'Woman, here is your son.' Then he said to the disciple, 'Here is your mother.' And from that hour the disciple took her into his own home... When Jesus knew that all was now finished, he said (in order to fulfil the scripture), 'I am thirsty.' A jar full of sour wine was standing there. So they put a sponge full of the wine on a branch of hyssop and held it to his mouth. When Jesus had received the wine, he said, 'It is finished.' Then he bowed his head and gave up his spirit.

Good Friday has always seemed to me a strange title for the day on which wretched human beings put to death the Son of God. Was it 'good' that out of spite, or envy, or misguided zeal for religion, a *completely* innocent man was executed as a criminal? Was it good that he should die by this most painful of all methods, joints and organs slowly torn apart while the body withered in the hot April sun? Was it 'good' that human justice was denied, that soldiers gambled for his garment? The answer has to be 'No' in each case, of course. The crucifixion of Jesus, as an event in its own right, was not good but utterly evil.

Yet 'Good' Friday it is, probably because 'good' and 'God' have the same root in Old English. This was *God's* Friday, the day when his great purpose of salvation reached its climax. Of all the Gospels, John's captures that note more obviously than the others. All through the betrayal, arrest and 'trial' of Jesus, the quiet prophet from Nazareth has somehow seemed to be in command. In our journey from Olivet to Calvary we have arrived at last at the 'Place of the Skull'. The scene is, of course, horrible: the three broken figures on the crosses, the distraught women, the callous soldiers. Yet out of the darkness, typically, light shines from the central figure on the cross. He quietly makes arrangements for his mother's future welfare, does everything to 'fulfil the scriptures', and finally says, 'It is finished' and—notice the phrase—'*gives up* his spirit'. That word 'finished'—*tetelestai* in Greek—doesn't mean 'ended' but *accomplished*. The work of salvation was done. He could rest at last.

Reflection

'Good' Friday is the day when the 'good' purpose of God for us was completed.

DW

John 19:38–42 (NRSV)

'There was a garden'

Joseph of Arimathea, who was a disciple of Jesus, though a secret one because of his fear of the Jews, asked Pilate to let him take away the body of Jesus. Pilate gave him permission; so he came and removed his body. Nicodemus, who had at first come to Jesus by night, also came, bringing a mixture of myrrh and aloes, weighing about a hundred pounds. They took the body of Jesus and wrapped it with the spices in linen cloths... Now there was a garden in the place where he was crucified, and in the garden there was a new tomb in which no one had ever been laid. And so, because it was the Jewish day of Preparation, and the tomb was nearby, they laid Jesus there.

Here are two of those 'secret' disciples of Jesus that we read about three days ago—Joseph of Arimathea and Nicodemus. Perhaps the manner of his dying had finally convinced them that he was the Messiah, or possibly they simply wanted to offer this last service to Jesus. There are some differences between the gospel accounts as to who anointed the body of Jesus, and when, but it would seem that 'the women', who had faithfully followed Jesus even when the male disciples fled, wished to share in this last duty as well.

'Now there was a garden in the place where he was crucified.' What an astonishing transformation from the sombre scene on Golgotha which John has just described. The Place of the Skull was a place of death, but a garden is a place of life. I was married to a very keen gardener, and began to see the appeal of working with living things, growing things, and things of beauty. Could there be a bigger contrast than Golgotha (Calvary) and a *garden*?

The human race made its first appearance in a garden: the 'garden of delights' which we call 'Eden'. That garden was spoilt by their disobedience, and they were driven from it. Now, in the wonderful purpose of God, the salvation of those men and women made in God's image, made to enjoy the delights of the garden, is to be brought to its conclusion in... a garden. 'There was a garden in the place where he was crucified.' In the place of death there was life.

Reflection

As we wait for the joy of Easter morning, let's visualize the garden, with the new growth of a Judean spring—waiting for the new life that would be spring-time for the human race.

DW

John 20:1–9 (NRSV)

Seeing and believing

Early on the first day of the week, while it was still dark, Mary Magdalene came to the tomb and saw that the stone had been removed from the tomb. So she ran and went to Simon Peter and the other disciple, the one whom Jesus loved, and said to them, 'They have taken the Lord out of the tomb, and we do not know where they have laid him.' Then Peter and the other disciple set out and went towards the tomb. The two were running together, but the other disciple outran Peter and reached the tomb first. He bent down to look in and saw the linen wrappings lying there, but he did not go in. Then Simon Peter came, following him, and went into the tomb. He saw the linen wrappings lying there, and the cloth that had been on Jesus' head, not lying with the linen wrappings but rolled up in a place by itself. Then the other disciple, who reached the tomb first, also went in, and he saw and believed; for as yet they did not understand the scripture, that he must rise from the dead.

Two of the great words in the resurrection stories in the gospels are found in this reading—indeed, they are linked together: 'saw', and 'believed'. The disciples, men and women, were given the priceless privilege of actually *seeing* the risen Lord, and as a result they believed. Like a repeated refrain, they say 'We have seen the Lord.' But at this point in John's narrative, they *hadn't*. All they had seen were the linen wrappings and the cloth that had been on Jesus' head 'rolled up in a place by itself'. Yet apparently that was enough to convince them: they 'saw and believed'. For now, it was the empty tomb, and the evidence of those cloths, that excited their faith. They didn't yet 'understand the scripture'. All they had was the evidence of their eyes!

Over recent decades there has been a tendency in theological circles to play down the 'empty tomb' and stress instead the disciples' experience of the risen Lord. But that is to ignore the Gospel record. For all the Gospel writers it was the stone rolled back, the empty tomb, the grave cloths, that were the first evidence that the greatest miracle in human history really had happened.

Reflection

Mary Magdalene couldn't wait to get to the tomb—'while it was still dark'. And that was, she thought, to anoint a corpse. At what hour would she have gone if she had known he was alive!

DW

John 20:11–18 (NRSV)

Why are you weeping?

But Mary stood weeping outside the tomb. As she wept, she bent over to look into the tomb; and she saw two angels in white, sitting where the body of Jesus had been lying, one at the head and the other at the feet. They said to her, 'Woman, why are you weeping?' She said to them, 'They have taken away my Lord, and I do not know where they have laid him.' When she had said this, she turned round and saw Jesus standing there, but she did not know that it was Jesus. Jesus said to her, 'Woman, why are you weeping? For whom are you looking?' Supposing him to be the gardener, she said to him, 'Sir, if you have carried him away, tell me where you have laid him, and I will take him away.' Jesus said to her, 'Mary!' She turned and said to him in Hebrew, 'Rabbouni!' (which means Teacher)… Mary Magdalene went and announced to the disciples, 'I have seen the Lord'; and she told them that he had said these things to her.

Mary Magdalene's role in the Easter story is fascinating. All the Gospel writers agree that she was the first to the tomb and the first to see the risen Lord. In an age and a culture where women were regarded as such unreliable witnesses that they were not permitted to give evidence in a court of law, that is an amazing fact, and one which must have been incontrovertible, or these (male) writers would surely have balked at it. And not only was she a woman, but the Gospels more than hint that she had had a disreputable past, and certainly record that Jesus had delivered her from 'seven demons' (see Luke 8:2). If God was looking for a witness to impress the society of the day, this was a strange choice… but a ringing endorsement of the loyalty of the women who followed Jesus, and of the richness of their faith in him.

This story is beautiful, and told with economy and restraint. Mary is distressed, and that distress is multiplied when she finds that someone has removed the body of 'my Lord'. Perhaps because of her tears, she neither recognized the angelic messengers nor, at first, Jesus himself, but his use of her name, 'Mary!' was enough to identify him to her. In the purest sense of the word, this is a love story.

Reflection

Perhaps every encounter with the risen Lord has to be as personal as this?

DW

John 20:19–23 (NRSV)

'Peace be with you!'

When it was evening on that day, the first day of the week, and the doors of the house where the disciples had met were locked for fear of the Jews, Jesus came and stood among them and said, 'Peace be with you.' After he said this, he showed them his hands and his side. Then the disciples rejoiced when they saw the Lord. Jesus said to them again, 'Peace be with you. As the Father has sent me, so I send you.' When he had said this, he breathed on them and said to them, 'Receive the Holy Spirit. If you forgive the sins of any, they are forgiven them; if you retain the sins of any, they are retained.'

This has been called 'John's Pentecost', though clearly it is quite different from the spectacular and public outpouring of the Spirit which was to occur some weeks later. Yet there is a 'pentecostal' element about this event, with Jesus 'breathing' on his disciples to endue them with the gift of his Spirit. 'Breath' and 'spirit' are the same word in Greek, so in effect he was transferring his 'living breath' to them. This action is followed by the promise that they would exercise, under the guidance of the Holy Spirit, a ministry of judgment and forgiveness. This is probably not directly related to any notion of apostolic authority—those involved were 'the disciples' (presumably the 120 to whom Luke refers in Acts 1: 15, including women, rather than just the 'apostles').

This endowment of the Spirit also relates to the earlier command: 'As the Father has sent me, I send you.' Their future ministry was to follow the pattern of the ministry of Jesus. He was 'sent' by the Father. Now he was 'sending' them. Just as Jesus, during his earthly mission, both forgave and judged sins, so his followers would continue to do so. This is not a matter of personal 'judging' (which Jesus had already warned them against—Matthew 7:1) but of being open to the guidance of the Spirit of God: 'When the Spirit of truth comes, he will guide you into all the truth' (John 16:13).

But whatever they did, they were to do *as Jesus would have done it*: that is the real test. They were not being 'sent' to be served, but to serve, and to give themselves for others as he had done. And what was true for them is true for us, their successors today.

Reflection

The risen Jesus sends his people to continue his 'mission'. What a calling!

DW

John 20:24–28 (NRSV)

Dealing with doubt

But Thomas (who was called the Twin), one of the Twelve, was not with them when Jesus came. So the other disciples told him, 'We have seen the Lord.' But he said to them, 'Unless I see the mark of the nails in his hands, and put my finger in the mark of the nails and my hand in his side, I will not believe.' A week later his disciples were again in the house, and Thomas was with them. Although the doors were shut, Jesus came and stood among them and said, 'Peace be with you.' Then he said to Thomas, 'Put your finger here and see my hands. Reach out your hand and put it in my side. Do not doubt but believe.' Thomas answered him, 'My Lord and my God!'

The story of Thomas, destined to be dubbed for ever 'Doubting Thomas', is intensely human, and true to experience. It would be very unlikely that in a group of eleven men not one would question the extraordinary claim that someone had appeared from the dead. Of course, and significantly, Thomas was 'not with them' when this appearance occurred, but we already know that he was the sceptic in the ranks—see, for instance, John 14:5. The others might be gullible, but however much he might have wished it to be so, he would not believe that Jesus was alive without incontrovertible proof.

Perhaps the clue to the whole story is in those words, 'however much he might have wished it'. Thomas, I'm sure, *wanted* to believe. His devotion to Jesus was no less than that of the others. But he had this inbuilt caution. It was all, as we say, 'too good to be true'. So he threw down this rather ridiculous challenge: 'Unless I see… unless I touch… I will not believe.' This was not a *refusal* to believe, but a genuine, honest inability to do so.

And then it happened! Not only did the risen Lord appear, but he directly confronted his sceptical disciple: 'Put your finger here… reach out your hand… do not doubt, but believe.' There is no record that Thomas responded to the first two commands, but he certainly did to the third, leaping in one dramatic moment from doubt to a faith that went beyond anything yet confessed by any of Jesus' followers: 'My Lord and my God!'

Reflection

We cannot see or touch the risen Jesus, but 'these things are written so that you may come to believe that Jesus is the Messiah, the Son of God' (John 20:31). It is those who have not seen, yet have believed who are to be 'blessed' (20:29).

DW

John 20:29–31 (NRSV)

Evidence for faith

Jesus said to him, 'Have you believed because you have seen me? Blessed are those who have not seen and yet have come to believe.' Now Jesus did many other signs in the presence of his disciples, which are not written in this book. But these are written so that you may come to believe that Jesus is the Messiah, the Son of God, and that through believing you may have life in his name.

Many scholars believe that these are the last words of the Gospel as John wrote it, and that what follows is a kind of 'post-script', perhaps by the same author, or possibly by another. Certainly the Gospel begins with a 'prologue' (1:1–18), which places Jesus, the 'Word', in the context of the eternal purpose of God. At the end, the Gospel, as we shall see, concludes with a rather similar look forward, into God's purpose for the emerging Christian Church.

Whether this is the 'end' of John's story or not is probably not important, because it certainly wasn't the end of the story of Jesus, which is still being told. But these verses do set out very concisely why the Gospel was written—and, perhaps, why the others were written, too. These are not academic histories, or cool biographies, but utterly committed writings, whose manifest intention is to awaken faith in their readers and hearers. 'These are written so that you may come to *believe*...' There is a shining honesty of purpose about that.

The writer also tells us that Jesus did 'many other signs in the presence of his disciples, which are not written in this book'. But 'these signs' are recorded not just for interest or to satisfy curiosity, but so that people would come to faith in Jesus, a faith which offers life 'in his name'.

John has told us of the resurrection experience of the disciples—of Mary Magdalene, of Peter and John, of Thomas and the others. Now, through this narrative, he offers the same experience to us, his readers. Those first believers felt that they were sharing in the risen life of the Lord. Well, says the writer, *so can you*.

Reflection

'Life' comes through believing in Jesus, the Son of God, crucified and risen. 'Whoever has the Son of God has life' (1 John 5:12).

DW

John 21:7–12 (NRSV)

A unique breakfast

That disciple whom Jesus loved said to Peter, 'It is the Lord!' When Simon Peter heard that it was the Lord, he put on some clothes, for he was naked, and jumped into the lake. But the other disciples came in the boat, dragging the net full of fish... When they had gone ashore, they saw a charcoal fire there, with fish on it, and bread. Jesus said to them, 'Bring some of the fish that you have just caught.' So Simon Peter went aboard and hauled the net ashore, full of large fish, a hundred and fifty-three of them; and though there were so many, the net was not torn. Jesus said to them, 'Come and have breakfast.' Now none of the disciples dared to ask him, 'Who are you?' because they knew it was the Lord.

Here is John's Galilee resurrection appearance story, the encounter of seven of the disciples with the risen Lord during a fishing expedition on the Sea of Tiberias. They had fished all night but caught nothing, until just after daybreak a strange figure on the shore advised them to cast their nets on the other side of the boat. They did, and suddenly had an enormous catch. No wonder 'the disciple whom Jesus loved' identified the stranger as 'the Lord', nor that Peter, on hearing this, should impulsively jump into the water and make his way to land. There they found a fire prepared, and a simple breakfast, which the 'stranger' invited them to share.

Why, we may ask, did the disciples still have problems about this person's identity? They didn't like to ask him who he was, because 'they knew it was the Lord'. This is the strongest possible indication that Jesus after his resurrection was in some way changed in appearance (an impression already given in this Gospel, and in Luke's—see 20:14, Luke 24:16). This should not surprise us. 'Flesh and blood cannot inherit the kingdom of heaven,' says the apostle Paul (1 Corinthians 15:50). 'We shall be *changed*...' The really encouraging thing is that despite this change (whatever it amounted to), in the end no one who knew Jesus well before his crucifixion was in any doubt at all that they had met the same man after his resurrection: 'they *knew* it was the Lord'.

Reflection

Shall we recognize our loved ones in heaven? Yes, in the same way as the disciples recognized the risen Jesus: by the sort of person he was, rather than by his appearance.

DW

John 3:14–17 (NRSV)

Lift high the cross

And just as Moses lifted up the serpent in the wilderness, so must the Son of Man be lifted up, that whoever believes in him may have eternal life. For God so loved the world that he gave his only Son, so that everyone who believes in him may not perish but may have eternal life. Indeed, God did not send the Son into the world to condemn the world, but in order that the world might be saved through him.

We have come to the end of our journey from Olivet to Calvary, and for this last reading we go back almost to the start of the story for John's explanation of its *meaning*. He uses a familiar Old Testament story to make the point—Moses saving the Israelites from a plague of snakes in the wilderness. People were dying from the deadly snake-bites until God told Moses to make a brass replica of a snake, nail it to a pole, and carry it through the Israelite camp. As the people looked up at the brass snake, so they would be healed, they would live (see Numbers 21:6–9).

In the same way, he says (or perhaps the words are those of Jesus, it is unclear whether this is direct or reported speech), Jesus was to be 'lifted up' to bring healing to those who are dying. 'For God so loved the world that he gave his only Son, so that everyone who believes in him may not perish but may have eternal life.' There is the same contrast, between death and life, between 'perishing' through the consequences of sin and being brought into God's great gift of eternal life.

When I did my National Service a *very* long time ago, I was in the RAF medical branch, and we proudly wore in our lapels the badge of Moses' brass snake on a pole. It told people that we were involved in the work of healing, perhaps even sometimes saving life. Of that healing work Jesus is the supreme example, not only in all the individuals whom he touched and restored to health, but in his great saving act on the cross when he was 'lifted up' so that the whole world could be rescued from perishing and enter into eternal life. That is John's story. This is our story, too.

Reflection

'Everyone who is bitten shall look at it and live' (Numbers 21:8). As the old Sankey and Moody hymn says, 'There is life for a look at the crucified one.'

DW

Ephesians 1:3–14 (NRSV, abridged)

Cosmic salvation

Blessed be the God and Father of our Lord Jesus Christ, who has blessed us in Christ with every spiritual blessing in the heavenly places, just as he chose us in Christ before the foundation of the world to be holy and blameless before him in love... With all wisdom and insight he has made known to us the mystery of his will, according to his good pleasure that he set forth in Christ, as a plan for the fullness of time, to gather up all things in him, things in heaven and things on earth...

Although this is wonderful doctrine, the apostle is not here writing as a systematic theologian, but rather singing a rhapsody of praise for the wonder of a salvation which embraces the whole created order. This whole section is practically one sentence, with wonder piling upon wonder, so that we become intoxicated with its glory. And, because we are used to modern, bite-sized thoughts, we become bewildered.

Paul says that the holy and loving will of the Father is the source and fountainhead of ultimate redemption. God is not distant, capricious or legalistic, but wholly involved with his creation. It is his perfect will that fallen humankind and the whole created order be redeemed.

Through Christ he accomplishes this wonder of redemption. It is not just a 'rescue package' for a few pious souls, but full and free forgiveness, a relationship of loving mutuality, and the possibility of all things being redeemed in the fullness of time. This is beyond our imagination, both in fact and time, but it does mean that we are given new birth through Christ as the first act in this cosmic drama, and that it will move, by grace, towards the ultimate end of the fullness of redemption.

The Holy Spirit is the agent through whom the will of the Father and the redemption of the Son are made real in our experience and in the world. We are sealed with the Holy Spirit. That 'seal' is the secret inward sign by which we are marked to show that we belong to God. And that same Holy Spirit is the pledge of our inheritance (vv. 13–14). That 'pledge' is the first advance payment, the guarantee that the rest will be paid in due time. It is a foretaste of heaven's glory.

Prayer

I am overwhelmed by the wonders of these verses, Lord. Enlighten my understanding, that I may enter into such experience, by your grace.

R/SSF

SECOND QUARTER

The New Life

Luke 4:16–20 (REB)

You and me too

Jesus stood up to read the lesson and was handed the scroll of the prophet Isaiah. He opened the scroll and found the passage which says, 'The spirit of the Lord is upon me because he has anointed me; he has sent me to announce good news to the poor, to proclaim release for prisoners and recovery of sight for the blind; to let the broken victims go free, to proclaim the year of the Lord's favour.' He rolled up the scroll, gave it back to the attendant, and sat down; and all eyes in the synagogue were fixed on him.

God appears in this passage to have a particular affinity with the poor, the blind, the broken, those who are captive and slaves. These are people whom God cares for especially.

Obviously the first hearers were astonished when Jesus read this particular scroll because of his claim to messiahship. Today what some people, particularly in churches, find difficult is that God has this passion for the poor and damaged.

I remember a gentleman on the church council becoming very angry because of the emphasis on helping the poor in this passage. 'We have to heat and maintain *this* church, otherwise there will be no help for anyone else,' was his argument. But such a comment fails to understand that what Jesus means by this is that *everyone* is poor, everyone is blind, everyone is a captive, broken and a slave.

Some are oppressed in very physical ways and Jesus demonstrated how his followers would need to face places of pain like Bethsaida or individual cripples or lepers. But he also made it abundantly clear that the disciples needed his care for their own souls. They were also the ones who were blind, imprisoned and enslaved in their attitudes, broken in spirit and so on. For us, this is not only about those who in Third World countries suffer oppression. We are all subject to and damaged by the evil in the world in which we live.

There are no favourites with God. It's just that those who admit their damage seem to grow closer to God. God recognizes in them a humility that accepts that 'I am in need'. The very categories of people whom the Spirit anointed Jesus to minister to are with us today. In fact they are *us*.

Prayer

Lord, heal me, and let me be
a healer for others.

GD

John 20:15–17 (RSV)

Don't touch

Jesus said to her, 'Woman, why are you weeping? Whom do you seek?' Supposing him to be the gardener, she said to him, 'Sir, if you have carried him away, tell me where you have laid him, and I will take him away.' Jesus said to her, 'Mary.' She turned and said to him in Hebrew, 'Rabboni!' (which means Teacher). Jesus said to her, 'Do not hold me, for I have not yet ascended to the Father; but go to my brethren and say to them, I am ascending to my Father and your Father, to my God and your God.'

The tomb is empty. Mary turns and appeals to a stranger, 'Tell me where you have laid him'—an image of despair and poignancy. Even the dead remains of a loved one are preferable to no trace at all.

Through the ages, many have grieved for runaway, kidnapped or aborted children, or lived with the uncertainty of an ambiguous telegram, 'Missing in action'. The denial of a final tactile goodbye piles grief upon grief.

Mary thought she was to be denied the healing process of a proper procedure of burial for her beloved Master. She longed to give that final 'touch' of love when nothing more could be offered to her deceased Lord. Perhaps that is why Jesus said, 'Do not hold me', which in Greek means 'Don't touch'. It is uncertain as to why he forbade her tactile contact. This was a master who gathered children into his arms to bless them, who touched lepers to heal them, and who, soon after his resurrection, had no qualms about inviting Thomas to place his fingers into the wounds in his hands and side.

Might his resurrected touch, at this stage, have been dangerous to her material body? Or perhaps he was addressing her psychological health as she showed signs of wanting to cling to a friend whom she must relinquish? We cannot tell.

But Mary had to learn to let Jesus go in order to keep him for ever. His Spirit would be sent to empower the disciples. We do not 'possess' God, he must be allowed unrestricted ownership of our lives and our wills.

Prayer

Dear Lord, whisper my name, as you did Mary's, and let me know your touch on my life by your Spirit's power. Loosen my grip upon all that I would seek to possess, that I may reach out for you and begin the long but certain journey from despair to hope. Amen

HMcD

John 20:18–21 (RSV)

'Peace be with you'

Mary Magdalene went and said to the disciples, 'I have seen the Lord.' ... On the evening of that day, the first day of the week, the doors being shut where the disciples were, for fear of the Jews, Jesus came and stood among them and said to them, 'Peace be with you.' When he had said this, he showed them his hands and his side. Then the disciples were glad when they saw the Lord. Jesus said to them again, 'Peace be with you. As the Father has sent me, even so I send you.'

Supposing you had been a first-century Christian who had just barricaded yourself in behind locked doors in hiding from the authorities? Suddenly a person materializes through the doors and stands beside you in the room. We cannot imagine how terrifying that experience must have been for the disciples, or the following sense of tremendous relief and joy when it became evident that the visitor was none other than Jesus himself.

No wonder his chosen words are both familiar and reassuring: 'Peace be with you.' What a contrast to what they were actually feeling. In the midst of a dynamic, unprecedented, almost sci-fi experience, superior to any script from the *X-Files*, Jesus brings an assurance of peace. It gives us additional evidence of the ongoing trauma with which the disciples wrestled during this momentous week in their lives. Jubilant a week previously on the Lord's triumphant ride into Jerusalem, devastated at his arrest, scattered in fear during the trial and crucifixion, in mourning and disarray until this very morning, when rumours had spread from the women that the tomb was empty. Now Jesus sends them to continue his mission to others. Do you think they were ready for *that*?

In our own lives we often feel we could do a great work for the Lord, if only... If only the kids were out of nappies, or the mortgage was paid, or the exams were over, or the illness was cured, or if we had more time, or less worries, or other talents, or maybe even if we could attain peace.

'Peace be with you,' says the Lord, and he means without anything else necessarily changing.

Prayer

Dear Father, thank you that if locked doors gave you no difficulty, then the solution to my problems is at hand. Help me claim your peace, not merely in the absence of troubles, but right in the midst of them. Amen

HMcD

John 20:24–29 (RSV)

'Unless I see...'

Now Thomas, one of the twelve, called the Twin, was not with them when Jesus came. So the other disciples told him, 'We have seen the Lord.' But he said to them, 'Unless I see in his hands the print of the nails, and place my finger in the mark of the nails, and place my hand in his side, I will not believe.' Eight days later, his disciples were again in the house, and Thomas was with them. The doors were shut, but Jesus came and stood among them, and said, 'Peace be with you.' Then he said to Thomas, 'Put your finger here, and see my hands; and put out your hand, and place it in my side; do not be faithless, but believing.' Thomas answered him, 'My Lord and my God!' Jesus said to him, 'Have you believed because you have seen me? Blessed are those who have not seen and yet believe.'

Poor old Thomas. First he gets a bad reputation by doubting and then, when he does confess that Jesus is Lord, he is superseded by the rest of us who call ourselves Christian, because he has seen the visual evidence and we have not.

Yet don't we often imagine that things were so much more 'real' for the disciples? If we could have just walked beside him through the cornfields, watched him bring the boat in on the beach, heard him teach those parables, put to him our own questions, our faith would be so much stronger. If one of us had actually taken bread from his hand at the Lord's supper and had our feet washed by him, wouldn't we believe he was God's Son?

Well, ask Thomas about that. Come to think of it, ask Judas! Jesus taught the importance of faith without proof. Yet we do have evidence: the Bible, the almost overnight transformation of frightened disciples, centuries of witness of the Christian Church with millions of individual followers of Christ testifying to a personal relationship with a living Lord. But scientific, empirical proof to place under a microscope and silence all doubters—this, according to Jesus, we must not covet. Not merely for God's sake, but for ours. Jesus says that the blessed are those who have *not* seen and yet believe.

Prayer

Dear Father, thanks for being there, whether I can see you or not. Amen

HMcD

John 21:1–6 (RSV)

'I am going fishing'

After this Jesus revealed himself again to the disciples by the Sea of Tiberias; and he revealed himself in this way. Simon Peter, Thomas called the Twin, Nathanael of Cana in Galilee, the sons of Zebedee, and two others of his disciples were together. Simon Peter said to them, 'I am going fishing.' They said to him, 'We will go with you.' They went out and got into the boat; but that night they caught nothing. Just as day was breaking, Jesus stood on the beach; yet the disciples did not know that it was Jesus. Jesus said to them, 'Children, have you any fish?' They answered him, 'No.' He said to them, 'Cast the net on the right side of the boat, and you will find some.' So they cast it, and now they were not able to haul it in, for the quantity of fish.

'Gone fishing!' Mouths need to be filled, and by all accounts Peter was a married man with family responsibilities, so the boat had to be got out.

They fished all night. Isn't it wonderful how Jesus chooses his moments carefully? 'Children, have you any fish?' he asked. The outcome of the interchange was that he gave advice, they took it, and the nets were full. Here was Jesus, having shortly beforehand given them a commission to 'catch fish' spiritually, now taking time to ensure that their material needs were met also. Instead of being angry that they were not spending more time preaching or witnessing, or nurturing the new followers, Jesus attends to their needs of body, mind and soul.

From the beginning of time, God has sustained his human creatures. He knows what we need on all fronts of our existence. Yet how often, in our imaginations, we attempt to restrict his concerns to the realm of the spiritual alone, arrogantly believing that we can fend for ourselves.

Jesus had come to the beach to help the disciples be fishermen in more ways than one. He was setting up a very special encounter with Peter. The Master meets us where we are, and in whatever condition he finds us. It's just as well, because instead of discovering our nets full of souls for the kingdom, he often finds a note pinned to our door, 'Gone fishing!'

Prayer

Dear Lord, where do I find the fish? Turn me round, use a strong but gentle hand on the rudder and send me out into depths of your choosing. Amen

HMcD

John 21:7–10 (RSV)

'It is the Lord!'

That disciple whom Jesus loved said to Peter, 'It is the Lord!' When Simon Peter heard that it was the Lord, he put on his clothes, for he was stripped for work, and sprang into the sea. But the other disciples came in the boat, dragging the net full of fish, for they were not far from the land, but about a hundred yards off. When they got out on land, they saw a charcoal fire there, with fish lying on it, and bread. Jesus said to them, 'Bring some of the fish that you have just caught.'

We often hear of the appearance to Mary Magdalene, to Thomas, to Peter, to the eleven, and so on, but I think of these verses as the appearance to John, the beloved disciple.

It is almost a throwaway remark in verse 7 when John records saying to Peter, 'It is the Lord.' Before this in the chapter, none of the disciples recognized Jesus and in the following verses the others were too scared, or too shy, to ask him, 'Who are you?' Yet, immediately the miracle of the net filled to capacity was obvious, John affirms his identity.

How slow we often are to recognize God's handiwork in the day-to-day circumstances of our lives. Like John, it is only with the eyes of faith and a loving heart that we can affirm the mark of our Master, even in the most trying of circumstances. Regardless of how the outward appearance of Jesus had altered (and he certainly did not appear to be instantly recognizable), John's relational love to his Lord had become so instinctive that he acknowledged him without question.

Peter rushes to land to authenticate the identification, just as he had rushed past John to be first into the empty tomb. The beloved disciple knew his master would wait, and helped his colleagues bring the catch to shore.

Could his assurance have originated from his experience of standing at the foot of the cross, the only male follower of Christ to brave the danger and scorn of public association with the victim? It is only by way of embracing the pain of the cross and its implications for each of our lives that we can move from despair to hope and fully experience the resurrection in our own living.

Prayer

Dear Lord Jesus, I acknowledge that you are the Son of God. I accept you as my Saviour. Come to breakfast each day in my home and feed the deep longings of my heart. Amen

HMcD

John 21:15–17 (RSV)

'Do you love me?'

When they had finished breakfast, Jesus said to Simon Peter, 'Simon, son of John, do you love me more than these?' He said to him, 'Yes, Lord; you know that I love you.' He said to him, 'Feed my lambs.' A second time he said to him, 'Simon, son of John, do you love me?' He said to him, 'Yes, Lord; you know that I love you.' He said to him, 'Tend my sheep.' He said to him, 'Simon, son of John, do you love me?' Peter was grieved because he said to him the third time, 'Do you love me?' And he said to him, 'Lord, you know everything; you know that I love you.' Jesus said to him, 'Feed my sheep.'

A miracle, a meal, and now a question. Having met their immediate physical and material needs, Jesus turns his attention to the deep psychological and spiritual wound which Peter was still carrying within himself.

I wonder if the sound of the cock-crow was in his mind on that beach at sunrise as Jesus asked him for the third time, 'Do you love me?' Peter could not have missed the significance of the three-fold question cancelling his previous threefold denial of the Lord, but it would have been with the eyes of faith that he could have made that connection. Isn't it wonderful to think that the God who knows what we need in every aspect of our life goes to such trouble to affirm his forgiveness of us?

In our own lives, God presents opportunities for us to reaffirm our commitment to, and service of, our Master, and to heal deep-seated memories of hurt and unforgiveness. Can our faith recognize these opportunities? Will we say an unequivocal 'Yes, Lord', and experience the healing?

We pray for health, and guidance, and successful life events, but how often do we pray for God-given opportunities to forgive and be forgiven? When Jesus heals, he heals completely, and that means he insists on dealing with the wounds of our past as much as our present, if we let him. Peter did, although it was painful for him, but after he felt grieved, he felt whole and went on to follow Jesus even to a martyr's grave. How far will you go when Jesus asks, 'Do you love me?'

Prayer

Dear Lord, teach me how to love you, whatever the cost. Thank you for never failing me like I fail you. Amen

HMcD

Matthew 28:16–20 (RSV)

'Go therefore...'

Now the eleven disciples went to Galilee, to the mountain to which Jesus had directed them. And when they saw him they worshipped him; but some doubted. And Jesus came and said to them, 'All authority in heaven and on earth has been given to me. Go therefore and make disciples of all nations, baptizing them in the name of the Father and of the Son and of the Holy Spirit, teaching them to observe all that I have commanded you; and lo, I am with you always, to the close of the age.'

After Jesus had appeared to Mary and the women, Matthew explains that they were sent to tell the disciples to go to a mountain in Galilee to meet with him. Some scholars suggest that this represents not a geographical mountain, but a mythological one. However, it would be very natural for Jesus to rendezvous with his disciples at or near a favourite familiar spot, mentioned a number of times in the Gospels, where he frequently went to pray and to teach. It would be a safe place, with good, positive associations to cement his continuing relationship with them after the resurrection.

Either way, he commissions them to take the gospel to the uttermost ends of the earth. Jesus has no qualms in affirming his authority now that his task is fulfilled and his time has come to take his role as the promised Messiah. He openly declares his intention to offer the gospel fully to the Gentiles, something which he seemed at first to do reluctantly.

The disciples had been in hiding; their families were vulnerable, both to the Jewish authorities and to the Roman government; their livelihoods were at risk; and Jesus was about to leave them to it, having given them the toughest job imaginable.

I wonder how we would have felt? Scared, angry, disappointed, inadequate, confused, maybe all of these. So how did these disciples later manage to 'turn the world upside down'? That's a good question to reflect on. Two incentives were given that day on the mountain. Jesus said, 'Go' and promised, 'I will be with you always.' They obeyed and he is still keeping his promise.

Prayer

Dear Lord, thanks for staying here by the power of your Holy Spirit. Where would you like me to 'go' next to witness for you? Please show me that the problems are not less than they were then—just different. Amen

HMcD

Luke 24:13–21 (RSV) (abridged)

'The third day since this happened'

That very day two of them were going to a village named Emmaus, about seven miles from Jerusalem, and talking with each other about all these things that had happened. While they were talking... Jesus himself drew near and went with them. But their eyes were kept from recognizing him. And he said to them, 'What is this conversation which you are holding with each other as you walk?' Then one of them, named Cleopas, answered him, 'Are you the only visitor to Jerusalem who does not know the things that have happened there in these days?' And he said to them, 'What things?' And they said to him, 'Concerning Jesus of Nazareth, who was a prophet mighty in deed and word before God and all the people, and how our chief priests and rulers delivered him up to be condemned to death, and crucified him. But we had hoped that he was the one to redeem Israel. Yes, and besides all this, it is now the third day since this happened.'

How long do you give God to work a miracle? According to the two travellers on the Emmaus road, three days is too long, despite the fact that they had hoped that he was the one to redeem Israel.

As the two people walked along, their whole concentration was upon rumours. They knew Jesus' name, his title, the manner of his life, prophecy and death, his reputation, his enemies, his executioners, the hopes of his followers and even the testimony from the witnesses at the tomb, both male and female. What didn't they know? They didn't know Jesus.

There he was, pacing the road step by step with them, and they knew him not. Whole generations of our present age are well versed in the 'rumours' about Jesus. In my country of Northern Ireland, many are educated from an early age in every aspect of his teaching and doctrine, in Sunday School and regular church worship. But, unless we are prepared for that personal encounter with the living Lord which requires an individual response from us, we will still be searching for God's promises to be fulfilled in our lives.

Prayer

Dear Father, I know only too well the evil effects of rumour and counter-rumour in the unstable situations of our present-day existence. Please bring me face to face with your reality, your claim upon my life, and my obedient allegiance. Amen

HMcD

Luke 24:28–32 (RSV)

'Did not our hearts burn...?'

So they drew near to the village to which they were going. He appeared to be going further, but they constrained him, saying, 'Stay with us, for it is toward evening and the day is now far spent.' So he went in to stay with them. When he was at table with them, he took the bread and blessed, and broke it, and gave it to them. And their eyes were opened and they recognized him; and he vanished out of their sight. They said to each other, 'Did not our hearts burn within us while he talked to us on the road, while he opened to us the scriptures?'

Walking home with Jesus, the two travellers were not treated to arguments from the Lord about who he was, or what he intended to do. Instead he opened the scriptures to them, reinforcing the continuity of prophecy, testimony and witness right from Moses to their time, illuminating again his long-foretold suffering and death and underlining his birthright of glory. Imagine their amazement and humility when they realized who had taken time to explain such things to them!

Their eyes were opened in the breaking of bread and they had felt their hearts burn during the revelation of scripture—two direct channels of Christ's revelation to his Church not only in those days but fully available to Christians today also. Yet how often we neglect one or other or both of these channels, preferring instead to wander the byways of the modern world, engaging in rumour and counter-rumour of spiritual novelty and fashion and dabbling in every innovation of faith and practice, desperate for that ancient 'burning of the heart' which tells us we are in the presence of the living Lord.

Meanwhile, Jesus himself quietly walks beside us, eager to make our acquaintance by means of the familiar firm foundations laid down through the ages even as far as the 21st-century Church and beyond.

Scriptural truth never fails; the fellowship of his supper remains. If we are determined not to be 'slow of heart' but to walk in step with Jesus all the way, until he enjoys full hospitality in our homes, in our churches, and in our lives, then we too will feel our hearts burn within us on the way.

Prayer

Dear Jesus, walk with me until my eyes are opened. I want no other destination but the one your will designs. Amen

HMcD

Luke 24:33, 35–43 (RSV)

'Have you anything to eat?'

And they rose that same hour and returned to Jerusalem; and they found the eleven gathered together and those who were with them... Then they told what had happened on the road, and how he was known to them in the breaking of the bread. As they were saying this, Jesus himself stood among them. But they were startled and frightened, and supposed that they saw a spirit. And he said to them, 'Why are you troubled, and why do questionings rise in your hearts? See my hands and my feet, that it is I myself; handle me, and see; for a spirit has not flesh and bones as you see that I have.' And while they still disbelieved for joy, and wondered, he said to them, 'Have you anything here to eat?' They gave him a piece of broiled fish, and he took it and ate before them.

Jesus appears to the eleven disciples at Jerusalem and at first they think he is a ghost. The Lord, contrary to his previous advice to Mary about not touching him, invites their tactile contact. He was no apparition, hallucination or ghost. To prove it further, he asks for food and eats some fish.

An early Christian heresy thought of the resurrected Christ in ghost-like terms, but in this appearance his resurrection body, however strangely changed in other ways, was still bearing all the hallmarks of its links to the planet. It was no ethereal spectre but a human body resurrected to the spiritual. What a reassurance it must have been for the disciples to see him take that broiled fish from their hands and watch him chew and swallow it.

They had 'disbelieved for joy'. What a lovely phrase. We might say they could not believe their eyes because it seemed too good to be true. In modern life also, many people turn away from salvation, or fail to embrace total healing, because it seems too good to be true. In an era where we are repeatedly offered every enticement to sample, to buy, to enter into contract with goods and services which cannot 'deliver', cynicism is rife.

Jesus' promises of resurrection prove faithful not only for first-century Christians, but still today to each individual who has faith enough to *believe* for joy.

Prayer

Dear Jesus, thank you that because your human body resurrected to the eternal dimension, I too, by your grace, can have hope of eternal life in your kingdom.
Amen

HMcD

Acts 1:6–11 (RSV)

'Why do you stand looking...?'

So when they had come together, they asked him, 'Lord, will you at this time restore the kingdom to Israel?' He said to them, 'It is not for you to know times or seasons which the Father has fixed by his own authority. But you shall receive power when the Holy Spirit has come upon you; and you shall be my witnesses in Jerusalem and in all Judea and Samaria and to the end of the earth.' And when he had said this, as they were looking on, he was lifted up, and a cloud took him out of their sight. And while they were gazing into heaven as he went, behold, two men stood by them in white robes, and said, 'Men of Galilee, why do you stand looking into heaven? This Jesus, who was taken up from you into heaven, will come in the same way as you saw him go into heaven.'

For every Jew, the restoration of the kingdom to Israel encapsulates a very political aspiration. But in answer to their question about this, Jesus steers their thoughts away from such earthly connotations and, instead of assuring his disciples of a position of prestige to rule the twelve tribes of Israel in a new earthly kingdom, he promises them authority of a very different kind—power from the Holy Spirit to be witnesses. They must have wondered how it would ever be possible to start in Jerusalem, move freely through Judea and even encroach upon the alien territory of Samaria with the gospel. They gazed heavenward, no doubt tempted to wish that Jesus might 'beam them up' with him, as in a *Star Trek* film, as he ascended.

Who would imagine that a question from two angels would bring them back down to earth? 'Why are you gazing into heaven?' they queried. Reminding them that Jesus would come again, the angels' retort implied that the disciples had better get on with the task in hand in the short time available.

The disciples of that era believed that the time would be very short indeed, and many followers went up mountains to 'sit and knit' (or whatever their cultural equivalent would have been) until his return. We know it will take a little longer, yet each of us has only the duration of our own lives to witness, and that time is short indeed.

Prayer

Dear Lord, if you see me gazing into heaven too long, prod me on to greater witness for you. Amen

HMcD

Acts 9:1–6 (RSV)

'Why do you persecute me?'

But Saul, still breathing threats and murder against the disciples of the Lord, went to the high priest and asked him for letters to the synagogues at Damascus, so that if he found any belonging to the Way, men or women, he might bring them bound to Jerusalem. Now as he journeyed he approached Damascus, and suddenly a light from heaven flashed about him. And he fell to the ground and heard a voice saying to him, 'Saul, Saul, why do you persecute me?' And he said, 'Who are you, Lord?' And he said, 'I am Jesus, whom you are persecuting; but rise and enter the city, and you will be told what you are to do.'

The surrounding cultures of that day called Christians many names. But 'followers of the Way' was a phrase adopted by the Christians themselves, with connotations from the Old Testament 'way of the Lord', but now meaning 'way of life'.

Paul also refers to his Damascus road experience in Acts 26 and 1 Corinthians 15 and quite definitely considers this one of the appearances of the risen Christ.

Jesus addresses him by the Hebrew translation of his name, 'Saul', most appropriately for a man who considered himself in the lofty position of 'Pharisee of the Pharisees'. One day, Paul would be known worldwide and for ever as the missionary to the Gentiles, but at this moment God touches him 'where he's at'.

He was spiritually blind. God had to render him physically blind before his spiritual sight could be restored. It is often at the point of our greatest vulnerability that we become open enough and humble enough to receive the most profound truths of God. No wonder this apostle wrote that God's strength is made perfect in weakness (2 Corinthians 12:9).

Paul was destined for a great ministry, but first he had to understand who deserved the glory and, most of all, he had to meet Jesus face to face. For three days his disability allowed him time to meditate and, no doubt, to pray and remember painfully all the ways in which his previous life's task had inhibited God's servants in their witness. But while Paul was making a quantum leap in his darkness, God had Ananias just around the corner to help him step again into glorious light.

Prayer

Dear Father, your timing is perfect,
and even your ways of reproof are tender.
Touch me where I am, gently, please.
Amen

HMcD

Acts 1:4–9 (NRSV)

The promise of the Spirit

While staying with them, [Jesus] ordered them not to leave Jerusalem, but to wait there for the promise of the Father. 'This,' he said, 'is what you have heard from me; for John baptized with water, but you will be baptized with the Holy Spirit not many days from now.' So when they had come together, they asked him, 'Lord, is this the time when you will restore the kingdom to Israel?' He replied, 'It is not for you to know the times or periods that the Father has set by his own authority. But you will receive power when the Holy Spirit has come upon you; and you will be my witnesses in Jerusalem, in all Judea and Samaria, and to the ends of the earth.' When he had said this, as they were watching, he was lifted up, and a cloud took him out of their sight.

In the forty days since his first sudden appearance in the upper room, the risen Jesus had been with the disciples many times, 'speaking about the kingdom of God'. They still didn't get it. They looked back over their shoulders, and wanted to know how the Jews stood with their special status as God's favoured people. In their minds this was linked with their hoped-for release from Roman domination. Their vision was small.

Jesus' picture was different. His disciples had indeed got a special place in his Father's kingdom. But this place was not as a favoured nation, at the apex of a pyramid. The Holy Spirit—who during Jesus' life on earth had been, as it were, wrapped up in him—would be released when he returned to his Father. That Spirit would put them at the centre of concentric circles, as his agents, his witnesses, so that the ripples of the message of his kingdom might spread worldwide.

It is easy to bemoan the disciples' slowness to grasp Jesus' teaching. But when the Holy Spirit came—wow!—they were transformed. We have the benefit of two thousand years of hindsight; yet we are often as slow to understand as they were. And we are even slower to allow the Spirit, released for all Christian believers as much as for those early followers, to flow through us in power and to make us his confident witnesses.

To think about

To what extent do we know or really want the power of his Spirit?

RG

Acts 1:10–14 (NRSV)

A new prayer group

Suddenly two men in white robes stood by them. They said, 'Men of Galilee, why do you stand looking up toward heaven? This Jesus, who has been taken up from you into heaven, will come in the same way as you saw him go into heaven.' Then they returned to Jerusalem from the mount called Olivet, which is near Jerusalem, a sabbath day's journey away. When they had entered the city, they went to the room upstairs where they were staying, Peter, and John, and James, and Andrew, Philip and Thomas, Bartholomew and Matthew, James son of Alphaeus, and Simon the Zealot, and Judas son of James. All these were constantly devoting themselves to prayer, together with certain women, including Mary the mother of Jesus, as well as his brothers.

Is there a surprise here? I don't mean the angels. They were no great surprise to the disciples; after all, there were angels at Jesus' empty tomb. The surprise comes in the little phrase 'as well as his brothers'. Earlier those very brothers had accused Jesus of being mad; they would have nothing to do with him. What a change now! Among them was James, who soon came into prominence in the Church. Another interesting phrase we might easily overlook is 'together with certain women'. These were the faithful, generous, resilient women who had travelled with him, had waited by the cross, had embalmed his body. Jesus' death, resurrection and now his final departure brought the Eleven, his brothers, these women and other followers—about 120 in all—together to pray and wait, as he had told them to do.

It is not easy to wait and pray, wait and pray, especially when we do not know what is ahead. I doubt if this group had any real comprehension of the Spirit whom Jesus had promised, despite his activity in the Old Testament. But they knew something was going to happen, and they were obedient. Many of us don't find this 'waiting' prayer easy. I don't. It's easier to be active, to do something, or at least to talk about what we might do! But when we pray, our focus is on God; we seek his direction, we are open to his power. And we will be more ready to fall in with his plans than if we get busy too quickly.

Prayer

Lord, help me to pray, wait and listen.

RG

Acts 1:15–26 (NRSV, abridged)

Making decisions

Peter stood up among the believers (about one hundred and twenty persons) and said, 'Friends, the scripture had to be fulfilled, which the Holy Spirit through David foretold concerning Judas... "Let another take his position of overseer." So one of the men who have accompanied us during all the time that the Lord Jesus went in and out among us... must become a witness with us to his resurrection.' So they proposed two, Joseph called Barsabbas, and Matthias. Then they prayed and said, 'Lord, you know everyone's heart. Show us which one of these two you have chosen to take the place in this ministry and apostleship from which Judas turned aside to go to his own place.' And they cast lots for them, and the lot fell on Matthias; and he was added to the eleven disciples.

Judas' suicide left a vacancy in the Twelve; they needed to complete their appointed number. Christians sometimes berate this group: 'Here are New Testament believers, just leaving it to chance.' But their selection of Matthias was not mere chance, and shows some good principles for decision-making.

- There was an appeal to scripture.
- The choice was made by the whole group, not by autocratic leaders.
- They had clear criteria.
- They used their minds to shortlist the possible candidates.
- They prayed and asked God for direction.
- They trusted God to overrule the way the lot fell.

Another complaint we hear is that Matthias is mentioned no more in the New Testament, so he must have been a mediocre choice, even a mistake. But neither do we hear about some of Jesus' selection: Bartholomew, or Simon the Zealot, or 'the other' Judas. We don't say that Jesus got it wrong with them!

Think about the way you make decisions, either personal or corporate —in your church council, perhaps. Are there biblical foundations? Do you make unilateral decisions or consult others? Do you use the mind God has given you? Do you pray, and trust the sovereign God to overrule events?

Prayer

Lord, I confess that I often disregard you in making decisions, and just want things my own way. Please show me/us your way over... [be specific about your own situation] so that what is done may glorify you.

RG

Acts 2:1–13 (NRSV, abridged)

Filled with the Spirit

When the Day of Pentecost had come, they were all together in one place. And suddenly from heaven there came a sound like the rush of a violent wind, and it filled the entire house where they were sitting. Divided tongues, as of fire, appeared among them, and a tongue rested on each of them. All of them were filled with the Holy Spirit and began to speak in other languages, as the Spirit gave them ability. Now there were devout Jews from every nation under heaven living in Jerusalem. And at this sound the crowd gathered and was bewildered, because each one heard them speaking in the native language of each. Amazed and astonished, they asked, 'Are not all these who are speaking Galileans? And how is it that we hear, each of us, in our own native language... about God's deeds of power?' All were amazed and perplexed, saying to one another, 'What does this mean?' But others sneered and said, 'They are filled with new wine.'

'You will receive power when the Holy Spirit has come upon you,' Jesus had told his followers. When the Spirit came, he didn't come with a whimper. He came with a bang! His power was unmistakable, demonstrated in this outpouring of new languages. And as the Christians praised God in this unexpected way, they were his witnesses to people from far away: people from Rome, from North Africa, from Turkey, from Egypt and Iraq were in the crowds who had come to Jerusalem for the festival.

Twenty years later Paul wrote to the Ephesians, 'Do not get drunk with wine… but be filled with the Spirit, as you sing psalms and hymns… giving thanks to God the Father' (Ephesians 5:18–20). These verses in Acts, very familiar to most of us, are not just about a unique event two millennia ago. Paul's injunction to the Ephesians to 'be filled with the Spirit' was not for them alone. It is for us, too. We will not all speak in tongues—though many modern Christians do. We will not all appear to be drunk—though there will certainly be some people who scoff at real Christianity. But we will know the joy and presence of God in a new way, and will want to be witnesses to others of his living power.

A question

Does my life show evidence of being filled with his Spirit?

RG

Acts 2:22–24, 32–33 (NRSV)

The heart of the message

'You that are Israelites, listen to what I have to say: Jesus of Nazareth, a man attested to you by God with deeds of power, wonders, and signs that God did through him among you, as you yourselves know—this man, handed over to you according to the definite plan and foreknowledge of God, you crucified and killed by the hands of those outside the law. But God raised him up, having freed him from death, because it was impossible for him to be held in its power... This Jesus God raised up, and of that all of us are witnesses. Being therefore exalted at the right hand of God, and having received from the Father the promise of the Holy Spirit, he has poured out this that you both see and hear.'

Peter was already (not surprisingly) emerging as the leader of this group. He immediately took control, and stood up to preach his first evangelistic sermon. He faced head-on the accusation of drunkenness: 'These men are not drunk.' He went on to declare that they were watching the fulfilment of Joel's prophecy that God would pour out his Spirit on all people. Then he moved to the kernel of his sermon—Jesus' resurrection, which was the linchpin of Jesus' life and death. Peter took great pains to show his hearers that Jesus was the Messiah, the Holy One, of whom David wrote. The power of the living God could not be contained in the stranglehold of death.

We often link Jesus' death and resurrection, as Peter does here. 'You crucified him. God raised him up.' Less often do we make the connection that Peter goes on to make, between the resurrection and the coming of the Holy Spirit. On Easter Day, do you commemorate a historical event of two thousand years ago, or do you celebrate a living Lord, now 'exalted to the right hand of God'? The more alive we are to the power of the resurrection, the more open we will be to the power of the Spirit in our lives.

Reflection

No one can say 'Jesus is Lord' except by the Holy Spirit.
1 Corinthians 12:3

RG

Acts 2:36–41 (NRSV)

A clear response

'Therefore let the entire house of Israel know with certainty that God has made him both Lord and Messiah, this Jesus whom you crucified.' Now when they heard this, they were cut to the heart and said to Peter and to the other apostles, 'Brothers, what should we do?' Peter said to them, 'Repent, and be baptized every one of you in the name of Jesus Christ so that your sins may be forgiven; and you will receive the gift of the Holy Spirit. For the promise is for you, for your children, and for all who are far away, everyone whom the Lord our God calls to him.' And he testified with many other arguments and exhorted them, saying, 'Save yourselves from this corrupt generation.' So those who welcomed his message were baptized, and that day about three thousand persons were added.

The Holy Spirit was active that day, not only in the visible wind and fire, in the audible praise and tongues, in the persuasive preaching, but also in many of the listeners. Before his death Jesus had talked to his disciples about the Spirit, the Comforter: 'When he comes, he will prove the world wrong... about sin, because they do not believe in me; about righteousness, because I am going to the Father (John 16:8–10). It was the Spirit at work in Peter's hearers who convinced them that Jesus had gone to his Father and who convicted them of their own sin. Hence their question 'What should we do?'—even before most evangelistic preachers would think that Peter had come to the crunch point of his sermon!

Peter was clear in his reply: 'Repent and be baptized.' John the Baptist had a similar message when he came 'proclaiming a baptism for the forgiveness of sins'. But there were differences. John was in the halfway house between the Old and New Testaments; for Peter, baptism was focused on Jesus. And whereas John knew that he was preparing for the one who would 'baptize... with the Holy Spirit and fire', Peter could proclaim with assurance, 'You will receive the gift of the Holy Spirit' here and now—and in future generations far and wide.

Prayer

Father, I rejoice in the promise extended to me, 2000 years later, and perhaps thousands of miles away. I pray that I may work out my baptismal promises in the fullness of the Holy Spirit.

RG

Acts 2:42–47 (NRSV)

A vibrant church

They devoted themselves to the apostles' teaching and fellowship, to the breaking of bread and the prayers. Awe came upon everyone, because many wonders and signs were being done by the apostles. All who believed were together and had all things in common; they would sell their possessions and goods and distribute the proceeds to all, as any had need. Day by day, as they spent... time together in the temple, they broke bread at home and ate their food with glad and generous hearts, praising God and having the goodwill of all the people. And day by day the Lord added to their number those who were being saved.

New believers joining the Church every day. Wow! That is something hard to imagine in most of our own churches. But there was such vitality in the church in Jerusalem that it was attractive to those outside who watched the enthusiasm, devotion and love portrayed by the Christians. Look at some of the marks of this church:

They devoted themselves: that implies whole-hearted commitment.

To the apostles' teaching: they were hungry to learn.

To the fellowship: their faith was corporate, not individualistic.

To the breaking of bread: holy communion was important to them.

To the prayers: they attended faithfully the formal, traditional temple daily worship.

Awe came upon everyone: there was great awareness of God's presence, great reverence for him.

Many wonders and signs were done: the disciples had watched Jesus' miracles. Now, empowered by the Spirit, they copied him.

They were generous with their possessions: they did not say 'mine' but 'ours'.

They used their homes: to share meals, to share the eucharist, to share their joy and love.

They were open in praise.

Although the Holy Spirit is not named in these verses, we see the signs of his life-giving activity. Paul warned the Thessalonians, 'Do not quench the Spirit' (1 Thessalonians 5:19.) Sadly, in many of our churches we do quench him. We fear the changes he might make; we fear being out of control. And then we wonder why, in our inhibited Western world, more people are leaving the church than joining it.

Reflection

When I have let down my guard of fear against the Spirit, he has freed me and enriched me. Can you say the same?

RG

Acts 3:1–10 (NRSV, abridged)

A mighty miracle

One day Peter and John were going up to the temple at the hour of prayer... And a man lame from birth was being carried in... When he saw Peter and John, he asked them for alms. Peter looked intently at him, as did John, and said, 'Look at us.' And he fixed his attention on them, expecting to receive something from them. But Peter said, 'I have no silver or gold, but what I have I give you; in the name of Jesus Christ of Nazareth, stand up and walk.' And he took him by the right hand and raised him up; and immediately his feet and ankles were made strong. Jumping up, he stood and began to walk, and he entered the temple with them, walking and leaping and praising God. All the people saw him and recognized him as the one who used to sit and ask for alms; and they were filled with amazement at what had happened to him.

Every day the forty-year-old cripple was carried to the temple entrance, to sit and beg from arriving worshippers. Born lame, his expectations were no higher than to receive enough money for a day's food. He didn't ask to be healed; he might even have been scared to contemplate such a radical change. But Peter was utterly confident in God's power. As soon as he spoke, he helped the man to stand. He didn't wait to examine his feet; he expected change. It happened. The cripple not only used his new-found strength to walk and jump; he went into the temple to pray, thanking and praising God.

I used to think that such miracles ended with the New Testament. I now know that God still intervenes in miraculous ways to answer prayer for healing—though not always as we want. We used to work alongside a clergyman who was specially interested in healing; I would say that God had given him the gift of healing of which Paul writes in 1 Corinthians 12:9. He prayed repeatedly with a lady with advanced cancer of the liver; successive scans showed that cancer shrink and disappear. Others with cancer died; but one young woman became a Christian, another had surprisingly little pain, a third died—and was released from pain altogether—more quickly than expected. All his prayers were answered... in different ways.

Reflection

'I have no silver or gold, but what I have I give you; in the name of Jesus Christ of Nazareth, stand up...'

RG

Acts 4:1–12 (NRSV, abridged)

The irrepressible gospel

While Peter and John were speaking to the people, the priests, the captain of the temple, and the Sadducees came to them, much annoyed because they were teaching that in Jesus there is the resurrection of the dead. So they arrested them... But many of those who heard the word believed; and they numbered about five thousand. The next day their rulers, elders and scribes assembled in Jerusalem... They inquired, 'By what power or by what name did you do this?' Then Peter, filled with the Holy Spirit, said to them, 'Let it be known to all of you that this man is standing before you in good health by the name of Jesus, whom you crucified, whom God raised from the dead. There is salvation in no one else, for there is no other name under heaven given among mortals by which we must be saved.'

The miracle attracted a crowd. Peter seized the opportunity to preach about Jesus and his power. The various Jewish authorities were all threatened: the priests, who thought they were finished with Jesus who had confronted their teaching and their traditions; the temple guard, who feared a riot; the Sadducees, who denied any possibility of resurrection. They arrested Peter and John. But even more people believed in Jesus than after Peter's Pentecost sermon!

Next day the two apostles were brought before the ecclesiastical court. Peter was fearless and clear. 'You crucified him. God raised him from the dead. Salvation comes through Jesus alone.' (In Greek, the words for 'salvation' and 'healing' are the same.) The good news about Jesus could not be stamped out—for Jesus himself was alive. They could not keep him down. Peter's clarity about the uniqueness of Jesus and his salvation confronts us in our pluralistic society, where many people—even Christians—say that there are many paths to God and it does not matter which one we take.

Notice that Peter was 'filled with the Spirit'. Hadn't he been filled with the Spirit on the Day of Pentecost? Yes, but he needed to be freshly empowered by the Spirit. When Paul wrote, 'Be filled with the Spirit' it was not 'Be filled once' but 'Go on being filled'. We too need a fresh refilling, like a plant that dies if it is not watered regularly.

Prayer

Spirit of the living God,
fall afresh on me.

RG

Acts 4:13–20 (NRSV)

Irrepressible disciples

Now when they saw the boldness of Peter and John and realized that they were uneducated and ordinary men, they were amazed and recognized them as companions of Jesus. When they saw the man who had been cured standing beside them, they had nothing to say in opposition. So they ordered them to leave the council while they discussed the matter with one another. They said, 'What will we do with them? For it is obvious to all who live in Jerusalem that a notable sign has been done through them; we cannot deny it. But to keep it from spreading further among the people, let us warn them to speak no more to anyone in this name.' So they called them and ordered them not to speak or teach at all in the name of Jesus. But Peter and John answered them, 'Whether it is right in God's sight to listen to you, rather than to God, you must judge; for we cannot keep from speaking about what we have seen and heard.'

The Jewish leaders were in a quandary. Here were two uneducated, courageous Galileans, members of the Jesus gang, now its leaders. Beside them stood a well-known cripple, undeniably healed. They hated the possibility of losing face with the ordinary people; they were terrified of this new sect with its supernatural power. I cannot help comparing them with some churchpeople today who so want to guard the safety of the status quo that they try to ignore, or to suppress, the enthusiasm of Christians whose deep joy and love for Jesus want God's Spirit to break past the barriers of convention. We don't all have to be 'happy-clappy' Christians. We do need to allow the Spirit of Christ to melt our reservations of fear, to take full control of our lives, to remould us according to our individual personality and his desires for each of us.

The weakness of the Sanhedrin's decision ('We'll let you go but you must stop preaching') contrasts with the confidence of Peter and John ('We've got to obey God rather than you. We can't stop speaking about Jesus'). The disciples could not be kept down—neither could the gospel.

Reflection

How do I compare with the Jewish leaders? With Peter and John? Do I want to take the risk of change?

RG

Acts 4:23–31 (NRSV, abridged)

The irrepressible Spirit

After they were released, they went to their friends and reported what the chief priests and elders had said to them. When they heard it, they raised their voices to God and said, 'Sovereign Lord, who made the heaven and the earth, it is you who said by the Holy Spirit through our ancestor David, your servant: "Why did the Gentiles rage, and the peoples imagine vain things? The kings of the earth took their stand, and the rulers have gathered together against the Lord and against his Messiah." ... Now, Lord, look at their threats, and grant to your servants to speak your word with all boldness, while you stretch out your hand to heal, and signs and wonders are performed through the name of your holy servant Jesus.' When they had prayed, the place in which they were gathered together was shaken; and they were all filled with the Holy Spirit and spoke the word of God with boldness.

'Go home and keep quiet.' That was the message the pair took back to the believers. Most of us would have spent time discussing the situation, planning our course of action. Not them! They turned straight to prayer, addressing God as sovereign. They were sure of his control in the world, as Creator, as the inspirer of scripture; above all, in control even of the evil machinations of Jesus' opponents. 'In this city, both Herod and Pontius Pilate, with the Gentiles and the peoples of Israel, gathered together against your holy servant Jesus, whom you anointed, to do whatever your hand and your plan had predestined to take place' (vv. 27–28). This fulfilled the psalm they quoted, which continues, 'He who sits in the heavens laughs; the Lord has them in derision' (Psalm 2:4).

This complete confidence in God was the foundation for their two bold requests. 'Help us to keep preaching your gospel. Continue to work your miracles.' His answer was unmistakable, with a fresh demonstration of the Holy Spirit and his power. Yet again, I am challenged to contrast the faith and vitality of these early Christians with my own Christian life. They had Jesus and the Old Testament saints as their models. We have, as well, the examples of Christians who have been risk-takers down two thousand years. Their secret was in the dynamic power of the Holy Spirit.

Reflection

Dare I make the apostles' requests my own?

RG

Acts 5:1–6 (NRSV)

Lies matter!

A man named Ananias, with the consent of his wife Sapphira, sold a piece of property; with his wife's knowledge, he kept back some of the proceeds, and brought only a part and laid it at the apostles' feet. 'Ananias,' Peter asked, 'why has Satan filled your heart to lie to the Holy Spirit and keep back part of the proceeds of the land? While it remained unsold, did it not remain your own? And after it was sold, were not the proceeds at your disposal? How is it that you have contrived this deed in your heart? You did not lie to us but to God!' Now when Ananias heard these words, he fell down and died. And great fear seized all who heard of it. The young men came and wrapped up his body, then carried him out and buried him.

This couple, Ananias and Sapphira, are to be wholly commended for one aspect of their lives. They discussed their financial affairs together, in a way that is unknown in many homes. We can tentatively commend them, too, for giving away part—probably quite a large part—of the proceeds of the sale. This was not their idea; many of the Christian landowners had sold property for the benefit of the poor.

But there our commendation stops. We don't know whether their initial motive was generosity or a desire to impress others. Mixed or ungodly motives are seeds from which large sins grow—yet how easy it is to deceive ourselves, let alone others, about our motives for any course of action. Peter makes it quite clear that there was no common ownership of property. The gifts were not demanded, even expected. If they had been open and above board about the sale and the gift, he would not have challenged them. Their sin was in their lies. They thought they could deceive people—but God's Spirit gave Peter a supernatural gift of insight. Did they think they could deceive God? That, of course, they could never do. They tried—with fatal results.

Reflection

God 'will bring to light the things now hidden in darkness and will disclose the purposes of the heart' (1 Corinthians 4:5). Does that alarm you (in fear of the God who judges) or encourage you (with assurance of a God who loves and forgives you)?

RG

Hosea 1:2–8 (NRSV, abridged)

Sharing in his sufferings

The Lord said to Hosea, 'Go, take for yourself a wife of whoredom and have children of whoredom, for the land commits great whoredom by forsaking the Lord.' So he went and took Gomer daughter of Diblaim, and she conceived and bore him a son. And the Lord said to him, 'Name him Jezreel; for in a little while I will punish the house of Jehu for the blood of Jezreel, and I will put an end to the kingdom of the house of Israel... She conceived again and bore a daughter. Then the Lord said to him, 'Name her Lo-ruhamah, for I will no longer have pity on the house of Israel or forgive them... When she had weaned Lo-ruhamah, she conceived and bore a son. Then the Lord said, 'Name him Lo-ammi, for you are not my people and I am not your God.'

Imagine how the average congregation would react if a prominent Christian leader announced that he was going to marry an unrepentant prostitute. I don't suppose Hosea's action went down any better with his contemporaries. If the prominent leader then announced that he was called to speak for God, he would probably be locked in a secure ward.

This was not the only time God asked a prophet to perform dramatic, even eccentric, actions. As in today's headline-grabbing demonstrations against Third World debt or the arms trade, unusual actions often speak louder than words.

Yet Hosea's strange marriage is more than an attention-seeking stunt to get people listening (which didn't work anyway). In his pain at his wife's betrayal, Hosea identifies with God's pain at Israel's 'adultery' with pagan gods and rituals. The pain spreads to his children, as he names the first after the site of a massacre (like calling your child 'Belsen') and the others 'Not-pitied' and 'Not-my-people'. His whole life was to be a parable of the wounded passion of God.

Paul writes to the Romans that we are only 'joint heirs with Christ *if in fact we suffer with him*' (Romans 8:17) and to the Philippians, 'I want to know Christ and the power of his resurrection *and the sharing of his sufferings*' (Philippians 3:10). When we suffer, we can glimpse something of God's pain—for the cross tells us that he suffers far more at our broken world than we can ever do.

Reflection

When Christ calls a person,
he bids them come and die.

Dietrich Bonhoeffer (1905–45)

VZ

Hosea 2:1–5, 8 (NRSV, abridged)

Judgment with mercy

Say to your brother, Ammi, and to your sister, Ruhamah. Plead with your mother, plead—for she is not my wife, and I am not her husband—that she put away her whoring from her face, and her adultery from between her breasts, or I will strip her naked and expose her as in the day she was born, and make her like a wilderness, and turn her into a parched land, and kill her with thirst... For she said, 'I will go after my lovers; they give me my bread and my water, my wool and my flax, my oil and my drink...' She did not know that it was I who gave her the grain, the wine, and the oil, and who lavished upon her silver and gold that they used for Baal.

What do people say when things go well for you? 'You've been lucky', 'Someone's looking after you', 'You've done well for yourself.' And what do *you* say?

In symbolic poetry, Hosea addresses the older brother Jezreel (the only one we are sure is Hosea's own son). He is to use his siblings as intermediaries to bring the adulterous mother to her senses. This is less about Hosea's family situation, more about God's erring 'bride', Israel. What hurts her 'husband' most is that she attributes the fertility of the land to the pagan gods. God's response may seem harsh: 'I will hedge up her way with thorns, and I will build a wall against her, so that she cannot find her paths… I will take back my grain in its time, and my wine in its season… I will uncover her shame in the sight of her lovers' (vv. 6, 9, 10). Famine will replace prosperity.

Yet there is mercy behind this stripping away of protection. Notice that the children's names have lost the 'Lo', which means 'not'. A hint of pity slips through. The punishment is meant to make the 'bride' say, 'I will go and return to my first husband, for it was better with me then than now.'

It is easy to thank capitalism, or secure defence, for our well-being. These are the gods we have affairs with today. But the only true giver of life and blessing is God—and he is generous beyond imagination to those who love him and follow his ways.

Reflection

Every generous act of giving, with every perfect gift, is from above…
from the Father of lights.
James 1:17

VZ

Hosea 2:14–20 (NRSV, abridged)

God's courtship

Therefore, I will now allure her, and bring her into the wilderness, and speak tenderly to her. From there I will give her her vineyards, and make the Valley of Achor a door of hope. There she shall respond as in the days of her youth, as at the time when she came out of the land of Egypt. On that day, says the Lord, you will call me 'My husband', and no longer will you call me 'My Baal'... I will make for you a covenant on that day with the wild animals, the birds of the air, and the creeping things of the ground; and I will abolish the bow, the sword, and war from the land; and I will make you lie down in safety. And I will take you for my wife forever... in righteousness and in justice, in steadfast love, and in mercy... and you shall know the Lord.

Two days ago, my husband came home bringing me roses. Actually they'd been given by a customer, but I was still deeply touched. After ten years of marriage, it brought back the days of 'dating', when little gifts could seem so very significant (and little disagreements cause huge traumas!)

We have just heard all about Israel's idolatry, and how God will punish and shame her—and then suddenly, the unexpected 'Therefore...' God will take her back to the 'honeymoon' times and woo her all over again. What inconceivable love, that responds to betrayal with renewed tender overtures...

Courting couples often have special names for each other. But Israel's name for God has deeper significance. 'My Baal', meaning 'My master', must be replaced by a more intimate title; for dominance and submission belong to the fallen world order ('your desire shall be for your husband, *and he shall rule over you*', Genesis 3:16).

Similarly, the people's relationship to the natural world will be restored to its Eden state—harmony between humans, creatures and environment (reconciliation with 'creeping things' poignantly recalls the serpent's role in the Fall story). Violence between human groups will end. Most importantly, the relationship with God will be re-established, never to be broken again.

These are universe-sized promises, going far beyond Israel in the eighth century BC. But their fulfilment begins now, with God's kingdom people.

Prayer

Imagine your family transformed in the way Hosea describes. Then your street, workplace, church, country, world. Pray, 'Your kingdom come.'

VZ

Hosea 3:1–5 (NRSV)

Redeemed

The Lord said to me again, 'Go, love a woman who has a lover and is an adulteress, just as the Lord loves the people of Israel, though they turn to other gods and love raisin cakes.' So I bought her for fifteen shekels of silver and a homer of barley and a measure of wine. And I said to her, 'You must remain as mine for many days; you shall not play the whore, you shall not have intercourse with a man, nor I with you.' For the Israelites shall remain many days without king or prince, without sacrifice or pillar, without ephod or teraphim. Afterward the Israelites shall return and seek the Lord their God, and David their king; they shall come in awe to the Lord and to his goodness in the latter days.

Once again, Hosea, having prophesied God's renewal of relationship with Israel, must act this out in his own life. That he must buy his wife back implies that she has become a 'sex slave'. 'Everyone who commits sin,' said Jesus, 'is a slave to sin' (John 8:34). But 'you were bought with a price' (1 Corinthians 6:20), 'not with perishable things like silver and gold, but with the precious blood of Christ' (1 Peter 1:18–19).

'You were bought… therefore glorify God in your body' (1 Corinthians 6:20). God's courtship of Israel takes place in the desert, the place both of Israel's beginning and of formative hardships; likewise, Hosea puts his wife (and himself) through a 'desert' experience. She must do without marital intimacy for a while, just as Israel must do without the 'trappings' of religion and the State. Is this to teach Israel that her relationship with God, and her nationhood, do not depend on these things, just as a male/female relationship is not just about sex? Special places and ceremonies, the delights of the physical, are good—but they are the expression of love, not its foundation.

Perhaps this also serves to draw a distinction between the mercenary sex that Gomer experienced with her lovers, and that of total commitment; between the 'grape festival' (with raisin cakes) of Baal and the true worship of the one God. The fake and the real thing may look alike but they are profoundly different.

Worship

My song is love unknown,
My Saviour's love to me,
Love to the loveless shown
That they might lovely be.

Samuel Crossman (1624–83)

VZ

Hosea 4:1–3 (NRSV)

Eden reversed

Hear the word of the Lord, O people of Israel; for the Lord has an indictment against the inhabitants of the land. There is no faithfulness or loyalty, and no knowledge of God in the land. Swearing, lying and murder, and stealing and adultery break out; bloodshed follows bloodshed. Therefore the land mourns, and all who live in it languish; together with the wild animals and the birds of the air, even the fish of the sea are perishing.

As I write, the new Northern Ireland assembly meets for the first time. Hopes of a lasting peace, disappointed so many times before, rise again, and many are praying that this will be the real thing. But—who knows?

Peace and justice require not just promises, but active working out of their implications. For Hosea, there have been promises of reconciliation; but his message of challenge and judgment is not yet over: 'The price of freedom is constant vigilance.' The people must be reminded frequently, and in detail, of how their abandonment of God has led to destruction.

It is a very contemporary picture. Traditional loyalty has gone out of the window—commercial criteria are all. Marriage commitment, respect for others' property, even the value of human life, are no longer given any thought. Human greed affects the natural environment: species die out and the land loses its fertility. It is as though there is a divine centre to the human and natural eco-systems; once that 'kingpin' is loosened, everything falls apart.

Where are the Hoseas today who will draw our attention to how much our desire for so-called 'growth' impoverishes others and the planet we depend on? They may come from unlikely quarters, and may not have any stated allegiance to Christ. The Spirit who leads us into all truth will help us recognize and hear them—if we are open.

As for Hosea, the prophet may often have to put his or her life on the line. It is not just the corrupt regimes that kill those who call for better values. According to Jesus, it is Jerusalem itself, the heart of religious life, that 'kills the prophets and stones those who are sent to it' (Matthew 23:37). Let us look to our own Jerusalems.

Prayer

Lord, send forth your light and your truth,
and let them lead us to your holy hill.

VZ

Hosea 4:4–9 (NRSV)

Blind leading the blind

Yet let no one contend, and let none accuse, for with you is my contention, O priest. You shall stumble by day; the prophet also shall stumble with you by night, and I will destroy your mother. My people are destroyed for lack of knowledge; because you have rejected knowledge, I reject you from being a priest to me. And since you have forgotten the law of your God, I also will forget your children. The more they increased, the more they sinned against me; they changed their glory into shame. They feed on the sin of my people; they are greedy for their iniquity. And it shall be like people, like priest; I will punish them for their ways, and repay them for their deeds.

In a theocratic (God-centred) society, the priests could be seen as the government and the (false) prophets as the 'official opposition'. Both, Hosea says, bear the full blame for the people's going astray. Power and prosperity have led the priestly class to complacency and corruption. And the prophets, who should stand out against this, are silent or give comforting thoughts with no cutting edge.

It is not easy to draw direct parallels with our very different society today. But we could think of governments who place political expediency above justice, or their own power above human rights. We could think of media (not all of them!) that derive entertainment from the worst human excesses but ration the air time given to deeper values. We could think of science that focuses its resources on keeping the rich alive longer and longer instead of helping the poor to live beyond infancy. We could also think of churches where arid disputes over ritual or doctrine have obscured the 'weightier matters of the law: justice and mercy and faith' (Matthew 23:23).

The priesthood was a hereditary one. But God would destroy both its ancestry and its posterity ('your mother... your children'). Today's leaders get there (mostly) by talent and perseverance. But those too are given by God, perhaps from birth—and they can be taken away. If those of us who lead others, in however small a way, fail to lead them rightly, our continued success is by no means guaranteed.

Reflection

'From everyone to whom much has been given, much will be required; and from the one to whom much has been entrusted, even more will be demanded.'

Luke 12:48

VZ

Hosea 5:3–6, 12–14 (NRSV, abridged)

God against us

I know Ephraim, and Israel is not hidden from me; for now, O Ephraim, you have played the whore; Israel is defiled. Their deeds do not permit them to return to their God. For the spirit of whoredom is within them, and they do not know the Lord... With their flocks and their herds they shall go to seek the Lord, but they will not find him; he has withdrawn from them... Therefore I am like maggots to Ephraim, and like rottenness to the house of Judah. When Ephraim saw his sickness, and Judah his wound, then Ephraim went to Assyria, and sent to the great king. But he is not able to cure you or heal your wound. For I will be like a lion to Ephraim, and like a young lion to the house of Judah. I myself will tear and go away; I will carry off and no one shall rescue.

'God will forgive me; that's his business,' quipped a French philosopher on his deathbed. Many of us unconsciously share his image of a 'service God', available just when we want him, like an all-night pharmacy.

Hosea here paints a much more disturbing picture: a God who has gone on strike, or appears only as a destructive force. 'It is a fearful thing to fall into the hands of the living God' (Hebrews 10:31). In their pride, the nation has taken God's favour for granted, whatever sins they commit. When God appears harder to approach than they expected, Israel turns to a powerful neighbour for help. Ironically, Assyria is the very nation that will destroy them. If God is against us (to reverse Paul's great statement), who can be for us?

Israel must accept that there are conditions to experiencing God's presence. 'If you close your ear to the cry of the poor, you will cry out and not be heard' (Proverbs 21:13). 'If you do not forgive others, neither will your Father forgive your trespasses' (Matthew 6:15). 'Whoever does not love does not know God, for God is love' (1 John 4:8).

Is God's love, then, conditional? No—he continues to love and know us infinitely: 'I know Ephraim, and Israel is not hidden from me' (v. 3). But unless we are willing 'to do justice, and to love kindness' (Micah 6:8), we cannot know his love.

Be encouraged

'Anyone who comes to me I will never drive away.'
John 6:37

VZ

Hosea 5:15b—6:6 (NRSV)

Cheap grace

In their distress they will beg my favour: 'Come, let us return to the Lord; for it is he who has torn, and he will hear us; he has struck down, and he will bind us up. After two days he will revive us; on the third day he will raise us up, that we may live before him. Let us know, let us press on to know the Lord; his appearing is as sure as the dawn; he will come to us like the showers, like the spring rains that water the earth.' What shall I do with you, O Ephraim? What shall I do with you, O Judah? Your love is like a morning cloud, like the dew that goes away early. Therefore I have hewn them by the prophets, I have killed them by the words of my mouth, and my judgment goes forth as the light. For I desire steadfast love and not sacrifice, the knowledge of God rather than burnt offerings.

Ever done one of those 'spot the difference' puzzles? To see what's missing in the second picture you have to compare it really closely with the first.

Israel's 'confession' here reminds me of one of those. It's got all the right language—attributing the hard times to God's punishment, 'claiming' God's mercy, persistence, even a tantalizing hint of the resurrection in the 'third day' theme. But there is just one problem: God rejects it. Why?

As in the puzzles, you have to know what to look for. Where is any acknowledgment of *why* God has 'struck down'? Any admission of guilt? Any commitment to give up the idols, to do God's justice in the land?

I have often met churches and Christian groups with 'formulae' for obtaining God's favour. When my friend's baby had leukaemia, her church pressurized her to 'claim' God's healing. The baby died, and my friend's faith was almost destroyed.

There is no magic formula for getting God to do what we want. If we think there is, we have our faith back to front: for it is about *us* doing what *God* wants. Spiritual aerobics will not impress God. Love of God and neighbour will always please him—even though the reward may not be this side of the grave.

Reflection and prayer

Little children, let us love, not in words or speech, but in truth and action.

1 John 3:18

Pray that this may be true for your church.

VZ

125

Hosea 6:11b—7:7 (NRSV, abridged)

God's passion, Israel's passion

When I would restore the fortunes of my people, when I would heal Israel, the corruption of Ephraim is revealed, and the wicked deeds of Samaria; for they deal falsely, the thief breaks in, and the bandits raid outside... By their wickedness they make the king glad, and the officials by their treachery. They are all adulterers; they are like a heated oven, whose baker does not need to stir the fire... On the day of our king the officials became sick with the heat of wine; he stretched out his hand with mockers. For they are kindled like an oven, their heart burns within them; all night their anger smoulders; in the morning it blazes like a flaming fire. All of them are hot as an oven, and they devour their rulers. All their kings have fallen; none of them calls upon me.

Medieval philosophers decided that God was 'impassible'—unaffected by emotions. This is not the God of the Old Testament, or the New. Hosea's God has a burning passion for the people he has created and called. The more they run away from him, the more he longs to bring them back.

The people of Israel have a burning passion too, but it is not for God. It is for doing exactly as their impulses dictate. Fraud, violence, theft, promiscuity, drunkenness—the corruption reaches all the way up to the head of State and his civil service. Images of the baker's fierce oven may recall the special cakes baked for pagan festivals. The picture is a powerful one that still resonates today: we speak of 'having the hots' for someone, 'blazing with anger', 'flaming desire'.

What fires us up, as the people of God today? Is it longing for God and God's ways? Do we hunger and thirst for righteousness? Or do we instead boil with anger because someone forgot they were doing the tea at church?

The passion of God's Spirit is a creative passion to make all things new. But human passions, when they're cut loose from God, soon become destructive, sinking into savagery. Our part is not to judge society's evils—that is God's job. Ours is to catch God's passion and let it fire us to build an alternative.

Prayer

O thou who camest from above,
The pure celestial fire to impart,
Kindle a flame of sacred love
On the mean altar of my heart.

Charles Wesley (1707–88)

VZ

Hosea 8:2–6a, 11–13 (NRSV, abridged)

Home-made religion

Israel cries to me, 'My God, we—Israel—know you!' Israel has spurned the good; the enemy shall pursue him. They made kings, but not through me; they set up princes, but without my knowledge. With their silver and gold they made idols for their own destruction. Your calf is rejected, O Samaria... For it is from Israel, an artisan made it; it is not God... When Ephraim multiplied altars to expiate sin, they became to him altars for sinning. Though I write for him the multitude of my instructions, they are regarded as a strange thing. Though they offer choice sacrifices... the Lord does not accept them. Now he will re-member their iniquity, and punish their sins; they shall return to Egypt.

What things are 'sacred' to your church? The form of worship? A particular belief about spiritual gifts? A leader who must never be questioned?

All human beings, including Christians, are prone to set up practices and ideas that are 'set in stone'. Israel had its own 'sacred places', in the capital Samaria and elsewhere; they were lavishly adorned, and the worship that took place there was nothing if not enthusiastic—generous animal sacrifices, and worshippers even injuring themselves to ensure fertility for the land (7:14).

With all this effort, Israel was proud to say, 'We know God'. The trouble was, God did not recognize in their worship or lives anything remotely connected with what he had commanded. His true commands—to worship only him, to make no idols, to respect life and the rights of neighbours—were now completely alien to them.

Their habits put them in danger of reversing the liberation of the exodus: not a literal return to Egypt, but a return to the conditions of poverty, sickness and oppression that they suffered in Egypt. This is the fate Moses predicted if the nation would not obey God (Deuteronomy 28:58–68).

It is easy to see this story as a far-off tale of a far-off people. But the danger of saying, 'We know God' while following human traditions is always around. 'Not everyone who says to me, 'Lord, Lord,' will enter the kingdom of heaven, but only the one who does the will of my Father' (Matthew 7:21).

Reflection

For freedom Christ has set us free. Stand firm, therefore, and do not submit again to a yoke of slavery.

Galatians 5:1

VZ

Hosea 9:7–8 (NRSV)

A prophet's lot

The days of punishment have come, the days of recompense have come; Israel cries, 'The prophet is a fool, the man of the spirit is mad!' Because of your great iniquity, your hostility is great. The prophet is a sentinel for my God over Ephraim, yet a fowler's snare is on all his ways, and hostility in the house of his God.

'There's none so blind as them that won't see,' goes a traditional English saying. It's natural to human beings to ignore unwelcome messages. We no longer go so far as to kill the bearer of bad news, but accusing the messenger of being mad—that has a very familiar ring!

Hosea's destiny is not only to live out God's message in his own life, but to be laughed at while he does it. After all, who'd listen to a prophet who married a prostitute—and then, of all things, accused the nation of immorality!

'No prophet is accepted in the prophet's home town,' observed Jesus. In Hosea's case, the rejection extends to his home country. Appointed as God's watchman, he has to watch his own step wherever he goes, for the people set political traps for him, and even in the temple there is open hostility to him.

How would a Hosea fare in our own churches—or in our Parliament? I fear it might be no better for him; we would all rather hear good news about our own church or nation, and bad news only about others 'out there'.

The prophet's lot is not a happy one, and Jesus himself is the prime example. 'A disciple is not above the teacher,' says Jesus. 'If they have called the master of the house Beelzebul, how much more will they malign those of his household!' (Matthew 10:24–25). While God still calls individuals in the Church and outside to alert the world to his values, it is through his body, the 'prophetic community', that we will mainly announce and demonstrate a different way of living. This will attract some and repel others; and in many places it will bring real danger to its adherents.

But beware: rejection doesn't guarantee that your words or ways are from God; you may just be expressing the message badly! 'What you are to say will be given to you' (Matthew 10:19); so pray for the Spirit's inspiration.

Reflection

'Do not fear those who kill the body but cannot kill the soul.'

Matthew 10:28

VZ

Hosea 10:1–2, 11–14a (NRSV)

Sowing and reaping

Israel is a luxuriant vine that yields its fruit. The more his fruit increased, the more altars he built; as his country improved, he improved his pillars. Their heart is false; now they must bear their guilt. The Lord will break down their altars... Ephraim was a trained heifer that loved to thresh, and I spared her fair neck; but I will make Ephraim break the ground; Judah must plough; Jacob must harrow for himself. Sow for yourselves righteousness; reap steadfast love; break up your fallow ground; for it is time to seek the Lord, that he may come and rain righteousness upon you. You have ploughed wickedness, you have reaped injustice, you have eaten the fruit of lies. Because you have trusted in your power and in the multitude of your warriors, therefore the tumult of war shall rise against your people.

As I write, $9 of debt repayment still goes back from Third World countries to the rich West for every $1 of aid that is given. National prosperity hardly seems to spur the prosperous nations to greater generosity to the poor!

As today, so in Hosea's day. Bumper harvests only led to more spiritual self-indulgence. Surplus wealth went on a huge military build-up, forgetting that the nation's true security was in God alone. Like the rich farmer in Jesus' parable (Luke 12:16–21), Israel was expert in building 'bigger barns', not to mention armouries. Are we any better, with our grain mountains, wine lakes and unusable nuclear arsenals, while millions starve and fall prey to preventable diseases?

Before Israel began to flourish and forget God, God was merciful to her (v. 11). But now there is no way back except by her own efforts. Nothing can be sown in ground that is already overgrown with weeds; Israel and her neighbour Judah must 'dig deep', breaking up their hard complacency, sowing the good seed that God provides. So the success of Israel's material crops becomes an ironic parable of her spiritual barrenness; while the vines yield hundredfold, in spiritual terms the ground isn't even ploughed.

This isn't God saying 'You must do it all by your own efforts now.' But a real commitment to change is the essential key to reformation. Then God will respond lavishly, raining righteousness.

Prayer

Lord, dig up our crops of self-indulgence and help us to sow the seed of faithfulness and justice.

VZ

Hosea 11:1–5, 8–9 (NRSV, abridged)

Father love

When Israel was a child, I loved him, and out of Egypt I called my son. The more I called them, the more they went from me; they kept sacrificing to the Baals, and offering incense to idols. Yet it was I who taught Ephraim to walk, I took them up in my arms; but they did not know that I healed them. I led them with cords of human kindness, with bands of love. I was to them like those who lift infants to their cheeks. I bent down to them and fed them. They shall return to the land of Egypt, and Assyria shall be their king, because they have refused to return to me... How can I give you up, Ephraim? How can I hand you over, O Israel? ... My heart recoils within me; my compassion grows warm and tender. I will not execute my fierce anger; I will not again destroy Ephraim; for I am God and no mortal, the Holy One in your midst, and I will not come in wrath.

In Western media there is still much debate about the 'new man' who changes nappies, cooks and cleans and may even stay home with the baby while his partner goes to work. Does he exist? Where can I get one?

I don't think the 'new father' would have been news to Hosea. His image of God's fatherhood is very much 'hands on': cuddling the baby, holding the toddler's leading reins as she takes her first tottering steps, kissing the 'hurties' better and doling out the parsnip purée!

I wonder if Jesus had this famous passage in mind when he told his even more famous parable of the prodigal son. God's passion for his wandering child here reminds us strongly of the father who, against all rules of decorum for that time, actually lifts up his skirts and runs to embrace his returning, pigsty-fragrant younger son.

We fear the anger of God in response to our frequent failures, and are quick to call down that anger on others' faults. 'Lord, shall we call down fire…?' (Luke 9:54). Indeed, God does blaze with anger at what sin does. But as with all the best fathers, love for the helpless child always wins out.

Prayer

Father of all, we give you thanks and praise that when we were still far off you met us in your Son and brought us home.

Common Worship

VZ

Hosea 14:1–9 (NRSV, abridged)

Re-rooted

Return, O Israel, to the Lord your God, for you have stumbled because of your iniquity. Take words with you and return to the Lord; say to him, 'Take away all guilt; accept that which is good, and we will offer the fruit of our lips. Assyria shall not save us; we will not ride upon horses; we will say no more 'Our God' to the work of our hands…' I will heal their disloyalty; I will love them freely, for my anger has turned from them. I will be like the dew to Israel; he shall blossom like the lily, he shall strike root like forests of Lebanon… They shall again live beneath my shadow, they shall flourish as a garden; they shall blossom like the vine, their fragrance shall be like the wine of Lebanon. O Ephraim, what have I to do with idols? It is I who answer and look after you. I am like an evergreen cypress; your faithfulness comes from me.

Is there a way back from the lostness of the desert, from a situation where God seems to have deserted us? Yes, says Hosea. But what is the difference between the words of Israel in chapter 6, which God said were 'like the dew that goes away early' (see page 134), and the words they bring here?

First, they acknowledge their guilt; earlier they only blamed God for their misfortunes. Second, they make specific commitments to change: they will give up their alliances with superpowers, abandon their military hardware (a horse was the equivalent of a tank), turn from worshipping gods of their own creation. Third, they recognize that it is only by God's power that their innocence can be restored.

For us this is a very 'Christian', grace-filled prophecy. In ourselves we have no power to stay faithful and be a source of blessing to others. Only God can replant us in good soil, in which we will grow and bear fruit.

Hosea's lovely poetry here picks up images from throughout his book. The dew that stood for impermanence becomes life-giving water. The vine whose luxuriance only caused self-indulgence (ch. 10) returns to being the special crop of God's planting. And nothing beats an established, fragrant, fruitful tree for an image of new life and growth.

Reflection

'Just as the branch cannot bear fruit by itself unless it abides in the vine, neither can you unless you abide in me.'

John 15:4b

VZ

Ezekiel 47:1; John 7:37–39 (NRSV, abridged)

River of God

He brought me back to the entrance of the temple; there, water was flowing from below the threshold of the temple toward the east...

On the last day of the festival, the great day, while Jesus was standing there, he cried out, 'Let anyone who is thirsty come to me, and let the one who believes in me drink. As the scripture has said, "Out of the believer's heart shall flow rivers of living water."' Now he said this about the Spirit, which believers in him were to receive.

One of the most wonderful conferences I ever shared in was on the island of Iona, when the theme was 'The Holy Spirit in Nature and Grace'. One early morning we all trod barefoot through the grass and sang together:

O River of God, flow down on me,
O River of God, flow out from me,
O River of God, I cry to Thee,
O River of God, flow down on me...

It is the same Spirit who raises the sap in the trees in springtime, who turns the cycle of the seasons, who causes the rising and setting of the sun and the waxing and waning of the moon.

This is the Spirit sent by Jesus to flow, not only into the world of nature, but into the experience of grace. This is the Spirit of natural order and beauty, the Spirit of virtue, power and love. The source of the Holy Spirit is the throne and altar of God in the temple, which is the symbol of God's loving heart—and the river flows, renewing and enlightening, wherever there is a receptive heart.

As the believer opens his or her heart to such spiritual indwelling, the river flows in, and through, and out in thirst-quenching, fertilizing and verdant beauty, to the whole world around.

We came away from Iona with a new vision and a new experience, carried along on the river of God's Holy Spirit, into a dry and thirsty world.

Prayer

Let your Spirit flow in and through me today, Lord. Overflow my heart, that I may minister to human need and become the channel of your fruitfulness and peace.

R/SSF

Ezekiel 47:2–3 (NRSV)

Ankle-deep

Then he brought me out by way of the north gate, and led me around on the outside to the outer gate that faces toward the east; and the water was coming out on the south side. Going on eastward with a cord in his hand, the man measured one thousand cubits, and then led me through the water; and it was ankle-deep.

In my Worcestershire hermitage, for fifty weeks of the year I miss wide expanses of water. But these last two weeks I have been cycling and swimming around the Gower Peninsula, from the shallows into the depths, with bracing water and tumbling waves.

However deep and far experienced swimmers may venture, they all have to begin at the shallows, with water ankle-deep. Here there is great excitement, playfulness mixed with laughter and shouting, as little children mingle with grannies and grandpas, paddling with skirts and trousers rolled up, accompanied by delighted screams as breakers roll in suddenly and catch them unprepared.

It was drizzling rain a few days ago, but this did not deter one little boy at the edge in his wellington boots, for he cried out in great jubilation, 'Daddy! This is the best day of our holidays, isn't it?'

You may only be ankle-deep in your life of prayer, feeling you've hardly begun, and yet even here on the edge of things the breakers roll in and carry messages from the great deeps.

Prayer

Father, I realize that there are depths beyond depths of your love and grace, and I've only just begun to paddle nervously on the edge of your sea. Let me rejoice in the breakers, and yearn for the depths.

R/SSF

133

Ezekiel 47:4a; Mark 1:16–18 (NRSV)

Knee-deep

Again he measured one thousand [cubits], and led me through the water; and it was knee-deep...

As Jesus passed along the Sea of Galilee, he saw Simon and his brother Andrew casting a net into the sea—for they were fishermen. And Jesus said to them, 'Follow me and I will make you fish for people.' And immediately they left their nets and followed him.

The progress into deeper waters is gradual; and from the paddling edge to knee-deep wading is not a great distance but it is progress in the right direction. Knee-deep is commitment, facing deeper water ahead. Ankle-deep is the place of prayers of petition in need, while knee-deep is deepening discipleship, from simple prayers of petition to a greater awareness and concern for those who cannot pray for themselves—the beginning of intercessory prayer.

It is also the place of repairing and casting nets. The fishermen-disciples were committed to the Lake of Galilee, and Jesus called them from fishing for fish to seeking for souls. It is only at the call of Christ that one can truly move into deeper water. True intercessory prayer is not pleading with a reluctant deity to grant favours to an unworthy humanity, but rather a participation by that humanity in the healing energies of the Holy Spirit on behalf of sick and sinful men and women throughout the world. Wading knee-deep into the river of prayer is my response to the needs and joys of my friends and neighbours... and on into the deep waters of my enemies and into the beginnings of universal love.

Prayer

Am I still in the kindergarten of prayer, Lord? Stir me up and deliver me from merely selfish concerns. Waken me to the joys and sorrows of the Church and the world—and teach me to pray.

R/SSF

134

Ezekiel 47:4b; Luke 5:4–8 (NRSV, abridged)

Waist-deep

Again he measured one thousand [cubits], and led me through the water; and it was up to the waist...

Jesu said to Simon, 'Put out into the deep water and let down your nets for a catch.' ... And they came and filled both boats [with fish], so that they began to sink. But when Simon Peter saw it, he fell down at Jesus' knees, saying, 'Go away from me, Lord, for I am a sinful man!'

After playing for a while at waist-deep level, I went floating on my back, out of the earshot of others, and began to sing:

O the deep, deep love of Jesus!
Vast, unmeasured, boundless, free;
Rolling as a mighty ocean
In its fullness over me.
Underneath me, all around me,
Is the current of Thy love;
Leading onward, leading homeward,
To my glorious rest above.

Here are mingled prayers of thanksgiving and adoration, and I thought of the Celtic monks who used to sing the psalter up to their chins in the sea. I rested in the Lord and allowed his love to flow over and around me. The border between waist-deep and waters to swim in is the place of meditation. It was in such deep waters that Peter realized his own unworthiness before Jesus, the man of glory, and he cried out in unworthiness and wonder, 'Go away from me, Lord, for I am a sinful man!'—though that was the last thing he wanted Jesus to do.

Then, floating in those mid-depths, a fellow flashed past me, swimming a powerful underwater, overarm stroke, and soon disappeared away towards the sea's horizon. And I began to yearn for a stronger stroke, and for deeper depths...

Prayer

Lord, I seem hardly to have begun. I see my own unworthiness, yet begin to rejoice in your forgiving love, and to adore you for your ineffable grace. I learn that there are deeper depths than I have ever imagined, and I ask, forgive my reticence, strengthen my arms and knees and gently lead me on, for I am afraid of deep waters.

R/SSF

Ezekiel 47:5; Mark 4:39–41 (NRSV)

Out of my depth

Again he measured one thousand [cubits], and it was a river that I could not cross, for the water had risen; it was deep enough to swim in. Jesus woke up and rebuked the wind, and said to the sea, 'Peace! Be still!' Then the wind ceased, and there was a dead calm. He said to them, 'Why are you afraid? Have you still no faith?' And they were filled with great awe and said to one another, 'Who then is this, that even the wind and the sea obey him?'

A few mornings ago I had a scary and salutary experience. Swimming in Langland Bay in the early morning, I went out too far, and on turning back found that the tide had also turned and was against me. After a breathless few minutes' hard swimming I thought, 'I don't think I'm going to make it! Shall my life end in drowning?' So I sent up some arrow prayers, and the resulting rush of adrenalin and effort landed me back breathless on the beach.

I have had a number of premature experiences of wading into the deeper waters of prayer over the years, and have sometimes found myself really scared, because I was both relatively unarmed against the powers of darkness (Ephesians 6:11), and relatively naked before the consuming fire of God's holiness and love.

Only over the past few years have I begun to allow myself to be taken by the Spirit into those deeper waters. It is scary, it is overwhelming—but it is inevitable for those who are seeking the depths of God's loving mystery.

Prayer

Lord, when I am in perilous deep waters of conflict and doubt, deliver me. When you call me into the deep waters of intercessory and contemplative prayer, enable me; for even the winds and the waves obey you.

R/SSF

Ezekiel 47:12 (NRSV) (read also Revelation 22:1–22)

River of fruitfulness

On the banks, on both sides of the river, there will grow all kinds of trees for food. Their leaves will not wither nor their fruit fail, but they will bear fresh fruit every month, because the water for them flows from the sanctuary. Their fruit will be for food, and their leaves for healing.

This vision in the book of Ezekiel and its eternal reality in the book of Revelation are of the same tree, its fruit and leaves for food and healing, fed by the river of God which flows from his throne. This river symbolizes the Holy Spirit flowing from the heart of God, made possible because the Son of God extended his arms of love upon the Tree of Life.

If we are to enter into that life of communion with God in the heavenly dimension beyond this mortal life, we must plunge into that river *today*. First we put our toes in to test the water, paddle ankle-deep, and then progress knee-deep, waist-deep, and so begin to swim as the Holy Spirit takes us deeper into prayer, deeper into the life of God.

If we begin here and now this adventure in prayer, the effect will be gentle but radical, for the river deepens as we progress. First there will take place the purging of our egocentric desires, a deepening of our awareness of God's loving action, an integration of all our finer faculties, and the experience of the permanent indwelling of the Holy Spirit. The result of all this will not be a pharisaic distaste of the world, but a fruitful life of compassion and healing, and a preparation for the fullness of joy beyond this dimension of space and time.

You know that experience of initial coldness when you first wade in; but take the plunge—it is well worth it!

Prayer

My Father, I believe the river of your love flows from your heart, through the world and into the dimension of eternity. Plunge me into that river, Lord, either gently and slowly, or by sudden and deep immersion, according to your will. Let me not be afraid, but bold in spirit, and make my life fruitful today and in eternity.

R/SSF

Acts 2:1–2 (NRSV) (read also vv. 3–21)

The breath of God

When the day of Pentecost had come, they were all together in one place. And suddenly from heaven there came a sound like the rush of a violent wind, and it filled the entire house where they were sitting.

In last week's readings the life of prayer was told out in creative symbols of river, ocean, trees and fruitfulness. This week we are caught up in the symbols of wind, fire and breath.

The disciples had received from Jesus the promise of the Holy Spirit's coming. They were gathered in the upper room in Jerusalem in a state of contemplative waiting, expecting the promise to be fulfilled but hardly knowing what would happen.

Suddenly, the breath of God enveloped them in a 'mighty rushing wind' (AV), filling the house and possessing their being. It was the new creation, recalling God's breathing into Adam the breath of life (Genesis 2:7), and consummating the action of Jesus breathing upon the disciples and saying, 'Receive the Holy Spirit' (John 20:22).

The mighty Spirit who proceeds from the Father through the Son swept into the midst of the nucleus of the New Testament Church, filling Mary, Peter and all the believers with the very life of God.

Every day is, in a sense, the day of Pentecost. It is an appropriate day for you, within the fellowship of the waiting Church, to receive afresh your inheritance, the breath of God which can breathe new life, power and joy into your body and spirit. The Holy Trinity is not meant to be a piece of complicated dogmatics, but a revolutionary experience which enabled the early Church to glimpse the very being and character of the living God.

Prayer

Breathe on me, Breath of God,
Fill me with life anew;
That I may love what Thou dost love
And do what Thou wouldst do.

E. Hatch (1835–89)

R/SSF

Acts 2:3–4; 4:31 (NRSV) (also read Acts 4:23–30)

Tongues of fire

Divided tongues, as of fire, appeared among them, and a tongue rested on each of them. All of them were filled with the Holy Spirit and began to speak in other languages as the Spirit gave them ability... When they had prayed, the place in which they were gathered together was shaken; and they were all filled with the Holy Spirit.

What a gathering! A violent wind fills and shakes the house, tongues and flames of fire envelop the waiting disciples, and they experience an infilling, a baptism, a fullness of the Holy Spirit—and the whole event erupts in a burst of mingled languages praising and adoring God.

Such a promise is ours too (2:39), if we are willing to wait in a contemplative state of prayer. The fire will come and do its purging, cleansing, irradiating and illuminating work within us. But we must not dictate the manner or consequences of such an experience. For some it may be a violent and fiery outburst accompanied by the gift of tongues; for others it may be a gentle rising of the river overflowing its banks, or a quiet deepening of trust in God and compassion for the world with no visible or emotional outburst.

According to the text, the united flame divided into separate tongues of fire which rested on each of them. Some of the Orthodox icons show Mary, our Lord's mother, with Peter and the apostles, lost in prayer as the tongues of flame hover over them. This is an apostolic vision, and our privilege is to enter into the pentecostal experience, not in an individualistic manner, but as part of the corporate Church of God. The separate tongues are meant to unite into the living flame which ascends again into the heart of God.

This is a powerful spiritual truth, and the human consequences are found in our second passage, from Acts 4, in which the Church prays under the pressure of persecution, and the Holy Spirit descends, shaking the very foundations of the house.

Prayer

Breathe on me, Breath of God,
Till I am wholly Thine;
Until this earthly part of me
Glows with Thy fire divine.

E. Hatch (1835–89)

R/SSF

Acts 2:6, 12–13 (NRSV)

Inebriated with joy

At this sound the crowd gathered and was bewildered... All were amazed and perplexed, saying to one another, 'What does this mean?' But others sneered and said, 'They are filled with new wine.'

Marvellous words: *bewildered*, *amazed*, *astonished*, *perplexed*—while the apostles were caught up in the inebriating joy of the new wine of the Spirit, telling the story of Jesus and of the mighty power of God to save, to heal and to fill with joy and glory.

You can identify today with one of the three groups. First there was the group of apostles—transformed from fearful and cowardly disciples, into a patient, hoping, praying band in the upper room who were filled and inebriated with love and boldness.

Then there was the crowd of bewildered, amazed, astonished, perplexed people who heard the wonderful words in their own languages, and were among the three thousand who responded to the Spirit's call in the preaching of Peter (v. 41).

But there was also that sneering and unbelieving group that looked for any alternative explanation, and came up with the conclusion, 'They are filled with new wine.' Well, of course they were, but it was the sweet, inebriating wine of the Spirit, the gift of the risen Jesus who had transformed water into wine at Cana in Galilee.

As I write these words from my hermitage today, I ask for you and myself that we may be filled with bewilderment, amazement, astonishment and even holy perplexity, at the mighty power of God, and then that we may drink deeply of the wine of the Spirit until we are inebriated with joy—and that for ever!

Prayer

Breathe on me, Breath of God,
So shall I never die,
But live with Thee the perfect life
Of Thine eternity.
E. Hatch (1835–89)

R/SSF

Acts 3:1–2 (NRSV)

The hour of prayer

One day Peter and John were going up to the temple at the hour of prayer, at three o'clock in the afternoon. And a man lame from birth was being carried in. People would lay him daily at the gate of the temple called the Beautiful Gate so that he could ask for alms from those entering the temple.

After all the hullabaloo and spiritual excitement of Pentecost and its aftermath, here are Peter and John settling into the regular and disciplined liturgical life of the temple. The new wine of the gospel was poured into the new skins of the new covenant, but the early disciples did not neglect regular, ordered and liturgical worship. We can see that charismatic joy was compatible with liturgical order in the best of New Testament worship.

It was while these expressions and manifestations of the Church's joy and worship were being experienced that it was confronted with human need. The man lame from birth was right in the path of Peter and John at the Beautiful Gate of the temple. And unlike the priest and Levite of Jesus' parable (Luke 10:31–32), Peter and John did not pass him by, or busy themselves with theological or liturgical matters while human need presented itself before their eyes.

So if we are faithful to the hour of prayer, setting heart and mind upon the glory of God, then human need will confront us, and in the power of the Spirit of Pentecost, we shall be able to act according to the will of God.

Prayer

Lord, let me not be so theologically and liturgically minded as to be of no earthly use. Rather, let the gifts of the Spirit and my faithfulness to prayer issue in compassionate concern and service to human need.

R/SSF

Acts 3:4–6 (NRSV)

Looking and gazing

When [the lame man] saw Peter and John about to go into the temple, he asked them for alms. Peter looked intently at him, as did John, and said, 'Look at us.' And he fixed his attention on them, expecting to receive something from them. But Peter said, 'I have no silver or gold, but what I have I give you; in the name of Jesus Christ of Nazareth, stand up and walk.'

Often, when I read a powerful text of scripture, I ask two questions: 1. What is happening? and 2. What is going on? The first relates to the *facts* that are recorded, and the second to the deeper *meaning* and dynamics that lie beneath the surface.

Here three different Greek words are used for opening one's eyes, and a further word for the opening of eye, mind and heart. We have to bear in mind that Peter and John have been the subject of God's gaze on the day of Pentecost and have their eyes fixed upon him.

So we read that the lame man simply *saw* them as they came by, and asked for alms. Peter and John then *looked intently* at him and said, '*Look* at us.' And obediently the man *gazed expectantly*—and wonderful things happened.

If you simply follow the story with the first question in mind, it yields a wonderful account of the first healing miracle in the early Church, and a coming together of the saving gospel of Pentecost with a crippled and wounded humanity. But if you look closer you will see that the quality of seeing permeates the story, and that we can play with such words as 'seeing', 'looking', 'gazing', 'perceiving', in the relationship between the lame man and the apostles. Different translations speak of Peter and John 'fixing their eyes', or 'gazing intently', and the lame man 'giving attention', 'paying heed' and 'looking expectantly' at the apostles. The fact was that the apostles gazed with the compassion of Christ upon the man, and he turned eyes, mind and heart upon the Christ within them. What qualities of power and response are perceived when you ask the second question, 'What is going on?'

Prayer

Anoint the eyes of my understanding,
Lord, that I may gaze upon your radiant
glory, and turn eyes of compassion upon a
needy world, for the healing of the sick
and the salvation of the lost.

R/SSF

Acts 3:7–8 (NRSV)

Walking, leaping, praising

And [Peter] took him by the right hand and raised him up; and immediately his feet and ankles were made strong. Jumping up, he stood and began to walk, and he entered the temple with them, walking and leaping and praising God.

I appreciate ordered, beautiful, liturgical worship, and if the psalms are set to Gregorian plainsong, all the better. Occasional participation or ministry in a charismatic gathering has also been part of my diet of worship, prayer and praise.

But can you imagine the effect on the assembled people (remember it was the hour of prayer) when into the temple came two men inebriated by the Holy Spirit, and a deliriously happy man who had been lame from birth, now immediately healed, who was walking, leaping and praising God?

I believe the Lord weeps at our divisions and exclusive attitudes towards the beliefs and worship of others. But there are times when he simply and humorously 'sets the cat among the pigeons'. Into the context of lofty Hebrew chanting of psalms bursts this liberated paralytic, this redeemed sinner, who had just tasted the new, sweet wine of Pentecost.

It is as if, at an aesthetically beautiful high mass in a traditional Gothic Anglican cathedral, a paralysed man suddenly began to dance and sing in tongues. What would we do?

Well, before the charismatics begin to chuckle, and traditionalists begin to debate—what about you and me? I mean, what if into the ordered habits, luxuries and sins of our self-indulgent lives (whether evangelical or Catholic) the Lord Jesus exploded a pentecostal firecracker? It would not only explode with illumination but with fire—both showing us the shabbiness of our hypocrisy and searing and purging our souls of sin.

Prayer

Lord Jesus, sometimes I wonder if I would prefer to cling to my comfortable paralysis than be set gloriously free. Help me to understand what it would mean to start walking and leaping and praising God.

R/SSF

Acts 3:9–10 (NRSV) (read also vv. 11–16)

Amazed and astounded

All the people saw him walking and praising God, and they recognized him as the one who used to sit and ask for alms at the Beautiful Gate of the temple; and they were filled with wonder and amazement at what had happened to him.

Yesterday I spoke of the sorrow of God at our petty divisions and seemingly exclusive *ordered* or *spontaneous* liturgies (as if they were incompatible!). I also spoke of the humour of God in confounding our liturgies and theologies. I am reminded of pentecostal worship in the midst of the *sobornost* (warm fellowship) of an Orthodox liturgy, of charismatic speaking in tongues at a Catholic mass, or the saying/singing of Compline at a Baptist gathering or at London Bible College.

The important thing is that we see and experience God at work—and he is at work among all the churches that constitute the great Church of God, which is the Body of Christ.

The fact that a hermit brother, who spends fifty weeks of the year in his enclosure, can write these last two weeks' of BRF notes with great joy is proof that God is at work in his Church. It is a matter at which we may be amazed and astounded, as were the Jews gathered in the temple when the well-known man, lame from birth, came singing and dancing into the midst of the worship. God is blessedly confusing us, amazing us, astounding us, for he is the God of order and beauty, of spontaneity and discipline, of oddness and symmetry, of autumn and springtime.

If we are following deeper into the life of prayer we shall continue to be amazed and astounded and, if the prayer is real, then we shall experience true sorrow for our dear world, and become the Lord's 'wounded healers' in living out his redeeming love.

Prayer

Lord, do not let me settle into a stagnant spirituality which lacks both enthusiasm and compassion; rather, give me the Spirit of pentecostal fire, and the discipline of an ordered life of prayer. Thus shall I glorify your name, and radiate your light into the dark places of the world.

R/SSF

Exodus 1:8–14 (NRSV)

Friend or foe

Now a new king arose over Egypt, who did not know Joseph. He said to his people, 'Look, the Israelite people are more numerous and powerful than we. Come, let us deal shrewdly with them, or they will increase and, in the event of war, join our enemies and fight against us and escape from the land.' Therefore they set taskmasters over them to oppress them with forced labour. They built supply cities, Pithom and Rameses, for Pharaoh. But the more they were oppressed, the more they multiplied and spread, so that the Egyptians came to dread the Israelites. The Egyptians became ruthless in imposing tasks on the Israelites, and made their lives bitter with hard service in mortar and brick and in every kind of field labour. They were ruthless in all the tasks that they imposed on them.

My younger son would tell you straight away that this new king would not make a good Jedi. The Jedi are the wise rulers in the *Star Wars* films. I was rather taken by one of the posters on his wall advertising the latest film. It says, 'Fear leads to anger, anger leads to hate, and hate leads to suffering.' One of the qualities which ensures that you will be a good Jedi is that you have no fear.

The kind of fear shown by Pharaoh is the fear of the unknown. If he had known Joseph, he would have discovered what a great partnership could have been forged, what an asset these people could be to Egypt, how much more successful things could be if they worked together in harmony. But he did not get to know any of them. Instead he saw them as a threat. A plague of Israelites! Pharaoh obviously feels very threatened. Afraid of them inside the country but equally afraid of them becoming enemies without. First, he works them so hard that they will have no strength left to rebel. Second, he attempts to 'cull' them. We have seen this 'ethnic cleansing' far too much in recent times too—the Holocaust, the troubles in the Balkans and Rwanda in recent years. The tension and unrest that still simmer in many multiracial communities are the result of suspicion, and fear of the unknown. It is a major part of our life as the faith community to welcome the alien, and make friends of strangers.

Reflection

There is no fear in love, but perfect love casts out fear.

1 John 4:18

RobG

Exodus 1:22—2:10 (NRSV)

Rescued

Then Pharaoh commanded all his people, 'Every boy that is born to the Hebrews you shall throw into the Nile, but you shall let every girl live.' Now a man from the house of Levi went and married a Levite woman. The woman conceived and bore a son; and when she saw that he was a fine baby, she hid him for three months. When she could hide him no longer she got a papyrus basket for him, and plastered it with bitumen and pitch; she put the child in it and placed it among the reeds on the bank of the river…

Moses has grown too big to be hidden, so his mother places him in a papyrus basket. The word for 'basket' is used in the Bible only here and in the story of Noah's ark (Genesis 6:14). In our Church life, the sign of rescue from death is, of course, baptism. The service of baptism in the 1662 Anglican prayer book includes the ark as a symbol of the Church. We recognize the child as a child of God and we offer our lives and those we love back into his hands, floating on the waters of faith. We are cleansed through the water of baptism, anointed as servants of Christ with his cross, and sent out into the world to serve him. Moses is placed in the safety of his basket and so rescued, that he might lead others in obedience to God. Named by Pharaoh's daughter (his name means 'drawn out'), he is rescued from the water. He was no 'ordinary child'.

It is so liberating when we place those we love into the loving hands of God, and trust in his rescue plan. Moses' mum couldn't have imagined in her wildest dreams that he would be returned to her briefly, before being freely given to lead their people out of slavery into the promised land.

Prayer

Heavenly Father, we thank you for the cleansing waters of baptism, and for the privilege of being anointed as your servants. May we serve you faithfully today and in the days to come. Amen.

RobG

Exodus 2:4–10 (NRSV)

Girl power

His sister stood at a distance, to see what would happen to him. The daughter of Pharaoh came down to bathe at the river, while her attendants walked beside the river. She saw the basket among the reeds and sent her maid to bring it. When she opened it, she saw the child. He was crying, and she took pity on him. 'This must be one of the Hebrews' children,' she said. Then his sister said to Pharaoh's daughter, 'Shall I go and get you a nurse from the Hebrew women to nurse the child for you?' Pharaoh's daughter said to her, 'Yes.' So the girl went and called the child's mother. Pharaoh's daughter said to her, 'Take this child and nurse it for me, and I will give you your wages.' So the woman took the child and nursed it. When the child grew up, she brought him to Pharaoh's daughter, and she took him as her son. She named him Moses, 'because,' she said, 'I drew him out of the water.'

I love it when I see God's plan coming together, especially when I witness his wonderful sense of irony. Pharaoh is a man who obviously thinks that women are an adornment to life but have no particular value. 'Kill any baby boy, but if it is a girl, she shall live,' says Pharaoh (1:16). He does not spare the girls' lives because they are precious, but because he believes them to be of no consequence. How wrong he could be. Every one is special in God's eyes and has a purpose in his plan. His only requirement is that they be obedient to him, whether man or woman. In chapter 1, Pharaoh commands the midwives to kill any baby boy. They fear God and so will not do this. Then Moses' mother and sister thwart his plans. And finally his own daughter shows compassion on baby Moses. The Pharaoh's impotence to destroy the people of God is ironically exposed through the wonderful compassionate ministry of the women he did not value. God is so eager to forgive, but cannot redeem anyone who hardens their heart against him or his people, for they will ultimately destroy themselves.

Mary's song

His mercy is for those who fear him from generation to generation. He has shown strength with his arm; he has scattered the proud in the thoughts of their hearts. He has brought down the powerful from their thrones, and lifted up the lowly.

Luke 1:50–52

RobG

Exodus 2:11–17 (NRSV, abridged)

Moses the fighter

One day, after Moses had grown up, he went out to his people and saw their forced labour. He saw an Egyptian beating a Hebrew... He looked this way and that, and seeing no one he killed the Egyptian... When he went out the next day, he saw two Hebrews fighting; and he said to the one who was in the wrong, 'Why do you strike your fellow Hebrew?' He answered, 'Who made you a ruler and judge over us? Do you mean to kill me as you killed the Egyptian?' Then Moses was afraid and thought, 'Surely the thing is known.' When Pharaoh heard of it, he sought to kill Moses. But Moses fled... He settled in the land of Midian... The priest of Midian had seven daughters. They came to draw water, and filled the troughs to water their father's flock. But some shepherds came and drove them away. Moses got up and came to their defence and watered their flock.

Here are three very important incidents in Moses' life which show that he is destined for a prophetic role. As a young man, outraged at seeing an Egyptian overseer beating a Jewish slave, he kills the overseer. The next day, he tries to make peace between two Hebrews who are fighting, but the aggressor takes offence and says, 'Do you mean to kill me as you killed the Egyptian?' That remark must have hurt. Moses was a peacemaker at heart. Word gets round about his recklessness and he is branded a rebel by the king. Indeed Pharaoh orders Moses' death, and he flees to Midian. At this point, Moses, I should think, wants nothing more than a quiet life, but immediately finds himself in another fight. The seven daughters of the Midianite priest are being abused by the Midianite male shepherds and Moses rises to their defence.

The incidents are, of course, related. In all three, Moses shows a deep commitment to fighting injustice. He intervenes when a non-Jew oppresses a Jew, when two Jews fight, and when non-Jews oppress other non-Jews. Moses cares deeply for any who are oppressed, and God is now ready to call Moses from shepherding sheep in Midian, to setting his people free.

A song

The Lord is my shepherd, I shall not want. He makes me lie down in green pastures; he leads me beside the still waters; he restores my soul. He leads me in right paths for his name's sake.

Psalm 23:1–3

RobG

Exodus 3:1–5, 10, 12 (NRSV)

Consuming fire

Moses was keeping the flock of his father-in-law Jethro, the priest of Midian; he led his flock beyond the wilderness, and came to Horeb, the mountain of God. There the angel of the Lord appeared to him in a flame of fire out of a bush; he looked, and the bush was blazing, yet it was not consumed. Then Moses said, 'I must turn aside and look at this great sight, and see why the bush is not burned up.' When the Lord saw that he had turned aside to see, God called to him out of the bush, 'Moses, Moses!' And he said, 'Here I am.' Then he said, 'Come no closer! Remove the sandals from your feet, for the place on which you are standing is holy ground... I will send you to Pharaoh to bring my people, the Israelites, out of Egypt... you shall worship God on this mountain.'

As Moses was going about his everyday business of tending sheep, little did he know he was acting out, as it were, the Exodus by leading his 'flock' closer and closer to God, through the wilderness to Mount Horeb, 'the mountain of God'. It was here that God got his attention—a mysterious moment in which he revealed himself in a burning bush that didn't catch fire.

A few years ago I was invited to a very exciting weekend at the convent in Ham, to participate in a 'Creative Arts Retreat'. It was the usual meditative weekend led by a spiritual director, going about the everyday business of a convent—except for one session, where I was taught how to eat fire without getting burnt. It seemed such an odd skill for a parish priest to learn! Later, at a eucharist in my church, I discovered a purpose. I ate fire and then read the Gospel. It was a very profound moment for me. It took quite a bit of courage. I did not want it to look like a circus trick or a bit of fun; I wanted this powerful symbol of fire-eating to express something of the task of evangelists—to speak the word of God in the power of the Holy Spirit. It certainly got everyone's attention! God wants us to hear his voice and act upon it, and will go to extraordinary lengths to do so.

Prayer

Let the words of my mouth and the meditation of my heart be acceptable to you, O Lord, my rock and my redeemer.

Psalm 19:14

RobG

Exodus 4:1–5 (NRSV)

The magician's assistant

Then Moses answered, 'But suppose they do not believe me or listen to me, but say, "The Lord did not appear to you."' The Lord said to him, 'What is that in your hand?' He said, 'A staff.' And he said, 'Throw it on the ground.' So he threw the staff on the ground, and it became a snake; and Moses drew back from it. Then the Lord said to Moses, 'Reach out your hand, and seize it by the tail'—so he reached out his hand and grasped it, and it became a staff in his hand—'so that they may believe that the Lord, the God of their ancestors, the God of Abraham, the God of Isaac, and the God of Jacob, has appeared to you.'

I used to be an entertainer on a cruise ship, and one of my acts was to be a mime and a magician. My one trick involved some very large playing cards and two volunteers from the audience. I would never touch the cards, but invited the volunteers to perform the trick. All I did was quietly to give the card holder some simple instructions. If my instructions were followed, he or she would discover which card the other volunteer had thought of! Everyone applauded them for the trick, but they knew who was really responsible for the magic. In the same way, God wants us to share in his work of creation by being obedient to his commands. We shall then share in his miracles.

Here we begin to learn how patient God is. Moses is full of doubts, fears and uncertainties about his own gifts of persuasion and oratory. But God, between gritted teeth, shows Moses ways of convincing the people that he is his man. Unfortunately Moses continues to be a wimp (4:10–17). 'I'm slow of speech': God assures him he will tell him what he needs to say. But no! Moses would prefer it if God sent someone else. But God has chosen him and offers him all the support he needs—Aaron to speak for him and then some persuasive signs, the trick with the staff, the leprous hand and the blood on dry ground.

Eventually Moses did all he was commanded and sure enough, everyone believed and bowed down and worshipped God. Moses had little confidence in himself and that's fine—that's humility. But God was insistent that he needed only to put trust in him. God creates the miracles; we just assist him.

A prayer

Lord, let us be your hands and feet.

RobG

Exodus 5:1–21 (NRSV, abridged)

Double trouble

Moses and Aaron went to Pharaoh and said, 'Thus says the Lord, the God of Israel, "Let my people go, so that they may celebrate a festival to me in the wilderness."' But Pharaoh said, 'Who is the Lord, that I should heed him and let Israel go? I do not know the Lord, and I will not let Israel go.' ... Pharaoh commanded the taskmasters of the people, as well as their supervisors, 'You shall no longer give the people straw to make bricks. Let heavier work be laid on them; then they will labour at it and pay no attention to deceptive words.' ... And the supervisors of the Israelites were beaten, and were asked, 'Why did you not finish the required quantity of bricks yesterday and today, as you did before?' ... As they left Pharaoh, they came upon Moses and Aaron who were waiting to meet them. They said to them, 'The Lord look upon you and judge! You have brought us into bad odour with Pharaoh and his officials, and have put a sword into their hands to kill us.'

At last, Moses agrees to tell Pharaoh to let God's people go, but Pharaoh refuses to listen and his heart is hardened, so much so that he makes life even more difficult than ever. 'Why did you ever send me?' cries Moses (5:22).

I remember, in prison ministry in Hong Kong, being impressed by many of the Christian inmates who would stand up against injustice, knowing they would suffer for it. Sometimes it lost them, and those associated with them, precious parole and privileges. That was the price of real freedom! They were the ones who eventually gained the respect of others.

Jesus warned his disciples that it would not be easy for them to be his followers. Life may be very hard, and discouragement is easy to catch, as Moses and the Israelites discovered. Crushed by the extra work and the impossibility of the task of making bricks without enough straw, the people were broken in spirit, so Moses prayed, because they had lost heart. How often I find a situation where people are bereaved and no words seem right. 'It'll be all right' is cold comfort. What they need is love, help and encouragement right then and there. God was and is always ready to send encouragement.

Prayer

Give us courage and hope in our troubles, and and bring us the joy of your salvation. Amen

Alternative Service Book 1980

RobG

Exodus 6:1–6, 8 (NRSV)

A promise is a promise

Then the Lord said to Moses, 'Now you shall see what I will do to Pharaoh. Indeed, by a mighty hand he will let them go; by a mighty hand he will drive them out of his land.' God also spoke to Moses and said to him: 'I am the Lord. I appeared to Abraham, Isaac, and Jacob as God Almighty, but by my name "The Lord" I did not make myself known to them. I also established my covenant with them, to give them the land of Canaan, the land in which they resided as aliens. I have also heard the groaning of the Israelites whom the Egyptians are holding as slaves, and I have remembered my covenant. Say therefore to the Israelites, "I am the Lord, and I will free you from the burdens of the Egyptians and deliver you from slavery to them... I will bring you into the land that I swore to give to Abraham, Isaac, and Jacob; I will give it to you for a possession. I am the Lord."'

'I am the Lord' is repeated three times in this passage, to assure Moses that although it may not seem like it, he can be absolutely sure that what God has promised will be fulfilled. God has heard the 'groaning' of the people of Israel and will set them free.

When we suffer, when we are sad, when we fear what may happen to us in the future, we can take courage by remembering that God has made promises to us his chosen people, through Christ Jesus, and he will not fail to keep them. God's love is constant and continuing, and his promise of rescue for us is certain too, through the cross and resurrection of our Lord.

We sometimes pass through dark and difficult times. It may be due to circumstances beyond our control, it may be because of blatant disobedience or because of foolishness, but that does not mean that God has forgotten us, or that he no longer loves us. We can be certain that he will reach out and give us the best.

For the Israelites, redemption means not only release from slavery and suffering, but also deliverance to freedom and joy.

Thanksgiving

We thank you that through the waters of the Red Sea you led your people out of slavery into the promised land; we thank you that through the deep waters of death you brought your son and raised him to life in triumph.

Alternative Service Book 1980

RobG

Exodus 7:1–13 (NRSV, abridged)

Encouragement

The Lord said to Moses, 'See, I have made you like God to Pharaoh, and your brother Aaron shall be your prophet. You shall speak all that I command you, and your brother Aaron shall tell Pharaoh to let the Israelites go out of his land. But I will harden Pharaoh's heart, and I will multiply my signs and wonders in the land of Egypt. When Pharaoh does not listen to you, I will lay my hand upon Egypt and bring my people the Israelites, company by company, out of the land of Egypt by great acts of judgment. The Egyptians shall know that I am the Lord...' Moses and Aaron did so; they did just as the Lord commanded them... Aaron threw down his staff before Pharaoh and his officials, and it became a snake. Then... the magicians of Egypt did the same by their secret arts... but Aaron's staff swallowed up theirs. Still Pharaoh's heart was hardened, and he would not listen to them.

So the battle begins—the battle between God and Pharaoh. I was once in a musical called *Annie Get your Gun*. One of the duets was between me and Annie. We sang a song entitled 'Anything you can do, I can do better'—a real battle of the sexes. In this situation it was a battle between Pharaoh who considered himself a god and God who *is* God, and there could only be one winner. Pharaoh was obstinate and defiant to the nth degree. So much so that he would have to learn the same lesson several times. The tale of the plagues at first sight may look like the actions of a God who continues to inflict pain and suffering to indulge in continuous punishment. But we soon discover a merciful God who gives Pharaoh chance after chance to soften his heart, repent and accept God's sovereignty. This theme of the sovereignty of God is linked with two other important ideas. First, that through the experience of his power the Egyptians will come to recognize that God is God, and second, that his power is used for and through those who obey him and against those who refuse to obey. God allows Pharaoh to do as he wants to do. But there is a heavy price to pay.

Reflection

'The price he paid for wood and nails cost his life, but the price was right for the Cross shows love that never fails.'

From a millennium song by Robyn Barnett

RobG

Exodus 7:20—8:19 (NRSV, abridged)

Blood, sweat and prayers

Moses and Aaron did just as the Lord commanded. In the sight of Pharaoh and of his officials he lifted up the staff and struck the water in the river, and all the water in the river turned to blood, and the fish in the river died. But the magicians did the same by their secret arts; so Pharaoh's heart remained hardened. So Aaron stretched out his hand over the waters of Egypt; and the frogs came up and covered the land of Egypt. But the magicians did the same. Then Pharaoh called Moses and Aaron, and said, 'Pray to the Lord to take away the frogs from me and my people.' But Pharaoh hardened his heart, and would not listen. Aaron stretched out his hand with his staff and struck the dust of the earth, and gnats came on humans and animals alike. The magicians tried to produce gnats by their secret arts, but they could not. And the magicians said to Pharaoh, 'This is the finger of God!' But Pharaoh's heart was hardened, and he would not listen to them.

In these last three days of my notes, I shall be looking at the nine plagues in three groups of three. Once you've experienced one plague, it just gets worse subsequently. There is a progression. One plague logically follows another. The river turns red and all life dies. The frogs hop out on to dry land and subsequently invade the houses and courtyards, and die from feeding off bacteria from the dead fish. This leaves rotting frogs, which in turn encourage disease and the breeding of mosquitoes in the stagnant flood waters.

Pharaoh's magicians were so eager to impress him that they simply added their trickery to the plagues and made the situation twice as bad. However, they were unable to imitate the third plague and gave up, acknowledging that 'this is the finger of God' (8:19). God had at least driven home his point with them. But with Pharaoh it was going to be a long-drawn-out saga before he would let the people go.

After the second plague, Pharaoh recognizes the power of the God of Moses and asks Moses to pray that he will take away the plague of frogs. Prayer is God's means of executing his will on earth. The plagues occurred at the initiative of God; the plagues ceased in answer to prayer.

Reflection

Let us pray.

RobG

Exodus 8:20—9:3 (NRSV, abridged)

Only fools and pharaohs

Then the Lord said to Moses, 'Rise early in the morning and present yourself before Pharaoh, and say to him, "Thus says the Lord: Let my people go, so that they may worship me. For if you will not let my people go, I will send swarms of flies on you, your officials, and your people... But on that day I will set apart the land of Goshen, where my people live, so that no swarms of flies shall be there, that you may know that I the Lord am in this land. Thus I will make a distinction between my people and your people..."' Pharaoh hardened his heart this time also. Then the Lord said to Moses, 'Go to Pharaoh, and say to him, "Thus says the Lord: Let my people go, so that they may worship me. For if you refuse to let them go and still hold them, the hand of the Lord will strike with a deadly pestilence your livestock in the field: the horses, the donkeys, the camels, the herds, and the flocks."'

The second set of three plagues followed a new pattern affecting only the Egyptians. God did this so that people might learn that he is the true God who controls the whole world and everything in it, even the livestock. The Egyptians thought that each god controlled a certain town or piece of land where he was worshipped. These plagues confirmed that the Israelites were the people of God and not the people of Pharaoh. Pharaoh had treated the Israelites as if he owned them. He forced them to act as slaves. He needed to learn that the Israelites belonged to a greater king, who was determined that they would be set free.

Pharaoh knows that Moses is not asking for a temporary freedom to offer sacrifices, but a permanent freedom from his service. So Pharaoh tries to set limits. They must worship the Lord in Egypt (8:25); they must not go far. Later he demands that only the men should leave (10:11). So he goes on, trying to retain control and authority. But because he is fighting with the true God, the battle is already lost. He is, however, facing a merciful God, and is given chance after chance after chance, until eventually he decides for himself to turn his back on God.

A thought for Pharaoh

When the wicked man turneth away from his wickedness that he hath committed, and doeth that which is lawful and right, he shall save his soul alive.

Ezekiel 18:27, AV

RobG

Exodus 9:22—10:29 (NRSV, abridged)

Hail and damnation

The Lord said to Moses, 'Stretch out your hand toward heaven so that hail may fall on the whole land of Egypt, on humans and animals and all the plants of the field.' And the Lord sent thunder and hail, and fire came down on the earth. Only in the land of Goshen, where the Israelites were, there was no hail. Pharaoh sinned once more and hardened his heart, he and his officials. So Moses and Aaron went to Pharaoh, and said to him, 'Thus says the Lord, "How long will you refuse to humble yourself before me? Let my people go, so that they may worship me."' Moses stretched out his staff and the locusts settled on the whole country of Egypt. The Lord said, 'Stretch out your hand toward heaven so that there may be darkness for three days.' But Pharaoh was unwilling to let them go. Then Pharaoh said to Moses, 'Get away from me! Take care that you do not see my face again, for on the day you see my face you shall die.' So Moses said, 'Just as you say! I will never see your face again.'

Here we have the last of the three sets of plagues. These are of cosmic proportions. Fire and brimstone, pestilence, and the darkness of death. After each plague Pharaoh offers concessions. First Pharaoh agrees to let the men go, but wants to keep the women and children and livestock. Then he agrees to let the men, women and children go, but not the livestock. But God has promised to deliver them all, and there is no room for negotiation. There can be no salvation without full repentance. Those who ignore God's word lose everything.

Pharaoh was free at any time to let Israel go, as he was no puppet in the hands of God. The Lord gives everyone the utmost respect. Yet God had promised to deliver his people. Pharaoh's rebellious nature and God's sovereignty were on a collision course of cosmic proportions. We should remember that God is the Potter and we are the clay. God is prepared to forgive Pharaoh each time he asks, but each time it proves not to be true repentance and so it changes nothing. Finally Pharaoh turns his back on Moses and on God. 'Just as you say! I will never see your face again,' says Moses. It is once again Pharaoh's free choice, and Pharaoh chooses death, not life.

Reflection

Choose life!

RobG

Romans 1:16–17 (NRSV)

The heart of the gospel

For I am not ashamed of the gospel; it is the power of God for salvation to everyone who has faith, to the Jew first and also to the Greek. For in it the righteousness of God is revealed through faith for faith; as it is written, 'The one who is righteous will live by faith.'

'The trouble is,' said the minister, 'my people do not believe that we have anything to offer that others really want.' Our culture is not gospel-friendly. We find ourselves apologizing for taking the gospel seriously, or keeping quiet about the fact that we are Christians.

It is said that the early Church grew because it never occurred to it not to. Convinced of the truth, relevance and power of its message, it went out boldly to proclaim it, believing that others would not want to miss out on the good news that was being offered. Paul himself suffered much for the faith. He was beaten, imprisoned and ridiculed but nothing could stop him proclaiming its truth. He would not be shamed into silence.

The message of salvation was not only the assurance of life beyond the grave, but also a present discovery of release from the tyranny of sin. Instead of feeling lost and confused we discover life full of meaning and purpose. As Charles Wesley writes, 'He breaks the power of cancelled sin, he sets the prisoner free.'

Note the crucial significance of faith. It helps salvation come alive in our own experience. It enables us to discover the very nature of God and his righteousness. Through faith we make our own what God offers us freely through the life, death and resurrection of Jesus. The goal is to live a righteous life. This means right behaviour based on a right relationship with God and a right understanding of his nature. It is the life of faith which begins with openness and receptivity to what God longs to share with us. It goes on to mental assent and understanding, which leads to total surrender and obedience. Faith, therefore, is the means of discovering God's salvation (through faith) and living out the life of discipleship (for faith).

Prayer

Thank you, Lord, for the gift of faith and the reality of salvation. Deepen my faith so that in total surrender I might live out the life of righteousness and true discipleship.

PG

Romans 1:18, 24–25 (NRSV)

The wrath of God

For the wrath of God is revealed from heaven against all ungodliness and wickedness of those who by their wickedness suppress the truth… Therefore God gave them up in the lusts of their hearts to impurity, to the degrading of their bodies among themselves, because they exchanged the truth about God for a lie and worshipped and served the creature rather than the Creator, who is blessed for ever!

Romans 1:18—2:16 does not make easy reading in our day. We do not like to think of judgment. Tolerance dominates our thinking and 'live and let live' is the order of the day. This passage is a healthy corrective to the secular values that permeate our culture. A moral God in a moral universe cannot blindly ignore our rebellion. If God were indifferent to moral questions, this would be an imperfection in his character and thus would deny his very nature. These verses show just how low we humans can sink. We fall deeper and deeper into sin almost to the point where we cannot tell good from evil. Paul is convinced that there is no excuse. Even the heathen should have seen the hand of God in creation and honoured the Creator. Instead we prefer to be our own God and bypass our maker.

The wrath of God is the opposite of salvation and faith. We are confronted by God but refuse to glorify and honour him. We long to be independent instead of recognizing his lordship, and so we manufacture other gods or idols so that we can obtain control.

It is not that God rejects us because of our sins. Rather he 'gives us up'. In other words he lets us stew in our own juice. As Leon Morris puts it: 'God pays us the compliment of taking our freedom seriously. He does not constrain us to serve him, but when we choose the wrong he sees to it that we go along with our choice and that we experience what that choice means.'

'In failing to make room for God,' says Graeme Rutherford, 'human nature self-destructs.'

Reflection and prayer

How deep is my commitment to Christian living? Have I really acknowledged Christ as Lord of all? What am I going to do about it?

Thank you, Lord, for loving us enough to care when we do wrong. Show us the better way and grant us the power to live it. Amen

PG

Romans 3:21–25a (NRSV)

God's work of salvation

But now, apart from law, the righteousness of God has been disclosed, and is attested by the law and the prophets, the righteousness of God through faith in Jesus Christ for all who believe. For there is no distinction, since all have sinned and fall short of the glory of God; they are now justified by his grace as a gift, through the redemption that is in Christ Jesus, whom God put forward as a sacrifice of atonement by his blood, effective through faith.

Here Paul considers the basic question: how can we get right with God?

To the Jews, it was through obeying the law. Unfortunately, though, we can never be good enough to keep it. The emphasis is always upon our struggle to earn God's acceptance. The Christian emphasis is on the grace of God and what he has done for us, especially through the cross and resurrection. He offers the free gift of love and forgiveness. Our response is simply one of humble acceptance and trust.

To help us understand Christ's work of salvation, Paul uses three images from contemporary life. The image of justification comes from the law courts. We stand guilty, arraigned before a judge. But instead of condemning us, he treats us just as if we had never sinned. He says in effect, 'You have been my enemy, but now you are going to be my friend.' It would have been shocking to the Jews to treat the bad person as though he were good, and yet this is exactly what Jesus does.

The next image is that of redemption. It comes from the slave market. A price is paid, the slave is set free. There is nothing superficial or sloppy about it. God does not treat sin lightly. After all, our salvation cost Jesus his life. The third image comes from the Jewish sacrificial system. The aim of temple sacrifices was to turn aside the punishment that should rightly fall upon us. Now the supreme sacrifice has been made. This opens the door to peace with God.

No wonder the gospel is good news. The cross makes us conscious of sin without being terrorized by it. We enter a right relationship through believing with all our hearts that what Jesus told us about God is true. We are no longer strangers cowering before an angry God but wayward children who trust the Father's love and seek his forgiveness.

For meditation

Amazing love! How can it be
That thou, my God, shouldst die for me?

Charles Wesley (1707–88)

PG

Romans 4:2–5 (NRSV)

The faith of Abraham

If Abraham was justified by works, he has something to boast about, but not before God. For what does the scripture say? 'Abraham believed God, and it was reckoned to him as righteousness.' Now to one who works, wages are not reckoned as a gift but as something due. But to one who without works trusts him who justifies the ungodly, such faith is reckoned as righteousness.

We can never earn God's favour, and never be justified by the works of the law. Salvation is completely dependent upon God's grace, made our own through faith. Responding to those who would insist that Christian converts keep the whole Jewish law, Paul skilfully uses Abraham to illustrate what true faith is like.

Many Jews would have seen Paul's emphasis upon trust rather than obedience to the law as a completely new idea. In reality, though, says Paul, this is the very basis of the Jewish religion. Abraham was the pattern of true faith. God had called him to leave his home and livelihood and challenged him to venture out in faith. Then he would become the father of a great nation. It was not his obedience to the law that put him in a special relationship to God, rather his willingness to cast himself totally on God's wisdom, promise, grace and power.

Today many would emphasize faithfulness at the expense of faith. Faithfulness is, of course, absolutely vital. Many a church would have closed but for the faithful service of a few devoted servants who kept going through difficulty. However, this is not the heart of the gospel. Faithfulness can degenerate into the plod of duty. It can be deeply committed to keeping things as they always have been and, as such, tends to be rather static. Faith, on the other hand, never gets bogged down in the limitations of the present but ever looks forward to what might be. It is always giving birth to a new dream. It is an adventure of love that involves putting our hands in the hand of God and letting him lead us forward into all truth. As Gerard Hughes has said, 'God is a beckoning word. He calls us out of ourselves and beyond ourselves. He is the God of surprises, always creating anew.'

Prayer

In the adventure of faith, Lord, help me to discover you as the God of surprises, ever leading me into new truth.

PG

Romans 5:1–5 (NRSV)

Peace and perseverance

Therefore, since we are justified by faith, we have peace with God through our Lord Jesus Christ, through whom we have obtained access to this grace in which we stand; and we boast in our hope of sharing the glory of God. And not only that, but we also boast in our sufferings, knowing that suffering produces endurance, and endurance produces character, and character produces hope, and hope does not disappoint us, because God's love has been poured into our hearts through the Holy Spirit that has been given to us.

Trusting faith brings peace with God. Jesus ushers us into his very presence. Indeed the word translated 'access' came to mean harbour or haven. It is as if by our own efforts we flounder in a stormy sea, but thanks to God's grace we are given the assurance of our salvation. We know we are accepted, loved and forgiven, which in turn leads to the peace which enables us to cope when the going gets tough. After all, 'if you want the rainbow, you have to put up with the rain'!

Unlike the Stoics, who approached their sufferings with a 'that's life, we must grin and bear it' approach, Christians can handle their troubles with joy. We know they are all part of a process which God uses to help us grow and discover more of his love and power. Indeed, positive faith recognizes that 'there is no oil without squeezing the olives, no wine without pressing the grapes, no fragrance without crushing the flowers, and no real joy without sorrow'.

Here Paul shows how faith helps us face suffering. Being under pressure, he says, fosters endurance—the determined spirit that actively overcomes and conquers trials and tribulations. This in turn fosters 'character', a word that speaks of metal which has passed through fire to be purged of impurities and thus strengthened. Such character produces hope. This enables us to meet life head-on, knowing that God will give us the strength we need. Such hope is a spur to triumphant action, and a challenge to true greatness. As Lord Reith put it, 'I do not like crises, but I like the opportunities they provide!' Thanks to God's love made real to us by the Holy Spirit, such hope will not fail us. It has a sure foundation!

Prayer

Thank you, Lord, for the relevance and power of positive faith. Strengthen me in times of trial and help me to keep on growing!

PG

Romans 5:8–11 (NRSV)

While we were yet sinners

But God proves his love for us in that while we still were sinners Christ died for us. Much more surely then, now that we have been justified by his blood, will we be saved through him from the wrath of God. For if while we were enemies, we were reconciled to God through the death of his Son, much more surely, having been reconciled, will we be saved by his life. But more than that, we even boast in God through our Lord Jesus Christ, through whom we have now received reconciliation.

One of the dominant notes of evangelical revival in the eighteenth century was the sense of sheer wonder and amazement that God actually cares for each one of us! The great hymn of Charles Wesley reflects this:

And can it be that I should gain
An interest in the Saviour's blood?
Died he for me who caused him pain,
For me who him to death pursued?

The initiative is always with God. The cross shows us how much he loves us and how far he was prepared to go to bring us wayward children home to the Father. It was while we were still in a state of enmity, hostility and rebellion as sinners that Christ gave his life for us.

Although Christ loves us just as we are, he loves us too much to leave us there. Through his death we are reconciled to God, loved, accepted, and treated 'just as if we had never sinned'. This, though, is but the beginning of a process of transformation. We need to be saved by his life (v. 10); to be open to the moulding of the Holy Spirit, so that as we participate in the life of Christ we become more like him. After all, Jesus is not just our saviour, but also the Lord, who deserves trust, honour and obedience. This is the process of sanctification about which John Wesley said, 'If we are looking for anything other than perfect love, we are looking wide of the mark.' As our love for God deepens, it is reflected in our love for our fellow human beings. The more we are transformed by the love of God, the more we can share that love with others.

Reflection

Were the whole realm of nature mine,
That were an offering far too small.
Love so amazing, so divine,
Demands my soul, my life, my all.

Isaac Watts (1674–1748)

PG

Romans 6:1–4, 11 (NRSV)

Continue in sin? Certainly not!

What then are we to say? Should we continue in sin in order that grace may abound? By no means! How can we who died to sin go on living in it? Do you not know that all of us who have been baptized into Christ Jesus were baptized into his death? Therefore we have been buried with him by baptism into death, so that, just as Christ was raised from the dead by the glory of the Father, so we too might walk in newness of life... So you also must consider yourselves dead to sin and alive to God in Christ Jesus.

If salvation is all of grace, it could well be argued that sin is good for us because it gives grace more chance to operate. Here Paul emphasizes that Christians are committed to a different lifestyle and must not make the mercy of God an excuse for disobedience. Jesus did not need to die so that we could merely tinker around with a basically secular lifestyle. Rather we need a life-transforming friendship with him.

Note that baptism in the first decades of the Church would normally have been for adults and was certainly intimately connected with a confession of faith. Many converts moved directly from paganism. Thus baptism marked a clear dividing line. Indeed, the practice of total immersion emphasized that discipleship was about dying and rising with Christ.

A group of young Latin Americans became Christians. All of them had been baptized as babies but none had ever been involved in the Church until their conversion. They now wanted a ceremony to set a seal upon the new life they had discovered. Realizing they could not be baptized again, the pastor developed his own service. He borrowed some coffins. Each of the new Christians lay down in one. The lid was closed until the Pastor banged three times upon the coffin lid and said, 'In the name of the Father, the Son and the Holy Spirit, arise to the new life in Christ.' They got out pretty quickly, but never forgot that Christianity is a matter of life and death and not just piecemeal improvement.

Prayer

In my heart of hearts, Lord, I know that discipleship means radical transformation. Forgive my superficiality and let the pattern of dying and rising with Christ grip my mind and mould my character. Amen.

PG

Romans 6:20–23 (NRSV)

True freedom

When you were slaves of sin, you were free in regard to righteousness. So what advantage did you then get from the things of which you now are ashamed? The end of those things is death. But now that you have been freed from sin and enslaved to God, the advantage you get is sanctification. The end is eternal life. For the wages of sin is death, but the free gift of God is eternal life in Christ Jesus our Lord.

In the Methodist Centre on St Simon's Island, Georgia, there are a few small slave huts that have now been restored as a kind of living museum. Looking through the window of one of them, I noticed on the wall a poster showing the Twelve Steps of Alcoholics Anonymous. Now every week a group meets to support each other as they journey from slavery to freedom.

Slavery is a somewhat dated term for modern ears. But we can understand the concept of addiction, which is very much a modern form of slavery. The way to wholeness begins with recognition of one's need. Speaking to the AA group, a member begins by saying, 'I am an alcoholic. It has been so many weeks, or years, since my last drink.' Such an acceptance of reality, matched with a commitment to transformation and determined action, leads to wholeness. Many would testify to the fact that it was only when they had acknowledged their need for help from a power outside of themselves that they were really set free for the first time. Resolution and commitment made all the difference in the world.

Human beings have a natural tendency to drift into sin and make all manner of excuses for doing so. In the eternal battle between good and evil, we have to choose our side. It is not the restraint of the law but the inspiration of grace that will liberate us from sin and inspire us to be better than we ever dreamed possible. As verse 23 reminds us, the wages of sin is death. That is the consequence that has been rightly earned. Alternatively, the free gift of God is eternal life. That involves a real commitment to Christ and a determination to journey on the way of discipleship.

Prayer

Teach me, Lord, that the way of true freedom can only come through commitment. Inspire me by your love to move forward on the way to holiness. Amen.

PG

Romans 7:19–20, 24–25 (NRSV)

The inner battle

For I do not do the good I want, but the evil I do not want is what I do. Now if I do what I do not want, it is no longer I that do it, but sin that dwells within me... Wretched man that I am! Who will rescue me from this body of death? Thanks be to God through Jesus Christ our Lord!

At great length he confessed the high ideals yet constant failure so typical of alcoholics. Having listened long, the minister simply began to quote the words of our Bible passage today. As he finished, the man said, 'I don't know who wrote that, but he must have been an alcoholic like me.' This true story beautifully illustrates the power of scripture to speak to human experience. We are all a bundle of contradictions, knowing what is right but powerless to do it.

Dominated by a sense of failure and weakness, many have interpreted Romans 7 as a description of life before conversion, whereas chapter 8 emphasizes the joy, freedom and optimism of the committed Christian.

Note that the verbs in verses 7–13 are all in the past tense, whereas verses 14–25 are in the present tense. Paul implies that even for Christians the battle against sin continues to be a real struggle. Indeed, we need ever to hold before ourselves, in creative tension, both the pain of imperfection and the joy of assurance, hope and victory.

Verses 24 and 25 are certainly a cry of anguish, but not despair. Although deliverance has been won by the unique sacrifice of the cross, our appropriation of it is all part of the process of sanctification—growing into holiness. At times we will lapse. Indeed, the more we grow in holiness, the more we realize our own sinfulness. This passage is full of realism. We dare not pretend but, with ruthless honesty, need to bring our sins openly to God. Our sin is a throwback to the old life, but it forces us to examine again our commitment and realize the need to trust God instead of relying on our own resources. Then we can acknowledge our need and seek his forgiveness.

Prayer

Lord, the more I grow the more I realize how much I need your help and strength. Help me to keep my eyes firmly fixed on you so that I can move forward in faith. Amen.

PG

Romans 8:14–17a (NRSV)

The spirit of adoption

For all who are led by the Spirit of God are children of God. For you did not receive a spirit of slavery to fall back into fear, but you have received a spirit of adoption. When we cry, 'Abba! Father!' it is that very Spirit bearing witness with our spirit that we are children of God, and if children, then heirs, heirs of God and joint heirs with Christ...

Michael was going through something of an identity crisis. At twenty years of age, away from home for the first time as a university student, he had to come to terms with his being adopted. He felt rejected and alone, wondering who he really was. With the skilful help of a counsellor, he was able to come to terms with his situation. Reflecting on that difficult time, he said, 'All my feelings were dominated by the anger I felt towards my natural mother. I should have focused on my adoptive parents. After all, they deliberately chose, loved and cared for me. Now I rejoice in what I have, rather than bemoan what I have lost. At long last I feel wanted, accepted, loved and free. Instead of taking my adoptive parents for granted, I am really grateful for them.'

Paul uses the image of adoption to stress the importance of relationships rather than natural parentage. Jesus is, of course, the unique Son of God but Christians are adopted as God's children. In the Roman empire, adoption was not uncommon. Once the complicated legal transaction was over, the adopted son gained all the rights of a legitimate child in his new family. He had legally become a new person. Consequently all the debts and obligations of the old life were abolished and all the privileges of the new were inherited.

Sin cuts us off from God, making us orphans. By grace we are forgiven, given eternal life and, by adoption, we become children of God again. This we can do with assurance. Adoption ceremonies were carried out in the presence of seven witnesses. Should a dispute arise, a witness would be called in to testify to the genuineness of the adoption. The Holy Spirit is our witness that we are adopted into the family of God and, as such, is a guarantee of our inheritance.

Prayer

We marvel, Lord of the universe, that you long for us to call you Father. Thank you for such wonderful love. Help us to respond with trust and obedience.

PG

Romans 8:18, 24–25, 28 (NRSV)

Working together for good

I consider that the sufferings of this present time are not worth comparing with the glory about to be revealed to us... In hope we were saved... If we hope for what we do not see, we wait for it with patience... We know that all things work together for good for those who love God, who are called according to his purpose.

These are just the verses to read in difficult times. They inspire hope and confidence in the God who can be trusted.

Note the tremendous stress on realism. The sufferings of the present time may be horrific. Indeed, the early Church endured persecution and martyrdom. However, belief in God inspires the kind of hope that has seen everything, endured everything and still has not despaired. As Bishop Trevor Huddleston puts it, 'Christian hope is not blind optimism. Optimism assumes things will get better. Christian hope is about looking life in the face and finding God at the centre.'

Such hope inspires trust. Not only is there the deep conviction of the reality of life beyond the grave but also the assurance that God can use even bad experiences to further his purposes. Indeed, it is as we find the strength to cope with our difficulties that we grow in our faith and discover more of the resources of God's love and power.

During the Second World War, a group of prisoners in the Nazi concentration camp at Ravensbrück gathered to read and study the Bible together. They read the challenge to thank God for everything. 'But how can we thank God for the fleas that invade this hut?' asked Corrie ten Boom. Her sister Betsy replied, 'It says in scripture we must thank God for everything. That surely includes the fleas!' With reluctant obedience, Corrie eventually thanked God even for the fleas. Much later, the prisoners realized that the only reason they had been able to have their Bible study meetings with such ease was that the guards were afraid of entering the hut. They were fearful of being infested by the fleas themselves! All things really do work together for good to them that love God.

Prayer

Thank you, Lord, for the way you have used difficult circumstances in my life and brought good out of them. Help me to be ever open to the work of your Spirit so that I might not lose heart but move forward in hope. Amen.

PG

Romans 8:35, 37–39 (NRSV)

Wonderful love!

Who will separate us from the love of Christ? Will hardship, or distress, or persecution, or famine, or nakedness, or peril, or sword? ... No, in all these things we are more than conquerors through him who loved us. For I am convinced that neither death, nor life, nor angels, nor rulers, nor things present, nor things to come, nor powers, nor height, nor depth, nor anything else in all creation, will be able to separate us from the love of God in Christ Jesus our Lord.

I recently saw a picture of the hands of God carefully holding a trusting child. The little one was surrounded by the love that gives security. This is very much the picture that Paul paints here. God's love upholds us.

Wilf had suffered much but, reflecting on his time in hospital, he said, 'It is not my hold on God that matters, but his hold on me. It is his love that has sustained me. I know I am not alone, but I am surrounded by his love. He understands and he will see me through.'

Paul had just summed up the themes of chapters 5 to 8 in a few brief sentences. He now draws his argument together by emphasizing that if we belong to Jesus we are safe in his love for all eternity. We have no need to fear condemnation, for Jesus is on our side, standing to plead our cause as our friend, interceding for us. With such support, no matter what life throws at us we will be able to cope. Be it persecution, the spiritual powers of earth and hell, or any of the uncertainties of life and death, nothing will ever be able to separate us from God's marvellous love.

Helmut Gollwitzer was carried off to Russia as a German prisoner of war. With his hopes of freedom fading daily, he wrote in his diary, 'The great ideas have vanished... It is essential that I have someone whom I love and who loves me. That is what gives meaning to my life and is therefore the ground of my happiness.' He knew something of the love about which Paul is speaking here.

Prayer

Thank you, Lord, for your love that knows no limits, and for your promise that 'underneath are the everlasting arms' which will never let me fall. Help me to trust and obey you so that my discipleship will be more real and vital. Amen.

PG

Romans 12:1–2 (NRSV)

Living sacrifice

I appeal to you therefore, brothers and sisters, by the mercies of God, to present your bodies as a living sacrifice, holy and acceptable to God, which is your spiritual worship. Do not be conformed to this world, but be transformed by the renewing of your minds, so that you may discern what is the will of God—what is good and acceptable and perfect.

Having considered the questions of righteousness, the way of salvation and the problem of the Jews as God's chosen people, Paul now opens a new section of his epistle and deals with practical questions of life and living. Chapter 11 closes magnificently with a wonderful ascription of praise to God for all his love and mercy. Now Paul calls for response.

In the Old Testament, Jews dealt with sin by offering animal sacrifices in the temple. Naturally this involved killing the beast. Although we have died with Christ, we have also been raised with him, so it is appropriate that our offering should not involve just a religious ritual but rather the living of our lives in such a way as to show our gratitude for all God's mercy. William Temple helpfully points out that many Christians think work is important and worship helps us do it. If, however, worship is the offering of our whole self to God, then our daily life is part of that worship.

J.B. Phillips translates verse 2, 'Don't let the world round about you squeeze you into its own mould, but let God remould your mind from within.' It really is too easy to go with the crowd. We all respond to peer group pressure. It takes a lot of courage to stand firm for our principles when others think them irrelevant or outdated. The way of Christian discipleship involves an inner transformation. It is as we seek to put Christ in the centre of our living, instead of our own selfish desires, that our mind and will are changed. In short, we take his teaching seriously and live under the guidance of the Holy Spirit. When God has given us so much, this is the least we can do to show our gratitude.

Prayer

Forgive me, Lord, that all too often I have let the world squeeze me into its own mould. Remould my mind from within, I pray, that I might live to your glory. Amen

PG

Romans 12:4–8 (NRSV)

Many members—one body

For as in one body we have many members, and not all the members have the same function, so we, who are many, are one body in Christ, and individually we are members one of another. We have gifts that differ according to the grace given to us: prophecy, in proportion to faith; ministry, in ministering; the teacher, in teaching; the exhorter, in exhortation; the giver, in generosity; the leader, in diligence; the compassionate, in cheerfulness.

As a young minister, I served for several years as an ecumenical chaplain at what is now a major university. Meeting with chaplains to other colleges in London, I can remember feeling overwhelmed by the different approaches, theologies and styles of ministry in which my colleagues were engaged. I felt strongly that I could never do all those things and some of them were just not in my nature. A great burden was lifted when I realized that I did not have to be a copy of anybody else. I could only be effective if I was authentically me. Although others had an approach that was valid for them, my approach had to be the one for my situation.

Here Paul is stressing the importance of every-member ministry. Each of us has been given gifts by the Holy Spirit to be used for the building-up of the body of Christ. We all have different functions, which need to complement each other so that the whole Church can move forward in harmony.

These verses emphasize our need to know ourselves, and to recognize and accept our gifts for what they are. It is not good to envy the gifts of others or complain about what we do not have. Rather we must celebrate the gifts God has given us and use them to his glory for the common good.

Note that the gifts of God are freely given by his grace. They are not achieved by our own efforts. Therefore there is no reason for us to boast in what we can do. Rather we must be sure to give of our best, develop our gifts and ensure that we use them in harmony with others. We all need each other if the body is to be united and effective in service.

Prayer

Thank you, Lord, for the gifts you have given me. Help me to develop and use them effectively in your service and also to encourage others so that together we work in harmony. Amen.

PG

Romans 12:9–13 (NRSV)

In trouble—stand firm!

Let love be genuine; hate what is evil, hold fast to what is good; love one another with mutual affection; outdo one another in showing honour. Do not lag in zeal, be ardent in spirit, serve the Lord. Rejoice in hope, be patient in suffering, persevere in prayer. Contribute to the needs of the saints; extend hospitality to strangers.

We stood in the church in the centre of Shanghai. It was an inspiration to experience its vitality and growth and know that God had used the awful years of persecution that Christians in China had experienced during the Cultural Revolution from 1966 to 1976. 'What did you do in those years?' we asked. Our guide simply replied, 'We could not worship or openly share our faith. But we could pray, read the Bible and hope: a hope that was richly fulfilled when the church reopened in 1979.' These words are a living illustration of Paul's teaching as translated in the New English Bible: 'Let hope keep you joyful, in trouble stand firm, persist in prayer.' They sum up the Christian way of facing difficulty.

Christian discipleship involves genuine and practical love which leads to enthusiastic service, but it is inspired by faith.

Joy comes from inner serenity, deep trust and forward-looking hope. It has been well said that 'peace is joy resting, and joy is peace praising'. Joy and peace are born of the conviction that God does not let us down but rather gives us the strength to cope, no matter what happens. This enables us to stand firm even when the going gets tough.

Prayer deepens our relationship with God. Because Jesus was a man like us, he understands our situation, gets alongside us in our need, and really cares for each one of us. It is through prayer that our relationship with God deepens. We not only discover new depths in our own personality, but also the strength that comes directly from him. 'Courage is fear that has said its prayers.' This enables us to move forward in faith, trust and confidence. As the old negro prayer says, 'Lord, help me to understand that there's going to be nothing coming my way that you and me together can't handle.'

Prayer

Thank you, Lord, for those in every age who have stood firm in time of trouble. Inspire me by their courage, and help me to stand firm when the going gets tough. Amen.

PG

Romans 12:14–17, 21 (NRSV)

Overcome evil with good

Bless those who persecute you; bless and do not curse them. Rejoice with those who rejoice, weep with those who weep. Live in harmony with one another; do not be haughty, but associate with the lowly; do not claim to be wiser than you are. Do not repay anyone evil for evil, but take thought for what is noble in the sight of all... Do not be overcome by evil, but overcome evil with good.

Make me a channel of your peace.
Where there is hatred let me bring your love;
Where there is injury your pardon, Lord,
And where there's doubt, true faith in you.

Have you ever noticed that in this famous hymn based on the prayer of Francis of Assisi, every negative is turned into a positive? This is a profoundly Christian approach to life. It gets to the heart of the teaching of Jesus, and is the core of the principles for human relationships that are the subject of Paul's teaching here.

We are challenged to meet persecution with prayer for the persecutor and to seek harmony and peace. Humility is vital. We should not only share the sorrows of others but also rejoice with those who rejoice. Sometimes that is harder than weeping with those who weep, for envy and jealousy are very negative emotions that can sometimes poison our own approach to the success of others.

When confronted with evil, injustice and hatred, it is all too easy to be twisted by the anger of the moment and want to do evil in return. Thus a negative spiral develops. It is imperative that someone nips the evil in the bud and tries to turn it into good. No one claims that this is easy but it is part of what is meant by love, and love is the heart of the gospel.

It is said that 'faith is the darkroom that changes our negatives into positives'. The following prayer applies this principle to life.

Prayer

Lord, grant me, I pray,
courage when the best things fail me,
calm and poise when storms assail me,
common sense when things perplex me,
a sense of humour when they vex me,
hope when disappointments damp me,
wide visions when life cramps me,
kindness when folk need it badly,
readiness to help them gladly,
and when effort seems in vain—
wisdom to begin again.

PG

Romans 14:13–15, 19 (NRSV)

Practical love

Let us therefore no longer pass judgment on one another, but resolve instead never to put a stumbling block or hindrance in the way of another. I know and am persuaded in the Lord Jesus that nothing is unclean in itself; but it is unclean for anyone who thinks it unclean. If your brother or sister is being injured by what you eat, you are no longer walking in love. Do not let what you eat cause the ruin of one for whom Christ died... Let us then pursue what makes for peace and for mutual upbuilding.

'For whom Christ died': T.R. Glover described these as 'four words that destroyed slavery'. On the cross Jesus shows how much he cares for each one of us. Every individual matters and we dare not treat another human being as if he were no more than our property or a tool to be used.

Chapters 12—15 deal with practical questions as we try to put Christian love into practice. In a Roman market it would have been virtually impossible to find meat that had not been slaughtered in a heathen temple. Christians asked if, by buying it, they were supporting paganism. Some gave up eating meat and became vegetarians. Others, however, felt it was *people* who were heathen, not meat, so there was no problem. Others would have been deeply concerned to keep the Jewish dietary laws. Paul says that these are not the important things. You may be liberal in your interpretation and that is probably right, for it is not the law but freedom which is at the heart of Christian experience. However, we may not use our freedom to ride roughshod over the genuine feelings of others. It is not our place to judge, attack or criticize those who have more scruples. We dare not give in to irritation, ridicule or contempt. We need to approach those with whom we differ in a spirit of sensitivity and love. We are our brother's keeper and we dare not put a stumbling block in the way of another.

Sincere Christians differ on a whole variety of moral questions. The important thing is that we should not offend those who differ from us. Sometimes it is good to abstain so as not to offend others and lead them away from the path of Christian commitment.

Prayer

Thank you, Lord, for those whose example has inspired me in my own pilgrimage of faith. Help me never to be a stumbling block to others, but rather a living example of the sensitivity and love of Jesus. Amen.

PG

Ezekiel 1:1–3 (NRSV)

The hand of the Lord

In the thirtieth year, in the fourth month, on the fifth day of the month, as I was among the exiles by the river Chebar, the heavens were opened, and I saw visions of God. On the fifth day of the month (it was the fifth year of the exile of King Jehoiachin), the word of the Lord came to the priest Ezekiel son of Buzi, in the land of the Chaldeans by the river Chebar; and the hand of the Lord was on him there.

What is 'the hand of the Lord'? It's a question you can't avoid in this book, where it occurs time and again. It seems to speak of God's involvement in human life (in this case, of course, Ezekiel's life)—his presence *with* him, his influence *on* him, his power *in* him. Rather like a parental hand on the shoulder, pushing in the right direction, the hand of the Lord isn't always what we, or Ezekiel, exactly *want*, but it is irresistible.

In these opening verses, we are introduced to the mystical involvement of God in the activity of prophecy. Ezekiel was already a priest (v. 3), but now, among the wretched Jewish exiles, he was to receive the gift of prophecy: 'The word of the Lord came to... Ezekiel.'

In many ways, this call is a picture of what all true vocation means—being 'called' to serve God, and given the necessary gifts to do it. That call comes at the right time—though nobody seems to know what the 'thirtieth year' actually refers to!—and to a specific person. It's for a specific purpose, too. And it requires a new openness to the will of God: 'The heavens were opened, and I saw visions of God' (v. 1).

Not all vocations involve such extraordinary and dramatic events, of course. My own call to ministry, for instance, occurred in a car during a late-night conversation outside a house in the West End of London—very prosaic! But however it comes, a call involves in some way or other a 'vision of God', a new perception of his purpose for us. And we shall feel 'the hand of the Lord' upon us.

Reflection

'The hand of the Lord' is pressure urging us in the right direction. But it is the pressure of love, not compulsion.

DW

Ezekiel 1:4–9 (NRSV)

The awesome power of God

As I looked, a stormy wind came out of the north: a great cloud with brightness around it and fire flashing forth continually, and in the middle of the fire, something like gleaming amber. In the middle of it was something like four living creatures. This was their appearance: they were of human form. Each had four faces, and each of them had four wings. Their legs were straight, and the soles of their feet were like the sole of a calf's foot; and they sparkled like burnished bronze. Under their wings on their four sides they had human hands. And the four had their faces and their wings thus: their wings touched one another; each of them moved straight ahead, without turning as they moved.

All sorts of things happen in storms in the Bible! The ark of Noah survived a storm, a stormy wind blew back the waters to let the Israelites escape from Egypt, Elijah sat through a storm before hearing the 'still, small voice of God', Jesus calmed the storm on Galilee… and a memorable storm marked his crucifixion.

Storms, for the people of the biblical world, spoke of the awesome power of God. Not knowing their explanation nor their likely outcome, for them storms put human power and majesty into a truer perspective. They would not have been surprised (though they might well have been apprehensive) to find God speaking to them in a storm.

Here the stormy wind came 'out of the north', a cloud with fire flashing from it, for all the world like the 'fire and cloudy pillar' of the wilderness journey. But in the middle of it were 'something like' four living creatures. ('Something like' is visionary or dream language, of course.) 'Living creatures' in Ezekiel are invariably angelic beings. As they approached, the prophet became aware of the details of their appearance. Their wings touched in perfect symmetry and unity of purpose. Yet 'they were of human form'.

God's power is as terrible and irresistible as a desert storm, true. But that power is not indiscriminate, nor crude, nor uncaring. God knows what he's doing!

Reflection

Perfect power, perfectly controlled.
This is our God.

DW

Ezekiel 1:10–14 (NRSV)

Images of the divine

As for the appearance of their faces: the four had the face of a human being, the face of a lion on the right side, the face of an ox on the left side, and the face of an eagle; such were their faces. Their wings were spread out above; each creature had two wings, each of which touched the wing of another, while two covered their bodies. Each moved straight ahead; wherever the spirit would go, they went, without turning as they went. In the middle of the living creatures there was something that looked like burning coals of fire, like torches moving to and fro among the living creatures; the fire was bright, and lightning issued from the fire. The living creatures darted to and fro, like a flash of lightning.

A few years ago I invited the top class in our village school to 'draw God'. I had tried to explain to them that no one had ever 'seen' God—that he is Spirit, not flesh and blood, as we are. But I suppose I thought they would still all draw old men with beards, kindly-looking grandpas —or, possibly, try to depict Jesus. I was quite wrong. When their drawings were revealed, they included a lion, an eagle, a mountain top, a smiling face, a sunrise—and not a single old man in the clouds! I realized that in their own way they were trying to draw not 'God', but the *qualities* of God—what God is 'like'.

I then read them this remarkable vision of God that Ezekiel had long ago. Unlike the average congregation or Bible study group, they seemed quite unfazed by it. Yes, this was how they 'saw' God, too: power, superiority, strength and personality. Or, to put it in pictures, a lion, an eagle, an ox—and a human being. They had added a few elements of their own, of course: beauty, kindness, love.

Of course, this vision—thus far—is of the cherubim who bore the mighty vehicle of divine majesty. Yet their faces seem to reflect the divine image in terms that even a child can understand. Powerful, like a lion; higher than we can ever soar, like an eagle; strong to help, like an ox; and yet relating to us, 'like a human being'.

Reflection

How do you 'see' God? Jesus said, 'He who has seen me has seen the Father.' Are these the qualities of the divine which we see in him, too?

DW

Ezekiel 1:15–20 (NRSV)

Wheels within wheels

As I looked at the living creatures, I saw a wheel on the earth beside the living creatures, one for each of the four of them. As for the appearance of the wheels and their construction: their appearance was like the gleaming of beryl; and the four had the same form, their construction being something like a wheel within a wheel. When they moved, they moved in any of the four directions without veering as they moved. Their rims were tall and awesome, for the rims of all four were full of eyes all around. When the living creatures moved, the wheels moved beside them; and when the living creatures rose from the earth, the wheels rose. Wherever the spirit would go, they went, and the wheels rose along with them; for the spirit of the living creatures was in the wheels.

The expression 'wheels within wheels' is quite well known in English—it usually refers to double-dealing—machinations beneath the surface! But it comes from this amazing vision of the 'vehicle' which carries the throne of God. It is a wheeled contraption driven, as it were, by the 'living creatures', splendidly adorned and gleaming. But its most important feature is its astonishing ability to move in any direction 'without veering'. This was engineering unknown to the ancient world, especially with its ability to move in all four directions, not only horizontally, but vertically as well. It 'rose from the earth'—like a helicopter!

The modern reader may well puzzle over the meaning of all of this. What possible relevance can this have to our daily life—to housework, or office or school? Yet essentially it's both clear and very relevant. The power and knowledge of God (his 'eyes all around') cannot be limited by space or time. He knows all, sees all and can respond to all. Nowhere is beyond the bounds of his involvement. His cherubic chauffeurs can take his 'throne' *anywhere*.

Reflection

The psalmist knew the meaning of this vision. Just look at Psalm 139! 'Where can I flee from your presence?'—not to heaven, because he's there. Not to Sheol, the place of the dead, because he's there too. In darkness or light, the God who knows and sees all can respond to every situation in which we find ourselves.

DW

Ezekiel 1:26–28a (NRSV)

A glimpse of God's glory

And above the dome over their heads there was something like a throne, in appearance like sapphire; and seated above the likeness of a throne was something that seemed like a human form. Upwards from what appeared like the loins I saw something like gleaming amber, something that looked like fire enclosed all around; and downwards from what looked like the loins I saw something that looked like fire, and there was a splendour all around. Like the bow in a cloud on a rainy day, such was the appearance of the splendour all around. This was the appearance of the likeness of the glory of the Lord.

At last the prophet is allowed to see the passenger in the marvellous vehicle! Everything in the vision so far has been a preamble to this. The cherubim, the wheels, the flashing fire, the eyes all round, the crystal dome: all are there to serve just one purpose—to be a splendid vehicle for the glory of the Lord, Yahweh.

And now Ezekiel is given just a glimpse of his glory. It is all described in visionary language, summed up in the beautiful simile of verse 28: 'Like the bow in a cloud on a rainy day, such was the appearance of the splendour all around.' This awesome 'likeness of the glory of the Lord', in other words, has the gentle beauty of a rainbow!

The other insistent image is of 'something like a human form' (v. 26). Mind you, this 'human form' is gleaming amber from the waist up and blazing fire from the waist down, so there was no danger of Ezekiel thinking of God as a 'mere mortal'. It reminds the Christian reader of the vision of Christ in Revelation 1:12–16. This is glory and splendour and power, but in a *Person*. God is much more than a cosmic dynamo!

Reflection

Seated on the throne of creation in glorious splendour is 'something that seemed like a human form'. Several hundred years later, people on earth were privileged to see that 'human form' of the divine in Jesus, the 'Son of Man'.

DW

Ezekiel 1:28b—2:5 (NRSV)

Shut off from the truth

When I saw it, I fell on my face, and I heard the voice of someone speaking. He said to me: O mortal, stand up on your feet, and I will speak with you. And when he spoke to me, a spirit entered into me and set me on my feet; and I heard him speaking to me. He said to me, Mortal, I am sending you to the people of Israel, to a nation of rebels who have rebelled against me; they and their ancestors have transgressed against me to this very day. The descendants are impudent and stubborn. I am sending you to them, and you shall say to them, 'Thus says the Lord God.' Whether they hear or refuse to hear (for they are a rebellious house), they shall know that there has been a prophet among them.

Here, for the first of many times in this book, God addresses Ezekiel as *ben adam*, literally 'son of man', or, as the NRSV translates it, 'mortal'. It was, of course, a title which Jesus took to himself, as one who was truly and completely human—indeed, all that a human being was meant to be. Here, in the context of divine messages and angelic figures, it serves to underline both Ezekiel's human status and also the tremendous responsibility which he, as a 'mere mortal', was being given.

At the voice of God he 'fell on his face', but he was commanded to 'stand up on his feet' in order to listen to the divine message. 'And when he spoke to me, a spirit entered into me and set me on my feet' (v. 2). A similar experience, in similar circumstances, befell the seer of Revelation (1:17). The 'son of man' fell to the ground before the voice of God, but the Spirit of God set him on his feet. Any call of God is always *both* humbling *and* enabling.

Then Ezekiel learnt what his task was to be. He was to speak in God's name to the people of Israel, in the midst of their suffering and torment. But his message would not, at first at least, be one of comfort. They had to learn that this suffering was the consequence of their rebellion. Now, 'whether they hear or refuse to hear', they would have the word of God spoken to them (v. 4) and 'know that there had been a prophet among them' (v. 5). They might be chastened, in other words, but they would not be abandoned.

Reflection

Refusing to hear the voice of God does not mean that what he has said is not true. It just means that we have shut ourselves off from the truth.

DW

Ezekiel 2:6–10 (NRSV)

Not popular, but faithful

And you, O mortal, do not be afraid of them, and do not be afraid of their words, though briers and thorns surround you and you live among scorpions; do not be afraid of their words, and do not be dismayed at their looks, for they are a rebellious house. You shall speak my words to them, whether they hear or refuse to hear; for they are a rebellious house. But you, mortal, hear what I say to you; do not be rebellious like that rebellious house; open your mouth and eat what I give you. I looked, and a hand was stretched out to me, and a written scroll was in it. He spread it before me; it had writing on the front and on the back, and written on it were words of lamentation and mourning and woe.

Before he could deliver God's message, Ezekiel needed to understand the extent of the resistance he would have to face. His message would be highly unpopular. Indeed, it would contain 'words of lamentation, mourning and woe' (v. 10). This must not dismay him nor deflect him from the task. God's prophets are not called to be popular, but faithful. That is never an easy lesson to learn, because it is a basic human instinct to want to be liked!

To reinforce the point, a 'hand' stretched out to the prophet, offering him a scroll with writing on it. He was told to eat it. (Think of the phrase about 'eating our words'!) It was not *his* message, but God's. But it would have to become part of him, as food becomes part of the body. He wasn't free to change, alter or water down the message, miserable though it might be, because it wasn't his. But he had to deliver it: that was his responsibility to the One who commissioned him. He was only, as Billy Graham memorably puts it, the 'messenger boy'.

Reflection

The church that sets out to be popular will probably only succeed in being superficial. The Christian whose decisions are shaped by popular approval will probably end up without either the approval of the people around or, more seriously, of God.

DW

Ezekiel 3:1–3 (NRSV)

A bitter-sweet message

He said to me, O mortal, eat what is offered to you; eat this scroll, and go, speak to the house of Israel. So I opened my mouth, and he gave me the scroll to eat. He said to me, Mortal, eat this scroll that I give you and fill your stomach with it. Then I ate it; and in my mouth it was as sweet as honey.

When Ezekiel was offered the scroll with words of 'lamentation, mourning and woe' his heart must have sunk. After all, the people to whom he was to carry God's message were already suffering—defeat at the hand of the Babylonians and a major deportation from Jerusalem and Judah. His own ministry was to be to the exiles 'by the river Chebar' (1:3) at Tel-Abib (3:15). Was there to be no word of hope for them, no comfort from the God of Israel?

Well, here we learn that if there *was* to be comfort, it would be from facing the truth, not continuing to avoid it. In a visionary moment, he was given this woeful scroll to eat—a bitter morsel, one would have thought! But he found to his surprise that in his mouth it was 'as sweet as honey' (3:3). In the words of Jesus, 'You will know the truth, and the truth will set you free' (John 8:32). There is, after all, no real comfort in delusion. Many of us have had to learn that in life the hard way, by painful experience. In the old saying, it's no use 'burying our heads in the sand'—nothing changes by shutting our eyes to it.

So this was to be Ezekiel's bitter-sweet message for the exiled Jews. There *was* hope, but only in repentance and obedience. Continued obstinacy and disobedience would bring even worse consequences, as we learn in the rest of his book—indeed, the destruction of Jerusalem itself.

Reflection

All through the Bible, and all through human history, the truth has been bitter-sweet: sweet if it is received and acted upon, bitter if it is ignored or rejected. In a nutshell, that is the message of this book.

DW

Ezekiel 3:4–7, 10–11 (NRSV)

The unwelcome message

He said to me: Mortal, go to the house of Israel and speak my very words to them. For you are not sent to a people of obscure speech and difficult language, but to the house of Israel—not to many peoples of obscure speech and difficult language, whose words you cannot understand. Surely, if I sent you to them, they would listen to you. But the house of Israel will not listen to you, for they are not willing to listen to me; because all the house of Israel have a hard forehead and a stubborn heart… He said to me: Mortal, all my words that I shall speak to you receive in your heart and hear with your ears; then go to the exiles, to your people, and speak to them. Say to them, 'Thus says the Lord God'; whether they hear or refuse to hear.

Now comes the moment of Ezekiel's prophetic commissioning. He has the message. He has felt the 'hand of the Lord' upon him. His mouth has discovered the sweetness of the truth. Now he must 'go'… but not very far! He is not being sent to an alien people, or to those who can't understand his language. These are *his* people (v. 11). He knows them, understands how they feel, identifies with them completely. Yet his message will not fall easily on their ears. They'll understand his words, no problem; but they won't be the words they want to hear, and, as my grandma used to say, 'There's none so deaf as those who will not hear.'

This is a familiar problem to God's people in every age. We ask God to speak to us, to show us what to do and where to go. But when he does, and we find it doesn't fit in with our own preferences, we reject it. In my own experience, it's seldom that I don't know what God is saying to me. The problem is, I don't want to do it!

Reflection

'Lord, show me the way.' But, more than that, when you have, help me to follow it.
DW

Ezekiel 3:14–17, 21 (NRSV)

Obedience—or compromise?

The spirit lifted me up and bore me away; I went in bitterness in the heat of my spirit, the hand of the Lord being strong upon me. I came to the exiles at Tel-Abib, who lived by the river Chebar. And I sat there among them, stunned, for seven days. At the end of seven days, the word of the Lord came to me: Mortal, I have made you a sentinel for the house of Israel; whenever you hear a word from my mouth, you shall give them warning from me. If I say to the wicked, 'You shall surely die,' and you give them no warning, and do not speak to warn the wicked from their wicked way, in order to save their life, those wicked persons shall die for their iniquity; but their blood I will require at your hand… If, however, you warn the righteous not to sin, and they do not sin, they shall surely live, because they took warning; and you will have saved your life.

So the prophet sets out on a mission that can spell either salvation or disaster to his fellow Jews, depending on their response to his message. He was a pretty reluctant messenger! 'I went in bitterness in the heat of my spirit, the hand of the Lord being strong upon me' (v. 14). But 'the spirit (surely this should have a capital S?) lifted me up and bore me away,' to the very people who were already suffering most, the Jewish refugees by the river Chebar. So the reluctant preacher meets the equally reluctant congregation!

For seven days he sat among them, silent and 'stunned' (v. 15). Why? Perhaps because he needed to know what it was like to be an exile before he could preach to exiles. Perhaps because he needed time to make God's message his own. Or perhaps (hinted at in verse 16) because the specific 'word of the Lord' for this situation had not yet come to him. When it did, at the end of the seven days, it came with a fresh commission and a renewed command: 'I have made you a sentinel for the house of Israel… you shall give them warning from me' (v. 17). Failure to give the warning would mean that he shared in the people's sin (see vv. 18–20). But faithfulness would bring its own blessings, both for them and for him: 'they shall live… and you will have saved your life' (v. 21).

Reflection

This passage may seem quite remote from my everyday experience. Yet it has an important spiritual lesson. Costly obedience is a better option than soft compromise.

DW

Philippians 4:4–7 (NRSV)

Peace through prayer

Rejoice in the Lord always; again I will say, Rejoice. Let your gentleness be known to everyone. The Lord is near. Do not worry about anything, but in everything by prayer and supplication with thanksgiving let your requests be made known to God. And the peace of God, which surpasses all understanding, will guard your hearts and your minds in Christ Jesus.

It was the end of term and a student came to discuss some personal problems. She was a deeply committed young woman in her early twenties. She was carrying problems far greater than most people her age would ever have to face. We talked and prayed together and I promised to see her again the following term. She returned a new woman. 'How's things?' I asked. 'They're OK now,' she said. 'It's not that the problems have gone away, but I have found the strength to cope.' She went on to speak about the peace that passes all understanding. The world wants to escape from problems and so did she, but now she had discovered true peace which comes from knowing that God is with us. After all, the verse does not say that he will take the problems away, but rather that he will guard our hearts and minds in Christ Jesus. The healing comes in the relationship that sustains and strengthens us. For 'sometimes the Lord calms the storm, but sometimes he lets the storm rage and calms the child'.

This passage also gives us the secret of success. Positive faith is emphasized by the words 'rejoice' and 'with thanksgiving'. This fosters trust, which is far more helpful than worry. After all, worry is like a rocking chair. It gives you something to do but it doesn't get you anywhere! Of course we need to be concerned, but whereas worry leads to panic, concern leads to action. Prayer is part of that concern. It must though be positive prayer. We pray with thanksgiving, not constantly dwelling on our problems but rather offering our problems to God and thanking him for strength and guidance to see us through. In short, we claim his victory and make it our own. In so doing, we find the peace that passes all understanding.

Reflection

Be still and know that I am God!
God is our refuge and strength,
a very present help in time of trouble.
Psalm 46

PG

8.3

PHILIPPIANS 4:4–7 NRSV

Peace through prayer

Rejoice in the Lord always; again I will say, Rejoice. Let your gentleness be known to everyone. The Lord is near. Do not worry about anything, but in everything by prayer and supplication with thanksgiving let your requests be made known to God. And the peace of God, which surpasses all understanding, will guard your hearts and your minds in Christ Jesus.

THIRD QUARTER

Under the Hand of God

Ecclesiastes 2:1, 4–11 (NRSV, abridged)

Seen this, done that

I said to myself, 'Come now, I will make a test of pleasure; enjoy yourself'... I made great works; I built houses and planted vineyards for myself; I made myself gardens and parks, and planted in them all kinds of fruit trees... I bought male and female slaves, and had slaves who were born in my house; I also had great possessions of herds and flocks... I also gathered for myself silver and gold and the treasure of kings and of the provinces; I got singers, both men and women... and many concubines... Whatever my eyes desired I did not keep from them... Then I considered all that my hands had done and the toil I had spent in doing it, and again, all was vanity and a chasing after wind, and there was nothing to be gained under the sun.

'You can have it all,' the smiling faces proclaim from the newsagent's shelves. The perfect body, the elegant lifestyle, the ideal partner, the designer baby—all these can be yours too, if you really try. If life is so futile, why not just live it up?

The Teacher (the author of this book), 'when king over Israel in Jerusalem' (1:12), had the money and the power to test it out. You name it, he did it. 'Work hard, play hard' could have been his motto.

It's a cliché to say smugly of the super-rich: 'Well, it doesn't bring them happiness.' The king was happy enough at the time. 'My heart,' he says, 'found pleasure in all my toil, and this was my reward' (v. 10). After all, he was 'creating wealth', wasn't he? But suddenly: 'I hated all my toil... seeing that I must leave it to those who come after me—and who knows whether they will be wise or foolish?' (2:18–19)

For throughout his punishing programme of pleasures, the king has kept a wider perspective: 'also my wisdom remained with me' (v. 9). However much wine he drank, he could never forget his mortality and his desire for a greater truth.

Be honest: at times we all fancy 'having it all' (well, I do...). Blessed are those who don't need to try it, in order to find out that 'fading is the world's best pleasure'.

Confession

Lord, I admit that part of me would like to give indulgence a try. Help me to keep in sight the 'solid joys and lasting treasure, none but Zion's children know'.

VZ

Ecclesiastes 3:1–8 (NRSV)

A sense of timing

For everything there is a season, and a time for every matter under heaven: a time to be born, and a time to die; a time to plant, and a time to pluck up… a time to kill, and a time to heal; a time to break down, and a time to build up; a time to weep, and a time to laugh; a time to mourn, and a time to dance; a time to throw away stones, and a time to gather stones together; a time to embrace, and a time to refrain from embracing; a time to seek, and a time to lose; a time to keep, and a time to throw away; a time to tear, and a time to sew; a time to keep silence, and a time to speak; a time to love, and a time to hate; a time for war, and a time for peace.

How long, O Lord? How long before I find the right partner… before I get another job? How long must I endure this illness… this unhappy relationship? How long before my children turn to you?

If only we knew exactly what was coming, we could prepare for it. Just give me a glimpse of the future, Lord. Tell me what's to become of me and I'll stop running around trying to fix everything.

Who's never glanced at their horoscope 'just to see what rubbish it is' or consulted a village fête fortune-teller 'for a laugh'? Congratulations if you haven't, but I confess I have. We all want to know about tomorrow, however much we remind ourselves that 'each day has troubles enough of its own'. 'Eye has not seen, nor ear heard, what God has prepared for those who love him'—but can't God give us a sneak preview?

The writer of Ecclesiastes has lived long enough to develop a wise, patient understanding of how life unfolds. This is not fatalism or resignation; it is a sense that every event of life has its place in God's overarching providence. One action may be appropriate for a young couple; another for an elderly widow. Wisdom weighs up all things with the aid of God's Spirit; for, as older translations say, 'he has set eternity in [our] hearts' (v. 11). Only from the eternal viewpoint will we understand.

Prayer

Teach us to number our days aright, that we may gain a heart of wisdom.

Psalm 90:12, NIV

VZ

Ecclesiastes 4:1–3 (NRSV)

'There's no justice...'

Again I saw all the oppressions that are practised under the sun. Look, the tears of the oppressed—with no one to comfort them! On the side of their oppressors there was power—with no one to comfort them. And I thought the dead, who have already died, more fortunate than the living, who are still alive; but better than both is the one who has not yet been, and has not seen the evil deeds that are done under the sun.

A rape victim, soon after her ordeal, stood on a beach and considered drowning herself. It is the ultimate protest against the injustice of life—to say, 'I wish I'd never been born, I'd be better off dead.' Job utters this cry when his troubles have come upon him: 'Why did I not die at birth... why was I not buried like a stillborn child?' (Job 3:11, 16). And often the voluntarily childless say, 'I wouldn't want to bring a child into this evil world'—a form, in my view, of 'suicide by proxy'.

Yet those in closest contact with suffering often have a much more positive attitude. Yesterday on television I heard someone observe that aid workers who return from war or disaster do not usually say, 'Because of the terrible things I have seen, I no longer believe in God.' On the contrary, they say, 'Only God can help this situation' or, 'Please pray for the people there.'

'The Teacher' too, for all his grim observations, does not leave us with 'Life's a bitch and then you die.' Like little gleams of golden thread woven into a tapestry, he keeps hinting at a more positive view of life:

'There is nothing better for mortals than to eat and drink, and find enjoyment in their toil. This also, I saw, is from the hand of God...' (2:24).

'I said in my heart, God will judge the righteous and the wicked, for he has appointed a time for every matter...' (3:17).

'Two are better than one... For if they fall, one will lift up the other' (4:9–10).

Satisfaction in work, the hope of eventual justice, the companionship of working together—these are everyday compensations for the apparent futility of life. And as we read on, there is yet greater hope to come.

Reflection

The light shines in the darkness, and the darkness has never mastered it.

John 1:5

VZ

Ecclesiastes 5:1–2; 8:2–4 (NRSV)

Talking religion and politics

Guard your steps when you go to the house of God; to draw near to listen is better than the sacrifice offered by fools; for they do not know how to keep from doing evil. Never be rash with your mouth, nor let your heart be quick to utter a word before God, for God is in heaven, and you are on earth; therefore let your words be few...

Keep the king's command because of your sacred oath. Do not be terrified; go from his presence, do not delay when the matter is unpleasant, for he does whatever he pleases. For the word of the king is powerful, and who can say to him, 'What are you doing?'

In the banqueting hall of a sixteenth-century house I sometimes visit, there is carved over one door, 'Dread God' and over the other, 'Honour the king'. Those two pieces of advice seem to sum up Ecclesiastes' recipe for a quiet life. In both religion and politics, less talk and more action might be a good policy.

The 'Wisdom' literature often suggests that to 'fear God' is the beginning of wisdom (Proverbs 1:7). We are getting our first glimpse of the wider perspective here, for we have turned from looking at 'the daily round, the common task' to how we encounter God. And the first lesson we need to learn is our own smallness: 'What are human beings that you are mindful of them?' (Psalm 8:4).

The political lesson is similar: don't rush in where angels fear to tread. Where government is sincerely trying to do good, we owe it respect.

But wait a minute—wasn't the writer biased? After all, he had been king! Don't most of us, by God's grace, live in a world where we can and should call the powers-that-be to account? Weren't the prophets appointed to do just that? And are we not encouraged by Job, and even Jesus, sometimes to ask God himself what on earth he's up to?

I suspect that the writer of Ecclesiastes, the great questioner, would not disagree. But here he is advocating a basic attitude of reverence. When we question or challenge those in authority, that itself expresses our respect for the concept of authority. When we question God, it should express our commitment to God.

Reflection

'Everyone must submit to the governing authorities, for there is no authority except that which God has established.'

Romans 13:1

VZ

Ecclesiastes 8:14–15, 9:7–10 (NRSV, abridged)

Don't worry, be happy

There is a vanity that takes place on earth, that there are righteous people who are treated according to the conduct of the wicked, and there are wicked people who are treated according to the conduct of the righteous... So I commend enjoyment, for there is nothing better for people under the sun than to eat, and drink, and enjoy themselves... Go, eat your bread with enjoyment, and drink your wine with a merry heart, for God has long ago approved what you do. Let your garments always be white; do not let oil be lacking on your head. Enjoy life with the wife whom you love, all the days of your vain life that are given you under the sun... Whatever your hand finds to do, do with your might; for there is no work or thought or knowledge or wisdom in Sheol, to which you are going.

During my time in an Anglican parish, I went every Ash Wednesday to the service of 'imposition of ashes'. The priest would smear a cross of ashes on our foreheads, reciting 'Dust thou art, and to dust thou shalt return.' I used to find it a curiously comforting rite, somehow putting life in proportion.

'The same fate comes to all' (9:2), 'the Teacher' tells us repeatedly in his musings on life and death. The Hebrew scriptures have little view of a life beyond death; 'Sheol' is a kind of half-life, a long way from the Christian hope of resurrection. 'Who knows whether the human spirit goes upward and the spirit of animals goes downward to the earth?' says Ecclesiastes in 3:21.

In the uncertainty and inequality of life, then, the best thing you can do is to make the most of the good gifts this earth offers: food, drink, dressing up, companionship. The writer is not advocating self-centred luxury, just a simple, unassuming life in which work is included among the daily satisfactions.

There is much to be said for this—as far as 'under the sun' goes. But what about beyond that? For all his perplexity, 'the Teacher' is sure that evil will not triumph, for, 'Though sinners do evil a hundred times and prolong their lives, yet I know that it will be well with those who fear God' (8:12).

Declaration

I know that my Redeemer lives...
in my flesh I shall see God.
Job 19:25, 26

VZ

Ecclesiastes 12:1–8 (NRSV, abridged)

Now or never

Remember your creator in the days of your youth, before the days of trouble come, and the years draw near when you will say, 'I have no pleasure in them'; before the sun and the light and the moon and the stars are darkened and the clouds return with the rain; in the day when the guards of the house tremble… and the women who grind cease working because they are few, and those who look through the window see dimly… because all must go to their eternal home, and the mourners will go about the streets; before the silver cord is snapped, and the golden bowl is broken, and the pitcher is broken at the fountain, and the wheel broken at the cistern… and the breath returns to God who gave it. Vanity of vanities, says the Teacher; all is vanity.

Have we returned to where we began? Are we left with nothing but 'vanity'? Not exactly. This wonderful poem (I wish we could include it all) may be about old age, or approaching death, or global disaster—or all three. It is a powerful picture of a world from which the joy and flavour has gone. But the crucial part is the opening line: 'Remember your creator in the days of your youth.'

I am one of those people who's planning to join the Society of Procrastinators… tomorrow. But at sixteen, when the minister asked me whether I was ready to be baptized, I had the strong feeling, 'If I don't do this now, I will regret it all my life.' So I did.

We have said that Ecclesiastes is the work of an ageing person. But it is ultimately addressed to the young. Our relation to God is not something we can shelve until we're less busy having fun. When the fun palls, we may no longer have the faith to approach God.

Throughout his writings, 'the Teacher' has tested the limits of what we can know as we live 'under the sun'. But he concludes with a much greater reality: 'The end of the matter; all has been heard. Fear God, and keep his commandments; for that is the whole duty of everyone. For God will bring every deed into judgement, including every secret thing, whether good or evil' (12:13–14).

Reflection

Abide in him, so that when he is revealed we may have confidence and not be put to shame before him at his coming.

1 John 2:28

VZ

Mark 11:1–6 (NRSV)

Preparing for the triumphal ride

When they were approaching Jerusalem, at Bethphage and Bethany, near the Mount of Olives, he sent two of his disciples and said to them, 'Go into the village ahead of you, and immediately as you enter it, you will find tied there a colt that has never been ridden; untie it and bring it. If anyone says to you, "Why are you doing this?" just say this, "The Lord needs it and will send it back here immediately."' They went away and found a colt tied near a door, outside in the street. As they were untying it, some of the bystanders said to them, 'What are you doing, untying the colt?' They told them what Jesus had said; and they allowed them to take it.

Jesus and his men had walked the long uphill road of over twenty miles from Jericho to Jerusalem. Little wonder, you might say, that he chose to *ride* into the city! But there is more to that choice than this. It was a well-planned gesture, the fulfilment of Zechariah 9:9: 'Lo, your king comes to you; triumphant and victorious is he, humble and riding on a donkey, on a colt, the foal of a donkey.'

There is a touch of the secret undercover operation here. The availability of the colt could have been set up beforehand. The theory that this is an instance of Jesus' 'supernatural prescience' seems unnecessary.

To us, the picture of Jesus riding on a donkey invites ridicule. Bring such a creature into the arena at an equine event and people will laugh, regarding it as an invitation to 'send in the clowns'. Donkeys in our culture are derided as one of God's creative jokes; and to dub someone a 'silly ass' is not exactly a compliment. But donkeys were more respectfully regarded by the Jews of Jesus' day.

To choose to ride into Jerusalem on a young donkey meant that he came as the Prince of Peace. It was a dramatic Messianic gesture. Generals victorious in war rode on horseback. And the reason why this colt had hitherto never been ridden was that the law required it of an animal to be used for a sacred purpose.

Reflection

In a 1631 edition of the Bible, Psalm 14:1 mistakenly omits the word 'not'. It reads, 'The fool hath said in his heart there is a God.' How far am I prepared to be a 'fool for Christ's sake'?

CE

Mark 11:7–11 (NRSV)

Cloaks and branches

Then they brought the colt to Jesus and threw their cloaks on it; and he sat on it. Many people spread their cloaks on the road, and others spread leafy branches that they had cut in the fields. Then those who went ahead and those who followed were shouting, 'Hosanna! Blessed is the one who comes in the name of the Lord! Blessed is the coming kingdom of our ancestor David! Hosanna in the highest heaven!' Then he entered Jerusalem and went into the temple; and when he had looked around at everything, as it was already late, he went out to Bethany with the twelve.

Were some of those who fêted Jesus as he rode into Jerusalem making fun of him? Mingling with his genuine supporters who hailed him with their hosannas, was there some kind of rent-a-mob mocking him? Was the crowd made up of two very different groups—the one, a smallish band of his true followers; the other, the others? A fanciful idea, granted; but it may explain the cloaks and branches.

Those who put their cloaks down on the road, the true followers, may have done so to prevent the colt from slipping, much as Jehu the fast charioteer had his fellow officers do the same on the steps when he was made king (2 Kings 9:13). Others wouldn't risk their own clothing under hoof, donkeys not being house-trained, so they snapped off branches from wayside trees, other people's trees. It is worth noting, however, that green branches were often waved about at festival time; and the 'Hosanna' verses from Psalm 118:25–26 were shouted out, 'Hosanna' meaning 'save now!'

Anyone can offer the Lord devotion with branches from someone else's field. The cross looms up darkly across the Christian way and confronts those who sport it as a trinket or wear it as a witness with the discomfiting question: is ours a cheap, undemanding religion—the kind with the cross removed?

The cloaks, by contrast, represent costly discipleship. We sing of it at Christmas: 'Say, shall we yield him, in costly devotion, odours of Edom and offerings divine.' The carol goes on to state that 'richer by far is the heart's adoration'. Truly to offer that is, in fact, more expensive than any external gift.

Reflection

What do I mainly expect from the ministry of the Church, and how far am I prepared to go in the service of the Church?

CE

Mark 11:12–14, 20–21 (NRSV)

Miserable non-producers!

On the following day, when they came from Bethany, he was hungry. Seeing in the distance a fig tree in leaf, he went to see whether perhaps he would find anything on it. When he came to it, he found nothing but leaves, for it was not the season for figs. He said to it, 'May no one ever eat fruit from you again.' And his disciples heard it... In the morning as they passed by, they saw the fig tree withered away to its roots. Then Peter remembered and said to him, 'Rabbi, look! The fig tree that you cursed has withered.'

Jesus may well have been hungry, but he must have known that figs would be out of season at that time of year (April–May). It is way out of character for him to be so petulant as to curse a tree because it didn't supply him with a little breakfast *en passant*. Nor was he, we believe, a kind of first-century Merlin with magic powers.

We are actually dealing here with a kind of parable, as in Luke 13:6–9. It is probable that Jesus saw Israel as a barren fig tree not yielding the fruit of righteousness and good works expected of it as the chosen people. Its fate under God was rejection. I remember, at school, the consequence of failing to do one's homework, or 'prep', as we called it. One teacher had you up before the whole class and scornfully arraigned you with the cry, 'Miserable non-producer!' Such was Israel in the sight of God.

We are in this world to use to the utmost our gifts, talents, energies and resources, all supplied by our Maker, as useful members of society. In the very first Psalm, the obedient and godly person is compared to a tree growing beside a stream and bearing fruit. When John the Baptist thundered out his hell-fire preaching on the banks of the Jordan, he warned his Jewish contemporaries, the chosen people, that every tree not bearing good fruit would be cut down and thrown on to the bonfire. Jesus made it clear that his followers must bear much fruit.

Prayer

Lord God, may our lives be fruitful in your service. Amen.

CE

Mark 11:15–18 (NRSV)

The upsetting of vested interests

And he entered the temple and began to drive out those who were selling and those who were buying in the temple, and he overturned the tables of the money changers and the seats of those who sold doves; and he would not allow anyone to carry anything through the temple. He was teaching and saying, 'Is it not written, "My house shall be called a house of prayer for all the nations"? But you have made it a den of robbers.' And when the chief priests and scribes heard it, they kept looking for a way to kill him; for they were afraid of him, because the whole crowd was spellbound by his teaching.

Pilgrims flocking into Jerusalem were faced with an annual temple tax. On average it amounted to two days' wages, to be paid in a particular currency known as the 'shekel of the sanctuary'. The temple, therefore, had its own foreign currency desk. A charge was made of half-a-day's wage to exchange currency for the correct kind. Some money changers undoubtedly took their cut by overcharging.

People also had to make a sacrificial offering of a pair of doves or pigeons, which could be bought outside for nine pence. The chances were that these would have been turned down as imperfect. The visitor then had to buy his birds from the inside sellers—at twenty times the outside rate. And, making the whole swindle considerably worse, the family of none other than the high priest Annas had a major share in the temple shops.

Enter an angry Jesus, throwing his weight about, rough-handling everyone and everything in sight and quoting Isaiah 56:7 ('My house shall be called a house of prayer for all peoples') and Jeremiah 7:11 ('Has this house, which is called by my name, become a den of robbers in your sight?'). The temple had become a thieves' kitchen of sleazy profiteering.

The temple, according to Isaiah, was intended by God to be a 'house of prayer *for all peoples*'. The precincts were patrolled by temple police, but only to ensure that the detailed *ritual* regulations weren't broken. The authorities confined Gentiles to their outer court far from access to the Holy of Holies, the very presence of God at the heart of the building.

Reflection

Bishop Runcie once criticized his Church for making it difficult for people to 'come to Christ' by, as he put it, tightening passport regulations to font and altar.

CE

194

Mark 12:1–5 (NRSV)

The vineyard allegory (part 1)

Then he began to speak to them in parables. 'A man planted a vineyard, put a fence around it, dug a pit for the wine press, and built a watchtower; then he leased it to tenants and went to another country. When the season came, he sent a slave to the tenants to collect from them his share of the produce of the vineyard. But they seized him, and beat him, and sent him away empty-handed. And again he sent another slave to them; this one they beat over the head and insulted. Then he sent another, and that one they killed. And so it was with many others; some they beat, and others they killed.'

Israel was a nation seething with unrest and risky to live in. A wealthy man with property might well let it out to others and then go and live in calmer, pleasanter surroundings—like those today who might live in Spain or the Bahamas and draw their wherewithal from land or business back home. Tenants of a vineyard could pay their rent in currency or by handing over an agreed percentage of the crop. Some tenants were known to refuse payment, and the owner's representatives were sometimes assaulted.

Like *The Pilgrim's Progress*, this story is an allegory. The vineyard is Israel, the landowner God, the tenants the priests and politicians; and the slaves sent to collect their master's share of the harvest are the prophets, who were often ill-treated, sometimes killed. The story highlights the abuse of privilege and the greed that drives human beings to appropriate what belongs to others. Those tenants were given every advantage. Their employer had fenced the vineyard to keep out marauding animals, provided a stone-lined hole for pressing grapes, and built a watchtower for security purposes. Yet out of their lust for possession they turned the vineyard into a scene of violence and murder.

We live in God's world, but he has entrusted it to us. 'I am putting you in charge,' says God to man early in Genesis: 'I have provided for you' (1:28–29, GNB). History, however, is, among other things, a record of humankind's attempt to play God in a power struggle between heaven and earth, as well as a smash-and-grab between person and person.

Reflection

'The sun, the moon and the stars would have disappeared long ago, had they happened to be within reach of predatory human hands.'

Havelock Ellis (1859–1939)

CE

Mark 12:6–11 (NRSV)

The vineyard allegory (part 2)

'He still had one other, a beloved son. Finally, he sent him to them, saying, "They will respect my son." But those tenants said to one another, "This is the heir; come, let us kill him, and the inheritance will be ours." So they seized him, killed him, and threw him out of the vineyard. What then will the owner of the vineyard do? He will come and destroy the tenants and give the vineyard to others. Have you not read this scripture: "The stone that the builders rejected has become the cornerstone; this was the Lord's doing, and it is amazing in our eyes"?'

The plotters knew what they were doing. Kill the son and dispose of the body, and the vineyard is ours, they reasoned. But Jesus made his point as sharply as the nails used in crucifixion. The chosen of God have repeatedly defied him, rejecting the message of the prophets and ill-treating them. Their murder of the Son was the last straw, but the Son will prevail (Jesus quotes Psalm 118:22–23). Now they will be 'destroyed'—the Greek word is unambiguous. And God will turn to others to be the special agents of his purposes for humanity.

We suppose that the Christian Church is meant to be the new Israel. But, through the centuries, have we Christians done any better? Jew and Gentile alike, we are all sinners. It was neither Jew nor Roman but sinner man who deliberately crucified the Son of God. Human beings are responsible for their actions, despite the fashionable theory that sin is an outdated concept. It is said that when we go wrong, do wrong, it's the fault of our genes. We have inherited primeval urges. One day they will be eradicated as man develops and climbs out of the mud and nearer to the stars.

True, we inherit tendencies and our glands may well drive us down wrong paths. But we are also the recipients of God's grace, empowered by him to conquer ourselves and the downdrag of evil within us. 'We are not permitted to choose the frame of our destiny,' said Dag Hammarskjold, 'but what we put into it is ours.' The picture within the frame is our responsibility. Will it be a portrait of Dorian Gray, or more akin to an angel?

Reflection

Toscanini once said to an orchestra, 'God has told me how he wants this piece of music to be played; and you—you hinder God.' In what ways do we 'hinder' God?

CE

Mark 12:13–17 (NRSV)

A catch-22 question

Then they sent to him some Pharisees and some Herodians to trap him in what he said. And they came and said to him, 'Teacher… is it lawful to pay taxes to the emperor, or not? Should we pay them, or should we not?' But knowing their hypocrisy, he said to them, 'Why are you putting me to the test? Bring me a denarius and let me see it.' And they brought one. Then he said to them, 'Whose head is this, and whose title?' They answered, 'The emperor's.' Jesus said to them, 'Give to the emperor the things that are the emperor's, and to God the things that are God's.'

The Romans imposed an annual poll tax on their provinces, Judea included. These Pharisees and Herodians referred to it in an attempt to trick Jesus either into trouble with the Roman authorities or into unpopularity with the crowds. By 'catch-22', the title of his 1961 novel, Joseph Heller meant a question which, whether answered yes or no, would land the victim in difficulties. In passing, we note that the Herodians were a political party supporting the dynasty of Herod and yet careful to keep in with the Romans.

The denarius was a silver coin used by Rome to pay their armies abroad, and recoverable through taxation. The Jews had their own copper currency and were reluctant to handle the hated occupier's. It was not allowed within the temple precincts, because it bore the head of the reigning emperor and acknowledged him as *divus*, divine. We may imagine the one handed to Jesus as inscribed '*Divo Tiberio*', a grievous insult to Jews whose only king was God. Significantly, the denarius, worth an average day's wage and half the annual tax, had to be fetched from somewhere. We suppose that no one present had one in pocket or purse.

The brilliant answer Jesus gave to the trick question prevented both his arrest by the Romans on a charge of treason and the accusation that he was a traitor to his own people. His followers are to 'fear God' and 'honour the emperor', according to 1 Peter 2:17. And bear in mind that when those injunctions were written, the emperor was Nero. It is a Christian duty to be a law-abiding citizen (Romans 13:1–7). Even so, our duty to the State does not supersede our duty to God.

Reflection

Cecil Spring-Rice's anthem 'I vow to thee my country' expects us to give our nation a 'love that asks no question'. Is this a truly Christian sentiment?

CE

Mark 12:41–44 (NRSV)

Small and all

He sat down opposite the treasury, and watched the crowd putting money into the treasury. Many rich people put in large sums. A poor widow came and put in two small copper coins, which are worth a penny. Then he called his disciples and said to them, 'Truly I tell you, this poor widow has put in more than all those who are contributing to the treasury. For all of them have contributed out of their abundance; but she out of her poverty has put in everything she had, all she had to live on.'

The temple authorities provided receptacles, shaped like trumpets, into which people dropped their gifts of money. There were thirteen of them, each relating to a different fund. The scene here has Jesus watching people come and go. We may wonder how he could see what amounts they were putting in. Is this, we may ask, a parable rather than an actual incident? No matter, for the point it makes is clear.

Widows in ancient Palestine had no State pension to save them from poverty and starvation. The early Church took daily care of them at first but had to ensure that they were really destitute and had no other means of support. Whatever their status, they were unlikely to be rich or even comfortably off. James, in his letter (1:27), defines 'pure and undefiled religion' as including the care of widows in distress. The widow here dropped her two small coins into the treasury. They would have been the smallest in the prevailing currency. We are informed that 128 of them were the equivalent of a single denarius. They were a quarter of an inch in diameter and very thin. Each was a 'lepton', the Greek word for 'thin'.

The donation of the poor widow is often misunderstood. A minister tells of his church's annual gift day when he would sit in his vestry and receive the monetary gifts of his people. Sometimes a widow would say, 'I must apologize. I'd like to give more, but I can only manage the widow's mite this year.' She meant a *small* contribution; but Jesus emphasized that the widow's mite, or more accurately her mites, amounted to a large one, the largest of them all, because they were her *all*.

Reflection

What difference is there between an offering made during an act of worship and a retiring collection at the close of a service?

CE

1 Thessalonians 1:2–7 (NRSV)

Patterns for prayer

We always give thanks to God for all of you and mention you in our prayers, constantly remembering before our God and Father your work of faith and labour of love and steadfastness of hope in our Lord Jesus Christ. For we know, brothers and sisters beloved by God, that he has chosen you, because our message of the gospel came to you not in word only, but also in power and in the Holy Spirit and with full conviction; just as you know what kind of people we proved to be among you for your sake. And you became imitators of us and of the Lord, for in spite of persecution you received the word with joy inspired by the Holy Spirit, so that you became an example to all the believers in Macedonia and Achaia.

A pattern for prayer. Paul wrote to the Ephesians (6:18), 'Pray at all times.' He was certainly a leader who practised what he preached! 'We always give thanks... constantly remembering you...' If anyone had the excuse that he was too busy to pray, it was Paul. He preached, travelled, wrote, trained leaders, worked with his hands; he was constantly on the go. But he prayed regularly for all the churches he had founded. What an example for me to follow in my supposedly busy life!

A pattern for preaching. 'Our gospel came to you with words... with power... We lived among you...' A modern preacher might start a sermon with this prayer: 'Lord, I ask that my words today may not be empty. Help me to speak in the power of the Holy Spirit so that your message is welcomed and that lives are changed.' Each of us can start each morning with a similar prayer: 'Lord, please help me today so that the words I speak reflect you and help other people.' Of course, words alone cannot communicate the reality of Jesus; our lives must give the same message. Paul's did. The quality of his life was such that they wanted to imitate it. And he was sure that in imitating him, they were imitating Jesus. What amazing confidence! It challenges me to look at my own life, to ask myself whether I am Jesus-like in my words, my deeds, my manner. The Thessalonian Christians grasped Paul's message so surely that they became examples in the region round them.

Reflection

How 'Jesus-like' am I in my words, deeds, manner?

RG

Luke 11:9–10 (NRSV)

Persistence in prayer

'So I say to you, Ask, and it will be given you; search, and you will find; knock, and the door will be opened for you. For everyone who asks receives, and everyone who searches finds, and for everyone who knocks, the door will be opened.'

Luke emphasizes that Jesus was a great man of prayer. Inspired by this, the disciples asked for guidance and were given the Lord's Prayer. Luke then follows with the story of the 'friend at midnight' and goes on to say that if an earthly father knows how to give good gifts to his children, then how much more will God give to those who ask.

It is the shameless persistence of the neighbour in need of bread that eventually forces an unwilling householder to get up and help him. This is in great contrast to our Father God who longs to give to his children. There is, though, a condition. We need to ask, seek and knock. These are all doing words. Jesus says, '*really* ask, *genuinely* search, and knock *hard*'. He does not say, 'be vaguely interested'.

This raises the question: if God longs to give, then why do we need to be persistent in prayer? A celebrated violinist asked a music student to give lessons to his daughter. When asked why he did not teach her himself, he replied that he longed to share with her all he knew, and would have done so, but she had never asked him. God cannot give until we ask, because he will not force himself on us. Furthermore, the very act of asking deepens our relationship with him and helps make us ready to receive what we really need. St Augustine said, 'God does not ask us to tell him our needs in order that he may learn about them, but in order that we may be made capable of receiving his gifts.'

Verse 13 goes on to stress the abundant generosity of God. He grants us not just gifts but the Holy Spirit himself, who is the source of all the gifts and graces we need to enable us to play our part in furthering the kingdom of God. In short, through prayer, Jesus wants us to have the same anointing with power that so enriched his own ministry.

Meditate

Pray as if everything depended upon God.
Work as if everything depended on you.

Ignatius of Loyola (1491–1556)

PG

Romans 8:22–27 (NRSV)

Paul at prayer

We know that the whole creation has been groaning in labour pains until now; and not only the creation, but we ourselves, who have the first fruits of the Spirit, groan inwardly while we wait for adoption, the redemption of our bodies... Likewise the Spirit helps us in our weakness; for we do not know how to pray as we ought, but that very Spirit intercedes with sighs too deep for words. And God, who searches the heart, knows what is the mind of the Spirit, because the Spirit intercedes for the saints according to the will of God.

Groaning and travailing in childbirth! Does that sound like a ministry of prayer? Only one who had entered into such an experience could have written the eighth chapter of Romans. When some Christians speak of being 'born again' as the result of an evangelistic rally or an individualistic human decision, I am reminded of the cosmic picture of the powers of the new birth in this chapter, in which the Holy Spirit groans and travails within the very fabric of creation, in yearning for the fullness of our redemption.

Paul's hidden life of payer was one in which the Holy Spirit carried him into such corporate dimensions of spiritual experience as can be expressed only in analogy and metaphor. He expresses the experience in a personal and pastoral sense when he speaks of the pain and burden of birthpangs for his congregation in Galatia: 'My little children, for whom I am again in the pain of childbirth until Christ is formed in you' (Galatians 4:19). On both a personal and corporate level Paul confesses that he does not himself know how to pray, but the Spirit draws him into the depths of travail and groaning—the creative process of spiritual childbirth, not only for those under his spiritual care but for the whole of creation.

This is what the great saints and mystics of the Church bear witness to, in the deeper reaches of the life of prayer. It is not simply petition, intercession, thanksgiving or even praise of God. It is being so transparently open to the interior movement of the Holy Spirit that the believer becomes possessed by the breath of God, caught up into the glory and pain of contemplative yearning. Totally available to God!

Prayer

Holy Spirit of God, I yield my life to you. Deal gently with me, but draw me closer to the heart of God, that Christ may be formed in me.

R/SSF

1 Corinthians 1:4–9 (NRSV)

The burden and joy of prayer

I give thanks to my God always for you because of the grace of God that has been given you in Christ Jesus, for in every way you have been enriched in him, in speech and knowledge of every kind—just as the testimony of Christ has been strengthened among you—so that you may be blameless on the day of our Lord Jesus Christ. God is faithful; by him you were called into the fellowship of his Son, Jesus Christ our Lord.

There are many problems at Corinth, and Paul does not shrink from facing them head on! But his first note here, and his final note (1 Corinthians 16:13 - 24) are of thanksgiving, encouragement and rejoicing.

I correspond with many people from my hermitage, and these are themes which are often sounded in my letters. But behind my words, holding the people up in prayer, there are sorrow and tears, and often wordless groaning in the Spirit for the pain, depression, terminal illness or various burdens which people share with me, in their letters and confessions.

In a later epistle Paul wrote to the same people, 'I wrote you out of much distress and anguish of heart and with many tears, not to cause you pain, but to let you know the abundant love that I have for you' (2 Corinthians 2:4).

There it is—joy, encouragement and thanksgiving up front, with tears, pain and profound intercession beneath the surface and in the secret place of intercessory prayer.

As I read through Paul's thanksgiving and rejoicing (and there are many passages like today's), I feel also the way in which Paul in secret yielded himself to the Holy Spirit—sometimes weeping, sometimes even laughing in prayer, as he became a channel of God's healing, enabling and dying grace.

Prayer

Father, stir up in me a spirit of profound intercession. Enable me to bear up my friends and loved ones, and the broken and oppressed people of our time. Make me a channel of healing, intercessory grace.

R/SSF

2 Corinthians 1:3–7 (NRSV)

Sharing consolation in affliction

Blessed be the God and Father of our Lord Jesus Christ, the Father of mercies and the God of all consolation, who consoles us in all our affliction, so that we may be able to console those who are in any affliction with the consolation with which we ourselves are consoled by God. For just as the sufferings of Christ are abundant for us, so also our consolation is abundant through Christ.

Paul has a wonderful way of praying out loud in his letters. Here he is blessing and thanking the Father of mercies, and at the same time allowing the consolation to flow from heaven, through his prayers and love, into the midst of the gathered community in Corinth.

Also, in doing that, there is a wonderful principle laid down—that the suffering Christ pours out consolation from the midst of his sufferings, and the receiving believer, in turn, pours out compassion to the needy soul who comes with burdens, sins and fears. So we are able to console with Christ's consolation, as channels and instuments of the grace of God.

A Baptist minister friend came to the monastery and asked if he could make his confession (these are days of ecumenical sharing). In the middle of it he began to weep and I remained silent and let him cry before the Lord until all that he needed to feel, say and confess was brought out into the healing presence of God. He felt my sympathy and understanding, and in the words of absolution and laying on of hands he received the consolation of assurance and forgiveness. In a letter that came a few days later he said that he had gone down the track singing, his feet hardly touching the ground because of the depth of mutual sharing and love.

This is what Paul is writing and praying about. That Baptist minister returned to his congregation and became to them a source of God's consolation, and this is what God desires for you towards your brothers and sisters in Christ. If you allow the healing of the risen Christ which you have experienced to be channelled to others, then you will create a new circle of love.

Prayer

Father of mercies, let your healing consolation flow through my life, and overflow to other lives, for the mutual healing of afflictions and the praise of your name.

R/SSF

2 Corinthians 13:11–13 (NRSV)

Apostolic benediction

Finally, brothers and sisters, farewell. Put things in order, listen to my appeal, agree with one another, live in peace; and the God of love and peace will be with you. Greet one another with a holy kiss. All the saints greet you. The grace of the Lord Jesus Christ, the love of God, and the communion of the Holy Spirit be with all of you.

These last chapters to the Corinthian believers are full of Paul's prayerful concern for them, for, as he tells them, 'I will most gladly spend and be spent for you' (2 Corinthians 12:15), and he prays that they may live rightly and attain perfection (13:7, 9). But the greatest prayer of all occurs in today's passage, and it is the ancient prayer we know as the Apostolic Benediction. It encapsulates in a marvellously succinct trinitarian prayer the highest, deepest and most profound blessings that can be bestowed upon a church or a believer this side of heaven. Here it is:

The grace of our Lord Jesus Christ. Grace is unmerited, undeserved and gratuitous favour, and it is directed towards undeserving, weak and helpless sinners. The result? They are made into forgiven, reconciled, rejoicing and faithful believers, whose lives are surrendered to their crucified and risen Saviour.

The love of God. God is not the projection of a Babylonian monarch, exercising a despotic tyranny of wrath upon offenders. He is the gracious Father of all, who loves poor sinners and longs for them to be drawn into the blessings of fellowship, into the family of believers, so that his love may be proclaimed and spread throughout the whole world. For loving begets love.

The communion of the Holy Spirit. The Holy Spirit, the life-giver, is the one who imparts and sustains life at all levels of the natural and spiritual orders, from the sap that rises in the spring, to the flaming outshining of the cherubim and seraphim. The 'communion' of the Spirit means that through the gospel poor sinners are drawn into the Holy Trinity, and become part of the cosmic and universal adoration offered by the whole creation to the God who is all in all.

Prayer

Subdue my heart by your grace, Lord; melt my spirit by your love; refresh my life by your gracious communion. Such a trinity of blessings will glorify your name in my life, Father, Son and Holy Spirit.

R/SSF

Ephesians 1:3–14 (NRSV)

Amazing grace!

Blessed be the God and Father of our Lord Jesus Christ, who has blessed us in Christ with every spiritual blessing in the heavenly places, just as he chose us in Christ before the foundation of the world to be holy and blameless before him in love. He destined us for adoption as his children through Jesus Christ, according to the good pleasure of his will, to the praise of his glorious grace that he freely bestowed on us in the Beloved... In him you also... were marked with the seal of the promised Holy Spirit; this is the pledge of our inheritance toward redemption as God's own people, to the praise of his glory.

This is almost too much to take in! It reminds me of St Augustine's *Confessions*, because both Paul and Augustine had been smitten by the overwhelming grace of Christ, and pour forth adoration, theology, spirituality and diamond-faceted precious stones of the truth they have experienced, from the abundance of their hearts. Read the whole passage slowly and pick up the themes. Here are three major truths:

- **God the Father** loved us, saved us, blessed us, before the foundation of the world (vv. 3–6).
- **God the Son** forgave, enlightened and redeemed us through the shedding of his precious blood (vv. 5–9).
- **God the Holy Spirit** called, marked and sealed us in our present experience of salvation, and as an assurance and pledge of the glory of heaven.

All the rest of the blessings come cascading down from these basic miraculous wonders. I find myself falling down with Paul and Augustine in tearful adoration of the God whose amazing good pleasure, in the fullness of time, is to gather up *all things* into a universal salvation. How broad and wide, how high and deep such a salvation is, only God can know—and we are overwhelmed.

This seal of the Holy Spirit is an experience of God's grace that brings with it an inward assurance that we are God's chidlren. It means we can *feel* and *know* that we are children of God, and we can be *assured* by his grace that we are his for time and eternity.

Prayer

Lord, I have only begun to taste these blessings, and I am overwhelmed by your mysterious purpose in gathering all things together in Christ. Help me to understand, help me to experience, and then let me shine with all its glory.

R/SSF

Ephesians 1:15–23 (NRSV)

Dynamic power!

I pray that the God of our Lord Jesus Christ, the Father of glory, may give you a spirit of wisdom and revelation as you come to know him, so that, with the eyes of your heart enlightened, you may know what is the hope to which he has called you, what are the riches of his glorious inheritance among the saints, and what is the immeasurable greatness of his power for us who believe, according to the working of his great power. God put this power to work in Christ when he raised him from the dead and seated him at his right hand in the heavenly places.

This is powerful praying! What is Paul asking for? At least three things:

- That God would grant the spirit of wisdom and revelation in increasing knowledge of him (v. 17).
- That with enlightened hearts the believer may grasp the great *hope* of God's eternal purpose, and the actual *experience* of the inheritance of grace in the fellowhip of the Church (v. 18).
- That the power (Greek: *dynamis*) of his great energies may become available in the Church and in the world (v. 19).

The first of these is revelation for the *mind*; the second is enlightenment for the *heart*; the third is power for *living* out the gospel in society. There are two contrasting 'powers' in this passage. The first is the power (*dynamis*) at the heart of the gospel which raised Christ from the dead, and the second is the power (Greek: *exousia*) of earthly rule and authority which will ultimately be put under the feet of Christ and offered to the Father.

The poor believers in Ephesus are called to be energized by the dynamic power of God. The Church, when filled with the fullness of God's power (v. 23), becomes the agent of grace, light and reconciliation in the world. After such a prayer as this, Paul tumbles into the full content of the Ephesian epistle—and this shows how poor sinners can be redeemed, reconciled and empowered by the Holy Spirit to bring about the world's salvation.

Prayer

Father, your servant Paul prayed for mighty things to be accomplished among the Ephesian believers. I hardly know where to begin, but grant Paul's prayers in my life, in my church fellowship, in the name, and by the resurrection power, of the Lord Jesus.

R/SSF

Ephesians 3:14–20 (NRSV)

Rooted and grounded in love

I bow my knees before the Father, from whom every family in heaven and on earth takes its name. I pray that, according to the riches of his glory, he may grant that you may be strengthened in your inner being with power through his Spirit, and that Christ may dwell in your hearts through faith, as you are being rooted and grounded in love. I pray that you may have the power to comprehend, with all the saints, what is the breadth and length and height and depth, and to know the love of Christ that surpasses knowledge, so that you may be filled with all the fullness of God.

Breadth and length and height and depth! A few evenings ago, after the night service of Compline in my hut chapel, I looked at the San Damiano Crucifix, and quietly sang the gospel hymn 'Beneath the Cross of Jesus' (English Hymnal No. 567). I reflected that the top of the cross pierces the very heart of God; the base of the cross reaches lower than the deepest depths to which humankind can sink; the arms of the cross extend in gospel invitation to the whole world. If you take up the hymn and read (or sing) it, you will see why I stretched out, face down, upon the floor, moved by the same compelling grace that transformed the life of Francis of Assisi and marked him with the wounds of Calvary.

Paul's prayer that we may know the dimensions of God's love in Christ leads to what he calls the 'fullness' of God. What is this fullness but the incomprehensible love which overflows from the heart of the Eternal, pouring its cascading glory into the dry and thirsty land of our world? In such irrigated gospel soil we may then be rooted and grounded in love, and will bear the fruits of the Spirit for the healing of the nations. The whole family of the Eternal Father needs to be drawn in, and the heart of God embraces each one.

Prayer

Father, I am scared when I think of exposure to the fullness of your love! Until now I have been content to paddle on the edge of your ocean. Give me courage to launch out into the deep, and don't let me sink!

R/SSF

Ephesians 6:18–20 (NRSV)

Pray in the Spirit!

Pray in the Spirit at all times in every prayer and supplication. To that end keep alert and always persevere in supplication for all the saints. Pray also for me, so that when I speak, a message may be given to me to make known with boldness the mystery of the gospel, for which I am an ambassador in chains. Pray that I may declare it boldly, as I must speak.

The malignant power of evil and of spiritual darkenss is the background to today's reading, with the need to be girded with the armour of God (Ephesians 6:10–17). Then comes the encouragement to pray in the Spirit, to pray for and with all the people of God, and to pray for the furtherance of the gospel.

All this comes from the apostle who is chained to a Roman guard—an ambassador in chains, he calls himself. But that doesn't stop him praying in the Spirit, rejoicing in the gospel, or asking that he may be filled with holy boldness. For after all, he is an ambassador of the King of kings!

Paul is well aware of the powers of darkness that surround us, imprisoning Christ's apostles and persecuting his saints. But there is no doubt in his mind where the victory lay. *If* (and it is a big *if*) we pray in the Spirit, the Spirit's power and boldness will flow. This is the power that raised Christ from the dead, and that was poured out on the 120 disciples on the Day of Pentecost. Praying in the Spirit is to allow your whole life to be caught up in the joyful adoration of God in prayer, and to allow his powerful presence to pervade your witnessing life. The separate tongues of fire which settled upon the disciples at Pentecost joined in one immense billowing flame (Acts 2:1–4). When Paul speaks of praying in the Spirit he intends that such prayer be made within the communion of saints, which is the Body of Christ on earth and in heaven. Praying in the Spirit will fill the Church with holy boldness, dispel the powers of darkness, and draw people to the crucified and risen Jesus!

Prayer

When the powers of darkness engulf me, Lord, gird me with the gospel armour. When my courage runs low, let me learn to pray in the Spirit. Then link me with all your believing people that Jesus may be glorified with holy boldness.

R/SSF

Philippians 1:3–11 (NRSV)

Freedom in the prison cell

I thank my God every time I remember you, constantly praying with joy in every one of my prayers for all of you, because of your sharing in the gospel from the first day until now. I am confident of this, that the one who began a good work among you will bring it to completion by the day of Jesus Christ. It is right for me to think this way about all of you, because you hold me in your heart, for all of you share in God's grace with me, both in my imprisonment and in the defence and confirmation of the gospel.

Paul speaks of God's grace in his imprisonment. I've been involved with the work of the Prison Phoenix Trust over the last eighteen months. Its main work is teaching meditation to inmates, and the Trust is in touch with over 2000 people at any one time. This week I had a letter from an inmate of Exeter Prison who has read my book *The Heart of Prayer* three times and asks for more. This is grace in the prison cell.

Paul is aware of enemies threatening his reputation, his integrity and even his life, in this epistle. But he is confident that God takes those very difficulties and uses them for the spread of the gospel (1:12–18). Look at three things, he says:

- First, that fellowship in prayer is a source of strength and comfort in his cell. I have a covenant with many people who pray for me (and I for them) by name every Sunday morning. It works!
- Then Paul says that the God who has *begun* a work of grace will *continue* it in the believer's heart—even until (and beyond) the coming of Christ.
- Thirdly, verses 3–11 show clearly that Paul is not the cold, legalistic kill-joy that some have made him out to be. He has a heart that loves, eyes that weep and a spirit of forgiveness for his enemies. It is difficult to stop at verse 11, so read on. Rejoice that the same Christ is at work in your dark situation, so that living or dying, all things may ultimately work together for good in the light of eternity.

Prayer

I pray today, my Father, for those in prison cells. Let your light pierce the darkness, setting the spirit free and renewing vision for love and service.

R/SSF

1 Thessalonians 1:2–10; 5:23–25 (NRSV)

Spirit, soul and body

We always give thanks to God for all of you and mention you in our prayers, constantly remembering before our God and Father your work of faith and labour of love and steadfastness of hope in our Lord Jesus Christ... May the God of peace himself sanctify you entirely; and may your spirit and soul and body be kept sound and blameless at the coming of our Lord Jesus Christ. The one who calls you is faithful, and he will do this. Beloved, pray for us.

Paul begins and ends this epistle with prayer! His opening prayer affirms three things about the Thessalonian believers:

- **Your work of faith**: this means a faith that works! It is the Holy Spirit at work within that produces faith (v. 5), and therefore it works and spreads and enthuses those around.
- **Your labour of love**: this reveals the validity of faith. Where faith is genuine it is bound to produce love. If love is lacking, then faith is doubtful.
- **Your steadfastness of hope**: this is not simply optimism for this life—indeed, persecution and martyrdom may be around the corner! It means that hope shines *now* in all our infirmities and sorrows, and beckons in the *future* at the coming of Christ in glory.

At the end of the letter, Paul's prayer is that believers may be sanctified wholly, as the old version expresses it. Paul is specific:

- **Sanctify your spirit** (Greek: *pneuma*). Part of the blessing of the new birth is that the Holy Spirit indwells the human spirit, restoring God's image in us and setting us free.
- **Sanctify your soul** (Greek: *psyche*). This is the thinking, feeling, deliberating part of our humanity, so that our minds may be set upon God's glory and our moral lives be irradiated by love.
- **Sanctify your body** (Greek: *soma*). This means that the body itself is the temple of the Holy Spirit, and that our physical powers may be harnessed to the service of God and our neighbours.

Prayer

Grant, Lord, that my spirit, soul and body
may be dedicated to your service of love—
wholly given and wholly blessed.

R/SSF

2 Timothy 1:3–7 (NRSV)

Victorious through prayer

I remember you constantly in my prayers night and day. Recalling your tears, I long to see you so that I may be filled with joy. I am reminded of your sincere faith, a faith that lived first in your grandmother Lois and your mother Eunice and now, I am sure, lives in you. For this reason I remind you to rekindle the gift of God that is within you through the laying on of my hands; for God did not give us a spirit of cowardice, but rather a spirit of pwer and of love and of self-discipline.

Paul is not having an easy time of it in prison. Former disciples have deserted him (2 Timothy 1:15), he is chained like a criminal (2:9), he is aware of imposters and deceivers in the church (3:13), and he misses his warm cloak (4:13). But in the midst of it all he is praying night and day, praising God for deliverance, and remembering the faithfulness of God.

As he prays, through waking and sleeping, Paul sees before him the tears of his beloved Timothy, the living faith of Timothy's mother Eunice and the loyalty of Lois, his grandmother. Paul's prayers remind him of the Holy Spirit which fell upon Timothy (1:14) when he laid his hands upon him, and he stirs up the flame by encouragement and expects Timothy to rekindle the fire and keep it burning.

Paul's expectation of his spiritual son is high, and when Timothy receives the letter, he will have before him the heroic example of the imprisoned veteran whose vision never seems to diminish and who encourages and exhorts his son from the midst of an imprisonment which he knows will lead to his death (4:6). Yet Paul's cry of victory rings out clearly, and he tells Timothy that victorious faith and sustaining strength can only be found in the gift of the Holy Spirit. It is by the same Spirit that Timothy will continue the battle and receive himself the crown of righteousness reserved for the faithful.

Prayer

I am surrounded, Lord, in heaven and on earth, by your saints in light, all caught up in the atmosphere of prayer.
Kindle again the gifts of your Spirit, forgive my cowardice, renew my vision, and grant me the power and discipline to serve you faithfully.

R/SSF

Philemon 4–9 (NRSV)

Answered prayer

When I remember you in my prayers, I always thank my God because I hear of your love for all the saints and your faith towards the Lord Jesus. I pray that the sharing of your faith may become effective when you perceive all the good that we may do for Christ. I have indeed received much joy and encouagement from your love, because the hearts of the saints have been refreshed through you, my brother. For this reason, though I am bold enough in Christ to command you to do your duty, yet I would rather appeal to you on the basis of love—and I, Paul, do this as an old man, and now also as a prisoner of Christ Jesus.

Paul is working up to something here! He is praying hard, but also making a good case. It is not a matter of God helping those who help themselves, but of making out a good appeal, a sound argument for action—and then crowning it with his powerful prayers!

Paul wants Philemon to grant his former slave Onesimus the liberty to serve Paul in his imprisonment, and thereby to serve the Lord Christ. Onesimus was a runaway slave, and he was arrested, convicted, converted and wonderfully transformed by Paul's preaching of the risen Christ. Onesimus means 'useful' and Paul is making the best use of his man. He prayed *for* Onesimus, he prayed *with* Onesimus, and now he is praying and pleading *on behalf* of Onesimus. And no doubt Onesimus is saying a hearty 'Amen' to Paul's prayers!

There is no doubt but that prayer is the pattern of Paul's life. He always laid great store by mystical prayers of adoration, mingled with much thanksgiving and intercession. And now a simple prayer of petition—and Philemon can hardly refuse such powerful praying.

There are blessings in a prison cell—and Paul's prayer life was enriched during his imprisonment. So much of it was channelled into his prison epistles and resounded around the prison cells. He may have been an old man and a prisoner, but he was full of spiritual vitality and as free as a bird!

Prayer

Give me a spirit of believing prayer, Lord.
Then I shall pray according to your will
and be astounded and encouraged by your
mighty response to my prayerful petitions.

R/SSF

Ruth 1:1–6 (NIV, abridged)

From sorrow to hope

In the days when the judges ruled, there was a famine in the land, and a man from Bethlehem in Judah, together with his wife and two sons, went to live for a while in the country of Moab... Now Elimelech, Naomi's husband, died, and she was left with her two sons. They married Moabite women, one named Orpah and the other Ruth. After they had lived there about ten years, both Mahlon and Kilion also died, and Naomi was left without her two sons and her husband. When she heard in Moab that the Lord had come to the aid of his people by providing food for them, Naomi and her daughters-in-law prepared to return home from there.

It's easy to miss the book of Ruth, tucked between Judges and the first and second books of Samuel. In these latter books, God's love for Israel is woven into a background of cruelty and tribal warfare—the sorts of stories we hear in our own times whenever we switch on the news. The writer hints at those bad days in verse 1, but Ruth in general paints a picture of love and compassion. A friend in Russia concluded that this little book prefigures the Gospels, and she was right: the key theme is redemption. The tender story of grace and blessing she found in Ruth brought great comfort to her in the hardship of life among desolate housing blocks.

However, Ruth opens with tragedy — famine. Bethlehem, 'the House of Bread', is empty. Naomi, too, will soon be emptied in another way by the death of her husband and sons. The loss of a family member is always devastating. The closer the relationship, the more desolate we feel. Where there was feast we have only famine. How much more for Naomi, who lived in a culture in which a woman's existence depended totally on her menfolk. Yet, the story overflows with the grace and protection of the Lord, who gave his people a just law by which even the poorest could win their bread (Leviticus 19:9–10). In the midst of her desolation, Naomi hears good news: the Lord has not forgotten his people, the famine is over and it is time to return home.

Reflection

When my heart is 'wintry, grieving and in pain', may I remember that 'our God is gracious, nor will leave the desolate to mourn'.

JR

Ruth 1:8–19 (NIV, abridged)

Along the road

Then Naomi said to her two daughters-in-law, 'Go back, each of you, to your mother's home... Why would you come with me? Am I going to have any more sons, who could become your husbands? ... It is more bitter for me than for you, because the Lord's hand has gone out against me!' At this they wept again. Then Orpah kissed her mother-in-law good-bye, but Ruth clung to her... So the two women went on until they came to Bethlehem.

Naomi can offer her daughters-in-law nothing except poverty and affliction. 'Return home,' she urges, unselfishly releasing them from a life in which they will only be losers. They are widows, too, but they are young and may yet make a new life, while she has no hope at all. I am amazed as I hear Naomi list the stark truths so objectively. She is right to do so, though, as we only begin to deal with pain, problems and anxieties when we confront them honestly. Remember the fairy-tale *Rumpelstiltskin*? It is when the girl calls the goblin by name that he loses his power over her.

Orpah consents to leave, but Ruth does not. We shall consider Ruth's response tomorrow. Today, we see her continuing with Naomi along the road. She has chosen poverty, but she has also chosen Israel's God (vv. 16–17); and I am reminded that blind Bartimaeus, having cast aside his cumbersome cloak, comes to Jesus and, healed, follows the Lord along the road (Mark 10:46–52). In fact, Mark's Gospel shows that much of Jesus' ministry takes place 'on the way', even the way of the cross.

The road leads home, but homecoming is hard when, like Naomi, we return with failure and loss. Our global village is full of people who leave home to make a living elsewhere. Life is often tough. Filipino and Sri Lankan women are exploited, even killed. Skinheads and neo-Nazis threaten immigrant workers. In Warsaw, where I live, charming, gentle Vietnamese sell cheap clothes, but they are taking jobs from Poles. Stephen of Hungary said a thousand years ago, 'A country of one language and one culture is weak and fallible. Therefore protect newcomers and hold them in high esteem.' Ruth honours the immigrant—do we?

Prayer

We pray for mercy and compassion for all who are exploited.

JR

Ruth 1:16–17 (NIV)

My God in whom I trust

But Ruth replied, 'Don't urge me to leave you or to turn back from you. Where you go I will go, and where you stay I will stay. Your people will be my people and your God my God. Where you die I will die, and there I will be buried. May the Lord deal with me, be it ever so severely, if anything but death separates you and me.'

Orpah returned; Ruth stayed with her mother-in-law. She is a pagan, yet she binds herself to the first and the sixth commandments. When I studied this book with children in Russia, we set it in the context of Psalm 19:7–11. The law of the Lord is more precious than gold; keeping it brings joy. Obedience to God's law gives this short book its harmony and happiness. We will see that Boaz honours the law and the Lord repays him richly by giving him a son whose line will produce the greatest king in Israel. However, the focus of the story is the foreign woman Ruth who refuses to abandon her destitute mother-in-law and flings herself totally on the God of Israel.

The poet John Keats may have described her as 'sick for home… in tears amid the alien corn', but Ruth is a strong woman and her great declaration of faith rings down the centuries and touches our hearts today.

We live in the age of the short-term contract and the professional carer, but Ruth makes her commitment for life. I am reminded of a promising young Jewish author in 1942 whose Polish friends offered to save her, but she refused to leave her widowed mother and went to the death trains with her in 1942. I think, too, of Aida Skripnikova in Leningrad in 1964. Youth leaders said, 'Forget all this religion. You have a brilliant future ahead.' Aida replied, 'I have chosen to suffer with my brothers and sisters in Christ.' Aida endured two terms in prison and then scrubbed long-distance trains. Now, in the Russia of chaos, she could live comfortably abroad with Christian friends, but she chooses to serve an elderly lady who shared her single room when Aida had nowhere to live.

Prayer

Father, when my faith falters, turn my thoughts to Ruth, who took the Lord as her refuge and shelter.

JR

Ruth 1:19–22 (NIV, abridged)

Homecoming

So the two women went on until they came to Bethlehem. When they arrived in Bethlehem, the whole town was stirred because of them and the women exclaimed, 'Can this be Naomi?' 'Don't call me Naomi,' she told them. 'Call me Mara, because the Almighty has made my life very bitter. I went away full but the Lord has brought me back empty…' So Naomi returned… arriving in Bethlehem as the barley harvest was beginning.

Naomi's arrival with her Moabite daughter-in-law creates a great stir. Life in a Middle Eastern village or town was never private. Jesus knew this when he told his stories. Although he does not mention them, the elders at the gate, the women at the well would also have watched the 'lost son' limp home empty, to be met by his father when he was still far off, be publicly embraced and welcomed to a feast (Luke 15:20–23). Naomi is empty, too. 'Call me Mara,' she tells the women. Naomi's husband Elim-elech's name means 'My God is King'. 'Naomi' means 'pleasant', while 'Mara' means 'bitter'. 'Ruth', appropriately, means 'friendship'.

Our names accompany us from birth to death. They are a very early gift from our parents. Sometimes young people wish they had another name. That's quite normal, part of establishing our sense of self, but I have met people who deliberately changed their Christian name. I felt that their parents must have felt rejected and sad. Our names define us so deeply that we feel lost if we do not know our birth names. Jewish children in Poland only survived the last war if they were given a new identity. One survivor wrote, 'Now I am old, but, increasingly, I feel that someone stole my name and with it my whole life.' Naomi uses the name change to highlight her changed circumstances: 'I went away full, but the Lord has brought me back empty.'

Redemption, though, is never far from this story. Naomi has a companion in her sorrows—Ruth is with her—and we have a glimpse of good things to come: 'the barley harvest was beginning.'

Prayer

'When we were still far off you met us in your Son and brought us home.'
My name and my deepest being are precious in your sight. You welcome me, empty or full. Help me to hold on to this and rejoice.

JR

Ruth 2:2–7 (NIV, abridged)

Ruth the gleaner

Ruth the Moabitess said to Naomi, 'Let me go to the fields and pick up the leftover grain…' … So she went out and began to glean in the fields behind the harvesters… As it turned out, she found herself working in a field belonging to Boaz, who was from the clan of Elimelech. Just then Boaz arrived from Bethlehem and greeted the harvesters, 'The Lord be with you!' 'The Lord bless you!' they called back. Boaz asked… 'Whose young woman is that?' … 'She is the Moabitess… She… has worked steadily from morning till now.'

On my first ever visit to my grandmother's home on the Orkney Islands, I travelled all night with my children. In the morning (it was 25 March), the sunrise stabbed the tossing water of the sea. Radiant snow-feathers drifted across naked moors. The annunciation of light brought satisfaction and peace. 'He has filled the hungry with good things,' sang Mary in a poem of blessing (Luke 1:53) that harks back to barren Hannah's praise (1 Samuel 2:7–8) and anticipates her son's Beatitudes (Matthew 5:3–12).

When a community honours God, 'the hungry are filled'. Ruth gleans behind the reapers because, although she is destitute, God's law has a 'bias to the poor' (Leviticus 19:9–10). Our God does not just give life, but life 'more abundantly'. Ruth, unknowingly, has found the fields of Naomi's kinsman. 'Boaz' means 'in him is strength'. The bountiful farmer, the plentiful harvest, the gracious exchange of blessings show that kindliness is next to godliness and are an annunciation of fullness to come.

A 14-year-old, Natasha, in densely populated St Petersburg with its six-month winter, pictured the scene like this: 'Ruth is in the field amidst the ears of barley. The warm breeze ruffles her hair. Swallows fly above her, singing marvellous songs. The bright sun burnishes the barley and the whisper of grain sets Ruth musing: "Naomi has become a second mother to me. I shall never leave her. I am doing for my mother no more than anyone else would have done. The Lord is merciful to me. He has given me a good harvest to glean for her."'

Reflection

Do you know of anyone to whom you can be a Ruth with flowers or a visit today?

JR

Ruth 2:8–16 (NIV, abridged)

Wings of kindness

So Boaz said to Ruth, 'My daughter, listen to me. Don't go and glean in another field and don't go away from here. Stay here with my servant girls… I have told the men not to touch you. And whenever you are thirsty, go and get a drink from the water jars the men have filled… May the Lord repay you for what you have done. May you be richly rewarded by the Lord, the God of Israel, under whose wings you have come to take refuge.' 'May I continue to find favour in your eyes, my lord,' she said. 'You have given me comfort and have spoken kindly to your servant—though I do not have the standing of one of your servant girls.'

When a community honours the Lord, the weak and poor are provided for. Boaz knows, however, that Ruth is very vulnerable—anyone could molest her and she doesn't have friends to offer her a drink from the jars: 'Our men filled these for us,' the other girls could point out. However, a word from the landowner gives Ruth instant protection and puts her in good standing with the whole village. Boaz embodies the protecting shelter of the Lord 'under whose wings' Ruth has taken refuge (v. 12). The nurturing, protective image will occur again in 3:9. It links back to Exodus 19:4 where God says, 'I carried you on eagle's wings'—the picture being a mother eagle teaching her young to fly. Jesus, too, compares himself to a mother hen protecting her brood (Matthew 23:37).

Ruth responds with gratitude (2:10, 13). In the faceless rush of our technological world, we have forgotten older courtesies. We do not, by and large, use them in church either. Paul says, 'Offer your bodies as living sacrifices, holy and pleasing to God—this is your spiritual act of worship' (Romans 12:1), but we have abandoned the gestures, truncated the prayers and cancelled the fasts so that the feasts have lost their meaning. 'Write the gesture out in full,' said the Austrian poet Rilke, 'the whole beautiful and weighty word: reverence.'

Reflection

Actions speak louder than words. Have you found any pattern of gestures or actions to help you express reverence, love and worship?

JR

Ruth 2:17–23 (NIV, abridged)

The grace of giving

So Ruth gleaned in the field until evening. Then she threshed the barley she had gathered, and... carried it back to town, and her mother-in-law saw how much she had gathered... Her mother-in-law asked her, 'Where did you glean today?' Then Ruth told her... 'The name of the man I worked with today is Boaz,' she said. 'The Lord bless him!' Naomi said... 'That man is our close relative; he is one of our kinsman-redeemers.' Then Ruth the Moabitess said, 'He even said to me, "Stay with my workers until they finish harvesting all my grain." ' ... So Ruth stayed close to the servant girls of Boaz to glean until the barley and wheat harvests were finished. And she lived with her mother-in-law.

Naomi is amazed when Ruth brings home a large amount of barley. She is even more amazed when she realizes that the man who offered his protection to Ruth is a 'kinsman-redeemer'. The Hebrew word 'redemption' appears 23 times throughout this short book. The kinsman-redeemer had to protect the weak and needy in the family (Deuteronomy 25:5–10; Leviticus 25:25–28). He could also avenge the killing of a relative (Numbers 35:19–21). Naomi knows the power of praise and calls down blessings upon Boaz (v. 20).

In today's highly mobile Western society, the extended family has largely gone and with it a level of care and protection. But care for the extended family can place limits on your freedom and constant demands on your hospitality. Relatives, a friend from Nigeria explains, expect to be housed, fed—and don't expect to pay bills. In chapter 4 we shall see another relative refusing the duty of caring for Naomi.

Boaz, by contrast, has even offered his protection throughout the barley harvest and the wheat harvest as well. A friend wrote, 'The way to give God thanks is to make room for more grace' and that is exactly what is happening here. Peace, satisfaction, courtesy and selfless commitment to others illumine the book of Ruth—and generosity adds an extra light. Ruth, Naomi and Boaz mirror in miniature the character of our God, who is infinitely generous. It was with outstretched arms and open hands that Christ was nailed to the cross.

Reflection

Excel in this grace of giving...
God loves a cheerful giver.
2 Corinthians 8:7; 9:7

JR

Ruth 3:1–5 (NIV, abridged)

The little foxes

One day Naomi her mother-in-law said to her, 'My daughter, should I not try to find a home for you, where you will be well provided for? Is not Boaz… a kinsman of ours? … go down to the threshing-floor… note the place where he is lying. Then go and uncover his feet and lie down…' 'I will do whatever you say,' Ruth answered. So she went down to the threshing-floor.

Naomi was desolate when she could not provide for her daughters-in-law. Now that she feels more hopeful, she starts to make plans. God is plainly providing, so why should Naomi start conniving? The answer is that she and Ruth belong to a culture with complex kinship ties. They are poor and those without power do not enjoy the freedom to organize their lives that many of the affluent and able-bodied take for granted. They are at the bottom, so Ruth must begin—with God's help—quite literally, at the bottom. She must slip into the threshing place, wait in the shadows and, when Boaz goes to sleep, good-humoured because his harvest is in and he has eaten and drunk well, she must lie at his feet, perfumed and wearing her best clothes. Essentially, they are asking Boaz to make Ruth his wife. Some of this behaviour may seem both manipulative and ambiguous, but Boaz will praise Ruth for her 'noble character' (3:10–11). She is showing the same unselfish devotion to Naomi as before.

In our relationships today, we are not generally called to go to these lengths of trust and obedience. However, our friendship and family ties are exposed to tensions Ruth and Naomi couldn't have dreamt of and they need to be guarded and nurtured. 'Catch us the foxes, the little foxes that spoil the vines, for our vines have tender grapes', cautions the lover in the Song of Songs (2:15, NKJV). Little niggles grow into major stresses. Can you think of any grudges you nurse? Do you see them threatening vulnerable areas in your relationships? Jesus calls us to guard the 'little ones', meaning our children, first of all, but we can extend it to mean our church, work and leisure life.

Reflection

Pause to take stock of your relationships, your hopes, your hurts. Have you allowed 'the little foxes' of resentment to harm tender feelings, immature faith, someone's trust?

JR

Ruth 3:7–13 (NIV, abridged)

The kinsman-redeemer

When Boaz had finished eating and drinking and was in good spirits, he went over to lie down at the far end of the grain pile. Ruth approached quietly, uncovered his feet and lay down. In the middle of the night something startled the man, and he turned and discovered a woman lying at his feet... 'I am your servant Ruth,' she said. 'Spread the corner of your garment over me, since you are a kinsman-redeemer.' 'The Lord bless you, my daughter,' he replied. 'This kindness is greater than that which you showed earlier... you are a woman of noble character. Although it is true that I am near of kin, there is a kinsman-redeemer nearer than I. Stay here for the night, and in the morning... if he is not willing, as surely as the Lord lives I will do it. Lie here until morning.'

Did Ruth sleep that night or did she lie awake, staring into the darkness, every sense attuned to the slightest movement Boaz made? In the middle of the night, Boaz wakens. Ruth makes herself known and places herself under his protection. 'Spread the corner of your garment over me' is a picture of shelter, like the one in 2:12, 'under whose wings you have come to take refuge'.

The structure of the book is tightly knit. We are midway through our readings in Ruth and the action now is towards provision and fullness, but the writer introduces an unexpected cliff-hanger. There is another, closer kinsman who has even more right to redeem the situation. Will Ruth marry Boaz? We must wait and see!

The mention of this kinsman highlights Boaz's moral goodness. Much as he respects Ruth (vv. 10–11), he will defer to the wishes of the kinsman (v. 13) in obedience to the law. However, if the nearer kinsman does not wish to marry Ruth, 'as surely as the Lord lives I will do it'. These words are the key to the book: faith in the living God is worked out in right actions, bringing blessings in the family and the wider community. Boaz and Ruth are both named in the genealogy of Jesus (Matthew 1:5) Boaz is also mentioned in Luke (3:31). Their gentle nobility prefigures the Gospels, when another 'kinsman-redeemer' will bring all things to fulfilment.

Reflection

Consider the beauty of Christ and rejoice that he has such beauty.

JR

Ruth 3:14–18 (NIV, abridged)

'Don't go back empty-handed'

So she lay at his feet until morning, but got up before anyone could be recognized; and he said, 'Don't let it be known that a woman came to the threshing-floor.' He also said, 'Bring me the shawl you are wearing and hold it out.' When she did so, he poured into it six measures of barley... When Ruth came to her mother-in-law, Naomi asked, 'How did it go, my daughter?' Then she told her everything Boaz had done for her and added, 'He gave me these six measures of barley, saying, "Don't go back to your mother-in-law empty-handed." ' Then Naomi said, 'Wait, my daughter, until you find out what happens. For the man will not rest until the matter is settled today.'

Boaz advises caution. Grain from the threshing floor was given in tithe offerings to the Lord (Numbers 18:27). Romans 14:16 counsels, 'Do not allow what you consider good to be spoken of as evil.' Tongues wag and Ruth's good name could be quickly compromised.

Then he pours grain into her shawl. Previously she has had to glean and thresh her own grain, toiling all day under the hot sun. Now Boaz pours out a generous measure of grain others have gathered and threshed. Jesus says, 'Give, and it will be given to you. A good measure, pressed down, shaken together and running over, will be poured into your lap. For with the measure you use, it will be measured to you' (Luke 6:38). Ruth has given everything to Naomi. Now she is richly rewarded. Boaz carries out this gospel precept to the letter, too—'a good measure, pressed down, shaken together and running over'. I demonstrated this with a youth group. We poured flour into a bowl so that the young people could see that when you press it down and shake it you can get more and more in. That is how God gives to us and that is how we must give to others—no half measures! No empty hands!

Reflection and prayer

He has filled the hungry with good things,
but has sent the rich away empty.
Luke 1:53

Lord, may I never go from you
empty-handed, but give and give from
your abundance, knowing that however
much I give, it is all too little and that
you will give me more and more.

JR

Ruth 4:1–8 (NIV, abridged)

The cost of redemption

Meanwhile Boaz went up to the town gate and sat there... Then he said to the kinsman-redeemer, 'Naomi... is selling the piece of land that belonged to our brother Elimelech... If you will redeem it, do so. But if you will not, tell me, so that I will know... I am the next in line.' 'I will redeem it,' he said. Then Boaz said, 'On the day you buy the land... you acquire the dead man's widow, in order to maintain the name of the dead with his property.' At this the kinsman-redeemer said, 'Then I cannot redeem it because I might endanger my own estate... Buy it yourself.' And he removed his sandal.

Boaz sat in the gateway where business was transacted. He gathered ten elders as witnesses. Every detail of the law was honoured. At first the kinsman was delighted to hear he had the right to more land—he was only too ready to profit from Naomi's misfortune. It's like playing Monopoly when the player with Mayfair and Park Lane buys up the rest of the board. However, the minute the kinsman heard that he had an obligation to marry Ruth and the land would pass to her son, he backed off. 'I might endanger my own estate,' he said.

Grasping on the one hand, grudging on the other, the unnamed kinsman is a complete contrast to Boaz. A Holocaust survivor has written a study called *The Altruistic Personality*, based on interviews with people who are honoured in Jerusalem as 'righteous among the Gentiles'. As a small boy fleeing for his life, barefoot and friendless, he had made his way to the house of a peasant woman who had bought his grandfather's cow. He remembered that she had given a good price and that there had been a mouthwatering smell of baking in her home. Now, when he appeared so unexpectedly at the door, she said, 'What are you doing? Don't you know how dangerous this is?' Like the other unselfish people in the study, she knew she would 'endanger her estate', but she said immediately, 'Come on in' and saved the boy's life.

Prayer

Lord Jesus, you knew the cost of our redemption and yet you paid the price. May I know you more clearly, love you more dearly and follow you more nearly, day by day.

JR

Ruth 4:9–12 (NIV, abridged)

'We are witnesses'

Then Boaz announced to the elders and all the people, 'Today you are witnesses that I have bought from Naomi all the property of Elimelech, Kilion and Mahlon. I have also acquired Ruth the Moabitess, Mahlon's widow, as my wife...' Then the elders and all those at the gate said, 'We are witnesses. May the Lord make the woman who is coming into your home like Rachel and Leah, who together built up the house of Israel. May you have standing in Ephrathah and be famous in Bethlehem... may your family be like that of Perez, whom Tamar bore to Judah.'

Was Ruth just a piece of property, thrown in with the sale of the land? To pull that out of today's reading is, of course, to misinterpret the whole book. Ruth had arrived landless and destitute in Judah. Now she has high social standing and she, a foreigner, is being compared with the Mothers of Israel, Rachel and Leah. She embodies a deep truth that the scriptures hammer home and the people of faith need always to relearn, which is that the Kingdom of God does not depend on birth or blood or the old school tie, nor on exam passes or promotion in the firm, but on 'the obedience which comes from faith' (Romans 1:5).

The story began on the road to Judah. The action took place in the fields and on the threshing floor, interspersed with dialogues between Naomi and Ruth. Now we are within the gates of the city, the place of the elders, whose courteous formalities are more than mere social niceties. They are the speech of a people familiar with their roots and they are words of prophecy, pointing to King David and, beyond, to a greater ruler to come. The prophet Micah proclaims, 'But you, Bethlehem Ephrathah... out of you will come for me one who will be ruler over Israel, whose origins are from of old, from ancient times' (5:2). And so it came to pass, and the one who was called the Ancient of Days was born as a homeless child (Matthew 2:1, 6).

The great themes of the scriptures roll like a Bach fugue throughout the book of Ruth, although it might at first sight have seemed small and insignificant, with no weight of doctrine.

Reflection

All scripture bears witness to the 'yes' of God—ancient, endless, ever new.

JR

Ruth 4:13–22 (NIV, abridged)

'Better... than seven sons'

So Boaz took Ruth and she became his wife... and she gave birth to a son. The women said to Naomi, 'Praise be to the Lord who... has not left you without a kinsman-redeemer... He will renew your life and sustain you in your old age. For your daughter-in-law, who loves you and who is better to you than seven sons, has given him birth.' Then Naomi took the child, laid him in her lap and cared for him... And they named him Obed. He was the father of Jesse, the father of David.

The story is rounded off with joy and fullness. Seven is the number of completeness (v. 15). The women who had watched Naomi return home a desolate widow rejoice with the proud grandmother and heap praises on Ruth and blessings on her son. However, the happy family circle is not a closed one: in the book of Ruth the characters, full and complete in and of themselves, mirror greater happiness, fuller redemption, perfect peace.

This is shown in the genealogy that closes the book. I'm never a great one for lists, so I found it helpful when I came across the following story. An old man recalled how, when he was small, he had watched his grandfather note the deaths of his relatives in the family Bible. 'Why do you write the names of the dead in the Bible?' asked the boy. 'Because it is the book of the living,' the old man replied, not ceasing to write.

The list of ten names (another symbolic number of completeness and rest) points to David (vv. 18–22). Ruth's unselfish care of Naomi brings fullness and joy, and her great grandson David will selflessly defend the name of the living God (1 Samuel 17:45–47) and bring Israel peace. The genealogy ultimately points to Jesus, who renews the life of his people (Ruth 4:15), our redeemer who opens the way to fulfilment and peace (Romans 5:1).

Reflection

God used Ruth and Boaz in his plan to bring about the birth of the Saviour. As I think back over the book, I recall Ruth in the barley fields. She illustrates words of Clare of Assisi: 'Make yourself beautiful, Daughter of God and Spouse of the King. Look at your face reflected in his and let your heart sing.'

JR

John 1:23–27 (NRSV)

The voice in the wilderness

He said, 'I am the voice of one crying out in the wilderness, "Make straight the way of the Lord,"' as the prophet Isaiah said. Now they had been sent from the Pharisees. They asked him, 'Why then are you baptizing if you are neither the Messiah, nor Elijah, nor the prophet?' John answered them, 'I baptize with water. Among you stands one whom you do not know, the one who is coming after me; I am not worthy to untie the thong of his sandal.'

It was 'priests and Levites from Jerusalem' whose question sparked these words from John the Baptist. It is the clearest possible statement of his mission: 'I am *the voice*'. His hearers, and certainly the priests, would have recognized the significance of his words, for this 'voice crying out in the wilderness' was the one prophesied by Isaiah, who would 'prepare the way of the Lord' (Isaiah 40:3). John was that 'voice', the forerunner of Yahweh, the Lord. This is undeniably messianic language. The one for whom John was preparing the way must be nothing less than the Messiah himself.

Elijah and 'the prophet' were figures whom Jewish tradition cast in the role of precursors of the Messiah. You may remember that the disciples asked Jesus about this on the way down from the mount of transfiguration, and Jesus told them that the promised Elijah had already come 'and they did what they pleased to him'—an obvious reference to John (Mark 9:13, and also see Luke 1:17). It was not a matter of blame that the Jews did not yet know the hidden Jesus ('among you stands one whom you do not know'), but it would be if they did not accept John's message about him. The 'voice' had spoken, and voices exist to be heard.

Reflection

'Among you stands one whom you do not know.' The tragedy is that it is still possible to say this of those who are near to Jesus, in one sense, yet do not 'know' him. And it may sometimes be true for all of us, when we shut our eyes to his presence.

DW

John 1:29–34 (NRSV)

The Lamb of God

The next day he saw Jesus coming toward him and declared, 'Here is the Lamb of God who takes away the sin of the world! This is he of whom I said, "After me comes a man who ranks ahead of me because he was before me." I myself did not know him; but I came baptizing with water for this reason, that he might be revealed to Israel.' And John testified, 'I saw the Spirit descending from heaven like a dove, and it remained on him. I myself did not know him, but the one who sent me to baptize with water said to me, "He on whom you see the Spirit descend and remain is the one who baptizes with the Holy Spirit." And I myself have seen and have testified that this is the Son of God.'

Here John the Baptist identifies Jesus in three ways. He is the one 'who ranks ahead of me because he was before me' (v. 30). He is the one who 'baptizes with the Holy Spirit' (v. 33). And he is 'the Lamb of God who takes away the sin of the world' (v. 29). The first statement tells us that Jesus was 'pre-existent'—he existed before his coming to earth (John 1:1)—a great theme of this Gospel. The second contrasts John's baptisms with those of Jesus. John baptized with water, according to Jewish tradition: a ritual which removed outward defilement and signified the desire for a new start. Jesus would baptize with (or 'in') the Holy Spirit, a baptism of heart and will that would change people radically and for ever.

The third statement tells us that Jesus is the 'Lamb of God', the sacrifice that God was to provide for the sins of the world—a sacrifice which, unlike the temple sacrifices, would take away sin for ever. For John, such a one must be 'the Son of God' (v. 34).

Reflection

God sent Jesus into the world to take away our sins and to give us new life through the Holy Spirit. This was his premeditated purpose, and in that purpose John saw himself as a small but vital cog. That's a healthy attitude for all of us, whatever our role in God's purpose, great or small.

DW

John 1:35–39a (NRSV)

'Come and see'

The next day John again was standing with two of his disciples, and as he watched Jesus walk by, he exclaimed, 'Look, here is the Lamb of God!' The two disciples heard him say this, and they followed Jesus. When Jesus turned and saw them following, he said to them, 'What are you looking for?' They said to him, 'Rabbi' (which translated means Teacher), 'where are you staying?' He said to them, 'Come and see.'

This is a rather strange piece of dialogue! Two of John's disciples (we learn later that they were John and Andrew) hear him speak of Jesus as the 'Lamb of God' and decide to investigate further. They follow Jesus until he turns and sees them. His question seems to embarrass them: 'What are you looking for?' At any rate, their answer is pretty lame! 'Rabbi, where are you staying?' He simply says, 'Come and see'.

As usual in this Gospel, there's probably more to all this than meets the eye! The two disciples are the seekers—that's the literal meaning of Jesus's question: what are you *seeking*? His invitation is the one he makes to all who truly seek him: 'come and see'. This reminds us of the psalmist's invitation: 'Taste and see that the Lord is good' (Psalm 34:8). Jesus doesn't ask us to believe 'in the dark', but to seek and explore and 'experiment' with faith. 'Come and have a look' is his invitation. 'See what a supermarket of delights there is in this new world of the Spirit. Try for yourself. Come and see!'

So the two men came and saw, and stayed that day—and went away convinced that they had found the Messiah. They didn't learn that from the furnishings of Jesus's undoubtedly simple dwelling, of course, but from the man himself. They 'saw' (one of the great words of John's Gospel) that he fulfilled all that John had spoken of, and with John they could now testify that he was the 'one who was to come' (1:27).

Reflection

Simply offering people the chance to experience the love and goodness of the Lord, without demanding any commitment from them, may often be the way into faith for them.

DW

John 1:45–51 (NRSV)

Heaven opened

Philip found Nathanael and said to him, 'We have found him about whom Moses in the law and also the prophets wrote, Jesus son of Joseph from Nazareth.' Nathanael said to him, 'Can anything good come out of Nazareth?' Philip said to him, 'Come and see.' When Jesus saw Nathanael coming toward him, he said of him, 'Here is truly an Israelite in whom there is no deceit!' Nathanael asked him, 'Where did you get to know me?' Jesus answered, 'I saw you under the fig tree before Philip called you.' Nathanael replied, 'Rabbi, you are the Son of God! You are the King of Israel!' Jesus answered, 'Do you believe because I told you that I saw you under the fig tree? You will see greater things than these.' And he said to him, 'Very truly, I tell you, you will see heaven opened and the angels of God ascending and descending upon the Son of Man.'

Here is another rather strange dialogue! It begins with Philip sharing with Nathanael his new-found faith in Jesus, the prophet from Nazareth. '*Nazareth?*' snorts Nathanael—'from that dump?' (Clearly he didn't know, nor perhaps did Philip, of the birth of Jesus at Bethlehem.) Philip wisely contents himself with the same invitation as Jesus had given him earlier: 'Come and see.' And Nathanael was sufficiently intrigued to do so.

When Jesus saw him, he took Nathanael aback by paying him a very beautiful compliment—that he was 'an Israelite in whom is no deceit'. Obviously Jesus 'saw' something in Nathanael which spoke of his sincerity and seriousness: 'I saw you under the fig tree'—perhaps praying, or wrestling with this question of a coming Messiah. Nathanael is so impressed by this that he utters words of faith beyond anything else we have yet heard. Why, says Jesus, you will see much 'greater things' than that—indeed, 'heaven opened'. What a promise!

Reflection

Jacob saw angels ascending and descending a ladder between heaven and earth (see Genesis 28:12, 13). Now Jesus himself would be the ladder, bridging the gap between where we are and where God is.

DW

John 2:6–11 (NRSV)

The new wine has arrived

Now standing there were six stone water jars for the Jewish rites of purification, each holding twenty or thirty gallons. Jesus said to them, 'Fill the jars with water.' And they filled them up to the brim. He said to them, 'Now draw some out, and take it to the chief steward.' So they took it. When the steward tasted the water that had become wine, and did not know where it came from (though the servants who had drawn the water knew), the steward called the bridegroom and said to him, 'Everyone serves the good wine first, and then the inferior wine after the guests have become drunk. But you have kept the good wine until now.'

Every year in the autumn the notice appears in shop windows, '*Le Beaujolais nouveau est arrivé*'—the new Beaujolais wine has arrived from France. This story or 'sign' (in John's language) is about the 'new wine' of the kingdom which has 'arrived' with Jesus. He took the 'old water' of the Jewish law—which filled the water jars for the rites of purification—and turned it into the rich, bubbling, effervescent wine of new life. Indeed, this new wine was so good that the MC couldn't understand why they hadn't served it first. Even in that remark one of John's 'deeper truths' emerges: 'You have kept the good wine until now.' All of God's dealings with us are good, but there has been nothing in all history to equal the sending of his Son into the world.

The miracle itself, like almost all of the gospel miracles, is a miracle 'with' nature rather than against it. After all, in the ordinary process of nature, water in the soil becomes juice in the grape and in due course wine in the jar. The word of the Master simply accelerates the process! But for John every miracle is a 'sign', evidence of deeper truth, testimony to the meaning of the great event which was unfolding before their eyes in the coming of Jesus.

A reflection

In life it is wonderful to hold to the truth that God always keeps the 'good wine' until now. He is not just a God of past blessings, but of the present, and with him it is always 'the best'.

DW

John 3:3–6 (NRSV)

Flesh and spirit

Jesus answered him, 'Very truly, I tell you, no one can see the kingdom of God without being born from above.' Nicodemus said to him, 'How can anyone be born after having grown old? Can one enter a second time into the mother's womb and be born?' Jesus answered, 'Very truly, I tell you, no one can enter the kingdom of God without being born of water and Spirit. What is born of the flesh is flesh, and what is born of the Spirit is spirit.'

The well-known conversation between Jesus and Nicodemus, the prominent Pharisee who came to see him secretly by night, is actually about the two worlds of 'flesh' and 'spirit'. Nicodemus's flattering greeting (v. 2) is met by what seems to be a bald statement by Jesus: 'You must be born from above'—or, as the NRSV margin translates it, 'born anew'. The conversation as it develops centres around this insistence of Jesus: people are both flesh and spirit, and human life is incomplete without the element of spirit. We have to be born of 'water and Spirit' (the capital letter 'S' is a tricky one in this passage!) Presumably the 'water' here is the water of physical birth. I remember one astonished husband remarking to me that he knew about the mother's 'waters breaking' before birth but he had no idea how *much* water there would be! We are all 'born of water', but we also need to be 'born of Spirit'. Without the spiritual element in our lives we are, in the teaching of Jesus, only half human.

That is the way we are made—'in the image of God'. So to concentrate in child development on physical, intellectual and emotional growth but to neglect the spiritual is to deprive the child of its human birthright. 'You *must* be born *from above*.'

Reflection

In a world that puts so much emphasis on education, health and mental stability, where does the life of the Spirit come in? Are we in danger of getting our values distorted?

DW

John 3:7–12 (NRSV)

The wind of God

'Do not be astonished that I said to you, "You must be born from above." The wind blows where it chooses, and you hear the sound of it, but you do not know where it comes from or where it goes. So it is with everyone who is born of the Spirit.' Nicodemus said to him, 'How can these things be?' Jesus answered him, 'Are you a teacher of Israel, and yet you do not understand these things? Very truly, I tell you, we speak of what we know and testify to what we have seen; yet you do not receive our testimony. If I have told you about earthly things and you do not believe, how can you believe if I tell you about heavenly things?'

My little granddaughter was looking out of the patio doors at the branches swaying in the wind, and the leaves being blown along by it. 'Grandpa,' she said, 'look at the wind!' And I did, of course, though what both she and I actually saw wasn't 'the wind' but the *effect* of the wind. The wind itself is invisible. All we can see—and feel—is what it does! That is the very simple and yet profound meaning of Jesus' words to Nicodemus. If you want to 'see' the Spirit of God, look at the results.

Jesus is driving home his point that 'you' (the word is plural—not just poor Nicodemus, who'd rather stuck his neck out!) must be born of the Spirit if you are to enter God's kingdom. Nicodemus was confused by this, but Jesus wanted him to understand that this wasn't some complicated piece of mysticism. It was simply the application in the spiritual realm of a truth he well knew in the natural world. There are some things, and wind is one of them, that you don't have to be able to explain or analyse in order to be deeply affected by them. Don't agonize over the Spirit of God, Jesus says, in effect, just be open to what he does.

Reflection

I can see the Spirit's work, in myself and in others, only by the effects. 'You will know them by their fruits.'

DW

John 3:14–17 (NRSV)

Why God sent Jesus

And just as Moses lifted up the serpent in the wilderness, so must the Son of Man be lifted up, that whoever believes in him may have eternal life. For God so loved the world that he gave his only Son, so that everyone who believes in him may not perish but may have eternal life. Indeed, God did not send the Son into the world to condemn the world, but in order that the world might be saved through him.

When I did my National Service in the RAF about five centuries ago, I served in the medical branch. We wore in our lapels a much-prized badge, which depicted a serpent coiled around a cross. I knew the biblical story from which this idea was drawn and there it was on our uniforms, the badge of healing. Moses healed the people of Israel of snake-bites by obeying God's command to fix a brass serpent to a post and carry it through the camp. All who looked on it were healed.

Here John (or is it Jesus himself?) uses that Old Testament story to introduce his answer to the question, 'Why did God send his Son into the world?' The answer is: in order to heal us from the fatal consequences of sin. And how would he do that? By bearing it himself. The serpent on the pole was both a picture of the cause of the trouble, and the cure for it. So is the death of Jesus. The cross shows us what sin is 'like'—this is what it does: it kills. But it also shows us the remedy, as the world's Saviour bears our sin and takes it away. Just as Moses lifted up the serpent so Jesus would be 'lifted up' on the cross—an image John comes back to later (see John 12:32). That is the measure of the love of God, and the commitment of the Saviour.

Reflection

However long we have known it, however familiar the story may be, these verses ought to lift the heart of the Christian. God did not send his Son to judge us, but to save!

DW

John 3:19–21 (NRSV)

Light and darkness

And this is the judgment, that the light has come into the world, and people loved darkness rather than light because their deeds were evil. For all who do evil hate the light and do not come to the light, so that their deeds may not be exposed. But those who do what is true come to the light, so that it may be clearly seen that their deeds have been done in God.

The moment of creation—what we might now call the 'Big Bang'—was when light drove back the darkness. 'Darkness covered the face of the deep… Then God said, "Let there be light"; and there was light' (Genesis 1:2, 3). And that, in a way, is the story of the Bible—a constant conflict between darkness and light, evil and good, death and life. John begins his Gospel with a reference back to that primeval darkness, in order to state triumphantly that in the coming of Jesus, the 'Word', the light has again shone into the darkness—'and the darkness did not overcome it'. This theme of Christ as the light of the world, challenging, judging and defeating its darkness, runs all through the Gospel, and indeed also through John's first letter.

Here John explains (or, again, is it Jesus?) how it can be that when the light of God is shining in the world through his Son there are those who prefer to stay in the dark. John's explanation is stark, but has the ring of truth about it: 'people loved darkness rather than light'. And the reason is not difficult to fathom: light exposes evil, and human nature doesn't like having its sins (even so-called 'little ones') exposed for what they are.

Of course, some light is harsh and hard on the eyes, but this is the light of Christ, who has not come to condemn and judge, but to save (v. 17). This is a light that we should not fear but gladly welcome, even if it does call us constantly to amend our lives and turn from the darkness.

Reflection

If we walk in the light as he himself is in the light, we have fellowship with one another, and the blood of Jesus his Son cleanses us from all sin.

1 John 1:7

DW

John 3:26–30 (NRSV)

John's witness

They came to John and said to him, 'Rabbi, the one who was with you across the Jordan, to whom you testified, here he is baptizing, and all are going to him.' John answered, 'No one can receive anything except what has been given from heaven. You yourselves are my witnesses that I said, "I am not the Messiah, but I have been sent ahead of him." He who has the bride is the bridegroom. The friend of the bridegroom, who stands and hears him, rejoices greatly at the bridegroom's voice. For this reason my joy has been fulfilled. He must increase, but I must decrease.'

It is not always easy to celebrate the success of another, especially when they are succeeding where we appear to have failed. It's a common problem in Christian work. One person runs the Sunday school or the Mothers' Union for years, faithfully and conscientiously. Then—perhaps through age, or tiredness, or circumstances—they have to give it up and their successor suddenly sees all the blessing that had somehow eluded them. Numbers increase, everyone in the church is talking about it. It's pretty hard to swallow our feelings and join in the applause, isn't it?

That's where John the Baptist is such a marvellous example. Reading the Gospels, we may not appreciate what a powerful figure he was in Jewish history—a prophet of enormous influence and stature. And then along comes the carpenter's son from Nazareth, and in a few days John's disciples are going over to Jesus and the crowds will soon have a new hero to follow. But John isn't hurt. After all, he says, he knew this would happen. Both he and Jesus were simply receiving the appointed gift of God, John as the 'friend of the bridegroom' and Jesus as the bridegroom himself. 'He must increase, but I must decrease.' John had faithfully done what God had sent him to do. Now the forerunner could step aside.

Reflection

May God help me to be glad when others enjoy his blessing.

DW

John 4:10–15 (NRSV)

Living water

Jesus answered her, 'If you knew the gift of God, and who it is who is saying to you, "Give me a drink," you would have asked him, and he would have given you living water.' The woman said to him, 'Sir, you have no bucket, and the well is deep. Where do you get that living water? Are you greater than our ancestor Jacob, who gave us the well, and with his sons and flocks drank from it?' Jesus said to her, 'Everyone who drinks of this water will be thirsty again, but those who drink of the water that I will give them will never be thirsty. The water that I will give will become in them a spring of water gushing up to eternal life.' The woman said to him, 'Sir, give me this water, so that I may never be thirsty or have to keep coming here to draw water.'

If you're not already familiar with it, this story of Jesus and the woman at the well is worth reading right through. It runs from 4:4 to 4:42. There are many ideas and pictures in it which are common in this gospel—the theme of 'living water', of course, and the priority of inner conversion over outward ritual. In dramatic terms, the woman is a well-rounded character, the sort of person who tries to laugh everything off with a flippant remark, but meets her match in Jesus.

The passage we are looking at today, however, introduces this theme of 'living water'. Most of the water available to people in Jewish towns and villages was well-water, very adequate for their needs, but lacking the zest and sparkle and freshness of spring water, 'gushing up' from the earth. That is what Jesus calls 'living water'—water that both keeps you alive and makes life worth living, water that adds that bit 'extra' (rather like the new wine of the earlier story). Just as Jesus offers the 'living bread' (bread that gives life—see John 6:35), so he offers the 'living water'. And, once given, that living water becomes self-renewing. The believer becomes, as it were, a 'spring' themselves, a constantly renewed source of inner life.

Reflection

'Sir, give me this water.'

DW

John 4:19–24 (NRSV)

True worship

The woman said to him, 'Sir, I see that you are a prophet. Our ancestors worshipped on this mountain, but you say that the place where people must worship is in Jerusalem.' Jesus said to her, 'Woman, believe me, the hour is coming when you will worship the Father neither on this mountain nor in Jerusalem. You worship what you do not know; we worship what we know, for salvation is from the Jews. But the hour is coming, and is now here, when the true worshippers will worship the Father in spirit and truth, for the Father seeks such as these to worship him. God is spirit, and those who worship him must worship in spirit and truth.'

It is a great breakthrough in our thinking about religion when we realize that God is not impressed by rituals, ceremonies and offerings but by true, inner commitment of heart and will. Anything else is, in essence, superstition. It was a lesson that the people of Israel resisted for centuries, somehow convinced that if only they offered the right sacrifices and performed the correct rituals God would accept and bless them. Time and again the great prophets of Israel warned them that it wasn't like that. 'Bringing offerings is futile; incense is an abomination to me… I cannot endure solemn assemblies with iniquity… Wash yourselves; make yourselves clean… cease to do evil, learn to do good' (Isaiah 1:13–17). What mattered was not the meticulous performance of *rites*, but doing *right*.

Here, the greatest prophet of Israel gives a Samaritan adulteress the most profound insight into the nature of true worship in the whole Bible. If God is 'spirit', then those who worship him must worship 'in spirit and in truth'. In other words, worship is an essentially spiritual activity, which expresses the deepest truths about ourselves and about God. It's not playing games, or jumping through hoops. Worship takes us into the very heart of things.

Reflection

In true worship, what we are in our deepest being meets—however fleetingly —with what God is in his deepest being.
DW

1 Corinthians 4:1–4 (NIV)

A clear conscience

So then, men ought to regard us as servants of Christ and as those entrusted with the secret things of God. Now it is required that those who have been given a trust must prove faithful. I care very little if I am judged by you or by any human court; indeed, I do not even judge myself. My conscience is clear, but that does not make me innocent. It is the Lord who judges me.

Paul makes three remarkable claims for himself in this passage. If they are justified he was a truly extraordinary man. My inability truthfully to make similar claims might go a long way towards explaining why 'being a Christian' can feel like such hard work at times.

First, he says he cares little whether he is judged by the people he is writing to, or by anyone else. Well, *I* do. I care whether I'm judged by you, and lots of other people as well. I sometimes pretend that I don't, because I dislike the image of myself as the kind of person who is concerned about the opinions of others. I'm certainly not like Paul, but I suppose it's something to aim for.

Second, Paul says he does not even judge himself. Well, I'm not doing quite so badly on this one. A while ago I did give up on trying to earn my way into God's good books, which was a great relief, but I'm still quite capable of voluntarily separating myself from God because I refuse to allow that his grace covers my current area of negative behaviour. This tendency towards self-judgment cripples more Christian lives than almost anything else, and, as usual, unbelief is at its root.

Paul's third and most staggering claim is that his conscience is clear, although he adds (thank God!) that this does not necessarily mean he's innocent. Now, does he mean that his conscience is clear because God is continually forgiving the sins that he commits, or that he is not aware of having committed any sins? If the former, then we can, in theory at least, line up with him, but if the latter, well—let's all huddle together and tell each other that we never really liked Paul much anyway…

Prayer

We want to be judged only by you.
Help us, Father.

AP

1 Corinthians 4:18–21 (NIV)

Whose power?

Some of you have become arrogant, as if I were not coming to you. But I will come to you very soon, if the Lord is willing, and then I will find out not only how these arrogant people are talking, but what power they have. For the kingdom of God is not a matter of talk but of power. What do you prefer? Shall I come to you with a whip, or in love and with a gentle spirit?

I know which I'd prefer. Paul on the warpath doesn't appeal at all, not because of the man, but because of the power he wielded. I expect these arrogant Corinthians felt the same. You can get away with murder while the boss is away, but when you know he's about to reappear, confidence tends to fade. Churches, then as now, are capable of building atmospheres, environments, ways of worship and even theologies that seem strong and impressive, until the genuine power of God reveals them as products of man's striving imagination.

Some of you will remember the Fountain Trust evangelist, Edgar Trout. I only heard him speak once, but I shall never forget it. I was sixteen, and quite excited as I headed for the meeting venue in Tunbridge Wells. Edgar Trout's reputation had preceded him, and I was intrigued to see what a 'modern apostle' looked like. I was disappointed at first. He didn't look very impressive. In fact, he seemed faded and colourless. He was introduced by two church leaders at the forefront of local spiritual renewal. I knew them. Now they *were* impressive men, full of inspiration and confidence. I wished one of them was doing the speaking.

Then Edgar Trout stood up.

Some of you will know what I mean when I say that the room was filled with the perceivable presence of God as this man spoke. The very air seemed to crackle with spiritual energy as he delivered a very simple message. The church leaders whom I had thought so impressive impressed me even more by listening to his voice like two small children who had never really believed or understood until this moment. In that room, on that night, we knew the power of God.

I do hope the Corinthians made the right choice.

Prayer

More power, Lord, as long as it's yours.

AP

1 Corinthians 5:1–3 (NIV)

An ill wind

It is actually reported that there is sexual immorality among you, and of a kind that does not occur even among pagans: A man has his father's wife. And you are proud! Shouldn't you rather have been filled with grief and have put out of your fellowship the man who did this? Even though I am not physically present, I am with you in spirit. And I have already passed judgment on the one who did this, just as if I were present.

One of the most immediately relevant passages in the book, this section rings with Paul's indignation and disgust that the church should be not just tolerating grossly incestuous behaviour, but appearing to be proud of it. Why would they have been proud, for goodness sake? What was there to be proud about—on any level? A brief look at what is happening in the modern church might help us to understand.

By and large, the church tends to reflect shifts and changes in society, even if it usually takes a little while to catch up. Sometimes these movements really are beneficial to Christians, but there are times when gusts of fresh air brought by the winds of change are closely followed by a very bad smell indeed. This has certainly been the case with what is loosely termed the 'sexual revolution'. A new openness about sex has been of great benefit to the church, which for years has needed a good spring-clean in an area that always tended to reek of guilt and unpleasantness. Unfortunately, this very positive adjustment of thinking has been accompanied by a relaxation of morality and standards that has left whole churches very confused and unsure about how to react to behaviours that were once (still are) clearly unfitting to a Christian lifestyle. As in Corinth, the generally increased carnality of the church environment has a paralysing effect on clear judgment, sometimes to the extent that a certain pride is taken in the fact that blatantly inappropriate behaviour is not condemned. Such tolerance can feel very Christian, but Paul is saying here with crystal clarity that it is not, and that something must be done about it.

Tackling this problem in the coming years without the option of reverting to our old pharisaical ways will need great courage and wisdom.

Prayer

Give us wisdom, and courage to be strong, Father.

AP

1 Corinthians 5:9–11 (NIV)

Staying pure

I have written to you in my letter not to associate with sexually immoral people—not at all meaning the people of this world who are immoral, or the greedy and swindlers, or idolaters. In that case you would have to leave this world. But now I am writing to you that you must not associate with anyone who calls himself a brother but is sexually immoral or greedy, an idolater or a slanderer, a drunkard or a swindler. With such a man do not even eat.

Some Christian groups have placed strict separation from the secular world at the very centre of their religious philosophies. It is almost as though there has been a wilful disregard of these clear indications from Paul that contact with the secular world is an inevitable and desirable part of Christian living. The reason for such avoidance? Perhaps people are fearful of having their hobbies disrupted. Mind you, Paul was not the first nor the most significant personage to convey this message. The ministry of Jesus involved regular contact with drunkards, swindlers, prostitutes and anybody else who would listen.

Paul's unequivocal statement that the Corinthian Christians must not even eat with people who claimed to be brothers but committed such sins is much more problematic, but just as important. Perhaps social editing of this kind was easier in Corinth, but in the superficially polite ethos of today's churches it can be tricky. I remember, just after being converted as a teenager, getting into conversation with an elderly man from my church about 'the state of society'.

'It's the blacks cause all the problems,' said my companion gloomily and unoriginally, 'coming over here, taking all our jobs off us.'

I was outraged. How could someone who called himself a Christian hold such blatantly racist and uncharitable views? I almost burst with indignation, but I didn't say anything. Since those early years of my faith, the same kind of situation has occurred many times, although on different subjects and usually in rather more subtle ways, and still, mainly for fear of appearing or feeling hypocritical, I have not protected the purity of the body of Christ by saying enough of what I really think—and I feel a little ashamed.

Prayer

Father, forgive us for letting your church become impure.

AP

1 Corinthians 6:1–5 (NIV)

The sticking point

If any of you has a dispute with another, dare he take it before the ungodly for judgment instead of before the saints? Do you not know that the saints will judge the world? And if you are to judge the world, are you not competent to judge trivial cases? Do you not know that we will judge angels? How much more the things of this life! Therefore, if you have disputes about such matters, appoint as judges even men of little account in the church! I say this to shame you. Is it possible that there is nobody among you wise enough to judge a dispute between believers?

Scratch a Christian and you'll find a human being, particularly where property is concerned. Paul seems amazed that these Corinthian Christians were resorting to secular courts to settle differences, but a lot of us Christians still have what we might call an 'All very well, but…' point in our lives. By this, I mean that point where we discover, perhaps with a stab of disappointment, that our 'game' of faith has ended, and we shrug sheepishly, and shake our heads and look knowingly at each other, as if to say, 'Come on, let's face it—we always knew we'd draw the line somewhere—you've got to live in the real world, you know.'

That line is usually drawn at the place where we will not surrender what we are determined to have in terms of sex, power or even personal problems that offer us a sense of identity, but money is more often the sticking point, and particularly any attempt to separate us from it. The very idea of genuinely opening up the issue of property to the church family is frightening and repugnant to those who find truly solid ground only in financial stability.

Controversy over the last decade about 'heavy shepherding' (close pastoral supervision of church members) must have been very welcome to members of churches where it was a problem. What a wonderful opportunity to submerge our reluctance to put Jesus above Mammon, by dropping it into that sea of righteous resistance to unwarranted interference by church leaders. This is why that particular movement was so destructive. It gave tentative members of the family a reason to move even farther from the centre, and to tell themselves that they were quite justified in doing so.

Prayer

Be our solid ground, Lord.

AP

1 Corinthians 6:9–11 (NIV)

On the list?

Do you not know that the wicked will not inherit the kingdom of God? Do not be deceived: Neither the sexually immoral nor idolaters nor adulterers nor male prostitutes nor homosexual offenders nor thieves nor the greedy nor drunkards nor slanderers nor swindlers will inherit the kingdom of God. And that is what some of you were. But you were washed, you were sanctified, you were justified in the name of the Lord Jesus Christ and by the Spirit of our God.

Here is Paul being quite categorical about what should *not* be permissible in the church, presumably basing his selection on problems that were actually emerging among Corinthian Christians.

When I began to write Bible notes a few years ago, I promised myself that I would do my best to be as honest as possible. Sometimes honesty is difficult because responses become habitual and are hardly visible. They fly past, as it were, before one has a chance to register or identify them. Well, I just caught one. I realized that on just about every occasion when I encounter lists of this kind, I work through the categories one by one to see if any of them apply to me. I really do. In this case I flicked through in order to discover if I am one of the wicked who will not inherit the kingdom of God.

Now, this is fatal for someone like me. Do you remember that wonderful passage in *Three Men In a Boat*, Jerome K. Jerome's great comic masterpiece, where a man reads a medical book from cover to cover and discovers that the only ailment he is not suffering from is Housemaid's Knee? It's a bit like that with this list of Paul's. I'm sure that I've never been a male prostitute or a homosexual offender, but all the other sins, well—isn't it possible that, by some definition or other, I've committed them *all*?

The answer to this kind of mild panic is, of course, contained in the same passage. Whether or not we have committed some or even all of these sins, the only truly important fact is that we are washed, and we are sanctified, and we are justified in the name of the Lord Jesus Christ and by the Spirit of our God.

Phew!

Prayer

Thank you for cleaning us up, Lord.

AP

1 Corinthians 7:1–7 (NIV)

Co-ownership

Now for the matters you wrote about: It is good for a man not to marry. But since there is so much immorality, each man should have his own wife, and each woman her own husband. The husband should fulfil his marital duty to his wife, and likewise the wife to her husband. The wife's body does not belong to her alone but also to her husband. In the same way the husband's body does not belong to him alone but also to his wife. Do not deprive each other except by mutual consent and for a time, so that you may devote yourselves to prayer. Then come together again so that Satan will not tempt you because of your lack of self-control. I say this as a concession, not as a command. I wish that all men were as I am. But each man has his own gift from God; one has this gift, another has that.

I don't think Paul would have been keen on our modern Christian dating agencies, do you? Still, he's not here, so never mind.

On first reading these verses one is struck by the singular lack of humanity and warmth. Sex appears to be an intrusive irritant, something which has to happen, but would really be better abolished altogether. Where is the romance? Where is the joy of togetherness? Where is the unity of mind, spirit *and* body? It all sounds a bit bleak, doesn't it?

However, two important factors (aside from contemporary literary conventions) help to explain Paul's very functional view of this matter. First, he believed, judging from other sections of the letter (see verses 29 and 31, for instance) that the world really was on the point of coming to an end. A general preoccupation with such matters as sex and marriage must have seemed maddeningly trivial, given the urgent task of evangelism on hand. Second, the Corinthian church was in such a tumultuous moral state that any teaching about sex had to be completely clear and uncompromising. If that was Paul's aim, he succeeded.

Quite apart from all that, Paul's comment about husbands and wives co-owning each other's bodies is worth reflecting on in an age when commitment has become a bit of a dirty word.

Prayer

Father, help us to bring life, romance and fidelity into our marriages.

AP

1 Corinthians 7:10–14 (NIV)

We know we've sinned

To the married I give this command (not I, but the Lord): A wife must not separate from her husband. But if she does, she must remain unmarried or else be reconciled to her husband. And a husband must not divorce his wife. To the rest I say this (I, not the Lord): If any brother has a wife who is not a believer and she is willing to live with him, he must not divorce her. And if a woman has a husband who is not a believer and he is willing to live with her, she must not divorce him. For the unbelieving husband has been sanctified through his wife, and the unbelieving wife has been sanctified through her believing husband. Otherwise your children would be unclean, but as it is, they are holy.

I can't read the first paragraph of this passage without experiencing a resurgence of the pain I have felt in sympathy with many folks who would dearly love to have done exactly what Paul says here. Of course Christians don't want their marriages to end in divorce. Of course they would rather have a lifelong, successful relationship reflecting that between Christ and his church. Of course we all fall woefully short of the ideal, and of course we thank God for Jesus who forgives sin and binds up the broken-hearted and understands and allows us to begin again.

In *Three Men in a Boat*, written around the turn of the century, Jerome K. Jerome describes how he discovers a corpse of a young woman in the river and learns later that, having given birth out of wedlock, she became so oppressed by poverty and loneliness that she ended her own life.

'She had sinned,' says Jerome. 'Some of us do that now and then, you know...'

Well, yes, we jolly well do, and most of us know well enough what we've done. Thank God Jesus is in charge.

As for the second paragraph—well, read it again. Do you believe what Paul says here? I do, and I think it's very good news indeed, don't you? Pass it on...

Prayer

Forgive us, hold us, heal us, save us.
Thank you.

AP

1 Corinthians 7:20–24 (NIV)

Staying put?

Each one should remain in the situation which he was in when God called him. Were you a slave when you were called? Don't let it trouble you—although if you can gain your freedom, do so. For he who was a slave when he was called by the Lord is the Lord's freedman; similarly, he who was a free man when he was called is Christ's slave. You were bought at a price; do not become slaves of men. Brothers, each man, as responsible to God, should remain in the situation God called him to.

When I was a young Christian these verses were hotly debated whenever the Christian sub-subculture managed to spend time away from those who told us what to think.

'What is Paul on about?' I might cry over my demonically strong coffee. 'Surely he's not saying that slaves simply have to accept the situation they're in. That's not radical Christianity—that's just disguised social control.'

We were terribly political in the 1960s, you know…

I look at this passage today and realize with a shock that we didn't notice the bit where he says slaves should gain their freedom if possible—I guess we didn't want to. It was much more fun getting hot under the collar. The thing that does strike me nowadays, though, is the distance between Paul's general recommendations and the thinking of many modern Christians, who express a desire to move into something called 'Full-time Christian Work'. One suspects that Paul's response to the vast majority of folk who say this would be something along the lines of, 'If you're not doing full-time Christian work in the situation you happen to find yourself in, you're unlikely to be able to do it anywhere else.'

Presumably, one of the primary needs in Corinth was exactly the same as it is now. For the benefit of the gospel, people in every walk of life were required to stay where they were and be salt and light to those they worked with and for. Clearly, as Paul himself indicates in verse 24, God might well call some out to perform particular tasks for him, but the majority were valuably involved with the unbelieving world and needed to stay put.

This will be a hard lesson for some of us.

Prayer

What is your agenda for me, Lord?

AP

1 Corinthians 7:29–31 (NIV)

The swing of the pendulum

What I mean, brothers, is that the time is short. From now on those who have wives should live as if they had none; those who mourn, as if they did not; those who are happy, as if they are not; those who buy something, as if it were not theirs to keep; those who use the things of the world, as if not engrossed in them. For this world in its present form is passing away.

I find this a very tough piece of teaching, tough to understand and to accept.

Look at this list. Married people should behave as if not married, mourners as if they've got nothing to mourn, those who are happy as if there's nothing to be happy about, those who buy things as if their purchases weren't really theirs, and those who use worldly things as if they weren't bothered with them. What's Paul talking about? Does he really want me to pretend I'm single after all the other stuff he says about sex? I don't think so, do you? Does he want me to go around pretending I'm miserable when I feel OK? Surely not. I do hope there isn't a church somewhere where everyone tries to obey these instructions to the letter, because, let's face it, the whole thing sounds like a recipe for producing a bunch of loonies.

No, to perceive and accept what Paul is really saying, we need to start with that phrase 'the time is short'. As we've seen, Paul expected the second coming at any moment. This 'unholy' Corinthian church had become heavily distracted from the simple truth of the gospel as originally preached by Paul. In this case the weighty spiritual pendulum needed to be swung from concentration on worldly matters to a new vision of that central truth expressed by Jesus as a need to seek the Kingdom of God above all things. To effect this swing the pendulum had first to be pushed to its farthest limits, so that it would then settle back into a central position of truth. The same ploy was used by Jesus when he talked about his followers needing to hate their families for his sake, and on the occasion when he publicly claimed that he had no mother and no brothers.

Paul's central message emerges as stark but essential. Absolutely everything is provisional, except Jesus.

Prayer

Lord, we loosen our grip on the world and look at you.

AP

1 Corinthians 7:32–35 (NIV)

Made in heaven?

I would like you to be free from concern. An unmarried man is concerned about the Lord's affairs—how he can please the Lord. But a married man is concerned about the affairs of this world—how he can please his wife—and his interests are divided. An unmarried woman or virgin is concerned about the Lord's affairs: Her aim is to be devoted to the Lord in both body and spirit. But a married woman is concerned about the affairs of this world—how she can please her husband. I am saying this for your own good, not to restrict you, but that you may live in a right way in undivided devotion to the Lord.

When you've been brought up as a Christian to believe that scripture is inspired to the extent that someone might easily be converted by a semi-colon in Leviticus, it's difficult to *see* familiar verses, let alone disagree with them. This can make Bible reading a barren experience, and is certainly not what God wants. We are to engage with scripture, not suck it like a thumb for flavourless comfort.

And here is an example. I have real problems with the dogmatic statements Paul is making here. I'm sure you're sick of the word 'context' by now, but it is true that the historical context is very different. (There wasn't much point raising families if the world was about to end!) Perhaps the Corinthians really were devoted to God when they were single and completely distracted when they married, but contemporary experience seems different. Most married people I know would say their spiritual lives have grown in authenticity through close commitment to another person, and we learn more about the fatherhood of God from the experience of parenthood than any book or sermon could teach us. In addition, Christian men who have wives clever enough to know them, and wise enough not to flaunt their knowledge indiscriminately, have been saved from disaster and foolishness again and again by intervention that's infuriating at the time, but essential in retrospect.

Of course, Paul has a point for today's church. Marriage and family life can become all-absorbing and distracting, just as singleness could, potentially anyway, leave more space for exclusive service to God. But, like just about everything else in the universe, it's not as simple as that.

Question

What do you think?

AP

1 Corinthians 8:4, 7–8 (NIV)

Rules and regs

So then, about eating food sacrificed to idols… Some people are still so accustomed to idols that when they eat such food they think of it as having been sacrificed to an idol, and since their conscience is weak, it is defiled. But food does not bring us near to God; we are no worse if we do not eat, and no better if we do.

We Christians should really rejoice about the fact that God is not silly. You may feel there is an air of irreverence in even suggesting that he might be, but from creation to the present day God has had his work cut out convincing us creatures made in his image that, in the most important sense (the one preceded by the adjective 'common'), he is more human than we are. God's dealings with his people throughout the Old Testament are shot through with his passionate desire to convey the essentially non-religious and quietly logical nature of our potential relationship with him.

Burnt sacrifices and that sort of thing are OK, says God, as he carefully places another fish over the fire to cook, but frankly, I'd prefer you to show mercy, and look after each other properly, and learn to love me as much as I love you, and generally practise for heaven.

These Corinthian Christians, fussing and fretting over the issue of food sacrificed to idols, had clearly not caught on to this at all. They credited God, as many of us do today, with the sort of irritable irrationality that demands meaningless adherence to redundant 'rules and regs'.

Surely nothing could be further from the truth, and yet I continually meet people who, perhaps because of a particular type of church upbringing, seem to devote their lives to the avoidance or observance of a whole set of behaviours that are actually quite neutral. If Jesus were to come into some of our church situations in the flesh today he might watch and listen for a while before saying with innocent puzzlement in his voice, 'You do this every Sunday? You never do this at all? You've never tried that? But—why?' The tragedy is that there would almost certainly be someone keenly, sternly ready to answer him.

Prayer

Help us not to be silly, Lord.

AP

1 Corinthians 8:9–13 (NIV)

Strengths and weaknesses

Be careful, however, that the exercise of your freedom does not become a stumbling-block to the weak. For if anyone with a weak conscience sees you who have this knowledge eating in an idol's temple, won't he be emboldened to eat what has been sacrificed to idols? So this weak brother, for whom Christ died, is destroyed by your knowledge. When you sin against your brothers in this way and wound their weak conscience, you sin against Christ. Therefore, if what I eat causes my brother to fall into sin, I will never eat meat again, so that I will not cause him to fall.

OK, here's the other side of the food-offered-to-idols coin, and we might as well spell it out before voicing an inevitable query.

Paul says that those who (wrongly) believe it a sin to eat food sacrificed to idols might be tempted to go against their beliefs if they see it being done by those who have understood that food is simply food. If these weaker brothers do this they *will* have committed sin, not because of the food, but because they have acted against their consciences. The stronger brother must abandon indulgence in any aspect of his freedom that might cause his weaker brother to sin.

That all makes sense. I have to confess that there was a period in my life when I read this passage like Little Jack Horner, pulling out the plums that suited me to throw them at the weaker brother, and make him feel silly because he felt unable to drink a glass of wine or see a film. That was mean, and foolish, because in crucial ways I'm a weaker brother myself, so I sincerely repent, which is a good thing, because it leaves me free to express the query that I mentioned just now.

Should the weaker brother be educated into the freedom that he is unable to enjoy, or should a whole church, for instance, happily conform to the views of a minority that is still imprisoned in this way? I have no universal answer to this question, although I notice that where good humour, mutual respect and a real willingness to be loving are present in Christian communities, there is much less of a problem. Where they are not—oh, dear!

Prayer

Help us willingly to share strengths and weaknesses, Lord.

AP

Judges 4:2–10 (NRSV, abridged)

Women of war

The Lord sold (the Israelites) into the hand of King Jabin of Canaan… the commander of his army was Sisera… At that time Deborah, a prophetess, wife of Lappidoth, was judging Israel… She sent and summoned Barak… from Kedesh in Naphtali, and said to him, 'The Lord, the God of Israel, commands you, "Go, take position at Mount Tabor, bringing ten thousand from the tribe of Naphtali and the tribe of Zebulun. I will draw out Sisera… to meet you by the Wadi Kishon with his chariots and his troops; and I will give him into your hand."' Barak said to her, 'If you will go with me, I will go; but if you will not go with me, I will not go.' And she said, 'I will surely go with you; nevertheless, the road on which you are going will not lead to your glory, for the Lord will sell Sisera into the hand of a woman.' … Barak summoned Zebulun and Naphtali to Kedesh; and ten thousand warriors went up behind him; and Deborah went up with him.

A woman in a man's society, Deborah is judge of Israel, and a prophet. Barak, though promised victory, is uncertain whether it can be achieved without her at his side, and is willing to give up the victor's acclaim rather than go it alone. And when Sisera is defeated, he meets his death at the hands of Jael, a Kenite woman whom he counted as an ally. Jael is even stranger than Deborah. We are not told why she kills Sisera, for she is no Israelite. Probably it is a political decision. The balance of power has shifted, and her people can no longer afford a dangerous alliance.

Whatever their background and motivation, two powerful women bracket the story, Deborah and Jael, each in a different way controlling the main male characters. It is a salutary reminder that God's ways are not ours. Women were normally of little account in that ancient society, but God chose Deborah as judge over Israel, and as the proclaimer of his word. Women did not usually make the important decisions, but Jael's bloody ruthlessness acted as God's judgment.

Happily, our age has seen great advances in sexual equality, but there are always those who are counted as less important. Christians cannot take this view, for God counts all as equal, and uses whomever he chooses to carry out his plans.

Reflection

Whom do we have little use for, and do we imagine God feels the same?

MM

Judges 6:11–17 (NRSV, abridged)

Mighty doubter

Now the angel of the Lord came and sat under the oak at Ophrah, which belonged to Joash the Abiezrite, as his son Gideon was beating out wheat in the wine press, to hide it from the Midianites. The angel of the Lord… said to him, 'The Lord is with you, you mighty warrior.' Gideon answered him, 'But sir, if the Lord is with us, why then has all this happened to us? And where are all his wonderful deeds that our ancestors recounted to us…?' But now the Lord has cast us off, and given us into the hand of Midian.' Then the Lord… said, 'Go in this might of yours and deliver Israel from the hand of Midian; I hereby commission you.' He responded, 'But sir, how can I deliver Israel? My clan is the weakest in Manasseh, and I am the least in my family.' The Lord said to him, 'But I will be with you, and you shall strike down the Midianites…' Then he said to him, 'If now I have found favour with you, then show me a sign that it is you who speak with me…'

Gideon is one of my favourite biblical characters. Confronted with the presence of God (the 'angel of the Lord' is God making himself visible rather than an angel in the sense we tend to use), his response is to question and to doubt. On the face of it, he sounds reasonable. How can God be with us, when we don't see any of the great things he's supposed to do? But the point, of course, is that God is about to do something great, if only Gideon will let him get a word in edgeways.

God is patient. He allows a test, then a couple more, but in the end he will have Gideon. Gideon will be a mighty warrior, whether he wants to or not. But first he needs to learn faith.

There is a lesson for us here. We are often led to question God. We rail against the injustice of the world, and shout our 'Why?' against an apparently silent heaven. As I write, I've just come back from conducting the funeral of a man whose inexplicable suicide has left his family distraught. Why? Like Gideon, we can ask, but we will probably receive no answer. No answer, that is, except to trust God and, like Gideon, become a means of bringing some measure of God's justice and love into the world.

Prayer

Father, we don't understand all your ways,
nor the problems of our world. In our
impatience we question you.
Help us, though, never to let our questions
become an excuse for inaction or
a substitute for trust.

MM

Judges 6:33–40 (NRSV, abridged)

Man of little faith

Then all the Midianites and the Amalekites and the people of the east came together, and crossing the Jordan they encamped in the Valley of Jezreel. But the spirit of the Lord took possession of Gideon; and he sounded the trumpet, and the Abiezrites were called out to follow him. He sent messengers throughout all Manasseh, and... to Asher, Zebulun, and Naphtali, and they went up to meet them. Then Gideon said to God, 'In order to see whether you will deliver Israel by my hand, as you have said, I am going to lay a fleece of wool on the threshing floor; if there is dew on the fleece alone, and it is dry on all the ground, then I shall know that you will deliver Israel by my hand, as you have said.' And it was so... Then Gideon said to God, 'Do not let your anger burn against me... let me, please, make trial with the fleece just once more; let it be dry only on the fleece, and on all the ground let there be dew.' And God did so that night.

What does this story tell us? That Gideon was hardly a man of great faith? Well, yes; rather like most of us, I suspect. You probably couldn't walk across my garden without stepping on soggy wool. Or is it telling us that God allows us to test him whenever we think he might want us to do something? In some Christian circles, 'putting out a fleece' is common practice: 'Lord, if you want me to do this, then let Elvis Presley arrive in my back garden on a flying saucer…'

Of course, it's right to ask God's will sometimes, and to seek carefully and prayerfully for a sense of calling before taking any drastic steps. Most of the time, though, we know perfectly well what God wants us to do. It isn't to smite Midianites. It is to live faithfully, honestly and lovingly, showing by what we do and say that we are followers of Jesus. Fleeces are not really needed most of the time.

Gideon knew what he had to do, too. And he tried to get out of it. But God didn't let him off the hook. And that's what the story is about. Not miraculous dewfalls, but the simple assertion that God calls us, has a role for us to play, and will bring us to it. When we are wondering about God's will, it's often best just to sit back, pray, and wait. God will arrange things. You just can't dodge him.

Prayer

Lord, help me to trust you, and to be willing to do what I know full well you want me to do.

MM

Judges 7:16–21 (NRSV, abridged)

Divine and human victory

After he divided the three hundred men into three companies, and put trumpets into the hands of all of them, and empty jars, with torches inside the jars, he said to them, 'Look at me, and do the same; when I come to the outskirts of the camp, do as I do. When I blow the trumpet, I and all who are with me, then you also blow the trumpets around the whole camp, and shout, "For the Lord and for Gideon!"' So Gideon and the hundred who were with him came to the outskirts of the camp at the beginning of the middle watch... and they blew the trumpets and smashed the jars that were in their hands. So the three companies blew the trumpets and broke the jars, holding in their left hands the torches, and in their right hands the trumpets to blow; and they cried, 'A sword for the Lord and for Gideon!' Every man stood in his place all around the camp, and all the men in camp ran; they cried out and fled.

At one time, there was a vogue for explaining events in the Bible in purely 'natural' terms. It looked for rational explanations of the miracles, for instance. Gideon's victory with just three hundred men was a good example. It was a stroke of military genius. The few Israelites would not end up fighting each other, but the Midianites would. Why suggest that it was the result of dreams or visions?

This approach misses the whole point of how God works. Of course Gideon's victory can be explained in 'natural' terms. Yet it was carried out in response to God's call, and by trust in him. Those who follow God do not expect miracles every step of the way. They do expect to find God in each situation they face, preparing the way, and providing strength, courage and inspiration.

Often enough, we face problems which seem impossible to solve. We pray, we think, we try things out—and lo and behold! the solution presents itself. Just luck? Coincidence? Human initiative? They are the very stuff which God uses to answer our prayers and guide us in our discipleship. The world is his. He is in it and through it. Where else would we expect to see him at work but in the processes of the world he has made and in which we are called to serve him?

Prayer

Lord open my eyes to what is going on around me, so that I can see you at work.

MM

Judges 8:22–35 (NRSV, abridged)

Ideals and realities

Then the Israelites said to Gideon, 'Rule over us, you and your son and your grandson also; for you have delivered us out of the hand of Midian.' Gideon said to them, 'I will not rule over you, and my son will not rule over you; the Lord will rule over you.' Then Gideon said to them, 'Let me make a request of you; each of you give me an earring he has taken as booty.' ... The weight of the golden earrings that he requested was one thousand seven hundred shekels of gold... Gideon made an ephod of it and put it in his town, in Ophrah; and all Israel prostituted themselves to it there, and it became a snare to Gideon and to his family... So the land had rest forty years in the days of Gideon... As soon as Gideon died, the Israelites relapsed and prostituted themselves with the Baals... The Israelites did not remember the Lord their God, who had rescued them from the hand of all their enemies on every side; and they did not exhibit loyalty to the house of Jerubbaal (that is, Gideon) in return for all the good that he had done to Israel.

Gideon's victory was marred by the bloody revenge he took on both his enemies and those allies who refused him help. Now that mixture of triumph and failure forms the pattern for his life and that of Israel as a whole.

First is the idealism. Gideon refuses to be made king; God's people should give their trust and obedience to God alone. God, though, can often seem hidden, and something more concrete seems to be needed. So Gideon goes astray, and makes an ephod (whatever that was in this case!) It seems to have been some kind of image (forbidden by God) and so Gideon, even if the ephod was intended as a reminder of God, was led into idolatry. Idolatry is not just the making of images representing God, but the belief that they can somehow control or contain God. And 'all Israel' soon forgot God too; or at least forgot that they could not keep him in a convenient place.

Yet Gideon had a point. What do we use to keep us on track, when God seems distant? In later Israel, that was the job of the king, the priests and the prophets. For us, perhaps, it is the structures of church, worship and daily prayer. Even these can be idols, when they become the end, rather than the means to knowing God.

Prayer

Lord, keep us faithful to you, and let us remember that you alone are worthy of our true worship.

MM

Judges 11:1–9 (NRSV, abridged)

Sins of the fathers

Now Jephthah the Gileadite, the son of a prostitute, was a mighty warrior. Gilead was the father of Jephthah. Gilead's wife also bore him sons; and... they drove Jephthah away, saying to him, 'You shall not inherit anything in our father's house; for you are the son of another woman.' Then Jephthah fled from his brothers and lived in the land of Tob... And when the Ammonites made war against Israel, the elders of Gilead went to bring Jephthah from the land of Tob. They said to Jephthah, 'Come and be our commander, so that we may fight with the Ammonites.' But Jephthah said to the elders of Gilead, 'Are you not the very ones who rejected me and drove me out of my father's house? So why do you come to me now when you are in trouble?' The elders of Gilead said to Jephthah, 'Nevertheless, we have now turned back to you, so that you may go with us and fight with the Ammonites, and become head over us, over all the inhabitants of Gilead.' Jephthah said to the elders of Gilead, 'If you bring me home again to fight with the Ammonites, and the Lord gives them over to me, I will be your head.'

Jephthah is one of the most ambiguous of the judges. Born as the child of faithlessness, he is an outcast and a leader of brigands. Rejected by his clan, he is punished not for his own misdeeds, but for those of his father, and so begins a tale of horror. Its roots lie in selfishness and lack of faith. His father may be unknown; 'Gilead' is the clan—a clan which rejects the illegitimate offspring of a whore. But the rejected son has a useful quality: he can fight mightily, and so has the chance for revenge. He will lead, provided that leadership is recognized as divinely given, and confirmed by victory. Once he is acknowledged as God's chosen, his position will be secure.

The faithlessness of Jephthah's father, the cruelty of kin to a child because of his parents' wrongs, and the outcast's desire for revenge are the moving force of the story. It could have been different. Acceptance, forgiveness, love could have been the cure. But as now, millennia later, they were hard to come by, requiring an openness of heart and spirit which are the so-often rejected gift of God.

In our story, God is a tool to be used; a useful ploy to get what Jephthah wants.

Prayer

God, let me not try to use you, but rather to be used by you.

MM

Judges 11:28–33 (NRSV, abridged)

Name in vain

But the king of the Ammonites did not heed the message that Jephthah sent him. Then the spirit of the Lord came upon Jephthah, and he... passed on to Mizpah of Gilead, and from Mizpah of Gilead he passed on to the Ammonites. And Jephthah made a vow to the Lord, and said, 'If you will give the Ammonites into my hand, then whoever comes out of the doors of my house to meet me, when I return victorious from the Ammonites, shall be the Lord's, to be offered up by me as a burnt offering.' So Jephthah crossed over to the Ammonites to fight against them; and the Lord gave them into his hand. He inflicted a massive defeat on them... So the Ammonites were subdued before the people of Israel.

Jephthah starts by trying diplomacy on the Israelites' enemies, but is rejected. It will have to be war. Then comes the startling moment. The spirit of God falls on Jephthah as on Gideon; victory is assured. God has been a ploy used by Jephthah to get status and acceptance, but he remains gracious. His act is unrequested, the loving gift of the heavenly Father. And it is not trusted.

How could Jephthah doubt? Yet he does, and tries to strike a bargain with God. It is not enough that God has empowered him for victory. Jephthah wants more. He wants to earn God's grace, to be sure that he is ultimately in control. And so he makes a pointless and foolish vow. 'If you really will give me victory...'

God is silent in reply. He has already spoken, in the act of anointing Jephthah with the spirit of victory, and has not been believed. The gift of grace has been flung back in his face, and replaced with an attempt to earn it. Victory comes, because it has been promised, but it is already soured, and greater bitterness is to follow.

We, of course, never make that mistake, do we? We never try to bargain with God, forgetting that he already wants to give us more than we can imagine? Of course we do. It's hard to grasp that God loves us despite our sins, and wants only the best for us. We like to think we can earn his grace, by being good, or saying our prayers. That's the wrong way round. We should do those, and much more, out of a loving gratitude for God's grace.

Prayer

Father, help me to know your love, and respond with trust and gratitude to your gifts.

MM

Judges 11:34–40 (NRSV, abridged)

Pride's victim

Then Jephthah came to his home at Mizpah; and there was his daughter coming out to meet him with timbrels and with dancing. She was his only child... When he saw her, he tore his clothes, and said, 'Alas, my daughter! You have brought me very low; you have become the cause of great trouble to me. For I have opened my mouth to the Lord, and I cannot take back my vow.' She said to him, 'My father, if you have opened your mouth to the Lord, do to me according to what has gone out of your mouth, now that the Lord has given you vengeance against your enemies, the Ammonites.' And she said to her father, 'Let this thing be done for me: Grant me two months, so that I may go and wander on the mountains, and bewail my virginity, my companions and I.' 'Go,' he said and sent her away for two months... At the end of two months, she returned to her father, who did with her according to the vow he had made. She had never slept with a man. So there arose an Israelite custom that for four days every year the daughters of Israel would go out to lament the daughter of Jephthah the Gileadite.

Jephthah's daughter comes to meet him, dancing in celebration of his victory. And so becomes the terrible fulfilment of his vow. It's often said that in those days a vow like that could never be taken back, but I wonder. Suppose the consequences of a broken vow were indeed dreadful; would they be more dreadful than the results of keeping it? For all that Jephthah is stricken, he is not moved to take the consequences on himself.

Indeed, he blames his daughter: '*You* have brought me low; *you* have become trouble...' It's a response we all know well. To be found to be wrong is to get angry, rather than to repent. We look for someone else to blame, even the victim of our wrongdoing. Perhaps God too gets blamed. He doesn't say anything in the story. But then, he's already said all he needs to. Jephthah persists in seeing his victory as the result of a bargain. It is not.

So Jephthah's daughter, a nameless victim of pride and false religion, becomes a memorial for the people of her nation. Perhaps a reminder of the folly of pride and power, as she surely should be to us.

Prayer

Father, let me trust your grace, and have the courage to answer for my own actions.

MM

Judges 13:1–5 (NRSV, abridged)

Samson

The Israelites again did what was evil in the sight of the Lord, and the Lord gave them into the hand of the Philistines forty years. There was a certain man of Zorah, of the tribe of the Danites, whose name was Manoah. His wife was barren... And the angel of the Lord appeared to the woman and said to her, 'Although you are barren, having borne no children, you shall conceive and bear a son. Now be careful not to drink wine or strong drink, or to eat anything unclean, for you shall conceive and bear a son. No razor is to come on his head, for the boy shall be a nazirite to God from birth. It is he who shall begin to deliver Israel from the hand of the Philistines.'

The story of Samson begins like the stories of Samuel, John the Baptist, and indeed of Jesus himself, with an angelic visitation. A barren couple are to be granted a child who will do great things for Israel. He is to belong from birth to an élite group who were totally dedicated to God. Yet all is not straightforward.

Samson will be a great hero, and the tales that follow are probably popular stories, handed down over many generations. Samson is Robin Hood, or William Tell—the leader of resistance to the occupying Philistines. Or again, he is James Bond—violent, ruthless and with a taste for women. Is he a man of God, though? To some extent, yes, but he is deeply flawed. He acts out of personal vengeance, and seems to have little desire either to help his people or to serve God.

What can we make of such a man? Perhaps it tells us that James Bond is not the answer to our problems, but there is surely something more. Although he is chosen by God, Samson goes his own way, often thoughtless, never less than reckless. God will call us, but he will not control us.

At the same time, God remains active. Samson disobeys, but God uses even his disobedience. The world rolls on, apparently subject to chaos and confusion, troubled by human sinfulness and damaged by human greed. Yet in the midst of it all, God works out his purpose, bringing good out of evil, and sin's downfall even out of sin's apparent triumph; resurrection out of crucifixion. And at the end, no matter how far we may move from God, there still remains the chance of redemption, for God hears all who call on him.

Prayer

Father, give me eyes to see you at work, and where I cannot see, grant me faith.

MM

Judges 14:1–8 (NRSV, abridged)

Strong sinner

At Timnah (Samson) saw a Philistine woman. Then he... told his father and mother, 'I saw a Philistine woman at Timnah; now get her for me as my wife.' But his father and mother said to him, 'Is there not a woman among your kin, or among all our people, that you must go to take a wife from the uncircumcised Philistines?' But Samson said to his father, 'Get her for me, because she pleases me.' His father and mother did not know that this was from the Lord; for he was seeking a pretext to act against the Philistines... Then Samson went down with his father and mother to Timnah. When he came to the vineyards of Timnah, suddenly a young lion roared at him. The spirit of the Lord rushed on him, and he tore the lion apart barehanded... Then he... talked with the woman, and she pleased Samson. After a while he returned to marry her, and he turned aside to see the carcass of the lion, and there was a swarm of bees in the body of the lion, and honey.

Samson's two most obvious attributes are introduced at the same time. His strength is a gift of God, to be used for the defence of Israel. It is subservient, though, to his own selfishness. It doesn't matter that the Philistines are the oppressors of his people, nor that they are worshippers of a different god. One of them has caught his eye, and he is determined to have her. Not even a lion is going to stand in his way.

His parents are dismayed, but we are told that God is working in this. Does that mean that God sends people to do what is wrong (in this case a disregard for God's own command against intermarriage) so that he can bring good out of it? A similar, more pointed question, is often asked about Judas Iscariot's betrayal of Jesus.

In both cases, the answer is not that God wants the wrong to be done, but that he is able to turn it to his purposes. It would be better if Samson paid attention to God, and challenged the Philistines in some other way. But as it is, the challenge will come.

There is hope here for most of us, all too often aware of our failings. They are not the end of the road, for God can use even them. There is a challenge too; for God would much rather have our willing co-operation. That is the route both to doing God's will, and to growing in faith.

Prayer

Lord, help me to be willing to be used in your service, and to seek what you want rather than what I desire.

MM

Judges 15:1–9 (NRSV, abridged)

Cycle of violence

At the time of the wheat harvest, Samson went to visit his wife... But her father would not allow him to go in. Her father said, 'I was sure that you had rejected her; so I gave her to your companion...' Samson said to them, 'This time, when I do mischief to the Philistines, I will be without blame.' So Samson went and caught three hundred foxes, and took some torches; and he turned the foxes tail to tail, and put a torch between each pair of tails. When he had set fire to the torches, he let the foxes go into the standing grain of the Philistines, and burned up the shocks and the standing grain, as well as the vineyards and olive groves. Then the Philistines asked, 'Who has done this?' And they said, 'Samson, the son-in-law of the Timnite, because he has taken Samson's wife and given her to his companion.' So the Philistines came up, and burned her and her father. Samson said to them, 'If this is what you do, I swear I will not stop until I have taken revenge on you.' He struck them down hip and thigh with great slaughter... Then the Philistines came up and encamped in Judah, and made a raid on Lehi.

We rejoin Samson in the midst of an escalating tale of revenge and counter-strike. Samson's Philistine wife has betrayed a secret, losing him a costly wager, which he pays by killing thirty Philistines before going off in a huff. From there, things go from bad to worse. It is hard for a Christian to read this story of blood-letting without a shudder. Earlier judges acted bloodily, but at least within the context of open warfare. Samson acts out of personal grudge, and the results become increasingly vindictive.

All through history we have seen similar actions. Northern Ireland is only one example of hatreds repaid by violence which begets more revenge. Only when the cycle of violence is broken can peace and reconciliation be established. But how to break it? Certainly it requires courage, and the determination to suffer without striking back. That is why Jesus' command to forgive is so hard, and so important. It is the only way to bring into reality the teaching of reconciliation which lies at the heart of the gospel. It is when Jesus' followers are seen to live reconciling lives that the message of reconciliation to God will be heard.

Prayer

Father, make me a peace maker,
not a peace breaker.

MM

Judges 16:4–6, 16–22 (NRSV, abridged)

Eyeless in Gaza

After this he fell in love with a woman... whose name was Delilah. The lords of the Philistines came to her and said to her, 'Coax him, and find out what makes his strength so great... so that we may bind him in order to subdue him; and we will each give you eleven hundred pieces of silver.' So Delilah said to Samson, 'Please tell me what makes your strength so great...' Finally, after she had nagged him with her words day after day... he was tired to death. So he told her his whole secret, and said to her, 'A razor has never come upon my head; for I have been a nazirite to God from my mother's womb. If my head were shaved, then my strength would leave me...' Then the lords of the Philistines... brought the money in their hands. She let him fall asleep on her lap; and she called a man, and had him shave off the seven locks of his head. He began to weaken, and his strength left him. Then she said, 'The Philistines are upon you, Samson!' When he awoke from his sleep, he thought, 'I will go out as at other times, and shake myself free.' But he did not know that the Lord had left him. So the Philistines seized him and gouged out his eyes. They brought him down to Gaza and bound him... and he ground at the mill in the prison. But the hair of his head began to grow again after it had been shaved.

To our minds, it seems strange that Samson's strength, especially since it is a gift of God's spirit, should be so apparently linked with his hair. Certainly it reflects a more 'magical' view than we would tend to hold. At the same time, though, the hair is symbolic of a deeper issue. Samson has been raised by God for a special task; to free the Israelites from Philistine domination. Much as he has been a thorn in the Philistines' side, he has not really made any impression on their rule. No decisive battle has been fought.

The loss of his hair symbolizes Samson's final break with his destiny. He has forsaken his calling once again for the sake of a Philistine woman. So Samson pays the price. Yet all is not over; in the darkness of his blinded self, perhaps faith once again is growing, as his hair too, symbol of his calling, regains its strength.

Reflection

What temptations most easily make you forget God's call?

MM

Judges 16:23–30 (NRSV, abridged)

Final victory

Now the lords of the Philistines gathered to offer a great sacrifice to their god Dagon… for they said, 'Our god has given Samson our enemy into our hand.' … And when their hearts were merry, they said, 'Call Samson, and let him entertain us.' So they called Samson out of the prison, and he performed for them… Samson said to the attendant… 'Let me feel the pillars on which the house rests, so that I may lean against them.' Now the house was full of men and women; all the lords of the Philistines were there, and on the roof there were about three thousand men and women… Then Samson called to the Lord and said, 'Lord God, remember me and strengthen me only this once, O God, so that with this one act of revenge I may pay back the Philistines for my two eyes.' And Samson grasped the two middle pillars on which the house rested, and he leaned his weight against them, his right hand on the one and his left hand on the other. Then Samson said, 'Let me die with the Philistines.' He strained with all his might; and the house fell on… all the people who were in it. So those he killed at his death were more than those he had killed during his life.

As Samson's hair grows back, so does his strength. Sadly, he still has not come to see the struggle in which he is involved as more than a personal one. His final prayer is still a prayer for vengeance for the injuries done to him.

And yet, he is at last in a place where he is able to fulfil his destiny. He has been Israel's judge for twenty years, and in that time has single-handedly fought the Philistines. Perhaps it would have been better if, like Deborah, Gideon and even Jephthah, he had mobilized the Israelites for a concerted struggle. However, it was not to be. Samson was a lone figure, seeking his own pleasures and his own revenge. Often forgetful of his calling, never a man of high ideals, none the less he is God's instrument. If his own folly brought him to destruction, yet it was an ending in which he did not forget God, however imperfectly he knew the Lord of Israel. More to the point, it was a place to which God had brought him. Bending with the direction of Samson's wayward will, God worked out his purpose, and rescued Israel, once again, and for a time.

Prayer

Father, you can work even through my sinful desires, but I'd rather you made your desires mine.

MM

263

Hebrews 1:1–4 (NIV)

Go on!

In the past God spoke to our forefathers through the prophets at many times and in various ways, but in these last days he has spoken to us by his Son, whom he appointed heir of all things, and through whom he made the universe. The Son is the radiance of God's glory and the exact representation of his being, sustaining all things by his powerful word. After he had provided purification for sins, he sat down at the right hand of the Majesty in heaven. So he became as much superior to the angels as the name he has inherited is superior to theirs.

In 1984, shortly after I was ordained, a very kind parishioner gave me a computer. Not only was I astonished by his generosity, I was also overwhelmed by the new technology. I remember word-processing a sermon one Saturday. Pleased to have completed it, I went to print it in the evening. Nothing happened. In a panic, I realized that I had wiped it off the machine. I have never tried to produce a sermon on a computer since.

In the fifteen years since that time, computers have advanced incredibly. The pocket computerized diary I carry is more powerful than the computer that took humans to the moon. When I think back to that basic computer I had, I wouldn't want to go back to it. In comparison it seems cumbersome, slow and unreliable, but, to be fair, it was the best it could be.

The whole emphasis of the book of Hebrews is summed up in the first few phrases. Why go back to the old when the new is so much better? The Christians, in the mind and heart of the writer, were in danger of what we might call backsliding. Quite possibly, Nero, that famous emperor and persecutor of Christians, was beginning his reign of terror. To be a Christian meant enduring hardship and, for some, it was tempting to go back to the old ways to avoid the flak.

To strengthen God's people, the writer encourages them to consider how much superior Jesus is to anyone of old—heir of the universe, radiance of God's glory, sustainer through his powerful word,. sitting at the right hand of Majesty. All these terms are inspirations to trust Jesus, and not fall away. The message is clear: don't go back, go on.

A task

Make a list of the benefits of being a Christian, and thank God for them.

GD

Hebrews 2:1–4 (NIV)

Pay attention

We must pay more careful attention, therefore, to what we have heard, so that we do not drift away. For if the message spoken by angels was binding, and every violation and disobedience received its just punishment, how shall we escape if we ignore such a great salvation? This salvation, which was first announced by the Lord, was confirmed to us by those who heard him. God also testified to it by signs, wonders and various miracles, and gifts of the Holy Spirit distributed according to his will.

We teach our Reader candidates to preach using one of three forms. They can preach in a story mode, or describe an image which might linger on in the mind, or they can argue a case. Here the writer wishes to convince readers of his case so, almost like a lawyer, he uses five potent arguments.

Firstly, he argues that we must be careful not to drift away. The sense is of a boat unanchored, or a person finding that a ring has fallen off a finger, or of water leaking out of a main. Are we to lose all we have worked for through carelessness?

Then he refers to the message declared by the angels. These creatures are the messengers who come directly from God. The authority of God travels with them and the words they speak are binding. Dare we disbelieve or disobey what they tell us?

Thirdly, he refers to the life of Jesus, which announces salvation. Jesus demonstrated in his life the opportunity for everyone to find eternal life. He was so convinced of what he was saying and doing that he was prepared to die for it. Shall we ignore his example?

Next, so many of those who heard him affirmed the truth of what he was saying. The Gospels and many other accounts have such a ring of truth about them, what more evidence would we want? But in case we do want more, fifthly, the Holy Spirit provides evidence in signs and wonders and gifts given to many people.

I have been involved with two schools going through OFSTED. In each case, they have been asked for cogent reasons why things are done, explanations and evidence to show that these things are being done. If the same criteria were to be applied to God's purposes, Jesus' ministry would be seen as an astonishing success.

Think

In what ways might I pay more attention to what I hear about God? (For example, by keeping a journal.)

GD

Hebrews 3:3–6 (GNB)

Outside and in

A man who builds a house receives more honour than the house itself. In the same way Jesus is worthy of much greater honour than Moses. Every house, of course, is built by someone—and God is the one who has built all things. Moses was faithful in God's house as a servant, and he spoke of the things that God would say in the future. But Christ is faithful as the Son in charge of God's house. We are his house if we keep up our courage and our confidence in what we hope for.

This passage helps us to date Hebrews. Surely, in speaking of houses, and likening the Christian to God's house, the author would have mentioned the enormously significant event of the destruction of the temple in Jerusalem, if it had happened. The fact that it is not referred to probably means that we can date the writing of Hebrews to somewhere in the forty years after Jesus' death and resurrection, and before the temple was destroyed.

The writer likens the Christian to a residence for God. It's a fitting picture. For instance, the character of the architect is expressed in the design and ambiance of the building. Looking at churches in Somerset, I notice the two-room shape. The larger room, normally called the nave, is where the people congregate. Often this is deliberately high-ceilinged, reminding us of the majesty of God. In the smaller room, the sanctuary, God's people experience a more intimate atmosphere when receiving Holy Communion. God's character is expressed in the design. He is closer than we can imagine, as well as being above all and beyond all.

When we lived in Bath, we experienced living in a famous area. Our rectory, like many other houses around us, was built by John Wood, a famous architect. However, many of the houses couldn't be kept as they were originally intended. All that remained of the original design was an outer façade.

If we are to be faithful to our creator, then we must be true to his likeness, outside and in. The temple was condemned by Jesus for its internal corruptions. Its fate was sealed when it was destroyed in AD70. In a similar fashion, Jesus, the head of the household, encourages us to a life of consistency which allows an inner and spiritual faith to be also an outward and physical action.

Meditation

Lord, renew me throughout my life, and let me be a living sacrament.

GD

Hebrews 4:9–11 (NIV)

Encountering Sabbath

There remains, then, a Sabbath-rest for the people of God; for anyone who enters God's rest also rests from his own work, just as God did from his. Let us, therefore, make every effort to enter that rest.

A great preacher, to my mind, is the author and Canadian professor of preaching, Herbert O'Driscoll. One of the things I admire about him is the cool, laid-back delivery he has. He gives the almost nonchalant air of saying, 'Let's just look a little at this passage and find out what it is trying to say. I suggest…'. It's a disarmingly attractive style, and should not be confused with, 'I've just thought this up as I approached the pulpit'. I know that behind O'Driscoll's delivery is deeply honed experience, reflection, hard work and patient prayer. I believe he lives a Sabbath experience.

We might be forgiven for thinking that Sabbath rest simply happens as we wake late on a Sunday, peruse the newspapers and calmly get ready for church. In contrast to that view, the writer encourages us to make every effort to enter the Sabbath with a positive attitude. We are to make a deliberate action to refrain from work and enter God's rest. Perhaps the problem for us is that we think of rest as lying back, whereas God means it as a reflective experience which is anything but laziness.

We live in a busy world which demands much of us. Our timetable gets crowded, our mind is filled with millions of images vying for priority, our responsibilities can overwhelm. In such circumstances it's hard to encounter God amidst all the 'noise in the system'. We need to open up space within ourselves. We need to find God's space within. If God could open himself to create our lives, so we can open space within our schedule, find the moments to encounter God, allow ourselves the permission to let go to him.

Our group of trainee Readers took time to look at and reflect on the community they were asked to observe, for a couple of hours on a Saturday afternoon. Later they turned their reflections into group tableaux. Each picture told a profound story of what they had seen and what had entered God's space within them.

Sabbath is not a day, it is a way of living.

Prayer

Lord, breathe your Sabbath way of life into all my activities and enable me to find rest.

GD

Hebrews 6:4–6 (NIV)

Once saved, always saved?

It is impossible for those who have once been enlightened, who have tasted the heavenly gift, who have shared in the Holy Spirit, who have tasted the goodness of the word of God and the powers of the coming age, if they fall away, to be brought back to repentance, because to their loss they are crucifying the Son of God all over again and subjecting him to public disgrace.

Hebrews contains some difficult passages and this is one of them. Does the writer mean that it is possible to fall away from God's love if we do not pay attention to our faith; or is it that once saved, we are always saved? Some great theologians, Calvin among them, emphasize the grace of God ultimately to save those who put their trust in him. On the other hand, others emphasize the need to *keep ourselves* in the love of God. One view emphasizes God's promise; the other, our response.

Arising from this debate is the knotty question of true faith. 'If someone appears to have fallen away from the love of God,' we might ask, 'were they ever really captured by that love in the first place?' The passage deserves more study than we can give it here, but personally I believe it is possible to fall away from God, if we really choose it. God will not allow us to do so unless we deliberately will it against him, but he doesn't force us to follow him. I prefer to think of it more as a trust relationship. We trust that he will not let go of us, even though from time to time we might let go of him.

If this appears complex, then one thing is clear. We can be assured of salvation if we continue to follow Jesus. To do so, we need to continue to develop and grow our faith. James Fowler, an American educationalist, has mapped out some stages of faith development. In two of the stages, he speaks of moving from believing what everyone else accepts to knowing what we believe ourselves.

Many of the most successful discipleship courses allow time for people to voice their own opinions. In so doing, we own or change our understanding of faith. Perhaps that's why the Alpha course appeals to those inside the Church as well as those outside.

Question

How might I do more to encourage the gift of faith within me, and how might I also encourage it in others?

GD

Hebrews 10:1–4 (NIV)

A shadow of things to come

The law is only a shadow of the good things that are coming—not the realities themselves. For this reason it can never, by the same sacrifices repeated endlessly year after year, make perfect those who draw near to worship. If it could, would they not have stopped being offered? For the worshippers would have been cleansed once for all, and would no longer have felt guilty for their sins. But those sacrifices are an annual reminder of sins, because it is impossible for the blood of bulls and goats to take away sins.

Throughout the Bible there are pictures of what is to come—for example, Abraham and Isaac. Isaac is a 'type' (picture) of Jesus, led towards the ultimate sacrifice. Interestingly, the picture changes when the angel prevents the sacrifice. A ram, caught with its head in thorns, is sacrificed instead. Another picture is Hosea, the faithful partner who buys back his wife from a life of prostitution. In a similar way, God also buys his people back from their enslavements. There are many more symbolic pictures in the Bible.

The writer here uses another picture. He likens the law to a shadow. His purpose is to show that God is real. This may seem strange, but a shadow cannot be formed unless there is something real and tangible standing before the sun. As the shadow is the effect of the real object, so the law is the effect of God's truth.

When Moses brought the law down from Sinai, it showed how the relationship between God and his people could be continued. The payment for breaking the law was bloodshed. But animal sacrifices were only a reminder of the true cost. The real cost was seen on the cross when Jesus fulfilled the law—literally, filled in the shadow.

I sometimes use clip-art for publicity. These are computer pictures that make posters look more interesting. Because I'm often working in black and white, they have to be silhouettes or greyscale. But when I have the opportunity of colour printing, the pictures are in another world.

Not only can we understand the law—the shadow—but we also see the body of Jesus hanging on the cross, and now we are glimpsing his glory when the full colour is revealed.

Imagine

If heavenly worship is in 'colour', rather than as we now experience it, in 'black and white', what will it be like?

GD

269

Hebrews 11:1–2, 8–10 (NEB)

Action faith

What is faith? Faith gives substance to our hopes, and makes us certain of realities we do not see. It is for their faith that the men of old stand on record... By faith Abraham obeyed the call to go out to a land destined for himself and his heirs, and left home without knowing where he was to go. By faith he settled as an alien in the land promised him, living in tents, as did Isaac and Jacob, who were heirs to the same promise.

One of the most challenging parts of being in the ministry is the lack of any tangible results to the work that is done. Sometimes it's just great to paint a wall or sweep out the garage—to see the result of my labours. One of the best activities I found, in one parish, was a practical Saturday morning when I got together with several men and women. We did as many nitty-gritty, practical jobs around the church as we could. We fixed hinges, cut down shrubs, mended door-bells. Sometimes the tasks were for people in the church, other times simply to keep the church building maintained. Generally, we felt well satisfied by lunchtime, none more so than I.

Now, as Lay Training Adviser, once a year I'm involved in a presentation of certificates for the diocesan course. Candidates come to Wells Cathedral to receive tangible evidence of their studies. It's a very proud moment for them, and also for me as I see the fruits of labour.

One of the main requests from those on the course is for practical learning about faith. The message comes across loud and clear: belief means more than simply knowing about Christ. It is about acting on what we know. Faith without some kind of action must be questioned as to whether or not it is real faith. When we pass by on the other side, leave the prisoner captive, leave the sick uncared for, are we demonstrating faith at all? Faith gives flesh to words, substance to hope, and reality to the concepts we believe.

Abraham followed God as a young and old man. When he was young, he left home and went to the place where God wanted him. In old age, he was tested almost beyond the limit of his faith, concerning Isaac. Faith was never simply intellectual for him; it always resulted in something practical.

Question

In what way is faith producing action in my church and life?

GD

270

Hebrews 12:1–3 (NIV)

Inspiration

Therefore, since we are surrounded by such a great cloud of witnesses, let us throw off everything that hinders and the sin that so easily entangles, and let us run with perseverance the race marked out for us. Let us fix our eyes on Jesus, the author and perfecter of our faith, who for the joy set before him endured the cross, scorning its shame, and sat down at the right hand of the throne of God. Consider him who endured such opposition from sinful men, so that you will not grow weary and lose heart.

When I find a Saturday free from holding courses, one of my favourite treats is to go up to Bath and watch the rugby. In recent years we've not done so well, but there are still enough world-class players to thrill us. When they are on form, Bath often have a cautious first half, wearing down the opposition, testing chinks in their defence, looking for a gap to let someone like Guscott fly through. Then in the second half they seem to up the pace and overwhelm their opponents, using knowledge gained earlier.

The context of this passage is that of a sporting event. The race is marked out, the athlete is flying down the back straight. What can slow him down? The author uses the word, literally, in the Greek, 'by weights'. Our sins are like weights around us, slowing us down and hindering us. We need to throw them off, and to do that we need support.

As supporters at Bath, we have a job to do. We need to encourage, applaud and cheer on the team. Of course, some will also offer tactical advice from the stand (not always taken up by the players, I may say)—but we're involved. What I love about the match is being caught up in the crowd, cheering and shouting.

Being a Christian is like being in an enormous stadium full of people cheering us on to win—the great 'cloud of witnesses'. At the trackside is Jesus, our coach, encouraging us and showing us how to do it.

As we fix our eyes on Jesus, let us remember all those who have been role models for us. Many will be the great saints mentioned in the Bible, but some will be the people we sit close to every day.

Question

Consider who you look to as a role model for faith, and thank God for their inspiration.

GD

Hebrews 13:5b–8 (NRSV)

A changeless God?

For he has said, 'I will never leave you or forsake you.' So we can say with confidence, 'The Lord is my helper; I will not be afraid. What can anyone do to me?' Remember your leaders, those who spoke the word of God to you; consider the outcome of their way of life, and imitate their faith. Jesus Christ is the same yesterday and today and forever.

A few years ago, I attended a conference which was entitled 'A Changeless God in a Changing World'. The main theme was that, as God does not change, we can rely on him as an anchor in our changing society. However, as I have grown up as a Christian, I wonder if the conference told the whole story. I wonder if it's really true that God doesn't change.

In recent years, I have read about an old branch of theology which has experienced a comeback in the last hundred years. It poses the possibility of God changing and growing. Developed by Peter Abelard in the eleventh and twelfth centuries, the theory is that, as God suffers with his people, his love grows deeper. This has led, in recent years, to a view of God being completely vulnerable to the world he created. He can only attempt to influence us by persuasion and attraction. He will never impose his will. But also, as he influences us, so he is also influenced by us, and thus changes.

Of course, there have been many critics of the theory, who say that Jesus is the same yesterday, today and for ever, so he doesn't change, and that these theologians have sold out the transcendence of God.

But before we dismiss the idea, perhaps we need to acknowledge that Jesus' being 'the same' does not prevent him from changing. We change, yet in some ways we are the same. Maybe change (in that sense) is part of God too. Or is perfection a state devoid of change? I recognize that all this is controversial, and I don't understand it completely. It would be very easy to veer away from the truth in thinking about it.

What is plain about the passage is that, as we grow, God tells us he will be alongside. As long as he never leaves us, and continues to be our helper, we can dare to explore new thoughts, in the knowledge that he will keep us.

Prayer

Pray that God will lead the Church to be open to new revelations of himself.

GD

Hebrews 13:11–14 (NRSV)

Outside the gate

The bodies of those animals whose blood is brought into the sanctuary by the high priest as a sacrifice for sin are burned outside the camp. Therefore Jesus also suffered outside the city gate in order to sanctify the people by his own blood. Let us then go to him outside the camp and bear the abuse he endured. For here we have no lasting city, but we are looking for the city that is to come.

It is significant that Jesus was taken outside the city gate to be crucified. It was outside the established capital, with all its organization and institutions, that Jesus was to be found, dying for the world.

I have often found, in parish ministry, that God wants us to search for him in places which we might term 'outside' the usual, normal places. I expect to find God in church on Sunday, and most of the time I do find him there. But he is just as present in other places, outside the 'camp'. In an interview with the leader of L'Arche community for disadvantaged people, Jean Vanier described to me finding God in the mud of life, the clouded, confused, sometimes even hostile environments.

Recently I needed to take our dog to the famous veterinary hospital near Bristol that has featured many times on television. As I sat in the surgery, waiting for the results of some tests, I mused on the incredible advances in veterinary science. Here I was, surrounded by some of the best scientific minds and equipment. The place was full of healing and hope. And yet, for a reason which I'm not entirely sure about, science and faith seem to have become opposed to one another in people's thinking.

As I mused, the hospital clock struck eleven with a quaint chime. I realized that it was playing the tune of 'All things bright and beautiful, all creatures great and small'. In the midst of this highly scientific community was the recognition of God: 'All things wise and wonderful, the Lord God made them all.'

Psalm 139 tells us that wherever we go, we never leave the presence of God. I must admit, often I don't want to leave the camp, but my experience tells me that when I do face the challenges the world offers, God is there.

Meditate

There is a green hill far away,
Outside a city wall,
Where the dear Lord was crucified,
Who died to save us all.

C.F. Alexander (1818–95)

GD

273

Hebrews 13:20–21 (NRSV)

Completion

Now may the God of peace, who brought back from the dead our Lord Jesus, the great shepherd of the sheep, by the blood of the eternal covenant, make you complete in everything good so that you may do his will, working among us that which is pleasing in his sight, through Jesus Christ, to whom be the glory forever and ever. Amen.

A phrase spoken at a recent conference in the diocese provoked much debate. The leader of the Spirituality workshop said, 'I take as my foundation that, in human beings, goodness is normative'. This caused almost an hour of debate, including an exposition of Augustine's doctrine of original sin and an exploration of the human state.

Personally I want to believe that goodness is normative in human beings—by which I mean that deep down inside, all of us want goodness, not evil, as the normal state. God has given us choice, a good thing in itself, and we deviate from the goodness of God if we choose evil. This choice is not only given but also supported by God. He entices us to follow his goodness and choose his life. His resurrection defeats death. As the great shepherd, he gently cares for us. His death forges the promise of eternal life and all these things serve to complete us.

I am not playing down the effect of sin. When we choose to hurt others or ourselves, it is devastating, destructive and disastrous. But to choose the wrong way doesn't make the fact that we are given choice wrong. Not to be able to choose would render us prisoners of God, and nothing is further from the truth.

Whatever we understand human beings to be like, it is understood by the writer of Hebrews that God wants to complete his goodness in everyone, in order that we may do his will. We are given freedom to choose, so that we may follow him into greater experiences of goodness.

I consider it to be the most encouraging thing in the Christian life to know that God believes in us enough to give us this freedom to choose, and the support to grow in our decisions. God believes in us. Why shouldn't he? After all, we are his children. This is the message which is shot through Hebrews from beginning to end. God is rooting for us. So go on, don't go back!

Prayer

Lord, complete in me what you have started.

GD

Deuteronomy 1:19–24 (NJB)

Learning dependence

So, as Yahweh our God had ordered, we left Horeb and made our way through that vast and terrible desert, which you saw on the way to the Amorite highlands, and arrived at Kadesh-Barnea. I then said, '...Look, Yahweh your God has given you this country. March in, take possession of it as Yahweh, the God of your ancestors, has said; do not be afraid or discouraged.' Then you all came to me and said, 'Let us send men ahead of us to explore the country; they shall report to us which way we ought to take...' I selected twelve men from among you, one from each tribe. These men made towards the highlands and went up into them; they reached the Valley of Eshcol and reconnoitred it.

The Israelites under Moses were making their way through the desert of the Negeb. Even today, when one can drive through it on a modern military highway, it is an awesome place, still 'a vast and terrible desert', nothing but coarse sand and bare little sandstone hillocks—just enough to destroy any sense of progress or control of their environment. A generation (for that is the sense of 'forty years') spent in such a place would surely teach a people their dependence on God for every wisp of life, every drop of water. That they should survive at all was irrefutable proof that the God of Abraham was protecting them. The blessed oasis of Kadesh-Barnea, which they made their centre, must have been a haven of security and life.

But allied to the sense of dependence on God seems to have come a complex of inferiority with regard to the dwellers in the fertile valleys of the Judean hill country, rich in olives, pomegranates and (today) oranges and grapefruit. To the ragged, defenceless nomads, wandering the desert with their scraggy goats, they seemed like well-nourished, powerful giants, dwelling in impregnable strongholds. They lost heart and refused to trust in Yahweh's power to lead them to victory. That meant for them more wanderings; they lost their way round to the East of Canaan, and entered north of the Dead Sea.

Prayer

Lord, the country around me sometimes seems bleak and severe, with nothing to welcome or encourage me. Grant that at such times I turn to you with full courage and confidence in your love for me and your power to save.

HW

FOURTH QUARTER

Waiting for the Lord

Amos 9:11–14 (NJB)

Restoration and comfort

On that Day, I shall rebuild the tottering hut of David, make good the gaps in it, restore its ruins, and rebuild it as it was in the days of old... The days are coming—declares Yahweh—when the ploughman will tread on the heels of the reaper, and the treader of grapes on the heels of the sower of seed, and the mountains will run with new wine, and the hills all flow with it. I shall restore the fortunes of my people Israel; they will rebuild the ruined cities and live in them, they will plant vineyards and drink their wine, they will lay out gardens and eat their produce.

The book of Amos ends with a codicil of hope. It was not part of the original prophecy, as the imagery and language show. When Amos proclaimed his message there was no threat against the 'hut of David', the royal dynasty of the southern kingdom around Jerusalem. By the time this prophecy came to be written it must already have been in ruins, in need of rebuilding.

The promise is a promise of boundless plenty, one continuous harvest, with soil so fertile that all the harvesting seasons run together. The Day of the Lord, once so threatening, has become a day of restoration and comfort. Restoration after the exile did indeed occur, but it was never near a fulfilment of these hopes. The community of the return remained harassed and poor, plagued by hostile neighbours and a prey to dictatorial superpowers, Egypt, Syria and finally Rome. For Christians, the imagery of this restoration flows into that of the messianic peace and plenty, the coming of the kingship of God proclaimed by Jesus. Not that this continuous harvest has yet come. There is shortage and famine enough remaining in the world. Enough of other, more gripping evils too, like avarice, corruption, torture. But the Christian faith is that, with the resurrection of Christ, the final reign of God has been inaugurated. No matter how slowly and fragmentarily, hope has begun to be fulfilled. These promises remain a banner of hope for the future.

Prayer

Lord Jesus, through all the collapses and disappointments of life, we retain the hope in your promise. It seems no more likely of fulfilment now than when you walked the earth, but the Christian hope is to trust in your power and your wisdom for its fulfilment in your own time.

HW

Revelation 1:4–6 (NIV)

Letters from the living Lord

John, To the seven churches in the province of Asia: Grace and peace to you from him who is, and who was, and who is to come, and from the seven spirits before his throne, and from Jesus Christ, who is the faithful witness, the firstborn from the dead, and the ruler of the kings of the earth. To him who loves us and has freed us from our sins by his blood, and has made us to be a kingdom and priests to serve his God and Father—to him be glory and power for ever and ever! Amen.

Many find the book of Revelation difficult to understand. This is not surprising, since it is written against the background of persecution and therefore uses coded language and symbolism. But it is worth the effort.

Our Easter readings focus on the seven letters written to churches in the Roman province of Asia with which the book begins. Although written to particular congregations that knew and loved John, they relate to the whole Church. Indeed, the number seven appears over fifty times. This is a 'perfect number' implying completeness, thus stressing that the message is for all.

We are not sure who John was. He wrote from the island of Patmos at the end of the first century. In a vision, the risen Christ gave him messages for the Church, and these he now communicates with the authority of the whole Godhead. The one who is, was and is to come is, naturally, God the Father. The seven spirits refer to the perfect Holy Spirit who gives sevenfold gifts to his people, and of course Jesus is the 'firstborn from the dead'. Through resurrection, he has inherited his Father's honour, glory and power.

Through his death, he offers once and for all freedom from sin. But his love is continuous, enabling us to enter a new living relationship with him and calling us to be a 'kingdom of priests'. As the old preachers would have said, 'We are saved to serve.' A priest has direct access to God, bringing the prayers of the people to him and making him real to the people. This is our privilege and our responsibility.

Prayer

Help us, risen Lord, to live out our high calling in the priesthood of all believers. Thus enable us to be bridge builders between you and your people. Amen.

PG

Revelation 2:2, 4–5 (NRSV)

Ephesus: first love abandoned

'I know your works, your toil and your patient endurance. I know that you cannot tolerate evildoers; you have tested those who claim to be apostles but are not, and have found them to be false... But I have this against you, that you have abandoned the love you had at first. Remember then from what you have fallen; repent, and do the works you did at first.'

'Their marriage after sixteen years had become a kind of "tired friendship".'

These telling words appeared in a novel. As I read them, I uttered an instant prayer—'Lord, don't let our marriage ever become a tired friendship. Keep it fresh, vibrant, and full of surprises.'

Alas, for many Christians, faith has become no more than a 'tired friendship'. There is always a danger that we let 'faith' become mere 'faithfulness' and, as such, a dull heavy plod when it should be a dance of joy. Of course, it is vitally important to be faithful, but this must never be at the expense of fresh, vibrant and expectant faith.

In this, the first of the letters to the seven churches of Asia, the risen Christ is proclaimed as the one who holds the seven stars in his right hand. In other words, he holds the churches in his love. His walk among the seven golden lampstands implies that he is active in the midst of the churches. As in all the letters, there is much encouragement, but the church had lost its first love. Freshness and vitality had gone and the relationship had become 'tired'.

Such backsliding could also refer to a general weakening of personal faith, or to specific problems faced by the Ephesian church. They had had to fight an insidious heresy involving sexual immorality. In a culture in which sexual relations outside marriage were regarded as completely normal, this is not surprising, After all, Ephesus was a great centre of paganism, and its temple to Artemis was one of the wonders of the ancient world. A fertility goddess, her cult included the use of temple prostitutes. If Christians had given in to such teaching, the world would have changed Christianity, instead of Christianity changing the world.

Had heresy-hunting killed love? Had orthodoxy been won at the price of fellowship?

Prayer

Grant, Lord, that my relationship with you and my fellow Christians might never become a 'tired friendship'. Keep my faith and love vital and expectant.

PG

Revelation 2:8–11 (NRSV)

Smyrna: 'faithful unto death'

'These are the words of the first and the last, who was dead and came to life: I know your affliction and your poverty, even though you are rich... Do not fear what you are about to suffer. Beware, the devil is about to throw some of you into prison so that you may be tested, and for ten days you will have affliction. Be faithful until death, and I will give you the crown of life... Whoever conquers will not be harmed by the second death.'

'I love my country and its people, but how I wish they could find Christ. Then their lives would have "so much more".'

The speaker was a Chinese Christian who, under Communism, had spent over twenty years imprisoned for this faith. It was the reality of that 'something more' which had sustained him throughout such terrible times. It had given him a depth of faith that could be learnt only on the anvil of experience. The same conviction would sustain the church in Smyrna during the persecution that was about to begin. The risen Jesus had experienced the worst that life could do to him, but had triumphed over pain and death. He therefore understands our situation and offers, through himself, the way of victory.

A missionary returned from forty years of faithful service in Africa. She faced a long and lonely retirement. On arrival at the airport, she heard screaming fans greet a pop group returning home from a successful world tour. All the mixed emotions of the moment rose to the surface and tears began to flow. 'There's nobody here to welcome me home,' she thought, but then heard a still small voice within, saying, 'But you're not home yet!'

Christians know their true home to be in heaven with the Lord. Here we are assured that the faithful will escape the 'second death', namely separation from God, and receive the 'crown of life'. To win the crown of victory in the games was one of the greatest honours the ancient world could give. It is this crown (*stephanos*) rather than the royal crown (*diadema*) which is spoken of here. We may have enormous troubles, for we live in a Good Friday world, but Christians are always Easter people. We know that evil has been conquered, and the ultimate victory already won. Such is resurrection faith!

Meditation

What a caterpillar calls the end of the world, the master calls a butterfly!

Richard Bach

PG

Revelation 2:12–17 (NRSV)

Pergamum: avoid compromise

'These are the words of him who has the sharp two-edged sword: I know where you are living, where Satan's throne is. Yet you are holding fast to my name, and you did not deny your faith in me... But I have a few things against you: you have some there who hold to the teaching of Balaam... (and) of the Nicolaitans. Repent then. If not, I will come to you soon and make war against them with the sword of my mouth... To everyone who conquers I will give some of the hidden manna, and I will give a white stone, and on the white stone is written a new name that no one knows except the one who receives it.'

Not all Roman governors had the power of life and death over their subjects, but those who did were said to have the 'right of the sword'. Although the proconsul of this, the administrative capital of Asia, had this right and could use it against Christians at any time, John's conviction is that the last word is with Christ. 'Satan's throne' probably refers to emperor-worship, for all had to worship him as Lord. However, Jesus has the two-edged sword. Rome could be satanically powerful, but the power of the risen Christ is much greater.

Our culture is not 'gospel-friendly'. The way of Christ is different from the ways of the world. The situation in Pergamum was similar. The same heresy that troubled the church in Ephesus is leading Pergamum into immorality. The Nicolaitans, or followers of Balaam, wanted a prudent adaptation to worldly standards. The risen Jesus goes to war with such heretics, but has pity on the seduced.

'I know where you are living,' reads verse 13, using the word for permanent residence rather than the more normal word for those who are just passing through. It is as if John is saying, 'Bloom where you're planted.' We are called to witness where we are. Our aim is not escape but conquest!

The 'two-edged sword' of the risen Christ brings conviction of sin, and assurance. Those who stand firm will receive 'hidden manna', not the seductions of this age with meat offered to idols, but the heavenly banquet of eternity. They will know the name and nature of God written on white stone, the colour of heaven, joy and victory.

Prayer

Lord, help me stand firm for truth.

PG

Revelation 2:19–21, 26–28 (NRSV)

Thyatira: obey faithfully

'I know your works—your love, faith, service, and patient endurance... But I have this against you: you tolerate that woman Jezebel, who calls herself a prophet and is teaching and beguiling my servants to practise fornication and to eat food sacrificed to idols. I gave her time to repent, but she refuses... To everyone who conquers and continues to do my works to the end... I will give the morning star.'

'I didn't realize anybody took all that religion stuff seriously these days. It's all so old-fashioned.'

The superior attitude may hurt, but such opinions are not uncommon today. Official religion is regarded as a hangover from less enlightened times. People may recognize the spiritual dimension of life, but do not realize the importance of revealed truth, or respect its authority.

We do not know to whom John was referring when he spoke of Jezebel, but she was obviously exercising an undue influence in the church. Doubtless, like Queen Jezebel, she would say that she did not wish to destroy the church but rather bring it more in tune with contemporary attitudes. The particular problem in Thyatira seems to have been the church's opposition to eating meat which had been offered to idols.

Even meat sold by butchers might previously have been offered to idols. The priests could not possibly eat all the meat to which they were entitled and so they sold much of it to butcher shops. Indeed, this was where the best cuts usually came from.

Thyatira was a commercial centre, famous for its dyes and woollen goods. Trade guilds were very important. Indeed, to abstain from joining one was the equivalent of commercial suicide. However, guild meetings were held in temples and began with sacrifices. This led on to meat eating, drunkenness and debauchery. Because Christians refused to be involved in such practices, they were cut off from social fellowship with unbelievers.

John is convinced that such accommodation to commercial pressures leads to infidelity. Christians must stand firm. Their authority comes from above. They march to the tune of a different drummer, and are called to influence the world for good. Jesus is the 'bright morning star', and in eternity the faithful will possess Christ in all his freshness and purity for ever.

Prayer

Forgive my petty compromises, Lord, and help me to put your teaching into practice, no matter what it costs. Amen.

PG

Revelation 3:1–5 (NRSV)

Sardis: lifeless and untroubled

'I know your works; you have a name of being alive, but you are dead. Wake up, and strengthen what remains and is on the point of death, for I have not found your works perfect in the sight of my God. Remember then what you received and heard; obey it, and repent... Yet you have still a few persons in Sardis who have not soiled their clothes; they will walk with me, dressed in white, for they are worthy. If you conquer, you will be clothed like them in white robes, and I will not blot your name out of the book of life.'

She loved the worship and liturgy of her new church, so went to see the minister and asked to join, because, so she said, 'I love your music and your lethargy.' If she did really mean 'lethargy', Sardis would have been her ideal church. It had a reputation for life but, in reality, was spiritually dead. Not surprisingly, there is no reference to being under attack or facing heresy. Such lifelessness was not worth attacking, and intellectual laziness does not lead to heresy. Only a church with a positive message draws forth opposition!

A group of Christian students in a university were undergoing much opposition for their faith. A sense of gloom and despondency hung over their weekly meeting until one student simply prayed, 'Thank you, Lord, that opposition has replaced apathy. At long last we are being noticed. Help us stand firm, and lead us through to victory.' That prayer marked a real change of attitude. Now the students felt they could win. They faced the challenge head-on and became far more effective than ever before. Lethargy became life!

To find such life, says John, we need to relive the thrill with which we first heard the gospel and felt its impact upon us. We then repent of our present slowness of heart and start obeying God's commandments. Thus living in the presence of Christ we are watchful, always on our guard against temptation and weakness.

Even in Sardis, the faithful few had the assurance of being with Christ for eternity. Their names were in the book of life. There are rewards for faithful service!

Prayer

Transform lethargy into life, Lord, and keep my faith fresh, vital and obedient. Amen.

PG

Revelation 3:8, 10–12 (NRSV)

Philadelphia: the city praised

'Look, I have set before you an open door, which no one is able to shut. I know that you have but little power, and yet you have kept my word and have not denied my name... I will keep you from the hour of trial that is coming on the whole world to test the inhabitants of the earth. I am coming soon; hold fast to what you have, so that no one may seize your crown. If you conquer, I will make you a pillar in the temple of my God; you will never go out of it. I will write on you the name of my God, and the name of the city of my God, the new Jerusalem... and my own new name.'

A patient with a notorious lifestyle asked to see the hospital chaplain and requested baptism. When asked about his beliefs, he replied, 'Don't ask me about the details. I believe what those nurses believe. All I know is that they are the best people I have ever seen. I want to finish up like them, so I believe what they believe. Now baptize me.' Their witness had earned them the right to speak.

Philadelphia, the youngest of the seven cities of Asia, was founded to be a kind of cultural 'open door', spreading Greek culture from Mysia to Lydia and Phrygia. The risen Christ now speaks of another 'open door' through which they were challenged to go and spread the gospel. Indeed, their faithful example and witness had earned them the right to speak. Now they must stand firm so as not to lose the crown they had already won!

Philadelphia is the only church to which no criticism is addressed. Indeed, the emphasis is very much on the reward that faithful Christians would have. They will become a pillar in the temple of God. They would thus be always in his presence and bear his name—a mark of honour and ownership. They would also bear the name of the new Jerusalem: a reminder of the gift of citizenship in the place where God dwelt. Furthermore, by gaining the new name of Jesus, they were availing themselves of all the benefits of his death and resurrection.

Prayer

Lord, help me by my faith and courage to bear a faithful witness to you so that others can see the attractiveness and power of your truth. Amen.

PG

Revelation 3:15–17, 19–20 (NRSV)

Laodicea: the lukewarm church

'I know your works; you are neither cold nor hot. I wish that you were either cold or hot. So, because you are lukewarm, and neither cold nor hot, I am about to spit you out of my mouth. For you say, 'I am rich, I have prospered, and I need nothing.' You do not realize that you are wretched, pitiable, poor, blind and naked... I reprove and discipline those whom I love. Be earnest, therefore, and repent. Listen! I am standing at the door, knocking; if you hear my voice and open the door, I will come in to you and eat with you, and you with me.'

Laodicea was well known for its poor water supply. It came mostly from the hot springs of Hierapolis, some miles across the plain. By the time it had flowed along the aqueduct to Laodicea itself, the taste of the minerals remained but the water had cooled down, and tasted foul. In the other direction, water came from cool mountain streams and was warmed up as it was piped in to Laodicea. In short, it was ineffective: not hot enough for healing or cold enough for refreshment in a hot climate. That summed up the church. Complacency ruled the day. Wealth and prosperity had blinded them to their need. The impurities needed to be refined away if they were to be really wealthy in the things that mattered. They must be clothed in purity and healed inside to see their real need. Such discipline comes from the love of God. Only the best is good enough for his children. His heart is saddened when we accept the second rate.

Reliant on its own resources, the church may have blindly closed the door to Christ. However, there is always the invitation to repent. Jesus knocks and waits for us to answer and then invites us to eat with him. To eat with someone in the ancient world was never a casual thing. It always implied a depth of relationship. So, every time we go to Holy Communion we respond to his invitation. We commit ourselves anew to him and ask that he will strengthen and deepen the transforming friendship that is the life of Christian discipleship.

Prayer

Forgive, Lord, the blindness that prevents my grasping the truth of your word. Keep the door of the Church and of my heart ever open to the transforming power of your love. Amen.

PG

Our next series of readings (pp. 298–315) offers an overview of the whole book of Revelation.

Colossians 1:24–26 (RSV)

The sacrifice of obedience

Now I rejoice in my sufferings for your sake, and in my flesh I complete what is lacking in Christ's afflictions for the sake of his body, that is, the church, of which I became a minister according to the divine office which was given to me for you, to make the word of God fully known, the mystery hidden for ages and generations, but now made manifest to his saints.

Lord Jesus, how can anything be lacking to your sufferings, your afflictions? We believe that your physical sufferings on the cross, your humilation, your loneliness, the desertion by your chosen disciples (an example we follow only too frequently) were the perfect sacrifice of obedience. In your perfect, loving obedience to your Father's will you fully compensated for the disobedience of the human race in Adam. It was the sacrifice 'once and for all'. How, then, can Paul say that he completes what is lacking in these afflictions?

Your body is the Church, spread through the world, men and women of every race and every language, plunged into your death by baptism and living by the Spirit of your risen life. You share with us all the rhythms of your life. Your experiences have become ours, and ours have become yours. You share our petty griefs. In our happiness you too rejoice. This is 'the mystery hidden for ages and generations, but now made manifest in his saints'. Is the love of Christ really made manifest in me, or do I do more to obscure and mask your saving love?

But if your Church is to be truly your body, to manifest your life in every generation, this cannot be without your sufferings. If there were no suffering in your body, the Church, it would be incomplete. The martyrs in every age, from missionaries in Zimbabwe to monks in Algeria, are to us a reminder and a witness of this vital role of suffering. They do not search for martyrdom, but their acceptance of it in your service mirrors and completes your acceptance of suffering in obedience to your Father. Did any of the martyrs of this century know, before their final crisis, that you were preparing them to be fully conformed to you in this way? Keep me faithful to your will now, and form me as a true sapling in your vineyard.

Prayer

Father, into your hands I commend my spirit.

HW

Revelation 1:4–11 (NRSV)

The prophet

John to the seven churches that are in Asia: Grace to you and peace from him who is and who was and who is to come, and from the seven spirits who are before his throne, and from Jesus Christ, the faithful witness, the firstborn of the dead, and the ruler of the kings of the earth. To him who loves us and freed us from our sins by his blood, and made us to be a kingdom, priests serving his God and Father, to him be glory and dominion forever and ever. Amen. Look! He is coming with the clouds; every eye will see him, even those who pierced him; and on his account all the tribes of the earth will wail. So it is to be. Amen. 'I am the Alpha and the Omega,' says the Lord God, who is and who was and who is to come, the Almighty. I, John, your brother who share with you in Jesus the persecution and the kingdom and the patient endurance, was on the island called Patmos ... I was in the spirit on the Lord's day, and I heard behind me a loud voice like a trumpet saying, 'Write in a book what you see and send it to the seven churches, to Ephesus, to Smyrna, to Pergamum, to Thyatira, to Sardis, to Philadelphia, and to Laodicea.'

While in exile on Patmos, John had a series of visions which formed the basis for his extended letter to the churches of his home district. Probably, though, he meant the message to travel further. It is addressed to seven churches, and seven is a number symbolic of completion—so perhaps it is addressed in fact to the the complete Church.

John prepares for that message in his description of God's people. They are those who know that Jesus died for them, and so have an insight into the depth and wonder of God's love for the world. They are called to be God's kingdom—not the whole kingdom of God, to be sure, but certainly its spearhead. In the Bible, a kingdom is not a place, but a rule. That is, wherever the king is acknowledged, that is his kingdom. So the Church is the body of people who are ruled by God, gladly recognizing his lordship over their lives. And they are priests, called to mediate God's presence to the world, through their words and their deeds. It should be enough to be going on with!

Reflection

What does it mean to you to be part of a 'royal priesthood'?

MM

Revelation 1:12–20 (NRSV)

Mighty risen Lord

Then I turned to see whose voice it was that spoke to me, and on turning I saw seven golden lampstands, and in the midst of the lampstands I saw one like the Son of Man, clothed with a long robe and with a golden sash across his chest. His head and his hair were white as white wool, white as snow; his eyes were like a flame of fire, his feet were like burnished bronze, refined as in a furnace, and his voice was like the sound of many waters. In his right hand he held seven stars, and from his mouth came a sharp, two-edged sword, and his face was like the sun shining with full force. When I saw him, I fell at his feet as though dead. But he placed his right hand on me, saying, 'Do not be afraid; I am the first and the last, and the living one. I was dead, and see, I am alive forever and ever; and I have the keys of Death and of Hades... As for the mystery of the seven stars that you saw in my right hand, and the seven golden lampstands: the seven stars are the angels of the seven churches, and the seven lampstands are the seven churches.

When Mary Magdalene met the risen Jesus in the garden, he came in gentleness, the good shepherd calling his grieving lamb by name, and turning her tears to joy. John's vision of the risen Christ is vastly different—a figure of awe and fear, clothed in power, whose words are a sharp sword. Yet his speech brings assurance of acceptance and love. There is no cause to fear, even faced with the Lord of the ages, the beginning and end of all things.

Jesus can be described in terms that the Old Testament reserves for God: in Revelation, both are the beginning and the end, and both will share the throne of heaven. Still, this picture of Jesus places him in the midst of the Church, symbolized by the seven lampstands. Though apparently alone in a hostile world, the spiritual reality of the Church is that it is held in the hand of the Son of God, who is its power and strength, its comfort and its joy.

John's vision strips away the mere seeming of our worldly view, and presents the way God sees us. We are his, called to have him at the centre of our lives and Church, to burn with his light as a witness to the world.

Prayer

Lord, may we see you as our strength and our keeper.

MM

Revelation 2:1–7 (NRSV)

Letters from heaven

To the angel of the church in Ephesus write: These are the words of him who holds the seven stars in his right hand, who walks among the seven golden lampstands: 'I know your works, your toil and your patient endurance. I know that you cannot tolerate evildoers; you have tested those who claim to be apostles but are not, and have found them to be false. I also know that you are enduring patiently and bearing up for the sake of my name, and that you have not grown weary. But I have this against you, that you have abandoned the love you had at first. Remember then from what you have fallen; repent, and do the works you did at first. If not, I will come to you and remove your lampstand from its place, unless you repent... To everyone who conquers, I will give permission to eat from the tree of life that is in the paradise of God.'

As we have seen (pp. 288–296), Jesus gives seven messages to be sent to the seven churches (and through them to the rest of the church). Each begins with a greeting from Jesus, described by one of the characteristics of John's vision. Each ends with a promise to the one who conquers—a promise which is taken up and fulfilled in the closing chapters of John's book. In general, they mix praise and criticism, warning and promise of blessing. Each addresses a particular issue in a given church, the solution to which will be spelt out in the rest of the book.

The letter to Ephesus shows the approach. The Ephesian Christians are morally upright and doctrinally sound. They are a church which no doubt prides itself on holding fast to the apostolic teachings and the message of Jesus. They face adversity with courage and determination. But there's a big problem. Love has faded. We are not told whether it is love for God, for each other, or for outsiders, but in the end there is little to choose between any of these, for all are tied together. Love for God overflows in concern for the fellowship and compassion for those around. It's a problem that we know only too well in the modern Church. It is often easy for a concern for truth and uprightness to turn into hard condemnation or self-righteousness; to be so concerned for what is right that we forget what is good for others. We need to remember that all Christian teaching must in the end spell, 'God is love.'

Prayer

Lord, keep us safe in the knowledge that you love us and call us to share your love.

MM

Revelation 4:1–7 (NRSV)

Behind the veil

After this I looked, and there in heaven a door stood open! And the first voice... said, 'Come up here, and I will show you what must take place after this.' At once I was in the spirit, and there in heaven stood a throne, with one seated on the throne! And the one seated there looks like jasper and carnelian, and around the throne is a rainbow that looks like an emerald. Around the throne are twenty-four thrones, and seated on the thrones are twenty-four elders, dressed in white robes, with golden crowns on their heads. Coming from the throne are flashes of lightning, and rumblings and peals of thunder, and in front of the throne burn seven flaming torches, which are the seven spirits of God; and in front of the throne there is something like a sea of glass, like crystal. Around the throne, and on each side of the throne, are four living creatures, full of eyes in front and behind: the first living creature like a lion, the second living creature like an ox, the third living creature with a face like a human face, and the fourth living creature like a flying eagle.

Now John is taken into heaven, to see the reality which lies behind the world we see every day. Heaven here does not refer to the final resting-place of the saints, as we tend to mean. It is the spiritual reality which lies behind the world, and it is ruled by God. Despite all appearances to the contrary, God remains in charge. So he is depicted as sitting on a throne, around which is the rainbow which symbolizes his mercy (Genesis 9:13) and before which are four creatures representing all creation, twenty-four elders standing for the people of God and seven torches which depict the Holy Spirit who empowers the Church.

God is at the heart of creation, watching over it (see the eyes in tomorrow's reading) and receiving the praise of his people, who wear golden crowns. The people of God may seem from a human perspective to be strange, weak and divided, but from God's point of view, they are his royal priests, called to worship him and proclaim his word to the world.

Prayer

Father, when the only reality seems to be
the world of sorrow and despair,
open my eyes to share your vision of
glory and wonder.

MM

Revelation 4:8–11 (NRSV)

Song of creation

And the four living creatures, each of them with six wings, are full of eyes all around and inside. Day and night without ceasing they sing, 'Holy, holy, holy, the Lord God the Almighty, who was and is and is to come.' And whenever the living creatures give glory and honour and thanks to the one who is seated on the throne, who lives for ever and ever, the twenty-four elders fall before the one who is seated on the throne and worship the one who lives for ever and ever; they cast their crowns before the throne, singing, 'You are worthy, our Lord and God, to receive glory and honour and power, for you created all things, and by your will they existed and were created.'

What is creation for? After all, God does not need to have anything else, presumably. And there's such a lot of pain and wrongdoing in the world, and presumably in the universe as a whole. So why bother? Why go to so much trouble, including the great act of salvation, with the incarnation and the cross?

There's no full answer to that sort of question, of course, but here John comes as close as anywhere in the Bible to answering it. Creation exists to sing God's praises. Of course, on one level, that sounds pretty daft. Does God really need to create a load of creatures just to tell him how great he is? It sounds narcissistic, at the least. To say that, though, is to miss the point of praise. It is not simply admiration, but the expression of love. A parent sees things in a child which no one else can, and yet calls them to others' attention. Lovers whisper outrageous compliments, because there is no other way of putting into words what love means, and what the beloved is to the lover.

Praise is the expression of love. For those who have encountered God, there can be nothing else but the outrageous extravagance of praise, for they have found the love they were created to know—and have met the love of the Creator.

When we worship, we are finally doing what we were created for—encountering God and expressing our love for him and his love for us.

Prayer

Father, may I worship you in spirit and in truth, and with angels and archangels and all the company of heaven.

MM

Revelation 5:1–7 (NRSV)

Conquering lamb

Then I saw in the right hand of the one seated on the throne a scroll written on the inside and on the back, sealed with seven seals; and I saw a mighty angel proclaiming with a loud voice, 'Who is worthy to open the scroll and break its seals?' And no one in heaven or on earth or under the earth was able to open the scroll or to look into it. And I began to weep bitterly because no one was found worthy to open the scroll or to look into it. Then one of the elders said to me, 'Do not weep. See, the Lion of the tribe of Judah, the Root of David, has conquered, so that he can open the scroll and its seven seals.' Then I saw between the throne and the four living creatures and among the elders a Lamb standing as if it had been slaughtered, having seven horns and seven eyes, which are the seven spirits of God sent out into all the earth. He went and took the scroll from the right hand of the one who was seated on the throne.

John's vision now moves on, and he sees a scroll, which will eventually turn out to contain God's plan for his coming victory over sin and death. But who is worthy to open (and therefore put into action) such a plan? John weeps in despair—itself a hopeful sign, for even in the midst of God's glory and power, there is space for human weakness and human feeling.

All is not lost, though. The Messiah has conquered, and so John is told this, in terms which reflect power and might. The Lion of Judah, the new king of David's line, has the victory. Yet what John sees differs from what he hears, as so often in this book. He sees a slaughtered Lamb, which is Christ.

To understand what this means, we have to put together what is seen and what is heard. The lamb, symbol of weakness and vulnerability, has turned out to be the conquering king. God's kingdom comes not through power and violence, but through suffering and apparent defeat. The cross on which Jesus was apparently put out of the way of the world's powers turns out to be the victory of God.

Prayer

Lord, do not let me be seduced into thinking in the world's ways. Enable me instead to see your definition of greatness, found in humble service.

MM

Revelation 5:8–14 (NRSV)

Victory song

The four living creatures and the twenty-four elders fell before the Lamb ... They sing a new song: 'You are worthy to take the scroll and to open its seals, for you were slaughtered and by your blood you ransomed for God saints from every tribe and language and people and nation; you have made them to be a kingdom and priests serving our God, and they will reign on earth.' Then I looked, and I heard the voice of many angels surrounding the throne and the living creatures and the elders; they numbered myriads of myriads and thousands of thousands, singing with full voice, 'Worthy is the Lamb that was slaughtered to receive power and wealth and wisdom and might and honour and glory and blessing!' Then I heard every creature in heaven and on earth and under the earth and in the sea, and all that is in them, singing, 'To the one seated on the throne and to the Lamb be blessing and honour and glory and might forever and ever!' And the four living creatures said, 'Amen!' And the elders fell down and worshipped.

Revelation 4 gave us a vision of creation worshipping its creator. As his creatures, we are made to worship God. But that is not our only reason to serve him. The song of heaven now celebrates the Lamb's victory. By his sacrifice he has bought us back from the power of death and sin. In the early Church, theologians used to argue about to whom the ransom was paid. Was it the devil? Personified death? But that misses the point. The biblical language of ransom is about the cost of salvation. God has not simply waved his hand and decided to forget matters. It has cost him dearly.

So the assembled hosts of heaven and all creation sing the praises of Jesus, for he is worthy of such praise. God does not simply demand our worship on the grounds that he has made us. He comes to us and says, 'Look what I have done for you; isn't that worth the response of praise? Doesn't that prove my love, and kindle yours?' It is his way of working throughout the Bible. He acts first to save, and then calls us to respond.

Prayer

Lord, your love is unimaginable. Forgive me that my response is often so cold, and inspire me to join the eternal song of heaven.

MM

Revelation 6:1–4 (NRSV)

Heralds of judgment

Then I saw the Lamb open one of the seven seals, and I heard one of the four living creatures call out, as with a voice of thunder, 'Come!' I looked, and there was a white horse! Its rider had a bow; a crown was given to him, and he came out conquering and to conquer. When he opened the second seal, I heard the second living creature call out, 'Come!' And out came another horse, bright red; its rider was permitted to take peace from the earth, so that people would slaughter one another; and he was given a great sword.

Once the seals of the scroll are opened, the process of salvation is set in motion. It may therefore seem strange that all we see at first is judgment. Four riders appear, bringing conquest, war, famine and death. The fifth scroll reveals the martyrs of God, crying for vengeance, and the sixth scroll brings the day of judgment, as the universe is torn apart and all have to face the wrath of God.

These few visions give an overview of the history of the world, not just a picture of some distant end times. Conquest, war, famine and death are the constant companions of the human race. God's saints are persecuted at all times (though happily not in all places at once). It is this sad history which leads to the final judgment.

What John is saying is that as we look at the turmoil that dogs history, and is the experience of so many at any time, we have a choice. We can see it as simply how things are, or as a pointer to our need for salvation, the need for humanity to be brought into a state where its full potential for good may be realized. For those with ears to hear, the suffering of the world is a cry of desperation, and God's call to repentance and faith.

For most, though, the call to repentance is not heeded. To see the sorrows of the world as judgments and warnings seems to be a perspective that is missed by many. Instead, God's goodness is doubted and the offer of salvation missed. Something else is needed, and to that John now turns.

Prayer

Father, look with mercy on the suffering of your creation, and uphold those whose work it is to relieve pain in the name of Christ.

MM

Revelation 7:1–4, 9 (NRSV)

God's army

After this I saw four angels standing at the four corners of the earth, holding back the four winds of the earth so that no wind could blow on earth or sea or against any tree. I saw another angel ascending from the rising of the sun, having the seal of the living God, and he called with a loud voice to the four angels who had been given power to damage earth and sea, saying, 'Do not damage the earth or the sea or the trees, until we have marked the servants of our God with a seal on their foreheads.' And I heard the number of those who were sealed, one hundred and forty-four thousand, sealed out of every tribe of the people of Israel... After this I looked, and there was a great multitude that no one could count, from every nation, from all tribes and peoples and languages, standing before the throne and before the Lamb, robed in white, with palm branches in their hands.

When John saw the Lamb, he heard a voice which proclaimed it to be a lion. Now, something similar happens. He hears a voice calling out that 144,000 must be marked as belonging to God, so that they will be protected from the coming judgment. Yet when he looks, he sees a numberless host in heaven. These, in fact, are the same group—the people of God.

The number is symbolic, seeing the church as a levy drawn from the tribes of Israel. In the Old Testament, the only time the people of Israel were to be counted was when an army had to be conscripted, and then the number of fighting men from each tribe was tallied. So John presents the Church as God's army, called to fight his holy war. The reality that he sees, though, is different. It is a numberless crowd, standing before God's throne, and singing his praises.

We are destined for the eternal presence of God, but here we confront the enemy. How? Not in fact by violence, as we shall see. The proclamation of the gospel, the call to justice, truth and peace, are the weapons of our struggle. When Christians speak against wrong, lobby their MPs, evangelize their neighbours, they are God's soldiers in the war between good and evil—a war whose outcome has already become certain, through Christ's victory on the cross.

Prayer

Lord, make me your faithful soldier and servant.

MM

Revelation 7:9–14 (NRSV)

Defeated victors

After this I looked, and there was a great multitude that no one could count, from every nation, from all tribes and peoples and languages, standing before the throne and before the Lamb, robed in white... They cried out in a loud voice, saying, 'Salvation belongs to our God who is seated on the throne, and to the Lamb!' And all the angels stood around the throne and around the elders and the four living creatures, and they fell on their faces before the throne and worshipped God, singing, 'Amen! Blessing and glory and wisdom and thanksgiving and honour and power and might be to our God for ever and ever! Amen.' Then one of the elders addressed me, saying, 'Who are these, robed in white, and where have they come from?' I said to him, 'Sir, you are the one that knows.' Then he said to me, 'These are they who have come out of the great ordeal; they have washed their robes and made them white in the blood of the Lamb.'

The Dead Sea scrolls are the library of a Jewish sect which lived a semi-monastic life at Qumran on the coast of the Dead Sea. One of their books is known as the War Scroll, and it sets out plans for the final conflict between the 'sons of light' (the Qumran sect) and the 'sons of darkness' (nearly everyone else). This was to be a literal battle in which God would intervene to bring victory to his chosen people, and re-establish the nation of Israel. The Qumran sect was wiped out by the Romans around AD70.

John's Revelation is in a sense a Christian War Scroll. He speaks of the army of God, and of conflict with the forces of darkness. But there the similarity ends. His battle is not fought with physical weapons—or at least, not on the Christian side. The victorious army, now standing in heaven, have come out of the great ordeal by being killed. They have washed their robes in their own blood, shed in martyrdom, like the death of the Lamb. (That this is John's meaning is clear from Revelation 12:11.) In other words, the victory is brought about not by force of arms, but by faithful witness to Jesus—a witness which is ready to end in martyrdom (a word which comes from the Greek *martys*—a witness).

Reflection

How faithful am I in my witness?

MM

Revelation 8:1–6 (NRSV)

Silence of the Lamb

When the Lamb opened the seventh seal, there was silence in heaven for about half an hour. And I saw the seven angels who stand before God, and seven trumpets were given to them. Another angel with a golden censer came and stood at the altar; he was given a great quantity of incense to offer with the prayers of all the saints on the golden altar that is before the throne. And the smoke of the incense, with the prayers of the saints, rose before God from the hand of the angel. Then the angel took the censer and filled it with fire from the altar and threw it on the earth; and there were peals of thunder, rumblings, flashes of lightning, and an earthquake. Now the seven angels who had the seven trumpets made ready to blow them.

The opening of the seventh seal brings the strangest response of all. Heaven itself falls silent. The seven seals are to be followed by seven trumpets which will introduce another series of warning judgments (which in turn are another way of viewing the world's history, this time focusing on spiritual evil). First, though, as the trumpets are prepared, there is the silence. In it, the prayers of God's people are offered.

John is using a Jewish tradition which says that at the daily hours of prayer, heaven falls silent to listen. The incense censer represents those prayers, and as it is flung back to earth, filled with heavenly fire, the prayers are answered.

Prayer is one of the great mysteries of Christian life. We can see that it is good for us, because it is always good to focus our thoughts, fears and desires on God. But we are often tempted to wonder whether those prayers make a difference. John has no such doubts. The prayer (here presumably for the vindication of the saints) is taken up and becomes a part of God's action in the world. God knows what he wants to do, and he knows what we want too. In his outworking of the history of the world, those prayers are taken into account, and worked into the pattern he is weaving (along, no doubt, with all the actions of people, both good and bad).

No, we do not always get what we want. Don't doubt, though, that without our prayers, things would be different.

Prayer

Lord, help me to keep praying,
and teach me that when you seem silent,
you are listening.

MM

Revelation 9:20–22; 10:8–11 (NRSV)

Bitter-sweet message

The rest of humankind, who were not killed by these plagues, did not repent of the works of their hands or give up worshipping demons and idols of gold and silver and bronze and stone and wood, which cannot see or hear or walk. And they did not repent of their murders or their sorceries or their fornication or their thefts ... Then the voice that I had heard from heaven spoke to me again, saying, 'Go, take the scroll that is open in the hand of the angel who is standing on the sea and on the land.' So I went to the angel and told him to give me the little scroll; and he said to me, 'Take it, and eat; it will be bitter to your stomach, but sweet as honey in your mouth.' So I took the little scroll from the hand of the angel and ate it; it was sweet as honey in my mouth, but when I had eaten it, my stomach was made bitter. Then they said to me, 'You must prophesy again about many peoples and nations and languages and kings.'

The seven trumpets sound, disaster walks the face of the earth, and the people fail to turn to God. The suffering of the world is not enough, terrible though it is, to bring about repentance. Something else must be tried. So John is told to eat a scroll, which is probably the same scroll as the Lamb has opened —it is God's plan of salvation for the world. John must speak it aloud; and while it is sweet, for it contains the word of God, it is a bitter pill to swallow, for it brings rejection, humiliation and persecution to the Church which must proclaim it.

The fact is that though much of what is wrong in the world is due to human sinfulness, it is not enough to point people to God. A word must be proclaimed which tells of God's love and mercy, his great sacrifice in Jesus Christ, and his welcome to all who turn to him. That message has a darker side, for it calls to repentance and a turning away from false gods, and may bring a backlash on those who preach it.

Prayer

Lord, let me see and seize the opportunity to speak of you, and keep me strong in the face of rejection.

MM

Revelation 11:3, 7–8, 11–13 (NRSV)

Costly witness

'I will grant my two witnesses authority to prophesy for 1,260 days, wearing sackcloth.'... When they have finished their testimony, the beast that comes up from the bottomless pit will make war on them and conquer them and kill them, and their dead bodies will lie in the street of the great city that is prophetically called Sodom and Egypt, where also their Lord was crucified ... But after the three and a half days, the breath of life from God entered them, and they stood on their feet, and those who saw them were terrified. Then they heard a loud voice from heaven saying to them, 'Come up here!' And they went up to heaven in a cloud while their enemies watched them. At that moment there was a great earthquake, and a tenth of the city fell; seven thousand people were killed in the earthquake, and the rest were terrified and gave glory to the God of heaven.

In our society, neither the proclamation of the gospel nor a backlash against it seem very strong. Yet most Christians know what it is to face, at the very least, derision and mockery for their message. The response to that mockery is a part of the message itself. It is by faithfulness that the Church shows the power of the message, and the strength of God. That is the message of today's reading, the central passage of Revelation. The two witnesses stand for the whole Church, which proclaims the gospel and is killed as a result. Does John really expect the whole Church to die under persecution? Perhaps not, though he is clear that effective witness does bring persecution. However, his point is this: even if all Christians died for their faith, God's message of salvation would only be preached more strongly by their testimony of faithfulness.

The witnesses are brought back to life and all but a small remnant of those who see this give glory to God. That is, as the Church's trust in eternal life enables it to face persecution, so the very persecutors are won over to faith, and confess God as their Lord and King. For John, the preaching of the gospel is essential to the salvation of the world. How seriously do we take that? How much of our churches' efforts is put into effective evangelism? How much of the lives of Christians really demonstrates trust in God?

Prayer

Lord, help us to recover a commitment to share your good news with the world around us.

MM

Revelation 12:1–8 (NRSV)

Dragon's defeat

A great portent appeared in heaven: a woman clothed with the sun, with the moon under her feet, and on her head a crown of twelve stars. She was pregnant and was crying out in birth pangs, in the agony of giving birth. Then another portent appeared in heaven: a great red dragon, with seven heads and ten horns, and seven diadems on his heads. His tail swept down a third of the stars of heaven and threw them to the earth. Then the dragon stood before the woman who was about to bear a child, so that he might devour her child as soon as it was born. And she gave birth to a son, a male child, who is to rule all the nations with a rod of iron. But her child was snatched away and taken to God and to his throne; and the woman fled into the wilderness, where she has a place prepared by God, so that there she can be nourished for 1,260 days. And war broke out in heaven; Michael and his angels fought against the dragon. The dragon and his angels fought back, but they were defeated...

In the ancient world there were several stories of a hero child who defeated a monstrous dragon or serpent. John uses it to tell God's story of salvation. The woman, the people of God, brings forth the Messiah, who is not devoured by the dragon, the devil, but ascends to heaven, making possible the devil's defeat. We already know that the child is the Lamb of God, who wins the victory by his death. Now Satan is defeated, and cast out of heaven to wage war on the earth, against the followers of Jesus.

By using a well-known (and pagan) tale, John is making two points. One is that the images of the world can be used by Christians to tell the gospel story in terms which non-Christians can understand.

More importantly, he is saying that all the hopes and longings of the world, told in whatever stories and dreams, find their fulfilment in Jesus Christ. What do people hope for today? Is it meaning or purpose? Assurance of love and acceptance? To be valued in a world which depersonalizes? All these are offered by God in Jesus Christ. The Church's task is to make the offer in terms which are as well understood today as the dragon story was in John's time.

Prayer

Lord, teach us to tell your story.

MM

Revelation 12:18—13:4 (NRSV)

Beastly power

Then the dragon took his stand on the sand of the seashore. And I saw a beast rising out of the sea, having ten horns and seven heads; and on its horns were ten diadems, and on its heads were blasphemous names. And the beast that I saw was like a leopard, its feet were like a bear's, and its mouth was like a lion's mouth. And the dragon gave it his power and his throne and great authority. One of its heads seemed to have received a death-blow, but its mortal wound had been healed. In amazement the whole earth followed the beast. They worshipped the dragon, for he had given his authority to the beast, and they worshipped the beast, saying, 'Who is like the beast, and who can fight against it?'

Most of John's fantastic images are drawn from the Old Testament, and the beast from the sea is a composite of the four beasts of Daniel 7. So his readers would know that here we see an empire, and moreover, one whose description is similar to that of the dragon. The beast is Rome, and it is an incarnation of Satan. In fact, it is not Rome exactly, but the power that Rome exercises, the power of military might and economic coercion. It is a power which demands worship, and whose glitter and glory backs up its claim to be all that is good in the world.

Rome, like all civilizations, brought many benefits, but it did so at a cost. The cost of its much-vaunted peace (the *Pax Romana*) was its absolute rule. The cost of its glory was the economic drain on its provinces. But the greatest cost for Christians was its claim to divine appointment. The blasphemous names on the beast are the claims to divinity of the emperor and the spirit of Rome. For Christians, this goes too far. There is one God, and one Lord to whom alone must be offered unswerving devotion.

Christians have to look critically at the powers of the world. Where they claim total allegiance, at the cost of conscience and freedom, they are demanding a service which can only be offered to God. It is no coincidence that totalitarian regimes, from Roman times till now, have been uneasy with the Christian Church.

Prayer

Lord of all, enable your people to serve you in the world, and to be a challenge to all that claims the power and sovereignty which are yours alone.

MM

Revelation 13:11–15 (NRSV)

False prophet

Then I saw another beast that rose out of the earth; it had two horns like a lamb and it spoke like a dragon. It exercises all the authority of the first beast on its behalf, and it makes the earth and its inhabitants worship the first beast, whose mortal wound had been healed. It performs great signs, even making fire come down from heaven to earth in the sight of all; and by the signs that it is allowed to perform on behalf of the beast, it deceives the inhabitants of earth, telling them to make an image for the beast that had been wounded by the sword and yet lived; and it was allowed to give breath to the image of the beast so that the image of the beast could even speak and cause those who would not worship the image of the beast to be killed.

As if the first beast were not enough, another now comes on the scene. Where the first represented unbridled political power, the second is the power of religion. For John's readers, this would be the state religion of Rome. When the great anti-Christian persecutions started, the acid test was whether a suspected Christian would burn incense to the emperor as a god. To acknowledge Rome's blessed status before the gods was a sign of true loyalty. The role of religion in the empire, then, was to bolster the political power of the day.

John presents us with a picture of an unholy trinity opposing the work of the true God. It consists of the devil, his incarnation in the power of the state, and the false religion which serves only to proclaim that all is well with the world. It is sobering to realize that John's second beast looks rather like Christ (with the horns of a lamb) but what it says is entirely the devil's speech. At times, the Church has itself succumbed to the temptation to become such a false prophet, working in the interests of political power, and ceasing to speak the word of God. (Under the Nazis, there were learned theologians who attempted to prove that Jesus was not a Jew!) When Christians give uncritical allegiance to worldly power, they lose the gospel, and the Church begins to worship another god altogether.

Prayer

Lord, hold safely all who are called to proclaim your word, so that they will not water it down to make it more palatable to a world which fails to worship you.

MM

Revelation 13:16—14:3 (NRSV)

Badge of allegiance

Also it causes all, both small and great, both rich and poor, both free and slave, to be marked on the right hand or the forehead, so that no one can buy or sell who does not have the mark, that is, the name of the beast or the number of its name. This calls for wisdom: let anyone with understanding calculate the number of the beast, for it is the number of a person. Its number is six hundred and sixty-six. Then I looked, and there was the Lamb, standing on Mount Zion! And with him were 144,000 who had his name and his Father's name written on their foreheads. And I heard a voice from heaven like the sound of many waters and like the sound of loud thunder; the voice I heard was like the sound of harpists playing on their harps, and they sang a new song before the throne... No one could learn that song except the 144,000 who have been redeemed from the earth.

Today's passage presents a call to choose sides. The beast which represents false religion demands that all people serve the earthly power, on pain of being cut off from society—unable to trade or get the goods necessary for daily life. This was an exaggeration, even in John's time, though for those who did not subscribe to paganism, membership of trade guilds and of respectable society would be difficult. John, though, is concerned with the spiritual reality underlying his image.

Conformity to the world which has no place for the true God is conformity with the devil. There is no neutral ground. We are called on the one hand to be stamped with the sign of the world, and on the other to be sealed with the sign of Christ.

So we are given a vision of the world in which all bear the mark of the beast, and against whom stand the army of the Lord, signed with his mark. The question is not who will win, for Christ has already won the battle. The real question is how many will be on each side. Revelation ultimately offers two possibilities—of the triumph of the kingdom through the repentance and conversion of the world, or simply the destruction of the world. Which it will be depends on the faithful witness of Christ's followers.

Prayer

Pray for those who are tempted by the pressures of the world, and for those who are called to be faithful witnesses— the Church of God.

MM

Revelation 21:1–4 (NRSV)

New creation

Then I saw a new heaven and a new earth; for the first heaven and the first earth had passed away, and the sea was no more. And I saw the holy city, the new Jerusalem, coming down out of heaven from God, prepared as a bride adorned for her husband. And I heard a loud voice from the throne saying, 'See, the home of God is among mortals. He will dwell with them; they will be his peoples, and God himself will be with them; he will wipe every tear from their eyes. Death will be no more; mourning and crying and pain will be no more, for the first things have passed away.'

For all its images of conflict and turmoil, the thrust of Revelation is toward the visions of the closing chapters, so it is best that we end with one of them. John's vision is of a final meeting between God and human beings, in which the people of God, personified as a city, become the dwelling place of God himself.

There is an end to all that opposes God (the sea symbolized chaos in Old Testament thought) and wounds and sorrows are healed. The tender image of God wiping away tears is in contrast to much of what goes before. Yet judgment, even in Revelation, is never God's desire, but the result of his being rejected by his creatures. Once we decide to cut ourselves off from the source of life, and to walk without the light of the world, our fate follows automatically.

It need not be that way, however. Here we see the beginning of a new creation, made from the best of the old, and destined for eternity in the presence of God. It is the light of this vision which draws people to it, and shines at the end of the road for all who trust God.

It is also the light by which we are to live now. Those who have caught a glimpse of the city of God have a model for their own lives and dwelling places. Even those who are exiled in Babylon may bring a little of Zion through their lives and words.

Prayer

Lord, let your light shine in me,
that others may catch the vision of
the city of God.

MM

Revelation 12:7–12 (NRSV)

St Michael and All Angels

And war broke out in heaven; Michael and his angels fought against the dragon. The dragon and his angels fought back, but they were defeated, and there was no longer any place for them in heaven. The great dragon was thrown down, that ancient serpent, who is called the Devil and Satan, the deceiver of the whole world—he was thrown down to the earth, and his angels were thrown down with him.

I wonder what you think about angels? Nowadays, just about the only time we use the word in ordinary converation is when we say, 'Be an angel and make me a cup of tea!' But angels are a constant feature in both Old and New Testaments, and if we can get behind the picture language of the Bible they can teach us a great deal about God and his care for us. The word 'angel' really means 'agent' or 'messenger', and at times, especially in the Old Testament, the angel of the Lord is virtually identified with God himself.

In this passage from Revelation we see the picture of angels as God's warriors, engaged in the cosmic battle between good and evil which is the backdrop to the whole story of the Bible. Satan or the Devil also has his 'agents', but they are doomed to defeat at the hands of Michael, God's archangel, and his troop. So angels speak of God's power over evil.

But they also speak of his care for us—think of the angels who, Jesus said, guard the well-being of little children (Matthew 18:10). And they remind us that God has 'messages' for us—he wants us to know and understand his purposes. Think of how the angel of the Lord guided Joseph through the trauma of Mary's pregnancy (Matthew 1:20, 21).

Reflection

Angels don't always (or often) come with wings and light! Sometimes they speak in much more mundane ways, if we are listening.

DW

304

John 14:1–9 (NRSV, abridged)

Troubled hearts

Do not let your hearts be troubled. Believe in God, believe also in me. In my Father's house there are many dwelling places. If it were not so, would I have told you that I go to prepare a place for you? And if I go and prepare a place for you, I will come again and will take you to myself, so that where I am, there you may be also. I am the way, and the truth, and the life. No one comes to the Father except through me.

How often I've used these opening words in the funeral service, and ministered the comfort and strength of Christ to mourning loved ones. The words have a profound power to impart hope and healing in the midst of death and bereavement.

In one sense this is very strange, because Judas had just gone out into the night to betray Jesus, and Jesus knew very well that his passion and death were before him. Yet he speaks of an untroubled heart and of his power to give peace and rest to those around him who were distressed, perplexed and afraid. It makes me want to cry out, 'What a wonderful Saviour!'—and that on the first day of what my mother used to call 'suicide month'.

At the end of today's passage we have those amazing words in which Jesus declares himself to be the divine Mediator between God and humankind. They are words for All Saints' Day, and ought not to be interpreted exclusively. We are not meant to say, 'Only immediate knowledge of the historical Jesus will bring us to salvation—therefore all others are damned.' We are meant to recognize that there are many 'other sheep who do not belong to this fold' which Jesus will bring home at last (10:16). None of the godly men and women of the Old Testament knew Jesus personally, but all of them came to the Father through the eternal *Logos* (the 'Word') who enlightens all those who come into the world (1:9).

This glorifies Jesus in whom the *Logos* became incarnate. It heightens our view of him, increases our love for him, and makes us realize that his was no parochial or exclusive task. That is why he is able to make such world-shaking claims as those found in John's Gospel.

Prayer

Jesus, you are the way of my going;
You are the truth of my knowing;
You are the life of my living.
Alleluia!

R/SSF

John 14:8–14 (NRSV, abridged)

Show us the Father

Philip said to Jesus, 'Lord, show us the Father, and we will be satisfied.' Jesus said to him, 'Have I been with you all this time, Philip, and you still do not know me? Whoever has seen me has seen the Father. How can you say, "Show us the Father"? Do you not believe that I am in the Father and the Father is in me? I will do whatever you ask in my name, so that the Father may be glorified in the Son.

Jesus was grieved at Philip's question. It was not that Philip got his theology or his catechism wrong, but that he had not recognized who Jesus really was!

The question reminds me of Moses' bold request to Yahweh (the Lord): 'Show me your glory' (Exodus 33:18). He hardly knew what he was asking, and he was only allowed to see the passing by of God's glory, for, as Yahweh said, 'You cannot see my face, for no one shall see me and live' (v. 20).

There were times when the outshining of God's glory in Jesus filled the onlookers with awe and fear, on the mount of transfiguration and in the garden of Gethsemane (Mark 9:6; John 18:6). But in the daily living, learning and ministering with his disciples, the simple humanity of Jesus was in the forefront, and Philip, like the others, had not yet understood or received the enlightenment which comes from the Holy Spirit.

The words Jesus spoke to him were for him to reflect upon, and for us to perceive at a far deeper level on this side of Easter. To look into the face of Jesus is to gaze upon the unutterable glory of God. As Michael Ramsey so wonderfully said, 'God is Christlike, and in him is no un-Christlikeness at all.' If you want to trace these words in a powerful theological unfolding, read John V. Taylor's book *The Christlike God*. I hope you'll do that—but today we are simply to gaze upon the face of Jesus, to behold the glory of the Father in our prayer, and to allow the wonder of it all to overflow into our daily lives.

If we seek, by God's grace, to do this, then the divine glory will shine from our lives, will irradiate our deeds of compassion, and even the 'greater works' of which Jesus speaks (v. 12) will point to the glory of God in our lives.

Prayer

Father, show us your glory in the face of Jesus, and let its radiance shine in me.

R/SSF

John 14:15–25 (NRSV, abridged)

The indwelling Spirit

If you love me, you will keep my commandments. And I will ask the Father, and he will give you another Advocate, to be with you for ever. This is the Spirit of truth, whom the world cannot receive, because it neither sees him nor knows him. You know him, because he abides with you, and he will be in you. On that day you will know that I am in my Father, and you in me, and I in you.

This fortnight's readings are in the context of the upper room where Jesus shared with his disciples the washing of their feet, the eucharist and the holy communion of intimacy and teaching before the darkness of Calvary fell upon him.

He entered into real darkness, suffering and agony, but was also aware that this would not be the end. Throughout these discourses he is preparing his disciples for 'the time between' and for the coming of the Holy Spirit.

There is no credal trinitarian formulation here, but there is the threefold thread which is woven throughout the New Testament, and especially in these chapters.

There is a basic simplicity and a profound spirituality in what Jesus is saying. It is that those who love him will, by the very nature of love, obey him. And to such disciples will be given the gift of the Holy Spirit in an interior indwelling which will be completely new. This gift will draw them into the fellowship which flows between the Father and the Son—the Spirit being the bond of union—a threefold circle of love.

The world can know nothing of this, but those who love can glimpse it, and begin to experience it: 'The Spirit is with you, and will be in you…'

The disciples would experience perplexity, fear, denial and abandonment before they would enter into any of this. Resurrection was no part of their thinking, and Pentecost was a world away. But in spite of all the darkness, pain and denial, they did love Jesus in a rough, human and poor manner, and the Spirit who was with them would lead them on to the fulfilment of the promise made in Ezekiel (36:26–27)—that the Holy Spirit would indwell them and lead them deeper into God.

Prayer

I see you among your disciples, Lord,
I glimpse you in your word; come and
dwell within my heart.

R/SSF

John 14:27–31 (NRSV, abridged)

Christ's own peace

Peace I leave with you; my peace I give to you. I do not give to you as the world gives. Do not let your hearts be troubled, and do not let them be afraid. You heard me say to you, 'I am going away, and I am coming to you.' If you loved me, you would rejoice that I am going to the Father because the Father is greater than I. And now I have told you this before it occurs, so that when it does occur, you may believe...

The disciples could not have known much of what Jesus was talking about, but he knew the sorrow and darkness through which they were to pass, and he was preparing them by planting in their memories such truths as would sustain them when they were in the valley of despair.

But information was not enough. They were also given an experience of peace. Not the kind of peace that is simply the absence of strife or which depended on outward circumstances. Together with memory's seed of truth he planted the bulb of peace. It was not immediately available because they needed to pass through the harrowing experiences which would bring them to an end of themselves. They had to realize their need of grace, to call upon God out of the depths of misery and helplessness.

Then the shoots of memory's words would appear, and the plant of peace would thrust itself up from the soil of their humanity. They would remember not only what Jesus had said but the promise he had given, and the peace of God which passes understanding would still their troubled hearts and open their eyes to the wounded hands and pierced side of a risen Saviour.

Jesus knows today the valley of sorrow, sickness or bereavement through which you may pass during the next year, and already he prepares you for the trials, so that you may not only be sustained, but experience that abiding peace which enables you to lay hold on eternal strength and values as never before. He does not *wish* you sorrow or pain, but *uses* it, and through it brings you greater blessing and joy than you had ever known before.

Prayer

Minister to me now, O Lord, that in the time of my need I may know that interior light and strength that will bring me through victoriously.

R/SSF

John 15:1–8 (NRSV, abridged)

Jesus, mystical Vine

I am the true vine, and my Father is the vinegrower. He removes every branch in me that bears no fruit. Every branch that bears fruit he prunes to make it bear more fruit. Abide in me as I abide in you. Just as the branch cannot bear fruit by itself unless it abides in the vine, neither can you unless you abide in me. I am the vine, you are the branches. Those who abide in me and I in them bear much fruit, because apart from me you can do nothing.

Here is an organic image which relates back to Israel's past as the vine of God (Isaiah 5:1–7; Psalm 80:8), and which Jesus uses to describe the relationship between himself and his disciples, for they are branches of the central vine.

Isaiah 5 speaks of degeneration and barrenness in the vine which was expected to bear fruit, and in contrast Jesus speaks of himself as the 'true vine'. What Jesus is saying is that no establishment religion of legalism and regulations can communicate life, but only vital, abiding fellowship with him. As the sap flows through the vine and into the branches, promoting sustenance and fruitfulness, so the Holy Spirit flows from the life-giving Jesus into the lives of those who live in his fellowship. 'Abiding' is the key word. The branch does not have to sweat and strive, as if it were independent of the parent vine. Jesus makes it clear: 'apart from me you can do nothing'. All the branch has to do is to abide, allowing the sap to flow, and the natural outcome will be that in the course of time, fruit will appear.

Jesus desires the pattern of his life to be our example, allowing his mystical life to be manifested in our body, mind and spirit. This is brought about by fellowship around word and sacrament, and by developing a contemplative life of prayer that will be the mainspring of a compassionate life in the world. He goes on to speak of stages in fruit-bearing: *fruit* (v. 2), *more* fruit (v. 2), and *much* fruit (vv. 5, 8), and this is brought about by disciplined pruning. Elsewhere Jesus speaks of fruitfulness in terms of thirtyfold, sixtyfold and a hundredfold (Mark 4:8). Such disciplined pruning is carried out by the vinegrower. The Father cuts away all that is unproductive and unloving in our lives, so that our fruitfulness may bring joyful fulfilment to us, and glory to him.

Prayer

Lord Jesus, let me abide in you and bear fruit to your glory. Prune me according to your will, but let it be a gentle severity, bearing the marks of your love.

R/SSF

John 15:9–17 (NRSV, abridged)

Love, joy and fruitfulness

As the Father has loved me, so I have loved you; abide in my love. I have said these things to you so that my joy may be in you, and that your joy may be complete. You did not choose me but I chose you. And I appointed you to go and bear fruit, fruit that will last, so that the Father will give you whatever you ask him in my name. I am giving you these commands so that you may love one another.

Yesterday we saw that fruitfulness depends upon disciplined pruning—and that hurts. When Augustine said, 'Love, and do what you will', Pelagius misunderstood him and was scandalized. Augustine meant that love was the key to discipline and fruitfulness. Jesus makes it clear here—pruning is the removing of all that is unloving, and love is the root, sap and fruit of the vine. It takes us a while to see that love is the name of pruning's secateurs, for all the painful pruning is for our ultimate good.

God can take all the negative factors that are part of our inheritance, upbringing and difficult lives, and weave them into the finished cloth on the loom of his providence. There are also times when he sends certain trials, withholds a *sense* of his loving presence, giving us an experience of absence. But he is never really absent, he is never unloving, he is always secretly gracious, but it may take us a long time to discover all this, in lives lived in the dark marketplace busyness of contemporary life.

Jesus never promised us a cosseted, comfortable, painless and sickness-free life. What he did promise was love, joy and fruitfulness in the midst of the pain and sorrow, and a basic meaning and pattern which may be traced with the insight of faith. This is what we have before us today. He has *chosen* us; he loves us; he has given us the gift of his loving friendship; he ordains us to fruitfulness. Out of all this emerges joy. It is not a glitzy happiness drug which masks the symptoms of our mortality, but an interior and abiding gift that will spring up as we look to him in faith and hope. Its source is the love between the Father and the Son, and it flows by the Holy Spirit into our lives, creating that spring from which flows healing and joy—for ourselves and those we contact day by day.

Prayer

You love me, Lord; you give me grace in trials; let me abide in your love.

R/SSF

John 15:26—16:4 (NRSV, abridged)

The Spirit and the world

When the Advocate comes, whom I will send to you from the Father, the Spirit of truth who comes from the Father, he will testify on my behalf. I have said these things to you to keep you from stumbling. They will put you out of the synagogues. Indeed, an hour is coming when those who kill you will think that by doing so they are offering worship to God. And they will do this because they have not known the Father or me.

Confrontation today! Not only did Jesus not promise an easy life, but he actually forecast conflict. Whenever love appears in our world it is rejected and persecuted, for love itself threatens all duplicity, evil power-systems and deeds of injustice. It may sound strange to us that Jesus prophesied that religion would be the greatest enemy of love—but it was religion, combined with the trappings of political power, that crucified him.

Religion has been responsible for holy wars, pogroms, jihads, holocaust and crusades, and religion without God is power without mercy. The antidote to all this is not more violence, greater power or an alliance of Church and State. The only antidote is true religion—and that means the love which flows from the source of the gracious Father, love which is mediated through the person of Jesus the Son, and love which is communicated and spread by the indwelling of the Holy Spirit.

Jesus calls the Spirit *Paracletos*, which means 'one called alongside to help and plead for us'. The NRSV renders it *Advocate*, which means the same thing. The old translation, *Comforter*, literally means the same, but it has lost its vitality as a word. The Holy Spirit not only comforts us, but fortifies, encourages and inspires us to face the dark power of the enemy.

A full-blooded trinitarian experience is the only answer to the false religion which persecutes, maims and kills in the name of God. Is this the faith which marks our lives? Here is a prayer to the Holy Spirit.

Prayer

Christ is our Advocate on high,
You are our Advocate within;
O plead the truth and make reply
To every argument of sin.

R/SSF

John 16:5–16 (NRSV, abridged)

Bad news and good news

It is to your advantage that I go away, for if I do not go away, the Advocate will not come to you; but if I go, I will send him to you. I still have many things to say to you, but you cannot bear them now. When the Spirit of truth comes, he will guide you into all the truth; for he will not speak on his own, but will speak whatever he hears. He will glorify me, because he will take what is mine and declare it to you.

The bad news for the disciples is that Jesus is going away. The good news is that the Advocate is to come. Thus the bad news becomes good, and the good news becomes better. But they have to prove that, and come out on the Easter and Pentecost side of experience—and the immediate future looks dark.

How easy it is for us to read the Gospel narrative with all the insight and spiritual experience which God has given us in his word and by his Spirit. Yet not only would we have been in a more desperate and perplexing spirit than they were, but even with all our insight we feel the Lord's absence in our dark days, and do not draw on the abundant source of strength, insight and experience which is our inheritance in the Holy Spirit.

The remarkable thing about John's Gospel is that the Evangelist is actually telling us, in the words of his text, those things which the Saviour could not communicate before Calvary and Pentecost. This Gospel is full of alleluias, and the good news floods the page and fills the reader with joy and glory. If we realize that Jesus is alive, that the Spirit has been given, then we are invited, even lovingly compelled, to enter into the fullness of gospel joy. 'These things are written,' says the Evangelist, 'so that you may come to believe that Jesus is the Messiah, the Son of God, and that through believing, you may have life in his name' (20:31).

This is the witness of the Spirit to Jesus, and we are the recipients of such good news. Do you believe it? Have you received it? Well then—rejoice!

Prayer

Holy Spirit of God, minister the things of Christ to me; fill me with joy; and make the risen Jesus real in my life.

R/SSF

John 16:16–24 (NRSV, abridged)

A little while

'A little while, and you will no longer see me, and again a little while, and you will see me.' Then some of his disciples said to one another, 'What does he mean by saying to us, "A little while..." and "Because I am going to the Father"? We do not know what he is talking about.' Jesus said to them, 'You have pain now; but I will see you again, and your hearts will rejoice, and no one will take your joy from you.'

The disciples are perplexed. How difficult for them not only to cope with the sorrow which enshrouded them in the upper room, but also to make sense of Jesus' words of peace, joy and hope when it became clearer by the moment that betrayal and arrest were at hand. Nevertheless, Jesus did not cease to encourage them and give them words and experiences to recall in the dark days ahead, so that then they may make sense of the surrounding darkness. He uses the image of a woman anguished in the pangs of labour which, in a little while, give way to the joy of childbirth—and the pain is remembered no more.

This 'little while' teaching is relevant for us. We are continually perplexed by the immediacy of the political and religious conflict and bloodshed on a daily basis in TV news, reports and documentaries—especially when our own nation is involved in bombing, shooting and killing, or sells arms and equipment used for the maiming and killing of innocent bystanders. Thus we cry, 'When will your kingdom come?'

The 'little while' is the period between our Lord's first and second comings, when, on the one hand, the gospel is proclaimed with works of compassion by people of good will, and on the other hand, violence and bloodshed increase on an ever greater scale.

During this 'little while' we must expend all our energies, giving time, talents and money to all agencies of compassion and reconciliation, and working by all means to alleviate suffering wherever it is to be found.

But in the midst of it all, let us remember that in 'a little while' our Lord will come, and the kingdoms of this world will become the kingdom of our God, and of his Christ. Then our joy will be complete!

Prayer

Let me live wisely, compassionately, sacrificially in this 'little while', Lord, and as I join in works of mercy, let me pray and look for your kingdom of justice and peace.

R/SSF

John 16:25–33 (NRSV, abridged)

Alone, yet not alone

Jesus answered, 'The hour is coming, indeed it has come, when you will be scattered, each one to his home, and you will leave me alone. Yet I am not alone because the Father is with me. I have said this to you, so that in me you may have peace. In the world you face persecution. But take courage; I have conquered the world!'

The further we go, the more amazed we become at the words of Jesus. The darker the shadow, the more he understands, sympathizes, forgives and encourages the distressed, fearful and failing disciples. He knows well enough that not only would one betray him—that one has already gone into the night—but that all would forsake and abandon him.

Yet in the face of all that, and of the closing in of his enemies, followed by suffering and death, he not only maintains his courage, but speaks of conquest and victory. His 'take courage' is not a 'cheer up, it may never happen' sort of counsel. It is rather directed to the stark reality of the situation, yet with an awareness that all is not what it seems to be. For there is the dimension of eternity, the power of God, the victory of the cross, to be taken into account.

The disciples could not yet see that, but they remembered all these words in the ensuing darkness. They recalled together the counsel he had given them, and as the darkness gave way to the glory which shone from the empty tomb, they entered into the wonders of his foreknowledge, his forgiving love, and the victory which he had promised. It was in this strength, energized by the gift of the Spirit, that they became witnesses, heralds and martyrs in days to come, so that the blood of these martyrs became the seed of the Church.

What is it that pulls you down today? Is it not so much the conflict of the nations and the expediency of mediocre or wicked politicians, but the struggles of daily living, the terminal sickness of loved ones, the awful loneliness that is the lack of loving relationships in your life? Stand with Jesus in the day of his darkness; listen to him and receive his words; let him work his miracle of grace, beginning in this small moment.

Prayer

In my darkness, Lord, you offer me not simply courage but joy; not only joy but victory. I cannot understand, but I believe, Lord. Help my unbelief.

R/SSF

John 17:1–5 (NRSV)

Glory! Glory! Glory!

Jesus said, 'Father, the hour has come; glorify your Son so that the Son may glorify you, since you have given him authority over all people, to give eternal life to all whom you have given him. And this is eternal life, that they may know you, the only true God, and Jesus Christ whom you have sent. I glorified you on earth by finishing the work that you gave me to do. So now, Father, glorify me in your own presence with the glory that I had in your presence before the world existed.'

When I was a boy we used to sing a hymn about white-robed children waving palms and singing around the heavenly throne, all crying, 'Glory! Glory! Glory!' That kind of hymn is unfashionable now, but it left me then with a sense of light and joy, of singing, waving and dancing —which isn't a bad picture of heaven!

The glory which is before us today is composed of both human suffering and divine exaltation—the one leading to the other. Through the Gospels, Jesus spoke of his 'hour' (John 12:23; Matthew 26:18, 45; Mark 14:41). It was the hour of his glory, and his glory was to be 'glorified' upon the cross!

How strange that crucifixion can be thought of as 'glory'. And yet when the dying thief gazed upon Jesus, he saw a king enthroned, lifted up and drawing all people to himself (Luke 23:42).

Jesus gave glory to God by utter obedience to the Father's will, and the Father raised him from the dead and gave him glory. Jesus had come from the glory, completed the work of redemption and returned to the glory. That glory is splendour, light, effulgence, dazzling holiness and the heavenly circle of the divine Love.

Eternal life is to know God in mind and heart, and thereby to enter into glory, and the light of that eternal glory sheds its beams upon the here and now, lighting up all the dark places as we pray and live and bless the name of God.

How is that accomplished? By yielding our lives so that his glory may be poured into and through us, that the Christ-life may shine in the dark places of our world, dispelling gloom, sin and sorrow.

Prayer

Jesus, Lord of Glory, light up my life, give me glory, and spread it all around.

R/SSF

John 17:6–19 (NRSV, abridged)

Believers in the world

I have given them your word, and the world has hated them because they do not belong to the world, just as I do not belong to the world. I am not asking you to take them out of the world, but I ask you to protect them from the evil one. As you have sent me into the world, so I have sent them into the world. And for their sakes I sanctify myself, so that they also may be sanctified in truth.

It is OK when the ship is in the sea, but when the sea gets into the ship, then the trouble starts! So with believers in the world. The 'world' here is not the world of nature in its beauty and order, not the world of human love and yearning, nor yet the world of music, art, poetry and true scientific endeavour and healing. It is the organized world-system based upon power, territory and money. How does one separate them?

It is as difficult as separating believers from worldlings, for none of us is wholly sanctified—we are a mixture. Let's say that those whose faces are towards the light, and whose hearts are set upon the love of God, are believers. Conversely, those whose faces are towards darkness, whose hearts are set on evil schemes and whose backs are towards the divine love, are 'of the world'.

Here is the line of separation, and Jesus calls believers to follow his way of love in the world, and into glory. Those who turn from him give their assent and their will into the keeping of the evil one. The purpose of our sanctification (that means growing in love) is that we might enter into the world of evil, as Jesus came from the Father into this world, to bring the hope of salvation and redemption to the children of darkness. The aim of Christ's death and resurrection is the salvation of the lost—and to that we are committed as believers. But that is only the beginning. If you want to know the fullness, read again through the whole of John 17, until its glory fills your vision, and your life is laid on the altar of service for the love of Christ.

Prayer

Lord Jesus, sent by the Father,
you call us into the fellowship of your love;
sanctify us by your Spirit; so send us out
into the world, that through us
the world may believe.

R/SSF

John 17:20–25 (NRSV, abridged)

Glorious remembrance

I ask not only on behalf of these, but also on behalf of those who will believe in me through their word, that they may all be one. As you, Father, are in me and I am in you, may they also be in us, so that the world may believe that you have sent me. The glory that you have given me I have given them, so that they may be one, as we are one, I in them and you in me, that they may become completely one.

Today is a day of remembrance. In the silence we shall reach out to all who have suffered, not only in the two World Wars, but in the wars and conflicts which have marked the last century. We shall also remember those left behind, whose memory is tinged with sorrow, pain and sadness. 'Remember' is the opposite of 'dismember', and our work today is the re-membering of all the wounded members of humanity, in order that they may be brought into one, in the unity of Christ's love.

The whole of John 17 is Jesus' 'high priestly prayer', where he prays to the Father not only for the disciples of his time, but for all those down through the ages who have sought to follow his way of love. It is their task to pray and work so that the redemption accomplished by Jesus on the cross may bring home all the lost, for the healing of their wounds, the drying of their tears, so that the mighty task of remembrance may be complete.

Read again the whole of our passage, and recognize the desire which filled Christ's heart as he laid down his life for the world: 'Father, I desire that those also, whom you have given me, may be with me where I am, to see my glory, which you have given me, because you loved me before the foundation of the world' (v. 24). This is the strong desire of the Son which the Father will grant in the ultimate glory of his kingdom. It is beyond anything we have yet imagined—and by grace we shall participate in it, and share the eternal circle of trinitarian love.

Prayer

Today, our Father, we remember all the lost, all the wandering, all those who have been wounded and killed in war and conflict in our fallen world. Bring us all home at last to you, when swords shall be beaten into ploughshares, spears into pruninghooks, and love shall reign eternal.

R/SSF

This reading can be used on 11 November or on Remembrance Sunday.

1 Timothy 1:1–7 (NRSV)

Partnership

Paul, an apostle of Christ Jesus by the command of God our Saviour and of Jesus our hope, To Timothy, my loyal child in the faith: Grace, mercy, and peace from God the Father and Christ Jesus our Lord. I urge you, as I did when I was on my way to Macedonia, to remain in Ephesus so that you may instruct certain people not to teach any different doctrine, and not to occupy themselves with myths and endless genealogies that promote speculations rather than the divine training that is known by faith. But the aim of such instruction is love that comes from a pure heart, a good conscience, and sincere faith. Some people have deviated from these and turned to meaningless talk, desiring to be teachers of the law, without understanding either what they are saying or the things about which they make assertions.

In 1998 I was appointed as Bishop's Officer for Evangelism. I was worried as to whether I had the right training and qualification. As part of the job, would I be required to be the next Billy Graham? I went off to the Anglican Conference for Evangelism and sat in on two evangelism master classes to find out how to do it. The only question that kept going through my head was, 'What if no one responds?' What an embarrassment that would be. I realized that if I was led into this ministry I could be famous as the evangelist to whom no one ever came forward!

Well, life was not easy for Timothy, either. He was shy, he was not well, and he had some difficult church members. So Paul wrote to offer encouragement. When God calls, it is by his *command* and not our choice, and our *hope* is in Christ, not ourselves. To have hope in Christ is to have security, confidence and peace. Knowing all this is one thing, but we need all the encouragement we can get. I have a 'soul friend' or 'spiritual director', who knows me very well and is there for me. I try to be the same for someone else. After all, Jesus sent out the first seventy disciples *two by two*.

Prayer

Pray that you may be a Paul to someone's Timothy and a Timothy to someone's Paul.

RobG

1 Timothy 2:1–7 (NRSV)

Public prayer

First of all, then, I urge that supplications, prayers, intercessions, and thanksgivings should be made for everyone, for kings and all who are in high positions, so that we may lead a quiet and peaceable life in all godliness and dignity. This is right and is acceptable in the sight of God our Saviour, who desires everyone to be saved and to come to the knowledge of the truth. For there is one God; there is also one mediator between God and humankind, Christ Jesus, himself human, who gave himself a ransom for all—this was attested at the right time. For this I was appointed a herald and an apostle (I am telling the truth, I am not lying), a teacher of the Gentiles in faith and truth.

Paul urges the church to pray for everyone, and cites as an example political leaders. During the beginnings of the troubles in Yugoslavia, I was invited to preach in a church that was very traditional in its form of worship. I suggested that they might share the peace with one another during the service by shaking hands (which was difficult enough) and at the same time we would pray lovingly for President Milosevic! Praying for the least likable isn't easy. The handshake would be a sign of God's wish for peace and reconciliation in that war-torn land —'lifting up holy hands without anger' (v. 8).

Paul encourages Timothy's congregations to pray for kings, even for godless, aggressive emperors. The church is called to pray for everyone—those who hurt us and those who are greatly loved. Do you pray only for the people you like? Jesus, who intercedes for us, gave himself as a ransom for all, not just a favoured few. The great preacher and pray-er, George Buttrick, recommends that we begin with prayer for our enemies: 'Bless So-and-so whom I foolishly regard as my enemy… banish my bitterness.' He encourages us to pray for leaders in 'statecraft'.

'Prayer' in our text (*proseuchi*) has as its root-meaning 'confidence'. We must speak what seems most appropriate in full confidence that God hears and answers. As Paul reminds us, Jesus promises to be present in great power whenever the community of faith is gathered in his name (Matthew 18:20). There is one mediator between God and us—the man Christ Jesus (v. 5).

Reflection

There is nothing that makes us love a person so much as praying for them… This will fill your heart with generosity and tenderness.

William Law (1686–1761)

RobG

1 Timothy 3:1–7 (NRSV)

Serving bishops

The saying is sure: whoever aspires to the office of bishop desires a noble task. Now a bishop must be above reproach, married only once, temperate, sensible, respectable, hospitable, an apt teacher, not a drunkard, not violent but gentle, not quarrelsome, and not a lover of money. He must manage his own household well, keeping his children submissive and respectful in every way—for if someone does not know how to manage his own household, how can he take care of God's church? He must not be a recent convert, or he may be puffed up with conceit and fall into the condemnation of the devil. Moreover, he must be well thought of by outsiders, so that he may not fall into disgrace and the snare of the devil.

I am fortunate at present to be serving a bishop who fits the requirements laid down by Paul, with the possible exception of the one suggesting that he should be 'sensible'! Even so, I don't think Paul means that bishops ('overseers') can't take risks, so perhaps my bishop is OK. The reason for having this list of leadership requirements written down was that the overseers of the church were forgetting their servant role. In the consecration service for a bishop, we pray to God, 'Fill this your *servant* with the grace and power which you gave to your apostles… that he will be given humility, that he may use his authority to heal, not to hurt; to build up, not to destroy.'

Although Paul admitted he was the worst of sinners, he was confident enough in his relationship with Jesus to write, 'I am sending to you Timothy… He will remind you of my way of life in Christ Jesus, which agrees with what I teach everywhere in every church (1 Corinthians 4:17, NIV).

Jesus' life was an excellent example to the disciples. As they worked alongside him day after day, they recognized that he was someone worth listening to and chose to obey him. When we find leaders modelling the truths they teach, then people will listen. Skills of leadership are, of course, important but here Paul stresses even more the character of the person who leads. Many leaders in the world separate their personal life from their public life. Jesus set the Church a different standard.

Prayer

Lord, let your priests be clothed with righteousness, that your faithful people may rejoice.

Psalm 132:9

RobG

1 Timothy 4:6–10 (NRSV)

The body beautiful

If you put these instructions before the brothers and sisters, you will be a good servant... Have nothing to do with profane myths and old wives' tales. Train yourself in godliness, for, while physical training is of some value, godliness is valuable in every way, holding promise for both the present life and the life to come. The saying is sure and worthy of full acceptance. For to this end we toil and struggle, because we have our hope set on the living God, who is the Saviour of all people, especially of those who believe.

Timothy is to train others in the way of godliness, not simply to serve the church but to serve well and be a 'good minister of Christ Jesus' (v. 6, NIV). If we are to teach others in the faith and share the truth of God's words, Paul suggests that we must also receive it for ourselves. We need feeding regularly. I have been reading *New Daylight* every day for many years and have found it to be such a blessing in my spiritual life. Now I have the wonderful opportunity to write for it, but I still read the other contributions every morning, for I need to be taught if I am to teach. But as we know, its not enough just to read the Bible daily and seek to interpret it.

If we are to be effective teachers of others, we need to 'walk the talk'. Those of you who don't like physical exercise will be jumping up and down with glee (or perhaps lying down with glee!) as you read that 'physical training is of *some* value' (v. 8). But it is necessary to understand the context to appreciate this remark. The image of athletic training was frequently used by Greek moralists to describe the effort required to attain moral or spiritual perfection. In our day, the gym is often seen as the place to seek perfection, in the belief that strict diets and punishing workouts will result in spiritual health too. Of course you need to take care of your body as the temple of the Holy Spirit, but so often the desire for fitness is to glorify yourself and not God. I thank God that he can work through weak earthen vessels as well as through those blessed with a 'body beautiful'!

Thanksgiving

For everything created by God is good, and nothing is to be rejected, provided it is received with thanksgiving; for it is sanctified by God's word and by prayer.

1 Timothy 4:4–5

RobG

1 Timothy 5:17–25 (NRSV)

Who wants to be a millionaire?

Let the elders who rule well be considered worthy of double honour, especially those who labour in preaching and teaching; for the scripture says, 'You shall not muzzle an ox while it is treading out the grain,' and, 'The labourer deserves to be paid.' Never accept any accusation against an elder except on the evidence of two or three witnesses. As for those who persist in sin, rebuke them in the presence of all, so that the rest also may stand in fear. In the presence of God and of Christ Jesus and of the elect angels, I warn you to keep these instructions without prejudice, doing nothing on the basis of partiality... keep yourself pure. No longer drink only water, but take a little wine for the sake of your stomach and your frequent ailments. The sins of some people are conspicuous and precede them to judgment, while the sins of others follow them there. So also good works are conspicuous; and even when they are not, they cannot remain hidden.

If I was Timothy's doctor, I would prescribe him a long holiday. He is sick, tired and very stressed. Paul recognizes this, suggesting perhaps that the church is not looking after him. Sometimes it is very difficult for the minister of a church to ask for help, especially personal financial help. After all, it's a vocation. He or she is not in it for the money but to serve God. Paul suggests that if the elder is doing well, he or she should be encouraged. It soon becomes 'conspicuous' when someone is in it for the money, but it is equally 'conspicuous' if they are not. If that person is exercising ministry to the best of their ability, then there should be no question that they should receive adequate remuneration. Timothy's church seems to have made a number of enemies, false teachers and preachers, who may have been making up all sorts of stories in order to discredit Timothy's team. There may have been a number of his elders who were behaving badly. The Church is not a society for the perfect, and sin needs to be rebuked. But when our servants in the Church are struggling with illness or hardship, or false accusations, the household of faith should rally. Take a moment with your minister on Sunday and give him or her your gift of encouragement.

Prayer

Make us worthy of our calling; through Jesus Christ our Lord. Amen.

RobG

1 Timothy 6:2–10 (NRSV)

Gains of godliness

Teach and urge these duties. Whoever teaches otherwise and does not agree with the sound words of our Lord Jesus Christ... is conceited, understanding nothing, and has a morbid craving for controversy and for disputes about words. From these come envy, dissension, slander, base suspicions, and wrangling among those who are depraved in mind and bereft of the truth, imagining that godliness is a means of gain. Of course, there is great gain in godliness combined with contentment; for we brought nothing into the world, so that we can take nothing out of it; but if we have food and clothing, we will be content with these. But those who want to be rich fall into temptation and are trapped by many senseless and harmful desires that plunge people into ruin and destruction. For the love of money is a root of all kinds of evil, and in their eagerness to be rich some have wandered away from the faith and pierced themselves with many pains.

Paul was not a mincer of words! Here he is demanding of those leading others in the faith accountability before the teachings of Jesus. Some leaders seem to be self-absorbed and self-centred, tuned into one radio station—WIIFM—'What's in it for me?'

I was invited to attend a 'Life Dynamic Skills' course in Hong Kong by one of my congregation, and he paid for it. He said he wanted me to see what certain people in business were being taught. (I thought perhaps he was implying that my life wasn't very dynamic!) I agreed to go, and while there I asked several of those attending why they had signed up. All of them said in one way or another, 'We want to be happy, successful and make lots of money.' I listened very carefully to those who were leading this course. I discovered that the slogan they used was, 'What do you want, and how can you get it, whatever it costs?' I became rather a thorn in their side as I kept challenging most of what they said. Eventually one of them asked me, 'What's your motivation for life?' I said, 'To find peace.' He then said, 'Have you found it?' Well, I said that I'd made a start by joining the life dynamic skills classes at our church. 'We learn from a chap called Jesus—oh, and the course is free!'

Reflection

'Where your treasure is, there your heart will be also.'

Matthew 6:21

RobG

1 Timothy 6:11–14, 20–21 (NRSV)

Action man

As for you, man of God, shun all this; pursue righteousness, godliness, faith, love, endurance, gentleness. Fight the good fight of the faith; take hold of the eternal life, to which you were called and for which you made the good confession in the presence of many witnesses. In the presence of God, who gives life to all things, and of Christ Jesus, who in his testimony before Pontius Pilate made the good confession, I charge you to keep the commandment without spot or blame until the manifestation of our Lord Jesus Christ... Timothy, guard what has been entrusted to you. Avoid the profane chatter and contradictions of what is falsely called knowledge; by professing it some have missed the mark as regards the faith. Grace be with you.

Timothy is encouraged at the end of Paul's letter to him to 'pursue...' and 'fight...', to 'take hold of the eternal life to which you were called'. To be a leader requires a tremendous amount of energy, so it is important not to waste it on things that don't matter. When Jesus appeared before Pilate, he did not waste energy on arguing with him. 'Are you the King of the Jews?' Pilate asked. Jesus said, 'You say so.' When accused by the chief priests, he 'did not answer' (Matthew 27:11–12). Stillness and silence seem to be keys which unlock the door into the presence of God so that his 'still small voice' can be heard, and we can be energized in his service. Then we won't be distracted by the 'profane chatter and contradictions' (v. 20).

Timothy is commanded to guard what has been entrusted to him. His example, of course, is Jesus who describes himself as the 'Good Shepherd'. A shepherd guards the sheep, not by rushing around shouting and arguing with the wolves, but by sitting quietly, brim full of energy, listening for the wolves as well as watching over his flock. If we rest in the presence of God 'who gives life to all things', then we shall be ready to 'fight the good fight of faith' (v. 12).

I was amazed to learn that butterflies *have* to spread their wings in the morning sunshine because the scales on their wings are actually solar cells. Without that source of energy, they cannot fly.

Prayer

Lord, light up my life, and 'fill me with life anew, that I may love as thou hast loved and do as thou wouldst do'.

RobG

Acts 11:2–4, 15–18 (NRSV)

Changing attitudes

When Peter went up to Jerusalem, the circumcised believers criticized him, saying, 'Why did you go to uncircumcised men and eat with them?' Then Peter began to explain it to them, step by step... 'As I began to speak, the Holy Spirit fell upon them just as it had upon us at the beginning. And I remembered the word of the Lord, how he had said, 'John baptized you with water, but you will be baptized with the Holy Spirit.' If then God gave them the same gift that he gave us when we believed in the Lord Jesus Christ, who was I that I could hinder God?' When they heard this, they were silenced. And they praised God, saying, 'Then God has given even to the Gentiles the repentance that leads to life.'

It is hard for us to imagine how far outside Jewish thinking was the concept that Gentiles could be included in God's fold. But if it had not been for this fundamental change of attitude in the early Christians, where would we ourselves be now? These next two chapters take us from this entrenched attitude to the beginning of deliberate widespread missionary outreach to non-Jews and Jews alike.

The story had started with two visions. Peter, praying on the rooftop in Joppa, at first remonstrated when a voice from heaven told him to eat the forbidden, 'unclean' animals. Cornelius, a Roman centurion, obeyed an angel's instructions when he sent messengers to bring Peter to his house. As Peter recounted the events 'step by step', his critical hearers had to acknowledge God's hand in it all, for even before Peter had finished telling Cornelius and his friends about Jesus they began to praise God in tongues—evidence that the Holy Spirit was a gift for the Gentiles as well as for the Jewish Christians.

It was like turning a key in a heavy door. No longer was the gospel confined to the Jews and proselytes (non-Jews who had accepted the Jewish faith). The door was open, and the good news about Jesus could spread worldwide. All credit to the circumcised believers who were willing to listen and to change their deeply held beliefs! Their example is a challenge to me.

Reflection

Are any aspects of my own beliefs, or my attitudes to people, steeped in prejudice and in need of change?

RG

Acts 11:19–24 (NRSV)

Church planting

Now those who were scattered because of the persecution that took place over Stephen travelled as far as Phoenicia, Cyprus and Antioch, and they spoke the word to no one except Jews. But among them were some men of Cyprus and Cyrene who, on coming to Antioch, spoke to the Hellenists also, proclaiming the Lord Jesus. The hand of the Lord was with them, and a great number became believers... News of this came to the ears of the church in Jerusalem, and they sent Barnabas to Antioch. When he came and saw the grace of God, he rejoiced, and he exhorted them all to remain faithful to the Lord with steadfast devotion; for he was a good man, full of the Holy Spirit and of faith. And a great many people were brought to the Lord.

After Stephen roused the Jews to enormous fury by his speech accusing them of disobedience to God, great persecution broke out in Jerusalem against the Christians. Far from stamping out this new faith, the persecution caused the believers to scatter in many directions—taking the gospel with them. Most of them still had tunnel vision: Jesus for the Jews. But some—who were not natives of Judea—had a wider aim: Jesus for all. The Hellenists were not ethnically Greek but had adopted Greek language and culture; now many of them joyfully adopted the gospel. From our perspective this seems natural; for these early Christians, it was a huge step. The principle that was accepted in theory when Peter explained about his meeting with Cornelius was now put into practice. God had clearly shown his hand in pouring out his Spirit on Cornelius and his friends. Now his blessing was equally clear among the Hellenists in Antioch, as 'a great number became believers'. When Barnabas came, he saw God's grace—his full, undeserved generosity—in action.

Barnabas, whose name means 'son of encouragement', may have been the brother of Mary, John Mark's mother. We meet him first bringing encouragement by his generosity (Acts 4:36–37). Next we find him encouraging the newly converted Saul, sponsoring him before the suspicious church in Jerusalem (9:27). Now we meet him encouraging the new Christians in Antioch by his teaching, his faith, his warmth. In what ways do you encourage others?

Prayer

Lord, please help me to be an encourager.

RG

Acts 11:25–30 (NRSV)

Church growth

Then Barnabas went to Tarsus to look for Saul, and when he had found him, he brought him to Antioch. So it was that for an entire year they met with the church and taught a great many people, and it was in Antioch that the disciples were first called 'Christians'. At that time prophets came down from Jerusalem to Antioch. One of them named Agabus stood up and predicted by the Spirit that there would be a severe famine all over the world; and this took place during the reign of Claudius. The disciples determined that according to their ability, each would send relief to the believers living in Judea; this they did, sending it to the elders by Barnabas and Saul.

The church in Antioch was planted by enthusiastic lay Christians who loved to talk about their faith in Jesus with anyone they met. It is interesting to watch how this infant Christian community then grew and got established. Barnabas had already begun to teach and pastor these new Christians. But, needing a partner in the growing work, he went to Tarsus (about 250 km away in southern Turkey) to find Saul, alias Paul. Here are some of the characteristics I notice in this church:

- They were eager to learn from the regular teaching.
- They were Christ-centred, so they were given a new name.
- They were open to the Holy Spirit and to prophecy.
- The prophecy came true, and they put their faith into action.
- They were generous towards fellow believers they had never met.

Not only did they collect money, they sent it to Judea with two of their own number. Here are some modern examples of similar visits: a couple in our congregation included in their holiday itinerary a visit to an Indian orphanage for which the church had raised funds; on their return they enthused us with firsthand news. A group of English teenagers worked for a fortnight in a youth club in Zimbabwe, then left behind musical instruments donated by fellow pupils. A hundred or more Anglicans from Malaysia came (at their own expense) to share in evangelistic mission in an English diocese. In these days of increasing overseas travel, might such visits happen more often?

Question

Do these characteristics of the Christians in Antioch mark our own lives, as individuals, or in the church to which we each belong?

RG

Acts 12:1–7 (NRSV, abridged)

Dictatorial leadership

About that time King Herod laid violent hands upon some who belonged to the church. He had James, the brother of John, killed with the sword. After he saw that it pleased the Jews, he proceeded to arrest Peter also… When he had seized him, he put him in prison and handed him over to four squads of soldiers to guard him, intending to bring him out to the people after the Passover. While Peter was kept in prison, the church prayed fervently to God for him. The very night before Herod was going to bring him out, Peter was sleeping between two soldiers, while guards in front of the door were keeping watch over the prison. Suddenly an angel of the Lord appeared and a light shone in the cell. He tapped Peter on the side and woke him, saying, 'Get up quickly.' And the chains fell off his wrists.

Herod's control of his country was almost out of control! 'These Christians… growing too fast… kill one of their leaders!' He calculated carefully to curry favour. 'James' death pleased the Jews: we'll execute another. But I mustn't offend them by defiling the Passover: better wait to kill him… I remember how the body of that fellow Jesus disappeared: we'll guard Peter extra carefully.'

Such tyrannical rulers are still around. The names of Hitler, Stalin, Pol Pot, Marcos, Idi Amin, Milosevic, all quickly come to mind. The lust for power is one of the 'big three' (with sex and money) that are the main keys to corruption. Our memory of these names reinforces Paul's plea for us to pray for national leaders if our world is to live in peace and harmony.

Herod's circumspection was God's opportunity. The Christians prayed; God acted. He tested them by waiting till the eleventh hour to free Peter, then he did it in a remarkable way. The angel came, cut Peter's chains, led him out past guarding soldiers and locked doors, and out into the street.

For prayer

I urge that supplications, prayers, intercessions and thanksgivings should be made for everyone, for kings and all who are in high positions, so that we may lead a quiet and peaceable life in all godliness and dignity. This is right and is acceptable in the sight of God our Saviour, who desires everyone to be saved and to come to the knowledge of the truth.

1 Timothy 2:1–4

RG

Acts 12:11–16 (NRSV)

Unbelieving prayer!

Then Peter came to himself and said, 'Now I am sure that the Lord has sent his angel and rescued me from the hands of Herod and from all that the Jewish people were expecting.' As soon as he realized this, he went to the house of Mary, the mother of John whose other name was Mark, where many people were gathered and were praying. When he knocked at the outer gate, a maid named Rhoda came to answer. On recognizing Peter's voice, she was so overjoyed that, instead of opening the gate, she ran in and announced that Peter was standing at the gate. They said to her, 'You are out of your mind!' But she insisted that it was so. They said, 'It is his angel.' Meanwhile Peter continued knocking; and when they opened the gate, they saw him and were amazed.

It was only when the angel left him, well away from the prison, that Peter realized that this was for real. God had acted! So he went to the home where he expected to find his friends (a mark of Mary's regular hospitality). There they were, holding an all-night prayer meeting—praying so fervently for his safety that when God answered their prayer they didn't believe it! And Rhoda was so excited that she forgot to let him in before rushing to tell the others. But she persisted: 'It's really Peter!' Peter persisted: 'Knock, knock!' And finally they saw that their prayer had indeed been answered.

We can laugh together at the absurdity of the situation. Then I have to turn round and ask myself about my own praying. Am I willing to lose sleep to pray for a particular need? Is my praying fervent and specific or (to be honest) is it feeble and unspecific? Do I really expect God to answer? Am I alert and sensitive to notice when he answers in ways I didn't expect? What about my quickly forgotten promises to pray for a friend?

Prayer

To him who is able to do immeasurably more than all we ask or imagine, according to his power that is at work within us, to him be glory!

Ephesians 3:20–21

RG

Acts 12:18–23 (NRSV)

Ungodly leadership

When morning came, there was no small commotion among the soldiers over what had become of Peter. When Herod had searched for him and could not find him, he examined the guards and ordered them to be put to death. Then he went down from Judea to Caesarea and stayed there. Now Herod was angry with the people of Tyre and Sidon. So they came to him in a body; and after winning over Blastus, the king's chamberlain, they asked for a reconciliation, because their country depended on the king's country for food. On an appointed day Herod put on his royal robes, took his seat on the platform, and delivered a public address to them. The people kept shouting, 'The voice of a god, and not of a mortal!' And immediately, because he had not given glory to God, an angel of the Lord struck him down, and he was eaten by worms and died.

Herod again! Furious at Peter's disappearance, did he disbelieve the guards' story? Or did he not dare risk tales circulating of yet another miracle? The guards outside Jesus' tomb were bribed to spread false stories; Peter's guards were killed. Behind Herod's rampage was a lust for power born of inner weakness. People whose strength lies in their core personality do not need to strive for power. It is those who are innately weak who throw their weight around as Herod did.

On Thursday we saw how Herod cultivated the Jews' approval. Now it was the inhabitants of Tyre and Sidon who curried favour with him. As Herod paraded at the games celebrated in the emperor's honour, they applauded: 'Marvellous! You're a god!' What a boost that gave his tiny ego!

Luke's story dovetails with a fascinating account of Herod's death from the Jewish historian Josephus. He too writes of the crowd's adulation of Herod as a god. The king accepted it—and was promptly seized by violent internal pains, and died five days later. Luke's message is clear. God himself acts against anyone who usurps his place and claims divine honour for himself. I may think, 'I'm in no danger of that.' But there are warnings for all of us from Herod's lust for power and his acceptance of unwarranted flattery.

Prayer

Lord, please help me to accept with gratitude and humility the position you give me.

RG

Acts 12:24—13:3 (NRSV)

Godly leadership

But the word of God continued to advance and gain adherents. Then after completing their mission Barnabas and Saul returned from Jerusalem and brought with them John, whose other name was Mark. Now in the church at Antioch there were prophets and teachers: Barnabas, Simeon who was called Niger, Lucius of Cyrene, Manaen a member of the court of Herod the ruler, and Saul. While they were worshipping the Lord and fasting, the Holy Spirit said, 'Set apart for me Barnabas and Saul for the work to which I have called them.' Then after fasting and praying they laid their hands on them and sent them off.

'But the word of God continued to advance' (v. 24). 'But'—that word sends us back to the preceding verses. 'But'—despite persecution, the gospel could not be muzzled. Herod died. The news of Jesus, risen from death, continued to spread.

In the last century, Communism and Islam have been Christianity's greatest rivals, yet even in Communist and Muslim countries the Church is not dead. A recent letter told us of an area in China where one missionary couple worked. When they left in 1951, there were about 5,000 Christians; now the estimate is 90,000!

Look at the leaders in the Antioch church—'prophets and teachers', with their contrasting gifts. Prophets speak what they hear directly from God: 'not a new message but a now message' is one way prophecy is described. It does not add to scripture but is used by God to show us the immediacy of a particular truth or need. Teachers patiently study and explain so that their hearers learn, absorb, obey.

Look at the variety of backgrounds represented: Simeon, the dark-skinned African; Lucius, an Arab from north Africa; Manaen, from high society; Saul, the deeply religious Pharisee—drawn together in shared leadership. With their priorities of worship (seeking to know God and put him first) and fasting (implying serious commitment), they were open to listen to God. It is not clear how the Spirit spoke—probably through a prophetic word. What matters is that they obeyed the surprising call to release their two main teachers for wider ministry.

Reflection and prayer

Look at the leaders in your own church. Do they show similar characteristics? Pray that they may exercise wise, spiritual leadership of God's people.

RG

Acts 13:4–12 (NRSV, abridged)

Missionary strategy

So, being sent out by the Holy Spirit, they sailed to Cyprus. When they arrived at Salamis, they proclaimed the word of God in the synagogues of the Jews... When they had gone as far as Paphos, they met a certain magician, a Jewish false prophet. He was with the proconsul, an intelligent man, who... wanted to hear the word of God. But the magician Elymas opposed them and tried to turn the proconsul away from the faith. But Saul, filled with the Holy Spirit, looked intently at him and said, 'You enemy of all righteousness, will you not stop making crooked the straight paths of the Lord? And now listen—the hand of the Lord is against you, and you will be blind for a while'. Immediately he went about groping for someone to lead him by the hand. When the proconsul saw what had happened, he believed, for he was astonished at the teaching about the Lord.

Barnabas and Saul, with John Mark, were not the first Christians on Cyprus (see 24 October). But they were the first who went intentionally as missionaries, called by God and commissioned by the Church. For many years, it remained Paul's policy to preach first in the synagogue before he went to the non-Jews.

Two men they met in Paphos were sharp contrasts. One, a Jewish magician, was deeply opposed to the gospel, probably under the influence of demonic powers; the other, a Roman official, governor of the island, was a thoughtful, intelligent man, open to the Christian message. One was temporarily blinded; the other had his spiritual eyes opened to the truth and power of the gospel. Saul was clear and bold in his denunciation of Elymas: 'filled with the Spirit', he was given a gift of prophecy, to speak a message he did not invent and would probably have preferred not to say.

We may ask, 'Why does God the healer act in such a hurtful way?' Elymas' temporary blindness had constructive purposes. Elymas was shown that his anti-God stance really mattered; whether that led him to repentance and faith, we don't know. The proconsul was converted when he saw the power that confirmed the teaching to which he had already listened.

Prayer

Lord, thank you that your long-term purposes for us are always good and righteous.

RG

2 Chronicles 6:12–14 (NIV)

Leaders on their knees

Then Solomon stood before the altar of the Lord in front of the whole assembly of Israel and spread out his hands. Now he had made a bronze platform, five cubits long, five cubits wide and three cubits high, and had placed it in the centre of the outer court. He stood on the platform and then knelt down before the whole assembly of Israel and spread out his hands towards heaven. He said: 'O Lord, God of Israel, there is no God like you in heaven or on earth—you who keep your covenant of love with your servants.'

Yesterday we went to our local Anglican church as usual, but as a child I went to the local Roman Catholic church every Sunday with my father. The mass was conducted in Latin at that time, and each service lasted about three days. I found it an excruciatingly tedious event, not least because I had been told that the priest did all the talking to God on our behalf. I found it difficult to believe that the Creator of the universe would be taking very much interest in a skinny, non-Latin speaking kid who spent most of the sacred hour yawning his head off.

I can recall, though, a feeling of something much warmer and more inspiring about the figure of the Pope. There was something rather awe-inspiring about the idea of a human being who was God's sort of second-in-command, a man who, like Moses, would do business with God, then produce the results for our benefit in a list of easy-to-understand points.

Nowadays, although I have a deep respect for my brothers and sisters in the Roman Catholic Church, I no longer think in that way. But I long for the nations of the world to have leaders like Solomon, who, despite enormous personal power and wealth, was prepared to kneel in the sight of the people humbly to petition the good favour of his God. Indeed, such a pattern of leadership might be adopted with profit by all in authority, including those at the front in our churches today, each of whom has the difficult task of shepherding his or her particular flock. Ministry that is not truly accountable to God is at best weak, and at worst, dangerous.

Prayer

Father, today we pray for our church leaders, that they may seek you constantly.

AP

2 Chronicles 6:36–39 (NIV)

On our behalf

'When they sin against you—for there is no one who does not sin—and you become angry with them and give them over to the enemy, who takes them captive to a land far away or near; and if they have a change of heart in the land where they are held captive, and repent and plead with you in the land of their captivity and say, "We have sinned, we have done wrong and acted wickedly"; and if they turn back to you with all their heart and soul in the land of their captivity where they were taken, and pray towards the land that you gave their fathers, towards the city you have chosen and towards the temple that I have built for your Name; then from heaven, your dwelling place, hear their prayer and their pleas, and uphold their cause. And forgive your people who have sinned against you.'

I wonder how many people actually heard this prayer when it was first said. Not many, I suppose, in an age without microphones, but presumably it would have been repeated over and over again. What a wonderful feeling it must have been to know that someone as close to God as Solomon was praying so determinedly on your behalf. When I read this passage just now I found myself wishing that someone would represent me to God with the same eloquence and passion, and for just a moment I felt a little sad.

Yes, all right, you're way ahead of me, as usual. How could someone like me, who has been bleating endlessly about the Son of God for years and years and years, forget that someone even closer to God is continously doing for you and me exactly what Solomon was doing here for the people of Israel? Because of Jesus' selfless act of sacrifice and redemption, we are never much more than a prayer away from the willing forgiveness of God, and the fulfilment of a promise that we can be with him for ever, stumbling prodigals though we may be.

It is worth just basking in that fact for a moment—the sunshine of the good news of the gospel.

Prayer

Father, thank you once again for Jesus. We owe our eternal lives to him, and we are truly grateful.

AP

2 Chronicles 7:1–3 (NIV)

Fire from heaven

When Solomon finished praying, fire came down from heaven and consumed the burnt offering and the sacrifices, and the glory of the Lord filled the temple. The priests could not enter the temple of the Lord because the glory of the Lord filled it. When all the Israelites saw the fire coming down and the glory of the Lord above the temple, they knelt on the pavement with their faces to the ground, and they worshipped and gave thanks to the Lord, saying, 'He is good; his love endures for ever.'

One of my favourite films of recent years was *Raiders of the Lost Ark*, a grippingly entertaining if hugely improbable account of the race between an American archaeologist and a group of Nazis to find the ark of the Israelites. In the film the ark is eventually discovered, but on being opened a violently destructive force is released, and, in a highly dramatic and rather satisfactorily gruesome scene, the chief baddies are—well—melted, I suppose. I remember sitting in the cinema smiling at the absurdity of this scene, trying to imagine how the real ark must have looked, and how prosaic any activities that surrounded it would appear to the modern eye. And yet…

Play around in your mind for a moment with this description of events at the dedication of the temple that Solomon had built to the glory of God. Here, if the writer is to be believed, is a spectacle that Spielberg, for all his wonderfully fertile imagination and millions of dollars, would never be able to emulate. After Solomon had entreated God to inhabit the building that had been prepared for him, God, who has always known when a really good effect is needed, was gracious enough to provide fire from heaven to consume the offerings, and to be present himself in such a startlingly vivid way that it was physically impossible to enter the temple.

It seems very important to me that we, who so often expect prosaic effects in a prosaic world, should remember that the glory of God would blow our socks off if we were exposed to a fraction of the power that these Israelites witnessed on that very special day.

I don't know about you, but I yearn to see the power of God electrifying the church in this country.

Prayer

Father, show your power in this flabby land.

AP

Malachi 1:1–5 (NRSV)

Loving God?

An oracle. The word of the Lord to Israel by Malachi. I have loved you, says the Lord. But you say, 'How have you loved us?' Is not Esau Jacob's brother? says the Lord. Yet I have loved Jacob but I have hated Esau; I have made his hill country a desolation and his heritage a desert for jackals. If Edom says, 'We are shattered but we will rebuild the ruins,' the Lord of hosts says: They may build, but I will tear down, until they are called the wicked country, the people with whom the Lord is angry forever. Your own eyes shall see this, and you shall say, 'Great is the Lord beyond the borders of Israel!'

Malachi begins by posing a problem for modern readers. Israel is doubting God's love. How can God really care for us when the kingdom is in tatters, subject to Persian rule, and the line of David is at an end? Look at the nation of Edom, says Malachi: there is a nation that really has endured God's punishment. If the chosen people, the descendants of Jacob, have it bad, how much worse has befallen the descendants of his brother Esau!

At the fall of Jerusalem, Edom had been on the side of Babylon, pursuing Israelite refugees and exploiting their deserted territory. Now, in turn, Edom has fallen to the invading Nabateans, and will not return. Their disaster is God's judgment for their role in Israel's downfall.

The problem for us, of course, is the idea that God should hate Esau and love Jacob. Doesn't God love all his creatures? Of course he does. The language here is not about personal animosity or liking. It indicates God's choice in calling the one to be his people, and rejecting the other. Both remain loved, and both are answerable to God. God's love for Israel is about his call to a people to act as his special agents in the world—and it carries a greater responsibility with it.

So Malachi reassures Israel of God's love—and they would know that they were being cared for if only they would worry less about their own problems, and look at the events of the world around them.

Prayer

Father, as your people, we know your love. Help us to realize the responsibility that this carries, and to live up to it.

MM

Malachi 1:6–9 (NRSV)

Easy giving

A son honours his father, and servants their master. If then I am a father, where is the honour due me? And if I am a master, where is the respect due me? says the Lord of hosts to you, O priests, who despise my name. You say, 'How have we despised your name?' By offering polluted food on my altar. And you say, 'How have we polluted it?' By thinking that the Lord's table may be despised. When you offer blind animals in sacrifice, is that not wrong? And when you offer those that are lame or sick, is that not wrong? Try presenting that to your governor; will he be pleased with you or show you favour? says the Lord of hosts. And now implore the favour of God, that he may be gracious to us. The fault is yours. Will he show favour to any of you? says the Lord of hosts.

One reason why Malachi is less well known than other prophets is his concern for the purity of the sacrificial worship of the temple. Compared with the great ethical concerns of the eighth-century prophet Amos, and the heart-rending exposition of God's love given by Hosea, this seems to many a backward step. Haven't the prophets already declared that God wants justice rather than sacrifices? Why this concern, then, for the temple offerings?

Malachi's point, though, is a very important one. The sacrificial system was part of God's law. It may have been less important than justice and compassion, but it was still a good indicator of people's attitude to God. The sacrifices were meant to be the best available, because God deserves the best. When the offerings become the weaklings, the diseased and the blighted, then there's a pretty good chance that God is not being taken seriously.

Try translating it into modern terms. How many churches are short of money, while their members are comfortable and well provided for? How many pieces of church furniture are cast-offs from someone's spring-cleaning? What does that say about God's importance in our lives? What does it say about offering him the best in terms of worship, and presenting the best picture of our love for him to our non-Christian friends and neighbours?

Words are easy to give. In Malachi's time and in ours, the challenge is to put our money (or our time or talents) where our mouth is.

Reflection

Stewardship is not a financial problem, but a spiritual one.

MM

Malachi 1:10–14 (NRSV, abridged)

Acceptable worship

Oh, that someone among you would shut the temple doors, so that you would not kindle fire on my altar in vain! I have no pleasure in you, says the Lord of hosts, and I will not accept an offering from your hands. For from the rising of the sun to its setting my name is great among the nations, and in every place incense is offered to my name, and a pure offering... says the Lord of hosts. But you profane it when you say that the Lord's table is polluted, and the food for it may be despised. 'What a weariness this is,' you say, and you sniff at me, says the Lord of hosts. You bring what has been taken by violence or is lame or sick, and this you bring as your offering! Shall I accept that from your hand? says the Lord. Cursed be the cheat who has a male in the flock and vows to give it, and yet sacrifices to the Lord what is blemished; for I am a great King, says the Lord of hosts, and my name is reverenced among the nations.

Do you ever feel that worship is a drag, that you have to heave yourself reluctantly out of the house to get to church? Of course. Everyone does, from time to time. For Malachi, though, this is a national attitude. The altar has ceased to be the focus of communion with God, and is treated with contempt. Such worship is no worship at all, and would be better not offered.

The Gentiles offer more acceptable worship than that! They may not know God, but at least they recognize his goodness and power, attributing it to their own false gods. Yet God finds that worship more wholehearted than the weary ritual of Israel.

The idea that God could accept such foreign worship would have been a shock to Malachi's hearers, but it is hopeful to us. It doesn't necessarily mean that God accepts the religion (or lack of it) in which such worship is offered. It does mean, though, that Christians have a common ground with other people of faith and a basis both for dialogue and evangelism. In our culture, many seek a form of spirituality, and express it in many ways. The task of God's people is to show that that which is worshipped is better known as the God who meets us in Jesus Christ.

Prayer

Father, kindle my enthusiasm for you, that I may share you with those around me.

MM

Malachi 2:1–5 (NRSV)

Failed priests

And now, O priests, this command is for you. If you will not listen, if you will not lay it to heart to give glory to my name, says the Lord of hosts, then I will send the curse on you and I will curse your blessings; indeed I have already cursed them, because you do not lay it to heart. I will rebuke your offspring, and spread dung on your faces, the dung of your offerings, and I will put you out of my presence. Know, then, that I have sent this command to you, that my covenant with Levi may hold, says the Lord of hosts. My covenant with him was a covenant of life and well-being, which I gave him; this called for reverence, and he revered me and stood in awe of my name.

If Malachi is unhappy with the worship and spirituality of the people as a whole, he knows where to place the blame. The malaise lies most firmly with the priesthood. They are failing to provide proper teaching, and are far from the ideal of their ancestor Levi, who was a true man of God.

Clergy may well feel some sympathy, since it is a well-known fact that the current minister is never a patch on the ones who went before! Malachi's complaint, though, is far more serious than simple nostalgia. The behaviour of the priesthood reverses all that they should stand for. By turning their blessings (a solemn and important part of worship, which became the only time the sacred name of God was uttered) into a curse, and by threatening to defile their ritually clean bodies, God declares their complete failure to live up to their calling.

Modern Church leaders are in a very different position, both in their function and their social status, from the Old Testament priesthood. In one way, though, they are similar. They face a temptation to lose their zeal and enthusiasm, to settle for less than their original vision, to become tired and disillusioned and to coast through their work.

All too often, they are left unsupported as well. They need prayer and encouragement just as much as the rest of the congregation.

Prayer

Pray for the ministers of your church (and even offer some positive comments!).

MM

Malachi 2:6–9 (NRSV)

Partial teaching

True instruction was in his mouth, and no wrong was found on his lips. He walked with me in integrity and uprightness, and he turned many from iniquity. For the lips of a priest should guard knowledge, and people should seek instruction from his mouth, for he is the messenger of the Lord of hosts. But you have turned aside from the way; you have caused many to stumble by your instruction; you have corrupted the covenant of Levi, says the Lord of hosts, and so I make you despised and abased before all the people, inasmuch as you have not kept my ways but have shown partiality in your instruction.

The meat of Malachi's accusation against the priesthood is concerned with their role as teachers and guardians of Israel's traditions, and most probably the Torah in particular.

Levi, the archetypal priest, is seen as one who taught both by word and example, and what he taught was righteousness—the proper walk with God. This is about both worship and morals, for the Law makes no distinction between them. The role of the priest is both to offer sacrifices and to keep the people aware of God's demands for their lives.

The melding of the spiritual and the moral remains a key part of Christianity. Worship and prayer reflect, and in turn affect, the way we live our lives. The charge of hypocrisy is levelled against the Church so often, and so automatically, that it is almost ludicrous. But, like many clichés, it has enough truth to make us sit up and think. How far do our lives openly reflect what we believe?

It is all too easy to slip into popular ways of thinking, without subjecting them to the questioning light of the gospel. So we encounter churchgoers who will happily display racist tendencies, believe that homelessness is just a disease of the work-shy and assume that single parents are feckless scroungers.

Malachi's priests seem to have taught an understanding of God's justice which was weighted too much in one direction (and if the picture of social conditions given in Nehemiah is accurate, we can bet it was not in favour of the poor!). Those who teach in God's name need to be aware that God is not partial—and all of us need to let God question the easy assumptions of the society in which we live.

Prayer

Father, let me live in a way that shows your love and justice.

MM

Malachi 2:10–12 (NRSV)

Faithless children

Have we not all one father? Has not one God created us? Why then are we faithless to one another, profaning the covenant of our ancestors? Judah has been faithless, and abomination has been committed in Israel and in Jerusalem; for Judah has profaned the sanctuary of the Lord, which he loves, and has married the daughter of a foreign god. May the Lord cut off from the tents of Jacob anyone who does this—any to witness or answer, or to bring an offering to the Lord of hosts.

Malachi's third area of condemnation focuses on the faithlessness of the people of Israel. Firstly, they are faithless in their lack of concern for God. God is the one who made a covenant with his people. He is the one who chose the patriarchs and promised them numberless descendants. He is the one who created them, both as part of his creation in general, and as his special people. If anyone can claim to be called their father, it is God himself.

This seems to count for little, though. The Israelites now look outside of Israel for their hope. The exile is over, but Israel is part of the vast Persian empire, and its claim to uniqueness probably rings hollow in many of its people's ears. So there is greater contact with the neighbouring nations, marriages are being contracted with non-Israelites, and the newcomers are bringing their own gods and religious practices with them. To many, this may have seemed sensible. It was a cosmopolitan age, open to new ideas where the old had failed. To Malachi, it was one more symptom of a lack of trust in God.

It is hard to trust God when nothing seems to be going well. The future seems bleak, and God has let us down. So we look for other sources of security and hope. The trouble is, they don't have any guarantee either. The future is a closed book to us, but not to God. The only truly sensible thing is to keep trusting him, knowing that his purposes are being worked out, come what may. But it's hard advice to follow, and it needs a strong foundation of prayer and worship. For the Israelites of the post-exilic period, that had already gone by the board.

Prayer

Father, help me to be constant in prayer and worship, so that I may build a foundation of faith which will weather all the uncertainties of life.

MM

Malachi 2:13–16 (NRSV)

Faithless husbands

And this you do as well: You cover the Lord's altar with tears, with weeping and groaning because he no longer regards the offering or accepts it with favour at your hand. You ask, 'Why does he not?' Because the Lord was a witness between you and the wife of your youth, to whom you have been faithless, though she is your companion and your wife by covenant. Did not one God make her? Both flesh and spirit are his. And what does the one God desire? Godly offspring. So look to yourselves, and do not let anyone be faithless to the wife of his youth. For I hate divorce, says the Lord, the God of Israel, and covering one's garment with violence, says the Lord of hosts. So take heed to yourselves and do not be faithless.

We often hear of old, wealthy men divorcing their not-so-young wives and hastily marrying a younger, prettier version. It's nothing new. The 'trophy wife' seems to have been known in Malachi's time. The impression here is of a fairly widespread phenomenon. Men were divorcing their Israelite wives and marrying younger and perhaps foreign (and therefore exotically alluring) ones. Part of the reason may have been a conscious effort to fit in with the new world order, to be part of the future which the God of Israel no longer seemed to provide.

Whatever the exact reason, it was an act of faithlessness which paralleled their abandonment of God. Of course, they didn't see it that way. The people knew they were estranged from God, and wondered why. The reason was once again that they could not separate their behaviour from their faith. The acts of worship, the sacrifices offered, had been invalidated by dalliance with foreign gods and faithlessness to their families.

God's response was immediate: 'I hate divorce and covering one's garment with violence.' The divorce issue was just part of the problem. Injustice in marriage reflected injustice in society as a whole. God's rejoinder is that we have whole lives, whose separate parts are separate only in appearance, but not in reality. There is no division between spiritual and physical, religious and ethical. There are only human lives, which can be lived to the glory of God—or not.

Prayer

May all my life be yours, O Lord.

MM

Malachi 2:17—3:4 (NRSV)

Refiner

You have wearied the Lord with your words. Yet you say, 'How have we wearied him?' By saying, 'All who do evil are good in the sight of the Lord, and he delights in them.' Or by asking, 'Where is the God of justice?' See, I am sending my messenger to prepare the way before me, and the Lord whom you seek will suddenly come to his temple. The messenger of the covenant in whom you delight—indeed, he is coming, says the Lord of hosts. But who can endure the day of his coming, and who can stand when he appears? For he is like a refiner's fire and like fullers' soap; he will sit as a refiner and purifier of silver, and he will purify the descendants of Levi and refine them like gold and silver, until they present offerings to the Lord in righteousness. Then the offering of Judah and Jerusalem will be pleasing to the Lord as in the days of old and as in former years.

I would like to think that God is infinitely tolerant, and will one day welcome me into heaven with open arms, asking no questions about the life I have lived, the deeds I have done or condoned, and the faith I have exercised. I would *like* to think so, but I'm sure that if I *did* think so, I would be in for a very rude awakening on the day of resurrection.

Yes, of course God is infinitely loving, and absolutely forgiving. He is also completely holy—a word which carries strong moral overtones—and totally pure. Our ultimate destiny is to spend eternity in the undiluted presence of God. How can we do that? By his grace, to be sure, but also by being the sort of people who do not find purity and holiness a discomfort.

One day, says Malachi, God will indeed come to his people, the people with whom he has the special relationship of the covenant. But that encounter will not be painless. It will be like the searing heat of a smelter. Words alone, the lip-service of religion, are not enough to prepare his people to meet him. Their lives must also fit into his pattern, be compatible with his very being. Those who have lived as though he were not present, or as though he could somehow be expected to condone their wrongdoing, will find the reality very different indeed.

Prayer

Lord, help me to live as one who trusts in you and works for you; refine me now, that I may delight in your eternal presence.

MM

Malachi 3:4–7 (NRSV)

Uncomfortable words

Then the offering of Judah and Jerusalem will be pleasing to the Lord as in the days of old and as in former years. Then I will draw near to you for judgment; I will be swift to bear witness against the sorcerers, against the adulterers, against those who swear falsely, against those who oppress the hired workers in their wages, the widow and the orphan, against those who thrust aside the alien, and do not fear me, says the Lord of hosts. For I the Lord do not change; therefore you, O children of Jacob, have not perished. Ever since the days of your ancestors you have turned aside from my statutes and have not kept them. Return to me, and I will return to you, says the Lord of hosts.

There's a sign that used to be found outside some churches: 'If God seems distant, who has moved?' Malachi makes a similar point here. If God had changed in his attitude to Israel, there would be no more Israel. It is his steadfast love which keeps him caring for them even in their waywardness. Indeed, his coming judgment is a sign of his love. It is not simply to wipe out those who rebel, but to call them back to himself and restore their true faith and worship.

By placing God's judgment and the purity of worship side by side, Malachi points out an aspect of worship which is often overlooked—that it should challenge us as well as give an opportunity for praise and thanksgiving.

In our age, with easy mobility, it is the simplest thing in the world to shop around for a church that suits us. We will no doubt look for somewhere with a warm welcome, a style of service we enjoy and teaching we can relate to. In doing so, we can easily miss the challenge. If we are made to feel uncomfortable, we can move on, possibly leaving behind God's message to us. For Malachi's audience, the message was a call to uprightness and justice. We need to hear that too. There are other areas where we may be challenged, though—to appreciate the riches of a tradition different from ours, or ways of praying which may initially be strange, but could lead to a closer walk with God, or a call to offer our time and abilities where we would rather not.

Prayer

Lord, do not let me seek only comfort and consolation from you, but open my ears to hear your call.

MM

Malachi 3:7b–12 (NRSV)

Putting God first

But you say, 'How shall we return?' Will anyone rob God? Yet you are robbing me! But you say, 'How are we robbing you?' In your tithes and offerings! You are cursed with a curse, for you are robbing me—the whole nation of you! Bring the full tithe into the storehouse, so that there may be food in my house, and thus put me to the test, says the Lord of hosts; see if I will not open the windows of heaven for you and pour down for you an overflowing blessing. I will rebuke the locust for you, so that it will not destroy the produce of your soil; and your vine in the field shall not be barren, says the Lord of hosts. Then all nations will count you happy, for you will be a land of delight, says the Lord of hosts.

So how to get back to God? Malachi's answer is simple: by restoring God to his rightful place. Because of his obvious concern for the temple's worship, he lights on the giving of the people in their tithes. These were the taxes payed for the upkeep of the daily worship, and it is clear that they were not being paid in full.

Interestingly, money matters are often seen as somehow not very spiritual. Once, when our church was planning a stewardship campaign, a church warden wanted nothing to do with it. She was devout, and indeed generous, but felt that highlighting the issue of giving was somehow impious. Yet it is a pretty good measure of what someone means to us. As Christmas approaches, many of us will be carefully searching for the perfect present to express our love for family and friends. Some of us will feel a little guilty or sad that we cannot afford to spend more. Of course, love has no cash value, and the simplest gifts are often valued for the love behind them, but still, if we are well-off, and spend as little as possible on others, it speaks as loudly as any protestations of devotion. Similarly, where God comes in our list of giving can tell us a lot about how much he means to us.

It is not simply about money, though. The basic question is how important God is to us. Where does he come in our priorities? Where do worship and prayer fit in on the 'must do' list?

Prayer

Father, let me put you at the top of the list, and learn that in giving myself to you, I receive far more in return.

MM

Malachi 3:16–17; 4:2, 5–6 (NRSV, abridged)

Preparing the way of the Lord

Then those who revered the Lord spoke with one another. The Lord took note and listened, and a book of remembrance was written before him of those who revered the Lord and thought on his name. They shall be mine, says the Lord of hosts, my special possession on the day when I act, and I will spare them... But for you who revere my name the sun of righteousness shall rise, with healing in its wings... Lo, I will send you the prophet Elijah before the great and terrible day of the Lord comes. He will turn the hearts of parents to their children and the hearts of children to their parents, so that I will not come and strike the land with a curse.

Malachi's perspective has slowly been changing. The condemnation of present-day Israel carries his vision to the coming rule of God. That judgment will result in a restoration of Israel, and a renewal of faith, of love for God and of true worship. At that time there will be a discovery: not everyone has forgotten God. There are always those who desire to serve him, and they, no less than the wicked, will receive their reward (or better, they will find the presence of God a joy, not a terror).

These two themes—the call to repentance, and the promise of coming salvation—make Malachi an appropriate book for Advent. It's a season when we examine ourselves and turn afresh to God, but we do so in the light of his promise of salvation, which comes into the world in Jesus and will be brought to full fruition at the last day. For Christians, the book of remembrance is the Lamb's book of life (Revelation 3:5) and inclusion in it is promised to all who put their faith in Christ.

It is hard to know exactly what Malachi envisaged in the return of Elijah. Perhaps, as one of the two biblical figures who went to heaven without dying, Elijah was seen as literally returning. Or perhaps Malachi saw his own ministry as being like Elijah's call to repentance and a preparation for God's rule. Jesus saw John the Baptist's work as that of the promised forerunner. Yet in a sense, that work is not finished. Jesus has brought in the presence of the Kingdom and the certainty of its fulfilment. Until that time, the work of the whole Church is that of Elijah—to prepare the way for the coming of the Lord in victory.

Prayer

Lord, make me a forerunner, so that in me others may be prepared to encounter Christ.

MM

Psalm 16:8–11 (NRSV)

Eternal blessing

I keep the Lord always before me; because he is at my right hand, I shall not be moved. Therefore my heart is glad, and my soul rejoices; my body also rests secure. For you do not give me up to Sheol, or let your faithful one see the Pit. You show me the path of life. In your presence there is fullness of joy; in your right hand are pleasures for evermore.

Generally speaking, the Hebrew scriptures have little to say about life after death, probably because the idea wasn't part of their religious heritage. The dead went to 'Sheol', literally the grave, the place of the departed, and the writers on the whole draw a veil over what that means in ultimate terms. It isn't until the great prophets of later centuries (Isaiah, Jeremiah, Daniel) that any real notion of what we would call 'eternal life' comes into the Bible.

Yet there are 'hints', and perhaps more than hints, that something better awaits the 'godly' than simply to 'dwell in darkness'. Here the psalmist, who may well have been the king, the Lord's anointed (see verse 6, 'I have a goodly heritage'), expresses a genuine confidence in a future joy beyond this life: 'In your presence there is fullness of joy; in your right hand are pleasures for evermore.' The language is slightly ambiguous, as befits the psalmist's generally rather hazy vision of a future life, but it is also very positive. Death ('Sheol') would not be, for him, the end of things. Despite the inevitability of death, his heart is 'glad' and his 'body also rests secure' (v. 9).

That is more than a vague hint of future blessing! Here is a man whose personal faith in God is so strong (see verse 2—'I say to the Lord, You are *my* Lord') that he cannot believe that even death can break that relationship. The God who instructs his heart in the night (v. 7) and is always at his 'right hand' (v. 8), will also be with him as he goes through the experience of death—an experience which he calls, very simply, 'the path of life' (v. 11).

Reflection

To believe that death is 'the path of life' is genuinely to have hope. Human destiny, in God's purpose, is not Sheol, the Pit, but 'fullness of joy' and 'pleasures for evermore'.

DW

This is the first of a series on 'Death and the Future'.

Daniel 12:1–3 (NRSV)

'Some to everlasting life'

At that time Michael, the great prince, the protector of your people, shall arise. There shall be a time of anguish, such as has never occurred since nations first came into existence. But at that time your people shall be delivered, everyone who is found written in the book. Many of those who sleep in the dust of the earth shall awake, some to everlasting life, and some to shame and everlasting contempt. Those who are wise shall shine like the brightness of the sky, and those who lead many to righteousness, like the stars for ever and ever.

This passage is a mysterious and elusive one, and scholars have argued at length over its interpretation. What is undeniable, however, is that out of a time of intense persecution of God's people—referred to here as 'a time of anguish'—he would bring them blessing. One can also see here, of course, ideas which are echoed in the teaching of Jesus about the 'tribulation' which would afflict the Jewish people (see Mark 13:19), but out of which would come their Saviour 'with great power and glory' (Mark 13:26).

'The book' (v. 1) is the record of God's 'elect', his chosen people. Those God has chosen he will deliver, even from a time of unparalleled suffering. And this deliverance will extend to those who have died during the suffering ('those who sleep in the dust of the earth'). In other words, God isn't defeated by death; he is its conqueror.

Those who are raised from death will either enjoy 'everlasting life' or 'everlasting contempt': their fate will depend on their relationship to the Lord. Those who have remained faithful will be saved, but the renegades and traitors (almost certainly those are the people the writer has in mind) will have to face the shame of what they have done. It's a harsh message, of course, but those were harsh and bitter times.

What rings clearly through this passage is the power of God even in the face of death. He is the Lord of the grave, as well as of all the earth.

Reflection

It would be in a time of suffering that blessing would come, just as it is in the moment of death that we shall experience the full wonder of the victory of God.

DW

Matthew 22:29–32 (NRSV)

The God of the living

Jesus answered them, 'You are wrong, because you know neither the scriptures nor the power of God. For in the resurrection they neither marry nor are given in marriage, but are like angels in heaven. And as for the resurrection of the dead, have you not read what was said to you by God, "I am the God of Abraham, the God of Isaac, and the God of Jacob"? He is God not of the dead, but of the living.'

This is the answer of Jesus to a question put to him by the Sadducees, a group of Jewish teachers who didn't believe in the resurrection. They based this on the teaching of the Pentateuch (the first five books of the Bible), in which, they claimed, no such belief could be found. In fact, their position was very similar to that of many modern people, who (if pressed on the subject) would say that when you die 'that's it'—*finis*, all over. They knew that Jesus shared the view of their arch-rivals, the Pharisees, who believed in the resurrection of the dead, a belief that had grown in Judaism from the time of the great prophets six or seven hundred years earlier.

Jesus, however, met the Sadducees on their own ground. If they wanted proof from the Pentateuch, they should have it—and what more central to those books of the Bible than the declaration of the very Name and nature of God: 'the God of Abraham, Isaac and Jacob'? But, said Jesus, God is not 'the God of the dead, but of the living'—and 'to be the God of' someone implies, in Jewish thought, a continuing caring and protecting relationship. If 'Abraham, Isaac and Jacob' can enjoy such a relationship with God, then they *must* be alive—to believe otherwise is to make a nonsense of the whole thing. So from their own scriptures Jesus was able to argue the truth of the resurrection: the patriarchs, though 'dead', were 'alive' to God, were still under his care and protection.

The reference to 'being like the angels' (not 'marrying or giving in marriage') does not imply that those who share in the resurrection are less than human! What it does emphasize is that the concerns, anxieties (and jealousies?) of earth will have no place in the kingdom of God.

Reflection

Jesus believed in the resurrection of the dead. That is beyond dispute. For a Christian to doubt the resurrection is to doubt Jesus himself.

DW

John 11:11–16 (NRSV)

Lazarus is dead

After saying this, Jesus told them, 'Our friend Lazarus has fallen asleep, but I am going there to awaken him.' The disciples said to him, 'Lord, if he has fallen asleep, he will be all right.' Jesus, however, had been speaking about his death, but they thought that he was referring merely to sleep. Then Jesus told them plainly, 'Lazarus is dead. For your sake I am glad I was not there, so that you may believe. But let us go to him.' Thomas, who was called the Twin, said to his fellow disciples, 'Let us also go, that we may die with him.'

This is the first part of the story of the raising of Lazarus, a narrative unique to John's Gospel. (Henry Wansbrough looked at it in the context of the passion narrative back in September.) As with everything in John's Gospel, we shall be looking for its 'deeper meaning', and quite clearly this story is intended as some kind of clue to understanding the resurrection of Jesus himself.

Jesus had had a message from Mary and Martha, in Bethany, that his friend Lazarus (their brother) was seriously ill, but for some reason ('so that the Son of Man may be glorified through it'—v. 4) Jesus decided to delay going to him. By the time he and the disciples arrived in Bethany, Lazarus had died—indeed, he had been dead four days. Jesus saw this event as an opportunity to strengthen the faith of the disciples ('so that you may believe'), but, not surprisingly, they found that a difficult notion. Thomas, ever the down-to-earth realist, saw the position as totally bleak: 'Let's go and die with him.'

Like all Christian ministers, I meet many people at the moment of bereavement, and Thomas's reaction is both normal and completely understandable. Even those with a very strong faith recoil in the face of the 'final enemy'—the most common reaction is, simply, 'No!' Thomas expressed the solidarity in grief that binds together all who mourn. Jesus didn't argue with him, and neither will the wise minister. He simply led the little party towards the beloved home of the grieving family, where other friends had also gathered to console Mary and Martha. It was an intensely human scene.

Reflection

What seems at the time cruel, bleak,
cold and final can become eventually a
means of strengthened faith,
provided Jesus is there.

DW

John 11:21–27 (NRSV)

'I am the Resurrection'

Martha said to Jesus, 'Lord, if you had been here, my brother would not have died. But even now I know that God will give you whatever you ask of him.' Jesus said to her, 'Your brother will rise again.' Martha said to him, 'I know that he will rise again in the resurrection on the last day.' Jesus said to her, 'I am the resurrection and the life. Those who believe in me, even though they die, will live, and everyone who lives and believes in me will never die. Do you believe this?' She said to him, 'Yes, Lord, I believe that you are the Messiah, the Son of God, the one coming into the world.'

As the coffin is carried into church, these words of Jesus ring out: 'I am the resurrection and the life. Those who believe in me, even though they die, will live, and everyone who lives and believes in me will never die.' But here is a person's body being brought into church for a funeral. How can we claim that they are 'alive' and will 'never die'? To all intents and purposes, they already have.

So the fact that it's well known doesn't make this an 'easy' saying. Far from it. But the clue is in the opening words: '*I am* the resurrection and the life.' This is to claim more than that Jesus will himself experience resurrection, or even that through him *we* can be raised. It is a claim that resurrection life is what Jesus *is*—it is an essential part of his nature. As John has already put it, 'In him is life' (1:4). So those who are united to him in faith—in Paul's language, those who are 'in Christ'—are united to life itself. It's in that sense that they can 'never die'—they are already living the 'resurrection life'.

Jesus asked Martha if she believed 'this'. Her reply was to a different question! 'Yes, Lord, I believe... *you*'. Perhaps, in the end, that's all any of us can say about the resurrection. We may find 'it' a baffling, elusive idea, but those who believe that Jesus is the Messiah, the Son of God, will trust his words and believe his promises. That is all he asks for.

Reflection

Like Martha, we may find the idea of a doctrine of resurrection a bit remote, but there is nothing remote about a Saviour who promises to give us eternal life, right now... and into eternity.

DW

John 11:32–36 (NRSV)

Jesus wept

When Mary came where Jesus was and saw him, she knelt at his feet and said to him, 'Lord, if you had been here, my brother would not have died.' When Jesus saw her weeping, and the Jews who came with her also weeping, he was greatly disturbed in spirit and deeply moved. He said, 'Where have you laid him?' They said to him, 'Lord, come and see.' Jesus began to weep. So the Jews said, 'See how he loved him!'

'Jesus wept'—the usual and most straightforward translation—is well known as the shortest verse in the Bible, but that doesn't make it by any means the most simple! *Why* did Jesus weep—'shed tears', as the Greek verb puts it? After all, he had already said that through the death of Lazarus he would be 'glorified' and the faith of the disciples would be strengthened, so presumably he knew that in a few moments his friend would be 'awoken' from the sleep of death (see v. 11). So what cause was there for tears?

The answer, as so often, is in the context. It was 'when Jesus saw (Mary) weeping, and the Jews who came with her also weeping' that he was 'greatly disturbed in spirit and deeply moved'. So it was not any lack of faith on the part of Jesus, nor doubt of God's power to raise Lazarus, but a deep and real sharing in ordinary human grief that tore at his heart and made the tears run from his eyes. This is the 'Man of Sorrows', the Son of God who shared human experience to the ultimate. Perhaps it was in this experience, this moment of a grief shared, that Jesus showed most fully what it meant to be 'incarnate'—to live as a human in the world as it is.

Here is the *real* comfort of Christ for the bereaved, the comfort of a shared sorrow. It makes a tremendous difference for the one who sheds tears at the death of a loved one to know that, in his Son, God himself has shared that experience. At that moment of grief it was little comfort to Mary to believe in the resurrection (though soon that would be the greatest of all comforts). The loss was human, and the pain is the pain of every human bereavement. And the Saviour knows all about it.

Reflection

'In every sorrow of the heart, the Man of Sorrows has a part…'

DW

Ephesians 1:20–23 (NRSV)

Christ the King

God put this power to work in Christ when he raised him from the dead and seated him at his right hand in the heavenly places, far above all rule and authority and power and dominion, and above every name that is named, not only in this age but also in the age to come. And he has put all things under his feet and has made him the head over all things for the church, which is his body, the fullness of him who fills all in all.

Just before Advent, we celebrate the feast of 'Christ the King', a concept which fits in well with the theme of these readings, 'Death and the Future'. For, as this marvellous passage from Ephesians reminds us, it was in victory over death itself that God 'put his power to work in Christ'. Without the resurrection, the story of Jesus would be yet one more in a long and dismal record of good men and women who died unjustly, victims of the triumph of evil over good and of death over life. But by raising Jesus from death God showed that Christ is above every 'rule, authority, power and dominion', in this world and the next. He is the Lord of life and the Conqueror of death.

And that is not just theory! I happened to spend most of yesterday afternoon with a young woman whose brother, in his twenties, had died suddenly of a heart attack. As we talked, it became clear that what she wanted was a reassurance that belief in life beyond death wasn't just a bit of the Creed, but something we could really believe and hold on to. And, as I said to her, the clue to that is Jesus. The power of God which raised him from the dead is at work in us, too: 'Because I live, you will live also.'

Reflection

Just as human birth is the gateway into earthly life, so human death is the gateway into heavenly life. Like the baby in the womb, we can't possibly begin to imagine the wonder of what lies ahead!

DW

John 12:20–24 (NRSV)

The 'dying' seed

Now among those who went up to worship at the festival were some Greeks. They came to Philip, who was from Bethsaida in Galilee, and said to him, 'Sir, we wish to see Jesus.' Philip went and told Andrew; then Andrew and Philip went and told Jesus. Jesus answered them, 'The hour has come for the Son of Man to be glorified. Very truly, I tell you, unless a grain of wheat falls into the earth and dies, it remains just a single grain; but if it dies, it bears much fruit. Those who love their life lose it, and those who hate their life in this world will keep it for eternal life.'

I remember, as a child, being given a packet of cornflower seeds, with a very beautiful picture of blue flowers on the front. I planted the seeds, and waited impatiently for these splendid blooms to appear. It seemed to take ages, but in due course little green shoots popped out, and eventually plants grew which produced flowers not unlike the ones on the packet. I couldn't resist finding out what had happened under the soil, so I dug one up, but no matter how hard I searched I couldn't find the seed I had planted—the seed which had made the whole thing possible!

That was the very simple yet profound lesson which Jesus wanted his followers to learn. 'Those who love their life lose it'—clinging to oneself is a negative, defeating process. It's by letting go that we find life. For Jesus, that meant that his own life had to be given up, the 'seed' of his body had to die and be buried, so that something more wonderful ('much fruit') could come into being. It's also the principle behind the very idea of resurrection. What we *are* comes to an end, so that what we *shall be* may come into being. It's a principle we'll be looking at later this week.

Reflection

To give something up in order to achieve something infinitely better is hardly to make a sacrifice.

DW

Acts 2:29–32 (NRSV)

'God raised Jesus'

'Fellow Israelites, I may say to you confidently of our ancestor David that he both died and was buried, and his tomb is with us to this day. Since he was a prophet, he knew that God had sworn with an oath to him that he would put one of his descendants on his throne. Foreseeing this, David spoke of the resurrection of the Messiah, saying, "He was not abandoned to Hades, nor did his flesh experience corruption." This Jesus God raised up, and of that all of us are witnesses.'

We began these reflections on the theme of 'death and the future' with a passage from Psalm 16, in fact the very words quoted on the Day of Pentecost by the apostle Peter which form today's reading. Peter attributes them to David and calls him a 'prophet'. A prophet is someone who 'sees' the purposes of God and 'speaks out' his truth. Here, David speaks of his own hope that he would not be 'abandoned to Hades' (the Greek version of *Sheol*, the grave) or 'experience corruption'.

For the first Christians, all devout Jews of course, the resurrection of Jesus was the glorious fulfilment of this 'prophecy'—a fulfilment that would have been beyond anything that David himself could have imagined.

David, Peter says, could not have been speaking about himself when he talked of not being 'abandoned to Hades', but of someone else—'one of his descendants', 'the Messiah'. David died and was buried, and they could visit his tomb. But this descendant *would* fulfil the prophecy. His flesh would 'not see corruption'. And who is that descendant? 'This Jesus!' After all, Peter has already argued (v. 24), 'God… freed him from death, *because it was impossible for him to be held in its power*.' The Lord of life cannot be conquered by death.

Reflection

'This Jesus God raised up.' That is the heart of our faith and the substance of Christian hope. What God did for his Son, he will do for all of those who belong to his Son.

DW

1 Corinthians 15:3–8 (NRSV)

Witnesses of the resurrection

For I handed on to you as of first importance what I in turn had received: that Christ died for our sins in accordance with the scriptures, and that he was buried, and that he was raised on the third day in accordance with the scriptures, and that he appeared to Cephas, then to the twelve. Then he appeared to more than five hundred brothers and sisters at one time, most of whom are still alive, though some have died. Then he appeared to James, then to all the apostles. Last of all, as to one untimely born, he appeared also to me.

The essential key to a Christian understanding of 'death and the future' is the resurrection of Jesus. That is Paul's argument in this splendid fifteenth chapter of 1 Corinthians—absolutely essential reading for anyone concerned about life after death. Everything hinges on the belief that Jesus rose from the dead, and Paul begins with a re-statement of the core Christian belief—what Paul had himself 'received' when he was baptized, a mere five years or so after the first Easter (v. 3). He doesn't present it simply as something to be believed irrationally, but as a *fact* based on *evidence*. And that evidence is compelling—eye-witnesses of unquestionable integrity, men and women many of whom were still alive and could be cross-examined about it. They actually saw with their eyes the risen Jesus. Paul himself, of course, was too late for that privilege—'untimely born' is his phrase for it! But he 'saw' the risen Jesus in his mystical encounter on the road to Damascus, and so feels able to add his name to the list of apostolic witnesses.

With such impressive testimony, Paul argues, how could people still doubt, as some of the Christians at Corinth did, the truth of the resurrection (see verse 12)? This was no wish-fulfilling fantasy, but demonstrable fact—truth to rely on.

Reflection

Christians believe in life beyond death not because it's a 'nice idea', or 'brings comfort', or offers us 'pie in the sky when we die'. We believe it because it's true, and it's true because truthful people have met the risen Jesus.

DW

1 Corinthians 15:13–14, 16–20 (NRSV)

Jesus the first of many

If there is no resurrection of the dead, then Christ has not been raised; and if Christ has not been raised, then our proclamation has been in vain and your faith has been in vain... For if the dead are not raised, then Christ has not been raised. If Christ has not been raised, your faith is futile and you are still in your sins. Then those also who have died in Christ have perished. If for this life only we have hoped in Christ, we are of all people most to be pitied. But in fact Christ has been raised from the dead, the first fruits of those who have died.

Five 'ifs' and one 'but'! That's the summary of this passage. The 'ifs' present the situation without the resurrection: a false and misleading message, a futile and empty faith, sins unforgiven, the Christian dead 'perished', the Christian faith a pitiable, hopeless thing. What a dismal catalogue!

But everything is altered by that resounding BUT: '*but* in fact Christ has been raised from the dead'. That is the truth to which they should hold firm. In the light of the resurrection, the Christian message is true, the faith is effective and full of comfort, our sins are forgiven and the Christian dead await, with us, a glorious resurrection. Easter changes everything!

Christ is risen, but that is only the first part of the triumphant message. He is the 'first fruits' of those who have died. That's to say, he's like the first sheaf of corn of a splendid harvest, the promise of marvellous things to follow. And what makes up the rest of the harvest? 'Those who have died'—their friends and fellow Christians in the church at Corinth who had 'fallen asleep' (Paul's actual words here), and about whom they had anxiously enquired of the apostle. They need not worry. The harvest was ripe. The first fruits had already been gathered from Christ's empty tomb. The rest would follow.

Reflection

Nearly two thousand years have passed,
and still that vast harvest of souls
is not yet fully gathered in. We wait, not
anxiously, but with hope and faith.

DW

1 Corinthians 1:3–9 (NRSV)

Waiting for the Lord

Grace to you and peace from God our Father and the Lord Jesus Christ. I give thanks to my God always for you because of the grace of God that has been given you in Christ Jesus, for in every way you have been enriched in him, in speech and knowledge of every kind—just as the testimony of Christ has been strengthened among you—so that you are not lacking in any spiritual gift as you wait for the revealing of our Lord Jesus Christ. He will also strengthen you to the end, so that you may be blameless on the day of our Lord Jesus Christ. God is faithful; by him you were called into the fellowship of his Son, Jesus Christ our Lord.

This reading makes a fitting conclusion to our reflections on 'death and the future'. It puts the future into the divine context, as it were.

For Christians, the past is the marvellous record of what God has done, above all, what God has done through Jesus—'the testimony of (or 'to'—see NRSV footnote) Christ' (v. 6). Through our experience of God in the past, we can trust him to be 'faithful' (v. 9). He is a God who keeps faith with us.

The present is a time of waiting (v. 7) and of being strengthened (v. 8). Although the Christian life always looks ahead, it is lived right here, in the present; and in this present scene God is strengthening us 'to the end'. That's where we are now—God's waiting people, living in 'the fellowship of his Son' (v. 9).

The future is in the hands of God, who in his own time will 'reveal our Lord Jesus Christ' (v. 7). We can't possibly imagine what that experience will involve, any more than the people of the first century could have imagined that his first 'revealing' would be in a stable in Bethlehem. But just as God has already 'enriched us' (v. 5), so we can be confident about the future. 'God is faithful'—that is our only guarantee, but what more could we want?

Reflection

Even so, come, Lord Jesus!

DW

Matthew 1:18–20 (NRSV)

Waiting

When his mother Mary had been engaged to Joseph, but before they lived together, she was found to be with child from the Holy Spirit. Her husband Joseph, being a righteous man and unwilling to expose her to public disgrace, planned to dismiss her quietly. But just when he had resolved to do this, an angel of the Lord appeared to him in a dream and said, 'Joseph, son of David, do not be afraid to take Mary as your wife, for the child conceived in her is from the Holy Spirit.'

When I was a little boy, I had a strategem to make Christmas come less slowly (it works the opposite way now!) I measured a novena (nine days) back from the early hours of Christmas morning and then counted down each day: 'Nine days and nine nights—Christmas!' The pain was taken out of waiting—or seemed to be.

No such boyhood stratagem could help Joseph, for he was caught up in a dilemma of apprehension and anticipation in which hope and trust were mingled with fear. Can you imagine the widening of his eyes, the race-beat of his heart, the cold clamminess of his skin as he looked, listened, and took Mary's hand in his own when she told him of the visit of Gabriel? How could he believe such a thing—but how could he distrust her? It was a matter of believing where you could not see, of trusting where you could not prove, and the whole of his life was in her hands now.

There is such a straightforward beauty about the account and such a ring of truth which shines through Mary's belief in Joseph as he wakes from the communicative truth of his dream, acting with integrity and quiet faith. This is the point at which the Gospel summons us to enter into the beauty of obedience and trust as we wait for his yearly miracle of grace which takes place in the celebration of the Church and within the secret mystery of our hearts.

Though Christ a thousand times
In Bethlehem be born—
Be he not born in thee
Thy soul is all forlorn.

So wrote the fourteenth-century German mystic Angelus Selesius, and we are on the brink of such a new birth. And we are waiting!

Prayer

I think too little of Joseph, Lord, but let those marvellous inward virtues of waiting, apprehension and anticipation shine in my heart at this brink of Incarnation—and let the light spread!

R/SSF

Luke 1:39–43 (NRSV, abridged)

Leaping

Then Mary went with haste to a Judean town where she entered the house of Zechariah and greeted Elizabeth. When Elizabeth heard Mary's greeting, the child leaped in her womb. And Elizabeth was filled with the Holy Spirit and exclaimed with a loud cry, 'Blessed are you among women, and blessed is the fruit of your womb. And why has this happened to me, that the mother of my Lord comes to me?'

This marvellous passage speaks of the initiative of God from first to last. And the central word, 'leaping', indicates that it is by direct action of the Holy Spirit that the babe leaps in Elizabeth's womb. It is not Elizabeth, nor even Mary, who leaps. Mary simply hears the words of Gabriel at the annunciation, receiving the word that she would be with child by the Spirit. She then communicates the message to Joseph as she hears his God-sent dream. And immediately she is moved mightily and with haste to go up to the hill country of Ain Karim. She shouts Elizabeth's name and baby John the Baptist leaps for joy. As I wrote in BRF's *When They Crucified My Lord*:

Leaping for joy is a consequence of being filled with the Holy Spirit. The amazing truth here, which pregnant women and mothers will understand best, is that there is something in conceiving, bearing, giving birth, which is unlike anything else in human life, and most like the activity of the Holy Spirit who 'is the Lord and giver of life'.

What can it possibly be like (I've wondered, as Franciscan friars will!) to carry within one's own body, to conceive, nurture, bear and bring to birth, another human being? Amazing!

Mary had a long time to wait, to move from the more active phases, though she was 'worked upon' by the Spirit, and enter more deeply into the physical, mental and spiritual work that was involved in bringing God to birth for our salvation and joy.

It is Christmas Eve and you are surely (especially if mother or father) caught up in the natural joys, sorrows, frenetic activities and arrangements of 'so many things and so many people' today. But it is our Lord's birthday and he desires from you a time of love and sharing. Let him work upon you, move you from phase to phase in his scheme of love for your life. May the Holy Spirit leap in your womb!

Prayer

Let there be an enclosed moment of stillness today, Lord. And speak in the midst of that stillness.

R/SSF

Luke 2:16–20 (NRSV)

Treasuring and pondering

The shepherds went (to Bethlehem) with haste and found Mary and Joseph, and the child lying in a manger. When they saw this, they made known what had been told them about this child; and all who heard it were amazed at what the shepherds told them. But Mary treasured all these words and pondered them in her heart. The shepherds returned, glorifying and praising God for all they had heard and seen, as it had been told them.

A fifth-century carol begins, 'A great and mighty wonder, a full and holy cure'. And in our passage it is Mary who is filled with the great and mighty wonder, for she is the contemplative, and it is the shepherds who begin to feel and experience in proclamation the full and holy cure of the gospel.

Of course, it is Mary who centralizes our thoughts upon Jesus today, for she has become, by the grace of God, the place where God enters the human race through a child, and who becomes the mediator, therefore, between God and humankind.

We may be drawn into all this by the dramatic excitement of the vision of angels and proclamations to shepherds, and we shall make our journey to crib and altar for the Christmas eucharist by the singing and revelation of scripture and choir. But when we come, then we shall be still with Mary, treasuring and pondering these things in our hearts.

People will be wrapping up before midnight and making the journey to Glasshampton monastery; the brothers and guests will be preparing the chapel, lights, vestments, flowers, incense, with visitors sharing the excitement of gathering, prayer and joy of midnight mass. You may gather in a cathedral or large church, simple chapel or meeting house. The important things are that we shall share the contemplative adoration of Mary of her dear Son, and that with the shepherds we shall enter into the glory and praise of God. You will find the baby Jesus wherever God is loved and worshipped today—but everywhere, wherever there is love. the universal Christ will manifest his joy, his hope and his peace.

Prayer

Let me see this great and mighty wonder—let me feel this full and holy cure, Lord.

R/SSF

Acts 7:55–60 (NRSV, abridged)

Surrendering

Filled with the Holy Spirit, (Stephen) gazed into heaven and saw Jesus standing at the right hand of God... But with a loud shout they dragged him out of the city and began to stone him... While they were stoning Stephen, he prayed, 'Lord Jesus, receive my spirit.' Then he knelt down and cried in a loud voice, 'Lord, do not hold this sin against them.' When he had said this, he died.

We celebrate the death of Stephen on the day after Christmas! Christ had surrendered himself in the glory of becoming human like you and me; Mary had surrendered herself into a humility and obedience that embraced you and me; Joseph had surrendered himself into an openness and simplicity that overshadowed you and me. And now it was the turn of Stephen.

Time and place were different, but the costliness of shedding one's blood for love's sake was the same. On their last birthday, I wrote to all my 'Stephen' friends and told them that their name meant 'martyrdom', and that as Stephen the first martyr had cast down his crown before the Lord, so their opportunity would come to surrender themselves to the Christ who had surrendered himself for them.

Stephen's assurance in witness was not arrogance, though he faced his enemies with the truth about themselves and about Jesus that made them very angry. It was an assurance which also was mingled with reconciliation, forgiveness and the very same spirit that Jesus manifested as the soldiers nailed him to the cross: 'Father, forgive them, for they know not what they do.'

Divine Love has been crucified. Stephen bears valiant witness. He is stoned to death for his witness, and as the light sparkles and then dies from his eyes, he cries, 'Lord, do not hold this sin against them.'

What a way to live, and what a way to die! On this day after Christmas day, this day of martyrdom, let us yield and surrender ourselves in such a way that our lives will be full of assurance and glory, and our dying be a simple and reconciling surrender to the loving will of God. The light of Christmas nativity will then shine on to the glory of martyrdom, and both will be resolved in the eternal birth and death which is the incarnation and resurrection of Jesus our Saviour!

Prayer

Lord of life and death, we behold your gift of life in the incarnation and your overcoming of death in the passion of Calvary. Both are told out in the story of Stephen. Help me to understand.

R/SSF

John 21:23–25 (NRSV)

Wondering

The rumour spread in the community that (the disciple whom Jesus loved) would not die. Yet Jesus did not say to him that he would not die, but 'If it is my will that he remain until I come, what is that to you?' This is the disciple who is testifying to these things and has written them, and we know that his testimony is true. But there are also many other things that Jesus did; if every one of them were written down, I suppose that the world itself could not contain the books that would be written.

'Wondering' in our title today does not only mean that dimension of wonder in which we become caught up when once the Spirit of God takes hold upon our lives in the pilgrimage from earth to glory. It also indicates the world of wonder in which the mighty acts of God are manifest—like the incarnation and the resurrection of Jesus, and all the wonders he has done, and will do, for us.

If there is a disciple in which both these senses of wonder are shown forth in the New Testament, it is 'the beloved disciple'. We have neither time nor place to identify John the evangelist with this disciple (see BRF's *People's Bible Commentary* on John), but we can accept it confidently for ourselves today.

John as disciple will enter into the wonder of the great experiences of grace that come to us through the incarnation, and John as evangelist will proclaim and record them in spoken and written word, so that those splendid words of our last sentence above can be written with joy.

We are called upon to enter into such apostolical experience of both senses of wonder. During this week we have been surrounded and indwelt by the wonder of the indwelling Christ—in Mary, in the Church of God and in our very selves! It brings us to tears and joy—and that is how the gospel is proclaimed. This sense of wonder is rooted in the indwelling facts of the gospel: Christ *was* manifested in the flesh; he *did* live a compassionate and healing life of miracle; he *was* taken in the body and crucified; and that body, risen yet glorified, *was* risen and will come again in the eternal kingdom.

The wonder of it all—and John the evangelist invites us ever deeper!

Prayer

Let the wonder of your love, O Lord,
and the wonder of your glorious
transformation, change my life from
glory to glory.

R/SSF

Matthew 2:16–18 (NRSV)

Innocent suffering

When Herod saw that he had been tricked by the wise men, he was infuriated, and he sent and killed all the children in and around Bethlehem who were two years old or under, according to the time that he had learned from the wise men. Then was fulfilled what had been spoken through the prophet Jeremiah: 'A voice was heard in Ramah, wailing and loud lamentation, Rachel weeping for her children; she refused to be consoled, because they are no more.'

I was studying theology in Zurich in the late 1960s when, over Swiss radio, I heard of the subsidence of the colliery pit waste down and over the whole school in Aberfan, South Wales. The area had lived under the shadow of miners' tragedies, but never one like this, and never one involving the multiple deaths of young children. It was a mini-holocaust.

About seven years later, I stood in the pulpit of the newly built Church of the Holy Innocents at Aberfan, preaching Evensong. As I looked through the window running below the roof, I could see the white graves on the side of the mountain, scores and scores of them in rows, in the evening light.

You have to understand the communal tragedy of something like an Aberfan to enter into the terrible suffering of a Ramah, just as you have to know the death of a beloved child to understand what that suffering means.

And what about the cruelty? We've been making excuses for community suffering and 'accidents' through commercial exploitation ever since, and increasingly; but here there is a Herod, just as today we could name half a dozen primary tyrants off the top of our heads if we chose to.

Yet all this is in the context of the embracing love of the incarnation at Christmas, of a child who came in order to suffer, to extend his two small arms of innocent mercy, in order that the world may be reconciled and redeemed.

It is not Ramah, nor Aberfan, today. It is the darker and crueller world which has succeeded them—but the light of Christ shines brighter, and the work of redemption continues... and we are at its centre.

Prayer

Lord, help me not to let bitterness take root in my soul because of the world's suffering; rather let me stand firm for the truth and live in reconciliation and nativity hope.

R/SSF

John 1:14–18 (NRSV, abridged)

Outshining

The Word became flesh and lived among us, and we have seen his glory, the glory as of a father's only son, full of grace and truth... From his fullness we have all received, grace upon grace. The law indeed was given through Moses; grace and truth came through Jesus Christ. No one has ever seen God. It is God the only Son, who is close to the Father's heart, who has made him known.

There is an immense joy and revelation in the Greek text which has been hidden from many Christians because of their lack of access and clear translation. My much loved King James Version said, 'No man hath seen God at any time; the only begotten Son, which is in the bosom of the Father, he hath declared him' (v. 18).

But the best (first and oldest) texts do not say here *hious* (Son), but *theos* (God). There are a number of textual reasons for this, and the KJV is a wonderful revelation of the Son declaring the Father. What we must note here is that the best and most primitive Greek reading does *not* say that it is the only Son who dwells at the Father's heart, but the only *God* who dwells at the Father's heart—he has made him known.

This is not about textual criticism but about light and glory and radiance. It is the outshining of the Father's heart. It is about the eternal source of love and creative joy which shines upon and into our dark world, so that *God himself* becomes human, and lifts up the human to the divine.

Today's title is 'Outshining', because the love continues to shine, the darkness cannot put it out, and it will shine in forgiveness, healing and peace until God brings in his eternal kingdom and brings his human family home at last. One of these Christmases will be the last—before Christ's coming in glory. And we are caught up in such outshining!

Prayer

You have given me not a religion, but yourself, dear Lord. And therefore you indwell me with your love, and allow your radiance to shine from me.

R/SSF

Luke 2:36–38 (NRSV)

Continuing

There was also a prophet, Anna the daughter of Phanuel, of the tribe of Asher. She was of a great age, having lived with her husband seven years after her marriage, then as a widow to the age of eighty-four. She never left the temple but worshipped there night and day. At that moment she came, and began to praise God and to speak about the child to all who were looking for the redemption of Jerusalem.

Anna was a prophet. She did not belong to any guild or rank of professionals, but was a hidden prophet, in the depths of the temple, whose ministry was fasting, prayer and the adoration of God. Hers was a continuing waiting—right up to the time of her dying when she could, with Simeon, depart in peace.

We have been waiting—it was our heading a week ago. And we have lived through the days and nights of Christmas, exposed to the revelation of joy and sorrow that the incarnation has brought to our world. Even in our few pages, it has touched the lives of kings, evangelists, martyrs and common people, preparing to shake and shape earthly realms until the coming of the realm of God which is foreshadowed in Anna's vision of redemption, beginning at Jerusalem.

At the end of this week, after our primary Christmas celebration, we have also reached the end of yet another year on the calendar. Last year some of us thought we'd never make it—and some of us didn't! But it doesn't matter, because we are on the borders of eternity, and the kingdom into which we enter is an eternal one.

Our task, with Anna, is to continue our prophetic ministry—one of prayer and worship, pouring out love into our dark world. Anna is the witness that as the prophetic word continues in the hidden place, so the light will dawn, the Kingdom will come, and all God's people will be brought home. This was why the Word was made flesh, and this is why Jesus is incarnated in your life and mine today. So let the light shine, let the love flow, until all are in its embrace of joy.

Prayer

Let me continue, Lord, in prayer and worship and love. And let your Christmas Kingdom come!

R/SSF

Colossians 3:15–17 (NIV)

A true resolution

Let the peace of Christ rule in your hearts, since as members of one body you were called to peace. And be thankful. Let the word of Christ dwell in you richly as you teach and admonish one another with all wisdom, and as you sing psalms, hymns and spiritual songs with gratitude in your hearts to God. And whatever you do, whether in word or deed, do it all in the name of the Lord Jesus, giving thanks to God the Father through him.

I must admit that every time I pass the sign outside our local branch of a certain DIY superstore, I think of that last verse: 'Do it all'—but do it 'in the name of the Lord Jesus'. I think it's a very good test of our actions, and a very good motto or resolution for the New Year, perhaps especially this one, the first (so the mathematicians tell me) of the new millennium.

It comes at the end of a lovely picture of the life of the early Church in fellowship, singing their songs and hymns, encouraging (and rebuking!) each other, and letting the word of Christ—his teaching, his message—soak into their lives. But this command extends beyond what we do together in church gatherings. This surely applies even more to the rest of the week—to work and home and hobbies and neighbours. 'Whatever you do'—that's a very comprehensive idea. But not *everything* we do *can* be done 'in the name of the Lord Jesus', because we can't tell lies in his name, or envy others, or lose our tempers, or hold a grudge. I have to admit that quite a few things I think and do in the week could not possibly be seen as being done 'in the name of the Lord Jesus'. So the message is plain (and, yes, I have tried to learn it)—*don't do them*!

A new year does give us a chance to address this kind of issue. It might be quite a positive step to apply to our ordinary everyday decisions this test: could I do this 'in the name of the Lord Jesus, giving thanks to God'? If the answer is no, then the decision is made for us!

Reflection

Our decisions about what we say and do in the rest of the week are much better tests of our discipleship than what we sing on Sundays!

DW

Contributors

CHRISTINE CHAPMAN
Christine Chapman was Director of Counselling for the Chester diocese. She is currently a member of the North-West Inter-Diocesan Counselling Team for clergy and their families, and is a lay Reader in her church.

MARGARET CUNDIFF
Margaret Cundiff has worked in the Church of England since 1973 as a lay worker, deaconess, deacon and finally priest. As well as her church work, she broadcasts regularly and serves as Diocesan Mother's Union Chaplain in the York Diocese. She is the author of fifteen books, including four published by BRF, the latest of which is *Still Time for Eternity*.

GRAHAM DODDS
Graham Dodds is Director of Reader Studies and Lay Training Adviser in the Diocese of Bath and Wells.

COLIN EVANS
Colin Evans is a former Moderator of the Eastern Province of the United Reformed Church, writer and broadcaster. He lives near Sudbury, in Suffolk.

ROB GILLION
Rob Gillion is Evangelism Officer for the Bishop of Kensington. He broadcasts regularly both nationally and locally, including BBC Radio's 'Pause for Thought'. He was formerly parish priest, prison chaplain, and responsible for religious broadcasting in Hong Kong.

PETER GRAVES
Peter Graves is Minister of Wesley Church, Cambridge and Chaplain to Methodist students at the University. He was formerly Superintendent Minister of the Methodist Central Hall, Westminster.

ROSEMARY GREEN
Rosemary Green is a popular speaker who is on the pastoral staff of Wycliffe Hall, Oxford. She is the author of *God's Catalyst*.

HILARY McDOWELL
Hilary McDowell exercises an independent lay ministry of evangelism, prayer, healing and reconciliation throughout Ireland and beyond. Based in Belfast, she is well known as a Christian communicator, Bible teacher, performance poet, dramatist and author. Her first book *Some Day I'm Going to Fly* made her name known internationally. She has also written *On the Way to Bethlehem* and *Visit to a Second Favourite Planet* for BRF.

MARCUS MAXWELL

Marcus Maxwell is Rector of St John's Heaton Mersey, Stockport, Cheshire and the author of *Revelation* in BRF's People's Bible Commentary series.

ADRIAN PLASS

Adrian Plass is a popular writer and speaker in many countries. His most recent book for BRF is *When You Walk*.

BROTHER RAMON SSF

Brother Ramon SSF died in early summer 2000, after a short battle with cancer. He wrote widely, especially on the subject of prayer and spirituality. He wrote *The Flame of Sacred Love* and *When They Crucified My Lord* for BRF.

JENNY ROBERTSON

Jenny Robertson lived for a number of years in Russia, working alongside her husband in St Petersburg. A prolific and experienced author, she has written many books for both adults and children, including *Windows to Eternity* for BRF. Her latest book is *Strength of the Hills*, an exploration of Scottish spirituality. She has also had a number of books of poetry published.

HENRY WANSBROUGH OSB

Henry Wansbrough OSB is the Master of St Benet's Hall, Oxford, a writer, broadcaster, and General Editor of The New Jerusalem Bible. He is also a Series Editor of the People's Bible Commentary and the author of *Luke* in that series.

DAVID WINTER

David Winter is retired from parish ministry. An honorary Canon of Christ Church, Oxford, he is well known as a writer and broadcaster. His most recent book for BRF is *After the Gospels*, and he has written BRF's Lent book for 2002, *With Jesus in the Upper Room*. He is one of the Series Editors for the People's Bible Commentary series and consulting editor of *New Daylight*.

VERONICA ZUNDEL

Veronica Zundel is an Oxford graduate, writer and journalist. She lives with her husband and young son in North London, where they belong to the Mennonite Church.

New Daylight is ideal for those looking for a fresh, devotional approach to reading and understanding the Bible. Each issue covers four months of daily Bible reading and reflection with each day offering a Bible passage (text included), helpful comment and a prayer or thought for the day ahead.

New Daylight is written by a gifted team of contributors including Adrian Plass, Margaret Cundiff, David Winter, Rob Gillion, Peter Graves, Helen Julian CSF, David Spriggs, Jenny Robertson and Veronica Zundel.

New Daylight is also available in large print and on cassette for the visually impaired.

NEW DAYLIGHT SUBSCRIPTIONS

❑ I would like to give a gift subscription
(please complete both name and address sections below)

❑ I would like to take out a subscription myself
(complete name and address details only once)

This completed coupon should be sent with appropriate payment to BRF. Alternatively, please write to us quoting your name, address, the subscription you would like for either yourself or a friend (with their name and address), the start date and credit card number, expiry date and signature if paying by credit card.

Gift subscription name ______________________________

Gift subscription address ______________________________

______________________________ Postcode ____________

Please send to the above, beginning with the January/May/September 2002* issue (* delete as applicable):

(please tick box)	UK	SURFACE	AIR MAIL
NEW DAYLIGHT	❑ £10.50	❑ £11.85	❑ £14.10
NEW DAYLIGHT 3-year sub	❑ £26.50		

Please complete the payment details below and send your coupon, with appropriate payment to: **BRF, First Floor, Elsfield Hall, 15–17 Elsfield Way, Oxford OX2 8FG**

Your name ______________________________

Your address ______________________________

______________________________ Postcode ____________

Total enclosed £ __________ (cheques should be made payable to 'BRF')

Payment by cheque ❑ postal order ❑ Visa ❑ Mastercard ❑ Switch ❑

Card number: ☐☐☐☐☐☐☐☐☐☐☐☐☐☐☐☐☐☐☐

Expiry date of card: ☐☐☐☐ Issue number (Switch): ☐☐☐☐

Signature (essential if paying by credit/Switch card) ______________________________

NB: BRF notes are also available from your local Christian bookshop. **BRF is a Registered Charity**

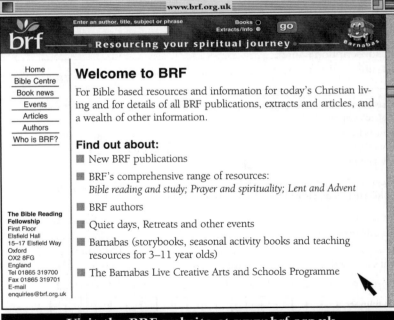